Most countries in Eastern Europe and the Baltics recorded healthy output growth in 1995 following a precipitous contraction during the early 1990s. Inflation in these countries has fallen sharply during the past two years. A sharp deceleration in the pace of price increases has also been recorded in many countries of the former Soviet Union, although the level of inflation in most of these countries remains substantial and, more importantly, output is still declining. The emerging picture is one of renewed growth in countries that showed early determination to implement market-oriented reforms and stabilize their macroeconomy, and of gradual and slow stabilization of output in those countries that entered the process only recently.

The essays collected in this book study in detail both the analytical underpinning of this process – the overall relationships between stabilization, reforms, and growth – as well as the specific stabilization experience in a number of Eastern European and former Soviet Union countries. In addition, the volume discusses some of the central policy issues related to enterprise behavior in postsocialist countries and looks at the longer-run dimensions of a successful transition.

MACROECONOMIC STABILIZATION IN TRANSITION ECONOMIES

MACROECONOMIC STABILIZATION IN TRANSITION ECONOMIES

Edited by

MARIO I. BLEJER
*International Monetary Fund
and Hebrew University*

MARKO ŠKREB
National Bank of Croatia

CAMBRIDGE
UNIVERSITY PRESS

CAMBRIDGE UNIVERSITY PRESS
Cambridge, New York, Melbourne, Madrid, Cape Town, Singapore, São Paulo

Cambridge University Press
The Edinburgh Building, Cambridge CB2 2RU, UK

Published in the United States of America by Cambridge University Press, New York

www.cambridge.org
Information on this title: www.cambridge.org/9780521581776

First published 1997
This digitally printed first paperback version 2006

A catalogue record for this publication is available from the British Library

Library of Congress Cataloguing in Publication data
Macroeconomic stabilization in transition economies / [edited by]
Mario I. Blejer, Marko Škreb.
p.   cm.
Papers presented at the first Dubrovnik conference
on transition economies.
ISBN 0-521-58177-X
1. Economic stabilization – Europe, Eastern.   2. Economic
stabilization – Former Soviet republics.   3. Europe, Eastern –
Economic policy – 1989–   4. Former Soviet republics – Economic
Policy.   5. Europe, Eastern – Economic conditions – 1989–   6. Former
Soviet republics – Economic conditions.   I. Blejer, Mario I.
II. Škreb, Marko, 1957–
HC244.M2254   1997
339.5′0947 – dc21   96-46103
                                                       CIP

ISBN-13 978-0-521-58177-6 hardback
ISBN-10 0-521-58177-X hardback

ISBN-13 978-0-521-02535-5 paperback
ISBN-10 0-521-02535-4 paperback

Contents

Contributors

Mario I. Blejer, *International Monetary Fund*
Velimir Bole, *Bank of Slovenia*
Martha de Melo, *World Bank*
Cevdet Denizer, *World Bank*
Alan Gelb, *World Bank*
Ardo H. Hansson, *Stockholm School of Economics*
Oleh Havrylyshyn, *International Monetary Fund*
Pero Jurković, *National Bank of Croatia*
János Kornai, *Collegium Budapest and Harvard University*
Robert A. Mundell, *Columbia University*
D. Mario Nuti, *London Business School*
Marcelo Selowsky, *World Bank*
Marko Škreb, *National Bank of Croatia*
Velimir Šonje, *National Bank of Croatia*
Vito Tanzi, *International Monetary Fund*
Nikica Valentić, *Prime Minister of Croatia*
Matthew Vogel, *World Bank*
Stanislaw Wellisz, *Columbia University*

Preface

Pero Jurković

It was a great pleasure to welcome all participants to the first Dubrovnik conference on transition economies.

In economics, a five-year period is considered to be long enough for macroeconomic stabilization and microeconomic structural changes to be activated. Five years have passed since the fall of the Berlin Wall. Not all of the former socialist countries immediately launched comprehensive reform programs in the autumn of 1989, but by 1990 several countries had already gained some experience in reforming socialist economies; others have joined "the club" only recently. Nevertheless, it seemed the right time to reflect on the results of transition programs and to draw lessons from the most successful (or the least successful) cases. Our main objective was to identify common principles and regularities, as well as common mistakes, in the transition process.

Conference presentations included papers on general issues and papers on country experience. The countries represented by the case studies were chosen so as to embrace extensively studied economies (such as Poland or Hungary) as well as economies about which not much is known but whose experience could still be very useful to other economies in transition.

The conference was organized by the National Bank of Croatia. Participants included senior officials from governments, central banks, and the World Bank and IMF, in addition to researchers from universities and academic institutes. The number of participants was limited in order to facilitate a "think-tank" atmosphere. The beauty and cultural richness of Dubrovnik provided a perfect environment for meeting with fellow economists and exchanging thoughts and ideas. The National Bank of Croatia intends to organize follow-up conferences in Dubrovnik in order to contribute to a continuing study of the progress being made in transitional economies.

Stabilization After Five Years of Reform: Issues and Experiences

Mario I. Blejer and Marko Škreb

> Stability is not everything, but without stability, everything is nothing.
>
> Karl Schiller
> Former German Minister of the Economy

More than any other single event, the fall of the Berlin Wall in November 1989 symbolized the beginning of the process of transformation of the economies of Central Europe and of the former Soviet Union from centrally planned, command systems to liberal, market-oriented economies. Although the "transition from socialism," as this process of transformation has been labelled, is centered around fundamental economic changes, transition is a multifaceted phenomenon that encompasses complex structural, institutional, and behavioral adjustments that go well beyond the realm of economics. For many countries, the demise of socialism signaled not only the start of a period of economic modifications but indeed the beginning of their nation-building process.

The analysis of the nature and causes of these tumultuous events has challenged virtually all established modes of studying human relations, from the purely ideological to the highly technical. Although transition is not an exclusively economic phenomenon, economics has taken center stage in the study of the postsocialist transformation; a complete new branch of economics – the *economics of transition* – has developed, focused on explaining and providing advice concerning this unprecedented process. Moreover, a special international financial institution, the European Bank for Reconstruction and Development, has been created to support and enhance the transitional process.

A large body of literature dealing with these subjects has appeared and numerous conferences have addressed these issues, so there is obviously no scarcity of empirical material on transition. However, no definite analytical framework has been established and much of what is discussed is largely based on conjecture, most of it immediately superseded by new hypotheses or rendered obsolete by current developments. This is to be expected since we are dealing, to a large extent, with unforeseen events and with a set of unfamiliar questions. The lack of historical precedents has hindered analysts' ability to draw viable conclusions relevant to the current circumstances of Eastern Europe and the former Soviet Union. The uniqueness of each country's experience, from its initial conditions to the specific nature of the constraints faced by their policy makers, makes generalized conclusions even more difficult to attain.

This does not imply, however, that one cannot try to understand the process of transformation. Because economists are dealing with a set of atypical problems does not mean that predictions and inferences cannot be made or that traditional analytical tools are not useful. In fact, after more than six years of reforms, an analysis and a comparison of actual experiences – and a detailed study of the design, implementation, and results of the various reform programs – could help to elucidate some of the most pressing questions and to draw some important theoretical and practical conclusions.

From the many dimensions of the transformation process, *macroeconomic stabilization* is the one where taking stock and deriving common lessons could be critical, and where the variety of experiences and results to date may allow extraction of the most valuable theoretical and policy insights. It is also the area where an early evaluation of the results could lead to conclusions that may help to avoid the repetition of mistakes. In the stabilization area, comparisons between the experiences of transition and market economies seem more relevant; the lessons obtained could lead to cross-fertilization and even to the advancement of general economic knowledge that could shed new light on existing theoretical debates.

Macroeconomic stabilization involves the achievement and maintenance of a reasonable degree of price stability and external balance, as well as a sensible rate of economic growth. In principle it could be claimed that macroeconomic stabilization is not an intrinsic component of postsocialist transition and would be relevant in this context only to the extent that the initial situation, at the outset of reforms, involved important macroeconomic imbalances. Yet in practice, for reasons that stem from the nature and functioning of the socialist system as well as from conditions created by the transition itself, all the postcommunist economies did emerge from their previous regimes with various – and sometimes very significant – degrees of macroeconomic imbalance (with inflation and output collapse the primary manifestation) that needed to be corrected. Therefore, macroeconomic stabilization has always been a major ingredient of the transition process.

It is evidently quite difficult to delineate the precise boundaries of stabilization policies during transition because, in practice, they interact closely with liberalization policies, with institutional adjustments, and with structural reforms. Nonetheless, it is still very important to distinguish and separate analytically the dominant features of the major macroeconomic developments and of the specific policy strategies that have been part of the transformation process. While recognizing the complexity of the interactions between structural and stabilization policies, this volume constitutes a substantial attempt to offer a comprehensive examination of postsocialist stabilization and to outline the principal inferences that can be derived from the experience to date.

In dealing with macroeconomic stabilization, the essays in this volume focus on five major issues: (1) the aggregative *trends* characterizing transition, particularly at the macroeconomic level; (2) the conception and strategy followed in the *design* of stabilization policies; (3) structural and external *constraints* faced by the economy; (4) *implementation* and instrumentation of specific stabilization policies; and (5) description and characterization of the *results* obtained.

The volume is divided into three sections. Part I contains four essays that are mainly concerned with the first three issues just listed (general macroeconomic trends, conceptual design of stabilization programs, and the nature of the constraints faced by reforms). Part II consists of seven detailed country studies, covering a wide range of experience and carefully examining the issues of design, implementation, and outcomes of stabilization programs. The volume concludes with an afterword that looks beyond the narrow aspects of stabilization to address some of the most important long-term issues connected with the process.

The opening chapter, by Martha de Melo, Cevdet Denizer, and Alan Gelb, is an ambitious undertaking aimed at analyzing the comparative experience of 28 transition economies over the 1989–94 period in order to draw conclusions about their progress regarding economic liberalization, inflation, and growth. Although the measurement of growth and inflation is relatively straightforward, the authors make a noteworthy attempt to develop a quantitative composite index for measuring economic liberalization. A "cumulative liberalization index" for each country is built by assigning numerical values, based largely on objective indicators, to the degree of domestic and external liberalization and to the extent that private-sector entry has been opened. The index is calculated to reflect both the intensity as well as the duration of reforms from 1989 onward.

Using their index, the authors obtain a number of important results regarding the patterns of transition. In the first place, they conclude that the extent of liberalization has a positive effect on the rate of growth of output. Second, it is observed that liberalization seems to induce an initial increase in inflation, but this increase is followed by a prompt and sustained decline. Third, there is marked negative relationship between inflation and output; that is, output recovery requires that inflation be reduced to moderate levels. Thus, their general conclusion is that liberalization is an important element in the success of stabilization policies and in prompting a resumption of output growth.

Two important policy implications arise from Chapter 1. First, fiscal pressures tend to be the most serious constraint on the road to stabilization; however, the more rapidly the economy is liberalized and reformed, the less binding this constraint becomes. In fact, rapid reformers have experienced smaller fiscal deficits. Second, the underdevelopment of monetary institutions and instruments has greatly limited the ability of monetary policy to play a central role in the stabilization process. As in the fiscal area, though, more-rapid reforms tend to reinforce the efficacy of this instrument and to enhance the ability of the government to cope with inflationary pressures. Although these implications are relatively straightforward and in accordance with conventional wisdom, the importance of the research by De Melo, Denizer, and Gelb is in providing quantified evidence and a solid empirical backing.

The opening chapter reconfirms the view that stabilization becomes a priority for the resumption of growth, but it also stresses that – in transitional countries – stabilization is rendered more difficult by the very acute output contractions often observed during the early stages of liberalization. The magnitude and the causes of these contractions are the subject of Chapter 2, by Robert Mundell. He observes that, between 1989 and 1994, the cumulative loss of output experienced by the economies of Eastern Europe and the former Soviet Union were on a scale never before experienced in modern history. After documenting the size of the output fall, Mundell elaborates on two central questions: What caused such an unprecedented contraction? Why have output contractions been so widely different across countries?

Mundell suggests six possible reasons for the loss of output: (1) flawed national statistics that do not correctly measure the rapid growth in private-sector output and overlook the probable increase in informal sector production that is brought about by economic liberalization; (2) the elimination of soft budget constraints that, combined with strict monetary policies, resulted in high real interest rates and strict credit restrictions; (3) the pervasive bureaucratic and red-tape legacies of the communist era that, combined with the scarcity of the appropriate human capital, resulted in negligible supply responses from the private sector; (4) collapse of foreign trade following the disintegration of the CMEA (Council for Mutual Economic Assistance) and of the Soviet Union; (5) deterioration of the terms of trade in a number of countries; and (6) lack of sufficient foreign support. Mundell suggests that all these factors have, to varying degrees, contributed to the reduction of output. But in his view the main cause behind the enormous collapse is the extraordinary decline in foreign trade and the effect of the foreign trade multiplier on both demand and aggregate supply. Mundell claims that the disintegration of export markets immediately reduces the capacity to import intermediary goods, inputs, spare parts, and machinery, leading to the emergence of bottlenecks and scarcities that result in the breakdown of the production chain.

The second question concerns the causes for the differential degree of contraction across countries (e.g., the cumulative decline of output over the 1990–93 period varied from less than 18% in Hungary to more than 80% in Georgia). Mundell enumerates four interrelated factors that influence the magnitude of output loss. He postulates that output declines will be larger when (a) the level of industrialization is higher, (b) the stock of human capital is lower, (c) the economy is more open, and (d) the country is more urbanized. Of course, specific country conditions (such as religious strife, war, and political unrest) have played a role, but initial structural conditions seem to be the most reliable predictors.

Chapters 3 and 4 stress the essential role played by state-owned–enterprise reforms in increasing the chances of success for stabilization programs in transition economies. It is generally agreed that the reform of state-owned enterprises is essential for the successful implementation of macroeconomic stabilization, but it is also evident that microeconomic restructuring and privatization are time-consuming and lengthy processes that cannot be completed overnight. Because stabilization policies cannot be postponed until the enterprise sector has been significantly restructured, interim procedures are required to moderate the inflationary pressures arising from that sector. Marcelo Selowsky and Matthew Vogel consider one such interim procedure in detail. They argue in Chapter 3 that large, loss-making enterprises must be isolated from the banking-system credit circuit and that budgetary resources should be directly allocated to finance the public goods that such enterprises are currently providing. In the socialist system, budgetary support for enterprises and cross-subsidization among them were common features, but a substantial number of money-losing enterprises become inviable as reforms and liberalization are set in motion. The authors argue that a significant number of large enterprises cannot be immediately closed down because they provide such public goods as artificial employment, public utilities, and social services to workers and their dependents. Political pressure to keep these enterprises alive is strong. The problem is worse in economies where no resumption of growth is imminent and so workers cannot be expected to be relocated as part of the normal evolution of the labor market. However, if those enterprises continue to borrow from the commercial banking system as before, they will have little incentive to restructure. Therefore, the best strategy may be first to isolate the enterprises from banking credit and second to allocate explicit resources to the budgetary provision of the public goods provided by these enterprises. Enterprise isolation programs can be, it is claimed, an efficient tool to achieve the needed downsizing.

Although there has been some experience with this procedure (in countries such as Albania, Kazakstan, and Kyrgistan), the authors warn about the dangers and tradeoffs present in the process. Selowski and Vogel argue that there is an appropriate sequence in the allocation of fiscal resources: they should first be used to support the downsizing of enterprises, and only later for the recapitalization of banks. If recapitalization of banks occurs before downsizing then there may be a delay in restructuring, significant moral hazard could be generated, and the stabilization process could be jeopardized.

The restructuring of the state-owned enterprises entails, to a large extent, the acceleration of the process of privatization, and the techniques used to accomplish this latter task may give rise to unexpected complications that will have both micro- and macroeconomic effects. Some of the consequences of observed privatization patterns in transitional economies are discussed by Mario Nuti. Chapter 4 deals first with some general problems of corporate governance, and then focuses on a particular form of intrashareholder conflict that may occur when employees own enough shares to control the company.

In Nuti's opinion a shareholder (or stakeholder) conflict constitutes a problem when control is in the hands of stakeholders who, individually, own less than a balanced share. In that case, the problem may take the form of overemployment and overpay (i.e., labor compensation is set above the levels warranted by profit maximization) and the stakeholders may eventually appropriate the entire present value of the company. Moreover, Nuti views the problems of corporate governance in recently privatized firms as part and parcel of the wider transitional problem of establishing law and order, of ensuring the legal protection of contracts, and of fighting against organized crime.

Part II of the book is composed of seven country-specific studies that analyze in detail the conception, implementation, and performance of various stabilization programs implemented throughout Eastern Europe and the former Soviet Union. Broad generalizations are usually suspect in the study of transition economies. However, the range of countries covered in this section, the variety of strategies adopted, and the differences in initial conditions, resource availability, historical experiences, and political constraints make the sample quite significant for any attempt to reach policy lessons and analytical conclusions.

In Chapter 5, Stanislaw Wellisz analyzes the post-1990 Polish stabilization program. Three different periods of exchange-rate regimes in Poland are described: the fixed–exchange-rate period, the "crawl-cum-mini devaluation" period, and the "pure crawling peg" period. Wellisz's main conclusion is that inflation in Poland was fiscal-deficit-driven until mid-1993 but that the chief causes of subsequent inflation were the policy refusal to let the zloty appreciate in real terms and the failure to sterilize the rapid accumulation of foreign exchange reserves. Wellisz reaches the interesting conclusion that, at least in the Polish case, it might be better to finance the fiscal deficit through monetization. His argument is that the monetization of the deficit imposes a generalized inflation tax on all money balance holders (i.e., on everyone), whereas deficit financing by issuing new government debt crowds out private borrowing and reduces investment.

Chapter 6 deals with the case of Hungary, which is (among the transition economies) the country where reforms started earlier and were implemented gradually over a long period of time. However, macroeconomic stability has not been achieved, and the Hungarian economy is in the midst of a new stabilization effort. In his study, János Kornai places the current Hungarian economic policies in an historical and political economy perspective. Toward this end he outlines Hungarian developments in the last three decades and distinguishes the transformation path adopted by Hungary from that followed by other postsocialist countries. Kornai emphasizes four distinct Hungarian characteristics: (a) the greater emphasis placed in Hungary on the material welfare of its population; (b) the creation of a paternalistic welfare state, as measured by a higher ratio of social entitlement spending to GDP; (c) the implementation of a gradual and extended process of transformation and reform; and (d) the preservation of relative political calm. These factors are closely related and, in Kornai's view, led to the creation of a significant social debt with the rest of the world, and with its own future generations, in the form of legislative commitments to maintain the consumption levels of the current generation.

Within this framework, Kornai analyzes the stabilization strategy of the current Hungarian government. He singles out three key elements in this strategy: a radical devaluation of the currency at the beginning of the program, coupled with a preannounced crawling peg; a substantial cut in budgetary spending, particularly on social expenditures and on the welfare system; and an income policy aimed at curbing the growth of nominal wages. These three components mark, in Kornai's view, a clean break with the four main features just described that until now have set Hungary apart from the other transition countries. Kornai notes this curious reversal of roles: the Socialist Party now in power, having won the elections by emphasizing its social sensitivity, is carrying out an almost "Thatcherite" program, while the conservative opposition is fighting the program and defending the overblown welfare state and wage demands of workers. Although it is still too early to assess the results of this shift in the Hungarian approach, Kornai delineates three possible scenarios: a return to the "muddling through" of the previous decades; perseverance in the current policies, leading to the government's political downfall; or success after some delays. Kornai does not weigh the chances of these three scenarios but clearly supports the program, and views abandoning the previous approach as a prerequisite to putting Hungary on the road to sustained development.

Chapters 7 and 8 deal with the case of Croatia, the host country to the Dubrovnik Conference. Croatia has, indeed, achieved remarkable results not only in stopping very high inflation (from more than 1000% per year before October 1993 to less than 5% currently) but also, and probably more importantly, in maintaining price stability afterwards. The preparations for launching the program are explained in the essay by Nikica Valentić (Prime Minister of Croatia); the implementation and achievements of the adopted policies are discussed by Velimir Šonje and Marko Škreb. The central claim of the essay by Šonje and Škreb is that the link between the exchange rate and inflation was very important in explaining Croatia's high inflation prior to the start of the stabilization effort. At the same time, they claim, the strength of this link was instrumental in achieving rapid disinflation. Indeed, the high degree of dollarization of the Croatian economy proved to be crucial in reducing inflationary pressures and in eradicating inflationary expectations and inflationary inertia once the exchange rate was credibly stabilized. The correlation between exchange-rate fluctuations and rising price is, of course, not perfect, owing to a number of factors that include changes in the ratio of tradable to nontradable prices and alterations in the exchange-rate regime. After analyzing the various transmission mechanisms between exchange rates and prices, and after testing empirically the proposition that domestic price changes are largely determined by exchange-rate fluctuations, the authors conclude that exchange-rate depreciations did indeed act as a significant cost–push factor. Based on this conclusion, Šonje and Škreb claim that a regime based on a floating exchange rate that allows nominal rate appreciation once confidence is restored is a superior stabilization strategy for a country that needs to accumulate international reserves and improve its fiscal position.

Like Croatia, and like almost every other transitional economy, Slovenia at the beginning of its transformation faced high inflation and widespread external and internal disequilibria. In addition, as stressed in Chapter 9 by Velimir Bole, Slovenia had neither foreign exchange reserves nor access to foreign financial markets. It was not possible, therefore, to adopt a standard or conventional stabilization approach. Thus, Slovenia was forced to build its stock of foreign exchange reserves and to stabilize simultaneously. The adopted program relied strongly on the reshaping of the foreign exchange market and on the adoption of a floating–exchange-rate regime, combined with a restrictive monetary policy. Tight fiscal discipline was also imposed, with the result that inflation dropped dramatically, reserves increased, and the economy started to grow. However, because income policies were introduced late and were very partial in nature, the relative prices of nontradables rose rapidly. Given this factor and the probably excessive inflow of foreign capital, inflation in Slovenia has remained above 20% per year. On the positive side, a clear lesson from the Slovenian experience is that its openness helped to mitigate the costs of stabilization by averting a serious impact on economic activity and employment.

Chapters 10 and 11 look at countries that were part of the former Soviet Union. In Chapter 10, Ardo Hansson offers a comprehensive comparative analysis of macroeconomic stabilization in the three Baltic states: Estonia, Latvia, and Lithuania. Following an extensive description of their stabilization plans that highlights the radical differences in the strategies adopted, Hansson offers some important conclusions. First, the passage from very high to controlled levels of inflation was largely due to the use of conventional macroeconomic policies: after tightening monetary policy and balancing the budget, inflation fell sharply in the three countries. Second, in the short run, the credibility of the program was an essential ingredient for success: public perception that the authorities were committed to lower inflation was a crucial element in attaining a significant reduction. Third, if the behavior of the money demand remains volatile, Hansson suggests that the exchange rate is a better nominal anchor than the money supply. Fourth, the relative price adjustment required in transition countries is probably larger than in developing market economies and could therefore lead to more prolonged inflationary pressures. Hansson notes that the sudden opening up of small countries, such as the Baltics, creates the potential for huge capital inflows that could jeopardize the authorities' control over the money supply and therefore over inflation; this has been observed in other transitional countries such as the Czech Republic, Croatia, Poland, and Slovenia (and more recently in Russia and Kazakstan). Hence the role of capital inflows in promoting inflation needs to be analyzed in more detail. In summarizing his comparative conclusions, Hansson strongly stresses that program credibility and a policy of gradual exchange-rate appreciation play central roles in slowing inflation.

In Chapter 11, Oleh Havrylyshin applies a political economy approach (similar to the one used by Kornai) to the analysis of Ukraine's stabilization. Two distinctive periods of Ukrainian reforms are identified and named after the respective contemporaneous political leaders, although more emphasis is given to the earlier Kravchuk period. Ukraine is an important comparative case because it is one of the slowest reformers. Havrylyshin offers three hypotheses for why reforms were delayed so long: intellectual debates, nation-building tasks, and the vested interests of the "new-old" elite to preserve an unreformed or half-reformed economy. In the author's view, this last factor – namely, the interest of what he calls the "post-Soviet rentiers patriarchs" – was primarily responsible for the delay in reforms. The period 1991–94 can be safely characterized as a nonreform period that contrasts with the current Kuchma period. Although Havrylyshin has great sympathy for the 1995 program, he stresses that it is too early to tell if the reform efforts will continue and will succeed in unthawing the frozen Ukrainian transition.

Like Kornai, Havrylyshin emphasizes the importance of political determination to pursue reforms, but the Ukrainian case exemplifies a different perspective. Whereas in Hungary it is considered necessary to abandon the benign, populist approach in order to reach sustainable stabilization and the resumption of growth, in the Ukraine what is viewed as essential is the adoption of policies aimed at weakening the position of the currently dominant interests *before* building a new, market-oriented economy. This is a difficult task, one that requires clear goals, political support, patience and determination.

Part III closes the book with a chapter by Vito Tanzi in which he calls attention to the longer-run dimensions of successful transition. In particular, Tanzi concentrates on the policies that are necesary to ensure that stabilization is indeed followed by economic reactivation and a resumption of growth. He points out that the process of economic growth, even in developed market economies, is surrounded by uncertainties and is, intrinsically, a very slow process. Therefore, there are political biases against paying too much attention to what must be done in this area. However, stabilization without growth may not be sustainable, so it is extremely important for policy makers to emphasize reform policies that contribute to enhancing growth prospects without hurting the stabilization effort.

In addition to the many reforms discussed in previous chapters that could contribute to future growth (such as redefinition of property rights and contracts, improvement in tax and expenditure policies, creation of appropriate fiscal and monetary institutions, etc.), Tanzi adds one area to which, in his view, policy makers should pay particular attention. This is the need to worry about the consequences of economic policies for equity and income distribution. In Tanzi's view, serious consideration of these aspects would ensure not only a better allocation of resources but also the political consensus needed to gear economic policy toward a path of sustained growth.

After studying both the variety of aggregate transition paths and the specific country cases, and after considering the analytical issues involving stabilization in a reforming environment, a number of significant messages emerge. In spite of the difficulties in making generalizations, it seems that the experience to date confirms that macroeconomic stabilization is a necessary condition for a successful transition, but that it is difficult to implement without a sufficient mass of structural reforms. Although it is hard to envisage a resumption of investments and growth without stabilization, macroeconomic stability is rarely sustainable without microeconomic restructuring, particularly at the level of state-owned enterprise. Without enough structural reforms, macroeconomic stability would induce less favorable supply responses than in a more fundamentally changed economy with a large private system in place. This, in turn, will politically weaken the reformers and reduce the chances of success. Even if stabilization initially succeeds in an unreformed environment, the sustainability of the effort is in doubt. Where old institutions of central planning have not been completely abolished, where quasimonopolistic market structures are common, and where prices as well as access to hard currencies have not been totally deregulated, an economy is very susceptible to inflation and so its macroeconomic stability is, indeed, very fragile.

An important insight that emerges from the various chapters is that, in practice, there are no nonstandard macroeconomic policies. The most successful stabilizations took place in the countries where, following the first postliberalization price increases, the government was determined to apply standard macroeconomic policies – based on a balanced government budget, stable monetary growth, and the principle of neutrality with respect to private-sector activities – in the way such policies are applied in most developed market economies.

It is clear that political economy considerations are essential in order to understand the design and performance of reforms. However, the relationship between changing political support and macroeconomic stabilization remains unclear. In Poland, for example, the defeat in the 1993 elections of the parties that had supported reforms since their inception took place in the context of an economic recovery in the country that has probably experienced the strongest rebound in output. On the other hand, the victory of the socialists in the recent elections in Hungary signaled the abandonment of populist, expansionist policies.

We remark in closing that, as in everyday life, simple rules seem to work best. Transitional countries would be well advised to suppress inflation, impose financial discipline, downsize large loss-making enterprises, maintain a sustainable balance-of-payments position, and so on. But, as in everyday life, the key issue is implementation – and here, generalizations are much more difficult. What is essential is to keep the final goal of the transformation always in mind and not to be distracted by short-run obstacles. The long path to a market economy contains many hurdles, but as has been said, "an obstacle is something that you see when you take your eyes off your goal."

PART I

General Studies

CHAPTER 1

From Plan to Market: Patterns of Transition

Martha de Melo, Cevdet Denizer, and Alan Gelb

1. INTRODUCTION[1]

The transition from a planned economy to a market economy involves a complex process of institutional, structural, and behavioral change. Formerly communist countries have moved along this transition to varying degrees.[2] This essay places these countries into a comparative perspective. It emphasizes the cornerstone of the early reforms – economic liberalization, for which an index is developed – and its interaction with growth and inflation: How do these outcomes relate to progress with reform? It also considers the macroeconomic and sectoral patterns underlying these interactions.

The findings here help to explain two paradoxes of transition. One is that the attempt to maintain employment and output by fiscal and quasifiscal transfers to enterprises results in larger output declines than a policy of hard budget constraints introduced along with economic liberalization. The other paradox is that the liberalization of prices results in lower inflation than do continued price controls. In both cases, liberalization leads to stabilization in a way that is not self-evident to policy makers accustomed to socialist pricing and output conventions.

The core countries analyzed are 26 in Central and Eastern Europe (CEE) and the former Soviet Union (FSU), plus Mongolia. China

[1] Stoyan Tenev developed the switching regression technique used here. We appreciate comments on the economic liberalization index by World Bank staff, and comments on other aspects of the paper by Leszek Balcerowicz, Stanley Fischer, Wafik Grais, Bert Hofman, Arvo Kuddo, Costas Michalopoulos, Branko Milanovic, Randi Ryterman, Tevfik Yaprak, and participants in the First Dubrovnik Conference on Transitional Economies, where the paper was presented in June 1995. A shorter version of this essay has appeared in the *World Bank Economic Review* (September 1996).

[2] See Fischer and Gelb (1991) for an early discussion of the elements of the transition process and Kornai (1993a) for a discussion of the multifaceted problems associated with the "transformational recession."

and Vietnam are also included for comparative purposes, although these countries are distinctive in many respects.[3] The period covered is 1989 through 1994. The starting point is the last year before the initial postcommunist transitions, although Poland, Hungary, the former Yugoslavia, and China had previously initiated significant reforms and other countries had also taken some reform steps.

What are the essential commonalities at the macroeconomic and broad sector level? Section 2 highlights four stylized features of the socialist legacy and predicts corresponding outcomes from transition.[4] Such changes are stimulated by a wide range of policy reforms collectively referred to as "economic liberalization," but a summary measure is needed to link liberalization to macroeconomic performance. In Section 3, we define a composite index that takes into account three dimensions of liberalization: internal markets, external trade, and facilitation of private-sector entry.[5] Countries are ranked on the depth of these policy reforms in each of six years of transition, 1989–94. Country classification is then based on *cumulative* liberalization – reflecting duration as well as depth of reform – because structural and institutional adjustment takes time, even when policy change itself is rapid. Countries are placed in one of four reform groups or in a "regional tensions" category for countries that have experienced major and persistent internal conflicts or conflict-related blockades.

Section 4 analyzes cross-country evidence on the interactions between liberalization, economic growth (or contraction), and inflation. Section 5 extends this by looking at the time profile of the transition experience. We first trace the experience of each reform group over the period, and then estimate a regime-switching equation to provide a profile for reformers and nonreformers. Section 6 considers macroeconomic and sectoral patterns underlying the (rather strong) relationships previously derived.

Section 7 addresses a deeper question: "What accounts for economic liberalization?" Many characteristics, including history and culture, affect policy choice, but here we look at politics. For CEE

[3] Transition countries in Southeast Asia, Africa, and Latin America are not addressed here, nor are the former GDR, rump Yugoslavia, and Bosnia.

[4] An important feature not mentioned is the widespread availability of basic human needs (education, health services, and housing) associated with a more equal distribution of income than in capitalist countries (Milanovic 1995). The transition has been accompanied by increasing inequalities in money income and a deterioration in social services, but these issues go beyond the scope of this chapter.

[5] EBRD (1994) provides a good overview of many dimensions of policy change and serves as a 1994 marker for the liberalization index developed here.

and the FSU, a close relationship is found between economic liberalization and political reform, as given by a widely used index of political freedom, and this is assessed. Section 8 summarizes main conclusions and their implications for some policy debates.

Data Limitations

Before proceeding with any empirical research on transition, one should note very serious data weaknesses.[6] Under socialism, *output* of state enterprises was often exaggerated, while during the transition, output – and especially the size of the private sector – tends to be underreported, sometimes by large margins according to recent studies.[7] Stockbuilding is frequently mismeasured. *Inflation* is also difficult to measure, with sharp changes in the quality and composition of goods and a base period characterized by serious shortages at fixed official prices. Problems encountered in estimating deflators mean that "real" wages are then hard to measure. Detailed reviews of individual countries suggest that official *unemployment* rates, which range from nearly 0% to 17%, reflect incentives to report as well as the actual level of unemployment. *Trade* and *balance-of-payments* data are difficult to interpret consistently over time in the transition from a planned trading system, owing to inconsistent bilateral exchange rates used in CMEA trade and problematic intra-USSR trade data. Cross-border trade is now hard to monitor.

We have some idea of the likely direction of most statistical biases, but their extent may differ among countries. Balcerowicz and Gelb (1994) argue, for example, that underreporting of output is likely to be larger in radical reformers, where private activity is growing fastest. Although this is not implausible, black markets thrive on pervasive regulation, and statistical systems have themselves adjusted less in certain slow-reforming countries (and also in those suffering from regional tensions), so that the opposite result could hold.[8] We test the robustness of the results of the regime-switching equation in

---

[6] For more discussion, see EBRD (1994) as well as Balcerowicz and Gelb (1994) and references therein.

[7] A separate problem is whether output is a useful welfare measure, since a proportion of its fall will involve the elimination of production that has little value in a market economy driven by consumer preference.

[8] Estimates of unrecorded economic activity exist for a number of countries but vary widely both between countries and, for individual countries, between sources. The difficulty in incorporating such estimates into growth rates is compounded by the lack of precise estimates of the size of unrecorded economies before transition.

Section 6 by simulating plausible adjustments for the underground economy. Given the more general uncertainties, however, this chapter emphasizes broad trends and large observed differences rather than fine ones.

2. THE COMMON LEGACY AND ITS IMPLICATIONS

The extent to which transition can be considered a common process depends on the relative strength of the common legacy of communism versus country-specific factors. Transition countries differed substantially in their initial conditions, which include the level of income and wealth, the nature and extent of economic distortions, and the level of institutional development.[9] However, they also had a strong common legacy that can be characterized by four features.

Macrobalance by Direct Control. Financial flows were the passive outcome of central directives that regulated credit and incomes. The financing of enterprises was set by a credit plan, taking into account investment targets, and implemented through the monobank financial sector. Surpluses were accumulated in large enterprises and were transferred to the budget to finance subsidies and transfers as well as direct expenditures, which accounted for up to 50–60% of GDP. Given fixed prices and consumption targets, wage control was the critical factor for the balance between output and demand. In the years prior to the collapse of the old regime, wage increases exceeded the ability of the economy to provide consumer goods, resulting in involuntary accumulation of financial assets, or repressed inflation.

Coordination through Plans. Economic activity was based on a central plan with quantitative output targets specified in physical units. Heavy industry was accorded priority over consumer goods, and service sectors were accorded low priority in the allocation of resources. The matching of income and expenditures with physical targets was achieved through coordinated, economywide plans, such as the central plan for material products, the manpower plan, the credit plan, and the investment plan. Domestic trade was carried out by centralized organizations, and the CMEA (Council for Mutual Economic Assistance) system linked most CEE countries and Mongolia into the highly planned economy of the USSR. These practices were softened

---

[9] See de Melo et al. (1995) for an exploration of the nature and importance of initial conditions and other country-specific factors in the transition experience.

Table 1. *From plan to market: the common legacy and systemic change during transition*

Common legacy	Changes occurring during transition
1. Macrobalance by direct control	Macroeconomic *destabilization*
2. Coordination through plans	*Output declines* resulting from disruption in the coordinating mechanism
3. Little private ownership	*Output gains* from private ownership and private-sector growth
4. Distorted relative prices	Microeconomic and sectoral *reallocations*

in "market socialist" countries; even there, however, discretionary ex post interventions by central authorities largely offset market forces.

Little Private Ownership. With limited exceptions, property rights were exercised by the state, and private ownership was not allowed. The lack of a profit motive – arising from the absence of private ownership – adversely affected efficiency, and the prevalence of planned allocations meant that communist economies had relatively few small firms.[10]

Distorted Relative Prices. Prices played an accounting role and were set in accordance with the central plan. Implicit prices of essentials – including housing, energy, transportation, education, and medical care – were kept low, and land prices were essentially zero.[11] Implicit trade margins were low, and prices of final goods failed to reflect differences in distribution costs.

What happens when a planned economy with the features just listed is replaced by a market system with liberalized prices?[12] Each of these features has its counterpart in systemic changes occurring during transition (see Table 1).

[10] For a comparison of industrial organization in Russia, see Brown, Ickes, and Ryterman (1994).

[11] Partly because of the suppression of prices in key nontraded sectors, the ratios of PPP-based GDP to exchange-rate based GDP tend to be high for communist countries. For discussion of China (where the ratio has been as high as 8 to 1), see Gelb, Jefferson, and Singh (1993) and World Bank (1994).

[12] Elements of an answer to this question appear in various works. See Aghion and Blanchard (1994), Berg (1993), Berg and Sachs (1992), Chadka and Coricelli (1994), Ickes and Ryterman (1993), Kornai (1993a), and Taylor (1994).

Macroeconomic Destabilization. Initial price liberalization typically leads to subsequent price increases, especially if it is undertaken under conditions of repressed inflation. The immediate challenge for macroeconomic policy is then to slow the rate of price increase and reverse the inflationary expectations and flight from domestic financial assets that follow the initial price spike. This requires introducing hard budget constraints on enterprises while introducing well-targeted social expenditures, including unemployment benefits. However, inflationary pressures may persist if and when the government's traditional tax base is eroded owing to: output losses (see next paragraph); further pressure on state enterprises' revenues due to their loss of monopoly position; and difficulties in imposing payment discipline through a previously passive financial system.

Output Declines from Disruptions in the Coordinating Mechanism. The sudden abolition of planning in a complex, highly interdependent economy can impair economic coordination, affecting both useful and unwanted production pending the establishment of a new, efficient system of market coordination.[13] The resulting increases in transaction costs can be imagined as a negative supply shock to an economy-wide production function that is specified to include coordination activities (such as trade and payments) as an intermediate sector. The severity of actual output decline would depend on the degree of interdependence within the economy, the extent to which the planning system was disrupted, and the speed at which the new, market-based coordinating system develops. In some countries, where plan coordination began to deteriorate prior to price liberalization, costs may occur over many years. For example, the planning process in the FSU deteriorated after *glasnost* and *perestroika* began to take hold in 1987.

Output Gains from Private Ownership and Private-Sector Growth. Efficiency gains come from the legalization of private ownership, which creates incentives to maximize returns, the establishment and enforcement of a legal framework to support private activities, and the facilitation

---

[13] Consider, for example, the case of the Kyrgyz Republic, which may have a comparative advantage in agriculture but has no institutional mechanism to allocate and recover agricultural credit. Other impediments to coordination have been introduced as a result of new national boundaries, which interfere with payment arrangements for the output from production monopolies now located abroad, or the allocation of previously centralized gas pipeline capacity.

of private entry. Much of the increased private-sector output would be produced by smaller firms. In the long run, the movement from (inefficient) plan to (efficient) market should be equivalent to a positive supply shock, raising the efficiency of resource allocation and creating a burst of economic growth, as well as increasing the "utility" of output. The latter would be expected to rise as output increasingly reflects individual preference rather than the demands of a plan.[14]

Microeconomic and Sectoral Reallocations. Microeconomic and sectoral reallocations occur in response to price changes resulting from liberalization and cuts in subsidies, as well as to changes in demand. Previously repressed sectors, notably energy and services, should expand and offset declines in industry – especially in defense-related industry, given substantial cuts in defense procurement, and in agriculture, which was heavily subsidized in many countries. Expansion of previously repressed nontraded sectors, including real estate, occurs despite large exchange-rate devaluations, which normally favor traded goods. Developments in the labor market would reflect the changes in the composition of sectoral output, and especially the growth of small private trade and transport activities.

These changes occur both as a result of disintegration of the old regime and in response to active measures of economic liberalization. An interesting question, which we address in what follows, is to what extent transition can be considered a common process, and in particular to what extent differences in experiences with growth and inflation are associated with economic liberalization.

3. COUNTRY EXPERIENCE WITH ECONOMIC LIBERALIZATION

In order to explore the broad cross-country relationships between growth, inflation, and liberalization, we construct an annual index of liberalization for the transition period starting in 1989. This index is then used to classify countries into reform groups, based on their cumulative experience with economic liberalization as of year-end 1994. Comparative analysis shows that recent experience with growth and inflation is broadly consistent within groups.

---

[14] If the posttransition distribution of income were very undesirable, the social utility of output could of course be judged as inferior to an inefficient planned output bundle.

Aggregate Indicators

Growth, inflation, and liberalization are defined as follows.

Growth is represented by annual changes in real, officially measured GDP.

Inflation is represented by average annual changes in the CPI.[15]

Liberalization is measured by an index of economic liberalization that has been constructed for purposes of our analysis. An annual liberalization index (LI) is calculated for each country for each year over the 1989–94 period. It ranges from 0 to 1, where 0 represents an unreformed and 1 a basically reformed country. The LI is the weighted average (with weights of 0.3, 0.3, and 0.4 respectively) of 0-to-1 rankings of liberalization in the following three areas:

I – *internal markets* (liberalization of domestic prices and abolition of state trading monopolies);[16]

E – *external markets* (currency convertibility and liberalization of the foreign trade regime, including elimination of export controls and taxes as well as substitution of low to moderate import duties for import quotas and high import tariffs); and

P – *private-sector entry* (privatization of small-scale and large-scale enterprises and banking reform).[17]

The values assigned to these three areas in each year are shown for 28 transition economies in the Appendix, which also explains how the values are derived.

The weights used in aggregating the components of the index are notional estimates of the relative impact of I and E, which represent liberalization through introduction of competitive, flexible-price markets, and P, which represents liberalization through chang-

---

[15] Substantial cross-country variation exists in the behavior of different price indexes. In Poland and especially Bulgaria, increases in the CPI have outpaced those in industrial prices, reflecting a sharp rise in the relative price of services (a previously suppressed sector). In Russia, on the other hand, price liberalization was followed by a sharp increase in the relative price of heavy industrial goods, probably reflecting strong monopoly power domestically reinforced by limited import competition due to a very depressed real exchange rate.

[16] Countries with an I rating near unity may still maintain price controls on a range of non-traded household essentials, in particular rents and household utilities.

[17] The indicators used for P are proxies for opening up the economy to private-sector development. They do not capture the overall quality of the legal and regulatory framework or the effectiveness of government in institution building or in the implementation of reforms, but only because of the difficulty of developing comparative measures. Also, land privatization is not included, although several countries (Romania, Armenia, Albania, and Lithuania) have privatized agricultural land, helping to stimulate agricultural growth.

ing ownership of fixed assets. The effects of these components differ slightly, as mentioned in Section 4 in the discussion of growth and inflation equations.

In the analysis that follows, a cumulative liberalization index (CLI) is defined to represent the duration as well as the intensity of reforms from 1989 onward. It is calculated as the sum of a country's LIs. The rationale for using the CLI is that, at any given moment, economic performance will not be determined by the degree of liberalization at that moment alone; it will also have been shaped by institutional and behavioral changes stimulated by prior policy reforms. The CLIs for 1994 are shown in the Appendix and are used in Table 2 (see Section 4) to rank CEE and FSU countries not affected by regional tensions into four reform groups, determined by natural breaks in the CLI values:

Group 1 – advanced reformers (CLI > 3);
Group 2 – (high) intermediate reformers (2 < CLI < 3);
Group 3 – (low) intermediate reformers (1.3 < CLI < 2);
Group 4 – slow reformers (CLI < 1.3).

Countries whose economies have been severely affected by regional tensions and the two East Asian countries are shown separately. The "regional tension" countries include former Yugoslav and Soviet republics that have experienced major and persistent internal conflicts during 1989–94 or, in the case of Armenia and FYR (former Yugoslav Republic) Macedonia, conflict-related blockades.[18] The macro and reform experiences of the East Asia countries, China and Vietnam, differ from those of CEE and the FSU. Although their 1993–94 LIs are lower than those of advanced reformers like Poland, their CLIs are quite high, reflecting their introduction of important reforms before many of the other countries included here.

Before turning to an analysis of the interactions between growth, inflation, and liberalization, we look more closely at the properties of the liberalization index. Figure 1a shows the evolution of means over the 1989–94 period, and Figure 1b shows the evolution of standard deviations. The means for I and E show large increases in 1991, reflecting reform in CEE countries, and in 1992, reflecting reform in

[18] Georgia and Armenia were relatively advanced among FSU reformers, but have since reverted to more state controls as a result of regional tensions. For example, Armenia maintained state orders to ensure a supply of goods to barter with Turkmenistan for vital energy supplies. In the regressions reported here, Moldova is included in this group for 1992.

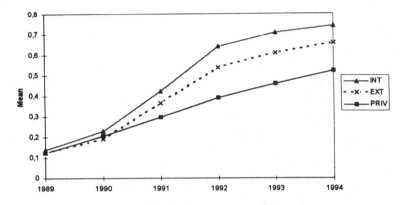

Figure 1a. Means of liberalization components.

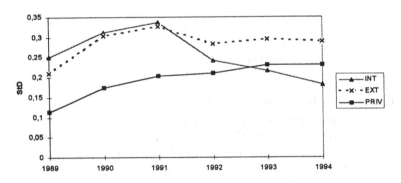

Figure 1b. Standard deviations of liberalization components.

FSU countries; the mean for P shows a more modest but steady increase over the entire period. Comparing means in 1989 with those in 1994, the most progress has been in the liberalization of internal markets and the least in private-sector entry. Standard deviations for I and E peaked in 1991 and have since declined, especially for I, reflecting the fact that most countries had moved ahead on internal price liberalization by 1994, even though no country had fully liberalized prices. The standard deviation for P increases over time as privatization leaps ahead in some countries but lags in others.

The three components of the liberalization index are also highly correlated with each other, suggesting that there is a high degree of complementarity in designing and implementing different types of reform and that any one component will perform almost equally well in

Matrix of simple correlation coefficients

	I	E	P	CLI
AVGR	0.57	0.52	0.60	0.59
AVLIN	-0.72	-0.67	-0.73	-0.74
GR93/4	0.72	0.69	0.67	0.73
LIN93/4	-0.80	-0.75	-0.79	-0.81

Note: AVGR is average real GDP growth and AVLIN is the average log of inflation over 1989-94; GR93/4 and LIN93/4 are the same variables for the period 1993-94.

regressions against growth and inflation. The correlation – as measured by the Pearson (or simple) correlation coefficient and the Spearman rank correlation coefficient – is somewhat higher between I and E than between either of these and P. Pearson correlations are 0.93 (I and E), 0.84 (I and P), and 0.82 (E and P); Spearman rank correlations are slightly higher. As shown in the matrix of (Pearson) correlation coefficients, the CLI is marginally more strongly associated with growth and inflation than the cumulative index of any one component (shown under I, E, and P).

The CLI is constructed to reflect the six-year period 1989–94, where the first year has historical significance for all CEE and FSU countries. A limitation on the time period is consistent with partial adjustment models, which show that the effect of reforms diminishes over long periods.

4. GROWTH, INFLATION, AND LIBERALIZATION

Following the dissolution of the Council for Mutual Economic Assistance (CMEA) and the ruble zone, each country in the CEE and FSU has followed its own path to reform, with varying speed and intensity. Here, however, we explore the hypothesis that despite the diversity in country circumstances, simple relationships exist between real GDP growth and economic liberalization, inflation and economic liberalization, and growth and stabilization. Our statistical analysis suggests that variations in country experience during the transition are in fact strongly associated with liberalization, and that the return to positive growth is associated with declines in inflation to double digits or less.

Table 2. *Liberalization, growth, and inflation, 1989–94*

Country	CLI 1994	Average liberal- ization 1993–94	Average inflation 1993–94	Average growth 1993–94	1993–94 GDP ÷ 1989 GDP	Lowest level of GDP ÷ 1989 GDP
Advanced reformers						
Slovenia	4.16	0.82	26	3.0	84	81
Poland	4.14	0.84	34	4.2	88	82
Hungary	4.11	0.84	21	0.0	81	80
Czech Republic	3.61	0.90	16	0.3	81	80
Slovak Republic	3.47	0.86	19	0.4	79	77
Average	3.90	0.85	23	1.7	83	80
High intermediate reformers						
Estonia	2.93	0.85	69	0.9	69	67
Bulgaria	2.90	0.68	81	– 1.4	73	73
Lithuania	2.72	0.79	231	– 7.3	44	44
Latvia	2.45	0.71	73	– 4.4	60	59
Albania	2.30	0.70	57	9.5	74	65
Romania	2.29	0.66	194	2.2	69	67
Mongolia	2.27	0.64	164	0.6	84	83
Average	2.55	0.72	124	0.03	67	65
Low intermediate reformers						
Russia	1.92	0.63	558	– 13.5	57	52
Kyrgyz Republic	1.81	0.68	744	– 13.2	61	57
Moldova	1.62	0.53	558	– 17.0	53	46
Kazakstan	1.31	0.37	1,870	– 18.5	57	49
Average	1.67	0.55	933	– 15.6	57	51
Slow reformers						
Uzbekistan	1.11	0.37	640	– 2.5	89	88
Belarus	1.07	0.35	1,694	– 16.6	73	64
Ukraine	0.80	0.20	2,789	– 18.6	56	48
Turkmenistan	0.63	0.19	2,751	– 15.0	69	62
Average	0.90	0.27	1,968	– 13.2	72	66
Affected by regional tensions						
Croatia	3.98	0.83	807	– 0.7	69	68
FYR Macedonia	3.92	0.78	157	– 10.7	57	55
Armenia	1.44	0.42	4,595	– 7.4	38	38
Georgia	1.32	0.35	10,563	– 24.6	24	23
Azerbaijan	1.03	0.33	1,167	– 17.7	50	44
Tajikistan	0.95	0.28	1,324	– 26.3	35	30
Average	2.11	0.50	3,102	– 14.5	45	34
East Asia						
Vietnam	3.42	0.78	10	8.5	145	100
China	3.08	0.64	13	11.7	157	100
Average	3.25	0.71	11	10.1	151	100

Note: CLI = cumulative liberalization index.

Growth and Liberalization

The data in Table 2 on growth and cumulative output declines show systematic variation by reform group (based on unweighted averages). Although outputs initially fell, advanced reformers were stable or growing in 1993–94; maximum output declines were about 80% of those in 1989. High intermediate reformers lost about a third of their GDP, but most have also stabilized or returned to positive growth. The highest growth was in Albania, which has benefitted from high external financing and, together with Romania, strong agricultural growth. Low intermediate reformers have fared the worst so far, with continuing strong output declines through 1994. The slowest reformers have managed to somewhat retard their output declines, and Uzbekistan appears to have so far defied the general pattern by avoiding a major decline. For the countries affected by regional tensions, huge cumulative output declines (which have quite distinctive sectoral features) highlight the cost of conflict and associated economic blockades. At the other end of the spectrum, the East Asian experience has been one of continuous development; both China and Vietnam have experienced high growth since 1989.

The overall relationship between recent output growth and the CLI is shown in Figure 2 for the 20 CEE/FSU countries not affected by regional tensions. A simple quadratic relationship shows a positive association between growth in 1993–94 and the CLI. It suggests that over half the variation in real growth is associated with increases in economic liberalization, with growth turning positive when the CLI reaches 3 or more. An analysis of the separate effects of the I/E and P components shows that although both show positive relationships similar to the one with the CLI, there is a slightly stronger association of growth with the cumulative I/E component alone than with the full CLI, and a weaker relationship with P.

The CLI in Equation (1), as well as in Equation (2) for inflation (see p. 33), results in a higher R^2 than similar equations where the independent variable is the annual LI for 1994 or the average annual LIs for 1993–94. This suggests that the duration, as well as the intensity, of reforms is important. Furthermore, substituting a CLI with graduated annual weights (giving greater weight to more recent years) for a CLI with equal annual weights results in a higher or equally high R^2. This suggests that the effects of reform dissipate over time, and that the use of a limited six-year period is reasonable even

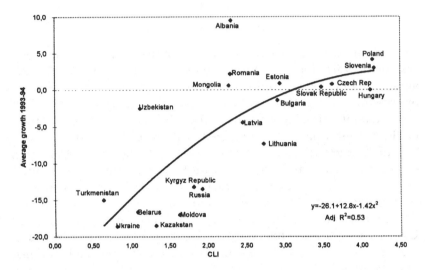

Figure 2. Growth and liberalization.

though some countries (Yugoslavia, Hungary, Poland) had a prior history of significant reform during the 1980s.

A multiple regression for average growth over the full six-year period, 1989–94, for all 26 CEE/FSU countries provides some additional insight into the relationship between growth and liberalization. Countries affected by regional tensions are identified by a separate dummy variable (RT). Per capita income in 1989 (PCY) is introduced to allow for the negative effects of more pervasive central planning and overindustrialization in the more highly developed CEE and FSU countries. As discussed earlier, output declines resulted from disruption in these centralized coordinating mechanisms.

$$AVGR = -9.1 + 2.6\,CLI - 0.54\,PCY - 6.5\,RT,$$
$$(5.4)\ (4.7)\qquad (1.9)\qquad\quad (4.8)\qquad\qquad (1)$$
$$adj.\ R^2 = 0.65.$$

The numbers in parentheses are t-statistics. The RT dummy shows that conflict and associated blockades are associated with average declines of an extra 6.5 percentage points. A linear relationship to the CLI fits better than a quadratic one, suggesting that the positive impact on growth of economic liberalization is equally strong in the upper ranges of growth, rather than declining as suggested by the quadratic relationship. To summarize:

Cumulative liberalization has a positive association with output changes in CEE and FSU, within the overall context of a "transitional recession."

The distinctive response patterns of China and Vietnam relative to those of CEE and FSU may be explained by several factors. Perhaps most important is the large rural economy in these countries, where decentralized incentives led to a big output boost from new firms and family farms. In China, an economy less centrally planned than the FSU as well as low integration into the CMEA trade bloc (and hence insulation from the shock of dissolution) were additional factors.[19]

Inflation and Liberalization

Recent inflation shows systematic variation by reform group in Table 2, and Table 3 provides further evidence of a strong relationship between inflation and cumulative liberalization over the full six-year period. This evidence shows that advanced reformers were relatively successful in containing the inflationary bursts that followed price liberalization, while intermediate performers have endured longer and more severe bouts of inflation. The continuing high levels of inflation in the slow reformers suggest that they have delayed, rather than avoided, adjustment.

Inflation seems to decline more slowly in the FSU in response to stabilization measures. In the non-Baltic FSU, for example, a widening of industrial price–cost margins is believed to reflect monopolistic pricing during the initial inflationary surge (Balcerowicz and Gelb 1994). However, the record of the Baltics – as well as of more recent stabilizers such as the Kyrgyz Republic and Moldova – suggests that, with determined policies, inflation can be brought down to moderate levels as quickly as in CEE.

Regression analysis indicates a strong negative association between inflation and economic liberalization. The R^2 of a simple log-linear relationship for the 20 CEE/FSU countries not affected by regional tensions is over 80%, suggesting a close relationship between economic liberalization and 1993–94 average inflation (Figure 3). An analysis of the separate effects of the I/E and P components shows that both have a strong relationship with inflation, although neither has as strong a relationship as does the CLI; the I/E component again shows a stronger association than the P component.

[19] See, for example, Sachs and Woo (1994) and Thuyet (1995).

Table 3. *Inflation experience by reform group, 1989–94*

Country	CLI	Inflation						Geo-metric average 1989–94
		1989	1990	1991	1992	1993	1994	
Advanced reformers								
Slovenia	4.2	1,306.0	549.7	117.7	201.0	32.0	19.8	213.3
Poland	4.1	251.0	586.0	70.3	43.0	35.3	32.2	117.2
Hungary	4.1	17.0	29.0	34.2	22.9	22.5	19.0	24.0
Czech Republic	3.6	2.3	10.8	56.7	11.1	20.8	10.2	17.5
Slovak Republic	3.5	0.0	10.8	61.2	10.1	23.0	14.0	18.4
Average	3.9	315.3	237.3	68.0	57.6	26.7	19.0	78.1
High intermediate reformers								
Estonia	2.9	6.1	23.1	210.6	1,069.0	89.0	48.0	125.8
Bulgaria	2.9	6.0	22.0	333.5	82.0	72.8	89.0	79.4
Lithuania	2.7	2.1	8.4	224.7	1,020.3	390.2	72.0	164.1
Latvia	2.5	4.7	10.5	124.4	951.2	109.0	36.0	106.5
Albania	2.3	0.0	0.0	35.5	225.9	85.0	28.0	47.9
Romania	2.3	1.1	5.1	174.5	210.9	256.0	131.0	105.2
Mongolia	2.3	0.0	0.0	208.6	321.0	183.0	145.0	111.7
Average	2.6	2.9	9.9	187.4	554.3	169.3	78.4	105.8
Low intermediate reformers								
Russia	1.9	2.2	5.6	92.7	1,353.0	896.0	220.0	214.3
Kyrgyz Republic	1.8	0.0	3.0	85.0	854.6	1,208.7	280.0	211.0
Moldova	1.6	0.0	4.2	98.0	1,276.0	789.0	327.0	220.2
Kazakstan	1.3	0.0	4.2	91.0	1,610.0	1,760.0	1,980.0	385.9
Average	1.7	0.6	4.3	91.7	1,273.4	1,163.4	701.8	257.8
Slow reformers								
Uzbekistan	1.1	0.7	3.1	82.2	645.0	534.0	746.0	201.8
Belarus	1.1	1.7	4.5	83.5	969.0	1,188.0	2,200.0	328.3
Ukraine	0.8	2.0	4.0	91.2	1,210.0	4,735.0	842.0	379.2
Turkmenistan	0.6	2.1	4.6	102.5	492.9	3,102.0	2,400.0	366.2
Average	0.9	1.6	4.1	89.9	829.2	2,389.8	1,547.0	318.9
Affected by regional tensions								
Croatia	4.0	2,520.5	135.6	249.5	938.2	1,516.0	98.0	544.5
FYR Macedonia	3.9	1,246.0	120.5	229.7	1,925.2	248.0	65.0	374.3
Armenia	1.4	0.0	10.3	100.0	825.0	3,732.0	5,458.0	492.9
Georgia	1.3	0.0	3.3	78.5	913.0	3,126.0	18,000.0	591.2
Azerbaijan	1.0	0.0	7.8	105.6	616.0	833.0	1,500.0	265.1
Tajikistan	1.0	0.0	4.0	111.6	1,157.0	2,195.0	452.0	289.7
Average	2.1	627.8	46.9	145.8	1,062.4	1,941.7	4,262.2	426.3
East Asia								
Vietnam	3.4	76.0	67.5	67.6	17.5	5.2	14.4	38.3
China	3.1	17.5	1.6	3.0	5.4	13.0	12.0	8.6
Average	3.3	46.8	34.6	35.3	11.5	9.1	13.2	23.4

Note: CLI = cumulative liberalization index.
Sources: World Bank, IMF.

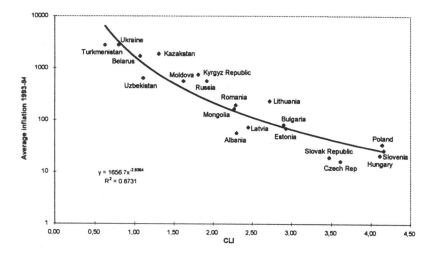

Figure 3. Inflation and liberalization.

A multiple regression for all 26 CEE/FSU countries shows that cumulative economic liberalization, output decline, repressed inflation, and regional tensions are all associated with average inflation. Output decline is included to capture the fact that a fall in the transactions demand for money will – other things being equal – result in higher inflation. The relationship is estimated only over the most recent four years to avoid the effects of inherited inflation:

AVLIN1/4

$$= 3.4 - 0.88\,\text{LCLI} + 0.64\,\text{LDROP} + 0.036\,\text{RINFL} + 1.2\,\text{RT},$$
$$(2.4)\quad(2.3)\qquad\quad(1.5)\qquad\qquad(2.1)\qquad\qquad(2.8)\qquad\qquad(2)$$

$$\text{adj. } R^2 = 0.76.$$

The numbers in parentheses are *t*-statistics. LDROP represents the log of the maximum drop in the annual index of real GDP for each country (1989 = 100); RINFL represents repressed inflation, defined as the increase in deflated wages less the change in real GDP during 1987–89; and RT is a dummy variable for countries affected by regional tensions. In general:

CEE and FSU countries that failed to liberalize experienced far higher inflation over the 1991–94 period.

In contrast, China and Vietnam experienced relatively stable prices over this period, even though the extent of liberalization was less than in the CEE and FSU advanced reformers. The policy of

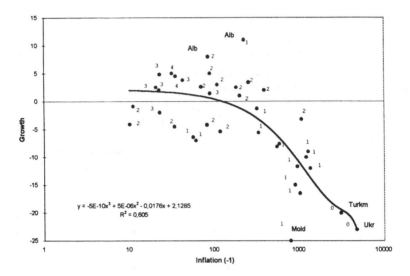

Figure 4. Growth and stabilization. (Numbers refer to the cumulative
liberalization index in the year of the observation of growth.)

gradual liberalization over a number of years – since 1978 for China
and since the mid-1980s for Vietnam – has created a less disruptive
environment, as has the lack of serious regional conflict. Moreover,
the absence of initial monetary overhang and subsequent output
drops allowed prices to be liberalized without provoking a sudden major burst of inflation and the associated flight from domestic currency.

Growth and Stabilization

In market economies, it is usually assumed that stabilization carries
a cost in terms of growth. But it is clear from the cross-country data
in Table 2 that output recovery in transition economies is associated
with declining inflation. A two-way causality between growth and stabilization is likely to exist, as recovery will have a favorable impact on
budget deficits, reducing inflationary pressures. For the 20 CEE/FSU
countries not affected by regional tensions, Figure 4 plots changes
in output against experience with stabilization, where the latter is defined as the year of highest inflation and all subsequent years. Inflation is measured as the annual average and is introduced with a one-
year lag. The statistical relationship suggests that a return to positive
growth requires inflation to drop below 100% a year.

The numbers on the graph refer to a country's CLI at the time of the observation. They confirm a strong relationship between liberalization and stabilization, which is consistent with the preceding discussion of liberalization and inflation. The most important outliers, notably Albania and Turkmenistan, benefit from growth led by primary sectors: agriculture and natural gas, respectively. An important policy implication is:

> *Output recovery in CEE and FSU countries requires stabilization of prices to moderate levels.*

A related issue is the perceived output cost of stabilization. Because transition economies initiated the reform process under negative growth conditions and all registered large declines of output, some policy makers argued during transition that stabilization would involve substantial output costs and hence adjustment should be gradual.[20] On the other hand, some analysts, noting that output falls coincided with tight stabilization programs in CEE, argued that such programs exacerbated output contraction.[21]

There are two factors that have made these concerns unwarranted. First, declines in the early stages of transition were largely attributable to permanent relative price changes and structural demand shifts, which turned a substantial portion of previous production into negative value added. This necessitated a change in output composition, which occurs at a rapid rate in high CLI countries (see Tables 7a and 7b in Section 6). As our research shows, this was accompanied by stabilization and lower output drops in high CLI countries; lower because output drops in this group were moderated by the rapid growth of previously repressed sectors. Second, the fall in output was greater in those FSU countries where stabilization was not attempted until recently. Taken as a whole, these factors suggest that stabilization programs are effective and that the output cost of stabilization has not been large.[22] Recent experience, for example, shows that stabilization policy can be surprisingly powerful in FSU countries (Kyrgyz

---

[20] Most FSU leaders subscribed to this point of view. See Fedorov (1995) in the case of Russia and World Bank (1993) for Uzbekistan.

[21] See Portes (1993).

[22] In his analysis of 28 high-inflation episodes, Easterly (1995) also found that inflation stabilization was expansionary on average. Sargent's (1992) analysis of hyperinflation in Austria, Germany, Hungary, and Poland also argued that output costs of stabilization programs in those countries were small.

Republic, Moldova), although these countries will remain fragile until structural reforms take hold and resources for restructuring become available. In CEE, since stabilization preceded growth, it seems that the opportunity cost of not stabilizing would have been potential growth, which in turn suggests that the cost of not stabilizing is actually higher than the cost of doing so.

Neither China and Vietnam nor countries affected by regional tensions are included in this analysis. Most of the latter were still suffering from high inflation in 1994 – although Croatia and the FYR Macedonia had recently introduced stabilization programs – and the East Asia countries were growing strongly throughout the 1989–94 period in an environment of low to moderate inflation.

5. THE TIME PROFILE OF GROWTH AND INFLATION

In this section we investigate whether there are common patterns in the time profile of country experience that go beyond the broad relationships proposed previously. We do this in two ways. The first way is to estimate "regime-switching" equations to provide stylized profiles of reformers and nonreformers. The second way is to trace the experience with growth and inflation of the four reform groups identified earlier. In both cases, we are looking at the interaction of growth and inflation over time. We exclude the East Asia experience, since patterns differ there.[23]

Under the first approach, we estimate regime-switching equations across all 26 CEE and FSU countries. However, to do this we must define the year in which the regime changes. This is easy for countries, such as Poland, that made a decisive change in a given year. It is harder for countries where reform has been more gradual or more partial. To avoid arbitrary specification of the switch points, we set the regime change on the basis of the CLI. First, the CLIs were rescaled so that Poland would have five years of reform by the end of 1994, implying that the new regime started in January 1990 (five years earlier), as was the case. Because all CLIs are normalized by the same factor (1.2), the implication is that each country's reform experience is being judged in "Poland-equivalent reform years."[24]

---

[23] When China and Vietnam are included in the regression analysis, for example, the signs and values of the equation coefficients are similar, but the overall explanatory value is slightly less; their experience does not fit the profile of the other countries.

[24] Two possible alternatives were considered: (i) setting the switch point according to the announcement of a comprehensive reform program (as in EBRD 1994), and (ii) setting the

Once rescaled, the new CLI is rounded off to the nearest year. Working backward from end-1994, each country has at least one observation in the reform regime and one in the nonreform regime. For example, Poland has one observation (1989) in the nonreform regime and five observations (1990–94) in the reform regime. Turkmenistan, with the lowest CLI, has five observations (1989–93) in the nonreform regime and one (1994) in the reform regime.

The equation specifying the time profiles of growth (GR) and inflation (INFL) relative to reform is as follows:

$$\text{GR(INFL)} = a + \sum_{i=89}^{R-1} b_i D_i^B + \sum_{j=R}^{94} c_j D_j^A + d\,\text{RT}, \tag{3}$$

where:

D_i^B are dummy variables for the successive years before reform begins for each country, starting in 1989;

D_j^A are dummy variables for successive years after reform begins;

RT is a dummy variable set equal to unity for each year when conflict or associated blockades seriously affect a given country; and

R is the year of reform.

Thus, dummy variables are used to define the variation in country experience in relation to the timing of reform and to capture the different economic experience of countries affected by regional tensions.

Table 4 shows the estimated coefficients of these equations.[25] When added to the intercept, they provide the growth and inflation time profiles of a regime of nonreform (the b coefficients) versus a regime of reform (the c coefficients). Caught in the deteriorating environment of a disintegrating economic system, nonreformers initially succeed in delaying the decline in output. Performance then contracts at an accelerating rate, so that after three years their position has deteriorated strongly compared to the reformers. Cumulative output declines are far higher than in the reform regime, indicating that the

switch according to the year of maximum increase in the LI. These procedures are unsatisfactory because they fail to take into account the actual degree of reform. In any case, the general pattern of results is surprisingly robust with respect to a variety of ways of deriving the switch point from the CLI index.

[25] We have attempted to assess the stability of coefficients between the earlier and later reformers. Preliminary results do not usually reject the hypothesis of stable coefficients, but such tests are problematic with limited observations, especially because, given the period covered, early reformers do not have many prereform years as observations and late reformers have few postreform years.

Table 4. *Switching regressions, 1989–94*[a]

| | Growth | | Log inflation | |
	Coefficients	Profile[b]	Coefficients	Profile[b]
5 years before reform	14.2 (6.7)	1.6	−4.4 (10.6)	1.6
4 years before reform	8.3 (3.7)	−4.3	−4.1 (9.3)	1.9
3 years before reform	2.5 (1.1)	−10.1	−1.5 (3.2)	4.5
2 years before reform	−6.6 (2.5)	−19.2	0.4 (0.7)	6.4
1 year before reform	2.8 (0.8)	−9.8	1 (1.5)	7.0
1st year of reform (intercept)	−12.6 (8.3)	−12.6	6 (20.2)	6.0
2nd year of reform	5.6 (2.5)	−7.0	−0.7 (1.6)	5.3
3rd year of reform	11.3 (4.5)	−1.3	−2.1 (4.3)	3.9
4th year of reform	13.8 (4.7)	1.2	−2.3 (4.0)	3.7
5th year of reform	15.5 (4.2)	2.9	−2.9 (4.0)	3.1
RT	−9 (4.7)	−21.6	1.4 (3.7)	7.4
R^2	0.51		0.65	
Adjusted R^2	0.48		0.63	

[a] Regressions are based on 26 observations; *t*-statistics are shown in parentheses. RT is a dummy variable for countries affected by regional tensions.
[b] Coefficient plus intercept: this is predicted annual growth or inflation rate.

status quo is not a viable option for countries experiencing the disruptions in internal and external economic coordination discussed in Section 2. Although it might theoretically be possible to follow a gradualist reform program, empirical evidence suggests that gradualism has not paid off.

The growth regression shown in Figure 5 has reasonably good explanatory power for what is essentially a cross-sectional relationship. The time profile shows that reforming countries experience a sharp contraction in the first year of reform but begin to recover after four years. The dummy variable coefficient for countries affected by regional tensions indicates a high and statistically significant additional cost of conflict. Each year of regional tensions reduces output by an additional 9 percentage points.

As indicated in Section 1, there are various hypotheses about the bias in underreporting of output. To assess sensitivity, we assume that official GDP not only (a) understates real GDP in transition countries, but also (b) understates the unofficial economy more for countries experiencing the largest declines, because such countries

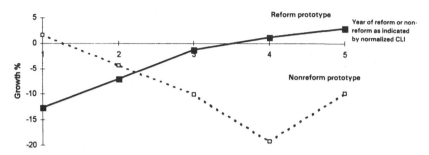

Figure 5. Growth profiles for reform and nonreform,
based on 26 countries' regression coefficients.

have the weakest statistical systems.[26] We have therefore undertaken
a simulation exercise to test the robustness of the growth profiles discussed previously. All countries are assumed to have a GDP adjustment coefficient of 1.15 with respect to their official economy in 1989,
and this coefficient in subsequent years increases proportionally
more in economies with the largest output drops. The resulting GDP
adjustment coefficients for underground economies range from 0.2
for Hungary to 0.5 for Georgia.[27] The results of the switching regression are quite similar for the adjusted data.

The implied inflation rates for reform and nonreform prototypes
are shown in Figure 6. The stage of liberalization is a surprisingly
strong predictor of inflation. As expected, liberalization is associated
with a sharp price spike in the first year. In subsequent years, inflation is usually brought down, typically to about 20% after four years.
Slow reformers initially manage to sustain inflation rates at moderate
levels. After three years, however, their inflation rates soar far above
the peak levels in the reforming countries as their economies contract
sharply. As might be expected from the severity of their output losses,
inflation is significantly higher in countries affected by regional tensions than would otherwise be expected, given their liberalization
profiles.

[26] This adjustment is the least favorable to our hypothesis, as it supports the view that the unrecorded economy is higher in countries that have liberalized less (and have the largest recorded output drops). Ongoing research by Daniel Kaufman of the World Bank provides
support for the view that the informal economy is higher in countries that have liberalized
politically but not economically; the adjustment here has the same feature.

[27] The formula for calculating the adjustment coefficient for 1994 is: $1.2 + (1.5 - 1.2) \times$
[(country i's drop in GDP since 1989) − (the minimum drop in GDP in sample)] ÷
[(maximum drop in GDP in sample) − (minimum drop in GDP in sample)]. Adjustment coefficients for intervening years are derived by interpolation.

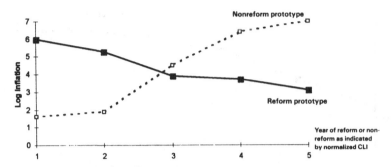

Figure 6. Inflation profiles for reform and nonreform,
based on 26 countries' regression coefficients.

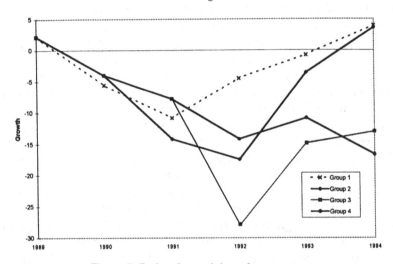

Figure 7. Paths of growth by reform group.

Under the second approach to exploring the time profile of transition, we analyze the experience of the 20 CEE and FSU countries in the four reform groups identified earlier and use regression analysis to trace the average experience of each of these groups, as it starts reform, over the reform period. Using the normalized CLI (which represents Poland-equivalent reform years), advanced reformers are assumed to start reforms in 1990, high intermediate reformers in 1991, low intermediate reformers in 1992, and slow reformers in 1993. The main finding is that each reform group follows a similar pattern. Figure 7 shows that advanced reformers effectively initiated reform in 1990, and that growth turned positive after three Poland-equivalent reform years. Output declines for other groups accelerate as each

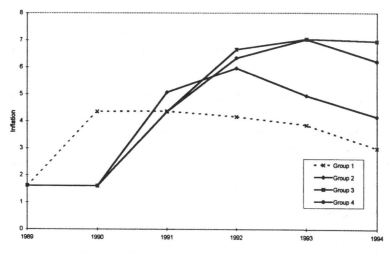

Figure 8. Inflation by reform group, 1989–94.

begins reform, and these declines were increasingly prolonged and/or severe for the slower reformers. By 1994, only the advanced and high intermediate reformers had returned to positive growth, on average. Low intermediate and slow reformers continued to experience major output declines.

A clear pattern can also be seen for inflation. In all groups, initial price liberalization led to a jump in inflation in the year of reform (Figure 8). In advanced reformers, inflation rose quickly and then declined; elsewhere, it rose after some delay but remains high. Some regional variation in inflation experience is evident. The highest inflation has occurred in the non-Baltic FSU, where participation in the ruble zone has resulted in imported Russian inflation. But experience in Eastern Europe suggests that even had the other former Soviet republics rapidly introduced their own currencies, many would not have been able to maintain price stability given the slowness of their liberalization programs. Indeed, the introduction of new currency in former Soviet states has frequently been marked by very high inflation.

6. UNDERLYING MACROECONOMIC AND SECTORAL PATTERNS

Patterns Underlying Growth

Why do growth rates seem to rise after a period of liberalization and stabilization? There are several possible explanations, which we examine in turn: (i) an increased flow of external finance; (ii) a recovery in investment levels; (iii) increases in employment; and (iv) an accelerated process of economic restructuring. Structural change appears to be the main factor.

External Finance. The role of external resources in the transition process has been debated (Dabrowski 1995; EBRD 1994; Sachs 1994). On the one hand, Dabrowski has argued that too much finance too early can weaken pressures for reform. On the other, external finance can encourage adjustment by providing investment resources and noninflationary financing of temporary fiscal deficits. The availability of foreign finance also depends on the reforms themselves, so that two-way causality is expected.

Table 5 shows the current-account balance of payments as a percentage of GDP in 1989–94 and in 1994. On (unweighted) average, current deficits have been modest over the period in groups 1 and 4, but larger both in the intermediate groups 2 and 3 and in the countries affected by regional tensions, especially those in the FSU. The picture in 1994 points to larger deficits among the least reformed countries.

Current accounts have varied a great deal between countries, however, for a variety of reasons. For example, Turkmenistan's 1994 deficit reflects repayment of previous involuntary export credits to natural gas importers, while that of the Kyrgyz Republic shows its ability to attract external assistance as the most advanced reformer in Central Asia. Mongolia, Albania, and Moldova have also benefitted from high external assistance.[28] In general:

> *Net external finance has little systematic relationship with the extent of reform or growth performance.*

Investment.[29] According to official data, fixed investment continues at moderate levels and varies only slightly, relative to GDP, across the four reform groups (see Table 5). Private investment and GDP are, of course, inadequately captured. Only Ukraine and Turkmenistan are reported as suffering a complete investment collapse.

[28] Between 1991 and 1994, some Central Asian republics received large export credits from Turkey while Ukraine, Belarus, Armenia, and several Central Asian republics received monetary transfers and "technical credits" from Russia to cushion terms of trade shocks from the liberalization of energy prices.

[29] The focus here is on fixed investment, since estimates of total investment are particularly unreliable for transition economies; changes in stocks are estimated for some countries to be ±20% or more of GDP.

Table 5. *Net external financing and fixed investment*

Country	Cumulative liberalization index	Current account[a] Average 1989–94	Current account[a] Level 1994	Fixed investment Change 1989–94	Fixed investment Level 1994
Advanced reformers					
Slovenia	4.16	3.4	4.0	1.0	19.0
Poland	4.14	– 1.0	– 1.0	– 0.8	15.6
Hungary	4.11	– 3.0	– 9.9	1.3	21.4
Czech Republic	3.61	– 0.5	0.0	– 5.6	20.4
Slovak Republic	3.47	0.7	5.8	– 14.3	15.4
Average	3.90	– 0.1	– 0.2	– 3.7	18.4
High intermediate reformers					
Estonia[b]	2.93	– 1.8	– 4.4	– 6.0	23.0
Bulgaria	2.90	– 2.5	1.4	– 7.3	18.8
Lithuania	2.72	3.6	– 4.7	– 14.0	18.0
Latvia[b]	2.45	0.4	– 2.0	– 19.8	11.2
Albania	2.30	– 9.2	– 8.3	– 16.0	12.6
Romania	2.29	– 3.4	– 2.4	– 9.0	21.0
Mongolia[b]	2.27	– 19.5	– 5.6	– 23.1	20.9
Average	2.55	– 4.6	– 3.7	– 13.6	17.9
Low intermediate reformers					
Russia	1.92	– 0.1	– 0.3	– 8.0	24.0
Kyrgyz Republic[b]	1.81	– 15.9	– 19.6	– 19.0	13.0
Moldova[c]	1.62	– 4.8	– 9.2	– 4.0	14.0
Kazakstan[c]	1.31	– 6.6	– 7.4	– 15.0	22.0
Average	1.67	– 6.9	– 9.1	– 11.5	18.3
Slow reformers					
Uzbekistan	1.11	– 0.8	– 2.0	– 5.0	26.0
Belarus[b]	1.07	– 5.2	– 8.9	5.0	27.8
Ukraine	0.80	– 1.3	– 1.8	n/a	3.0
Turkmenistan[c]	0.63	1.1	– 14.0	– 24.3	3.0
Average	0.90	– 1.6	– 6.7	– 8.2	15.0
Affected by regional tensions					
Croatia	3.98	2.4	0.3	0.5	14.3
FYR Macedonia	3.92	– 11.9	– 4.1	0.0	17.0
Armenia	1.44	– 16.0	– 36.6	– 16.5	10.0
Georgia[c]	1.32	– 19.1	– 45.1	– 8.0	16.0
Azerbaijan	1.03	– 2.1	– 15.6	– 3.6	17.8
Tajikistan	0.95	– 20.0	– 14.0	n/a	n/a
Average	2.11	– 13.8	– 27.8	– 5.5	15.0
East Asia					
Vietnam	3.42	5.6	– 7.2	10.2	24.2
China	3.08	1.8	7.2	8.9	36.5
Average	3.25	3.7	0.0	9.6	30.5

Note: n/a = not available.
[a] For FSU, change is over 1991–94.
[b] For fixed investment, change is over 1989–93 and level for 1993.
[c] For fixed investment, change is over 1989–92 and level for 1992.
Sources: IMF, World Bank.

Fixed investment was high in most of the countries prior to reform, ranging from 21% of GDP in Hungary to 44% in Mongolia (which received transfers from the USSR equivalent to 30% of GDP). Levels were higher in the Soviet Union than in Eastern Europe, however, so that the decline between 1989 and 1994 was only 4% of GDP in group 1, compared with 14% and 12% in groups 2 and 3, respectively. While the more buoyant economies of group 1 may have sustained investment spending, the larger declines in the less advanced reformers mainly reflects their higher – and more wasteful – prereform levels. In general:

> *Fixed investment rates differ only slightly among reform groups. Investment is at moderate levels for many transition countries, but far below previous highs.*

Employment. It is very difficult to obtain a reliable time series of employment in transition countries, but initial levels of labor force participation in transition countries were very high. Statistics on unemployment do exist, however, and Table 6 shows the association between registered unemployment levels in 1994 and the CLI. Unemployment is a noisy transition indicator, and there is considerable cross-country variation in the incentives to report. Registered unemployment varies greatly from any pattern that might be expected from recorded declines in output; indeed, it tends to be higher in the countries where output has recovered the most.

This apparent anomaly may reflect the success of these countries in downsizing or closing loss-making firms and in freeing up resources for new activities. Part-time employment, wage arrears, and reluctance to register all contribute to the lag between firm adjustment and unemployment statistics. At the same time, unemployment statistics in some countries may fail to capture re-employment of state-sector employees in the private sector, where many firms remain unregistered. These factors may explain a tendency for recorded levels to be higher in Eastern Europe than in FSU countries that are comparably advanced in the reform process. For example, a considerable proportion of the unemployed recorded in Hungary are believed to have been working, and Orazem and Vodopivec (1994) find evidence in Slovenia that the duration of registered unemployment is closely associated with the duration of benefits, with many people finding work in the last months of eligibility. In contrast, limited unemployment benefits in Armenia and the stigma associated with being unemployed

Table 6. *Registered unemployment through transition*[a]
(as percentage of labor force, end of year)

Country	CLI	1989	1990	1991	1992	1993	1994
Advanced reformers							
Slovenia[b]	4.16	2.9	4.7	8.2	11.1	14.5	14.5
Poland	4.14	0.1	6.1	11.8	13.6	16.4	16.0
Hungary	4.11	0.3	2.5	8.0	12.3	12.1	10.9
Czech Republic	3.61	0.0	0.8	4.1	2.6	3.5	3.2
Slovak Republic	3.47	0.0	1.5	11.8	10.4	14.4	14.8
Average	3.90	0.7	3.1	8.8	10.0	12.2	11.9
High intermediate reformers							
Estonia	2.93	0.0	0.0	0.1	4.8	8.8	8.1
Bulgaria	2.90	0.0	1.5	11.1	15.3	16.4	12.8
Lithuania	2.72	0.0	0.0	0.3	1.3	4.4	3.8
Latvia	2.45	0.0	0.0	0.1	2.1	5.3	6.5
Albania	2.30	1.9	7.7	8.6	26.9	28.9	19.5
Romania	2.29	0.0	0.0	3.0	8.4	10.2	10.9
Average	2.60	0.3	1.5	3.9	9.8	12.3	10.3
Low intermediate reformers							
Russia	1.92	0.0	0.0	0.1	0.8	1.1	2.2
Kyrgyz Republic	1.81	0.0	0.0	0.0	0.1	0.2	0.7
Moldova	1.62	0.0	0.0	0.0	0.7	0.8	1.2
Kazakstan	1.31	0.0	0.0	0.1	0.5	0.6	1.0
Average	1.67	0.0	0.0	0.1	0.5	0.7	1.3
Slow reformers							
Uzbekistan	1.10	0.0	0.0	0.0	0.1	0.2	0.3
Belarus	1.07	1.0	1.0	1.0	0.5	1.5	2.1
Ukraine	0.80	0.0	0.0	0.0	0.3	0.4	0.4
Turkmenistan	0.63	0.0	0.0	0.0	0.0	0.0	n/a
Average	0.90	0.3	0.3	0.3	0.2	0.5	0.9
Affected by regional tensions							
Croatia	3.98	0.0	9.3	15.5	17.8	17.5	18.0
FYR Macedonia[b]	3.92	n/a	n/a	18.0	19.0	19.0	19.0
Armenia	1.44	1.0	1.0	3.5	3.5	6.2	5.6
Georgia	1.32	0.0	0.0	0.0	5.4	8.4	n/a
Azerbaijan	1.03	0.0	0.0	0.1	0.2	0.7	0.9
Tajikistan	0.95	0.0	0.0	0.0	0.3	1.1	1.7
Average	2.11	0.2	1.7	6.2	7.7	8.8	9.0
East Asia							
Vietnam	3.42	n/a	n/a	n/a	n/a	n/a	n/a
China	3.08	2.6	2.5	2.3	2.3	2.6	2.8
Average	3.25	n/a	n/a	n/a	n/a	n/a	n/a

Notes: CLI = cumulative liberalization index. n/a = not available.
[a] End-of-year percentage of labor force.
[b] Annual average.
Sources: EBRD (1995), World Bank, IMF.

result in low recorded unemployment, even though energy shortages have heavily constrained industrial activity.

Unemployment estimates must be interpreted with caution, but the positive relationship with growth is striking, particularly since higher unemployment in market economies is typically associated with lower labor force participation because of the "discouraged worker" effect. In general:

> *The positive association between registered unemployment and growth makes it unlikely that large increases in employment underlie output recovery.*

Structural Change. Table 7a shows the shifts of output in current prices between broad production sectors, and Table 7b shows the corresponding shifts in constant prices. The more advanced reformers have experienced an accelerated shift from industry, which was overbuilt, toward services, which were repressed. This shift reflects higher profitability in the growing sectors and leads to faster output recovery. On average, the share of current price services in GDP has increased by 15 percentage points in the advanced reformers, 10 percentage points in the high intermediate reformers, and 7 percentage points in the low intermediate reformers.[30]

These structural shifts have occurred despite the fact that services fell, relative to GDP, in almost all FSU countries between 1990 and 1992, owing to a precipitous decline in government (including military) services. Growth in services has been concentrated in private trade, finance, and other business and consumer services. These activities represent a major locus for accumulation of private wealth, which – in some countries – is now starting to be used to acquire industrial assets.[31] Service growth is undoubtedly severely understated because of the underreporting of private activity, but its growth may also be exaggerated by the fact that many services were previously incorporated into industrial firms and not separately distinguished.

In the more advanced reformers, the fall in industry's share has been across-the-board, including military production, heavy industry, and consumer manufactures that are uncompetitive with imports. A striking development has been the sharp deconcentration of industrial employment by firm size (see e.g. Balcerowicz and Gelb 1994 and Kornai 1994). This has resulted from a combination of new

---

[30] Not much weight can be put on differences between current and constant price data for services; even for market economies, deflators for many services are problematic.

[31] One example is the 1995 purchase of Russian energy companies by a consortium of Russian banks.

Table 7a. *Sectoral shifts at current prices, 1989–94*

Country	Cumulative liberalization index	Change in share as percentage of GDP		
		Industry	Agriculture	Services
Advanced reformers				
Slovenia[a]	4.16	– 5.8	0.0	5.8
Poland	4.14	– 14.6	– 7.2	21.8
Hungary	4.11	– 4.6	– 7.2	11.8
Czech Republic[b]	3.61	– 8.7	– 2.3	11.0
Slovak Republic	3.47	– 22.5	– 1.6	24.1
Average	3.90	– 11.2	– 3.7	14.9
High intermediate reformers				
Estonia	2.93	– 8.4	– 10.0	18.4
Bulgaria[b]	2.90	– 25.0	1.7	23.3
Lithuania[b]	2.72	– 3.4	– 6.7	10.1
Latvia[b]	2.45	– 13.1	– 4.3	17.4
Albania	2.30	– 20.1	14.8	5.3
Romania	2.29	– 20.8	5.2	15.6
Mongolia	2.27	13.5	4.0	– 17.5
Average	2.55	– 11.0	0.7	10.4
Low intermediate reformers				
Russia	1.92	– 7.8	– 10.3	18.1
Kyrgyz Republic	1.81	– 11.9	1.8	10.1
Moldova	1.62	– 0.3	7.5	– 7.2
Kazakstan	1.31	12.3	– 18.5	6.2
Average	1.67	– 1.9	– 4.9	6.8
Slow reformers				
Uzbekistan	1.11	– 5.8	– 2.6	8.4
Belarus[b]	1.07	6.2	– 5.6	– 0.6
Ukraine	0.80	– 12.2	17.1	– 4.9
Turkmenistan[b]	0.63	23.4	– 14.6	– 8.8
Average	0.90	2.9	– 1.4	– 1.5
Affected by regional tensions				
Croatia[a]	3.98	2.1	2.1	– 4.2
FYR Macedonia[b]	3.92	0.2	4.2	– 4.4
Armenia	1.44	– 27.4	44.5	– 17.1
Georgia[b]	1.32	– 21.1	36.6	– 15.5
Azerbaijan[b]	1.03	– 2.8	– 1.6	4.4
Tajikistan[c]	0.95	1.5	6.2	– 7.7
Average	2.11	– 7.9	15.3	– 7.4
East Asia				
Vietnam	3.42	1.8	– 12.8	11.0
China	3.08	4.2	– 8.7	4.5
Average	3.25	3.0	– 10.8	7.8

[a] Change over 1990–94.   [b] Change over 1989–93.   [c] Change over 1989–91.

Table 7b. *Sectoral shifts at constant prices, 1989–94*

Country	Cumulative liberalization index	Change in share as percentage of GDP		
		Industry	Agriculture	Services
Advanced reformers				
Slovenia[a]	4.16	– 23.3	– 3.8	27.1
Poland[a]	4.14	– 21.4	– 2.0	23.4
Hungary	4.11	– 0.2	– 1.7	1.9
Czech Republic	3.61	– 10.5	– 0.5	11.0
Slovak Republic	3.47	– 14.8	0.2	14.6
Average	3.90	– 14.0	– 1.6	15.6
High intermediate reformers				
Estonia	2.93	– 12.7	– 10.1	22.8
Bulgaria[a]	2.90	– 10.3	4.3	6.0
Lithuania[b]	2.72	– 11.5	2.6	8.9
Latvia[a]	2.45	– 18.8	1.9	16.9
Albania	2.30	– 20.1	14.8	5.3
Romania	2.29	– 6.5	6.2	0.3
Mongolia	2.27	3.0	4.3	– 7.3
Average	2.55	– 11.0	3.4	7.6
Low intermediate reformers				
Russia[b]	1.92	3.5	6.5	– 10.0
Kyrgyz Republic	1.81	– 7.8	7.2	0.6
Moldova	1.62	3.5	6.5	– 10.0
Kazakstan	1.31	– 6.3	17.5	– 11.2
Average	1.67	– 1.8	9.4	– 7.7
Slow reformers				
Uzbekistan[a]	1.11	– 7.6	12.7	– 5.1
Belarus[a]	1.07	5.8	– 2.8	– 3.0
Ukraine	0.80	– 11.2	10.0	1.2
Turkmenistan[c]	0.63	– 4.5	0.1	4.4
Average	0.90	– 4.4	5.0	– 0.6
Affected by regional tensions				
Croatia	3.98	– 4.0	0.8	3.2
FYR Macedonia	3.92	9.1	– 6.0	– 3.1
Armenia[c]	1.44	– 6.4	0.0	6.4
Georgia	1.32	– 8.7	18.3	– 9.6
Azerbaijan	1.03	– 14.8	0.2	14.6
Tajikistan	0.95	n/a	n/a	n/a
Average	2.11	– 5.0	2.7	2.3
East Asia				
Vietnam	3.42	– 1.1	– 6.0	7.1
China	3.08	18.6	– 6.1	– 12.5
Average	3.25	8.8	– 6.1	– 2.7

[a] Change over 1989–93. [b] Change over 1989–92. [c] Change over 1989–91.

private entry, layoffs from the state sector, and the breakup of large state firms, sometimes in the course of spontaneous processes separating good and bad assets prior to privatization.[32]

According to official statistics, the shift away from industry has not taken place in the countries with low CLIs. Indeed, industry's measured share has actually risen for some low intermediate and slow reformers. Service sectors are certainly larger than officially estimated, as some services are included in the unofficial economy, but they are less well developed than in countries with high CLIs. Also, where reforms are slow, service-sector growth may not signal private-sector growth; government-owned monopolies have been known to absorb previously autonomous firms (tourism in Uzbekistan) and to have created higher regulatory barriers to entry.[33]

The relative performance of agriculture varies considerably among countries. Prereform agriculture was inefficiently organized but benefitted from subsidies, including credit, energy, and other inputs. Performance during the transition reflects a variety of effects, including privatization in some countries, relative price changes (which have especially hit the livestock sectors), and a critical emerging shortage of liquidity at the farm level. Widespread drought in Eastern Europe in the early 1990s also complicates the picture. High intermediate reformers with a strong agricultural response include Romania, Albania, and Mongolia; all are leaders in agricultural privatization. Among the slow reformers, Ukraine has experienced a substantial shift from industry to agriculture, reflecting a strong comparative advantage in farming. Recorded output patterns for the countries affected by regional tensions are distinctive. Faced with overestimated (but still very large) declines in aggregate activity, populations have retreated toward subsistence farming. In general:

Dramatic changes in the sectoral composition of GDP underlie the recovery in real output.

Patterns Underlying Inflation

Why has inflation come down in some countries following a period of liberalization but remained high for others? Several possible explana-

---

[32] Such processes have been especially powerful in Hungary; see Brada, Singh, and Torok (1994).

[33] Statistical measures of the transition between "socialist" (generally public) and "market" (generally private) sectors of the economy are not readily available for all countries, but rough measures confirm a picture of higher private-sector shares as liberalization progresses.

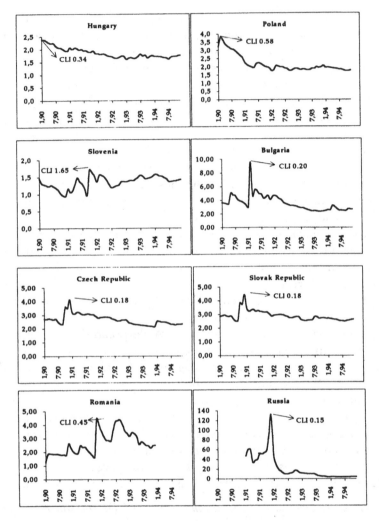

Figure 9. Ratio of market exchange rates to PPP rates.
Source: PlanEcon, monthly data.

tions will be examined in turn: (i) exchange-rate movements; (ii) conventional budget deficits; (iii) quasifiscal deficits; and (iv) monetary developments. The main spur to inflation appears to have been from quasifiscal deficits and the associated monetary expansion.

Exchange-Rate Movements. Figure 9 shows the ratio of the nominal exchange rate to an estimated purchasing power parity (PPP) rate as an indicator of the real exchange rate.[34] In both floating-rate and pegged-rate countries, large real exchange-rate depreciations occurred during the early stages of reform in conjunction with price liberalization and elimination of the money overhang. These huge real devaluations sustained external balance but surely exacerbated inflationary pressures at the time. Subsequently, however, exchange rates strengthened toward a market rate of twice the PPP rate, a ratio consistent with comparable ratios for countries at comparable levels of PPP income (Balcerowicz and Gelb 1994). In general:

> *Substantial depreciation of the real exchange rate occurred during the early stages of liberalization, but the ratio of real rates to PPP rates was subsequently fairly steady.*

Conventional Budget Deficits. As Table 8 indicates, revenue shares in GDP averaged 50% for the advanced reformers in 1994, some 4% lower than in 1989.[35] At 33% of GDP on average, revenues in high intermediate reformers had stabilized in 1994 but at far lower levels than before. At 24% of GDP, revenue shares were lowest in the low intermediate reformers. In Mongolia and some former Soviet republics, revenue declines reflect the elimination of previous large budgetary transfers from the center.

In the slow reformers, reported revenue shares have fallen only in Turkmenistan, where trading partners failed to pay for gas exports. However, revenue performance is partly spurious – reflecting payments to the budget taken out of credit subsidies from the central bank. The surprisingly strong performance of countries affected by regional tensions was largely due to the inclusion of foreign grants: in Georgia, revenues net of grants collapsed to 3% of GDP in 1993.

Except in the advanced reformers, expenditures typically fell less than revenues and in some cases they increased substantially relative to GDP. The largest increases in expenditure shares were in the countries affected by regional tensions, although slow reformers also showed some increases on average. In advanced reformers, cuts in subsidies ranged from 7% to 10% of GDP, although these were offset by rising social expenditures.[36]

---

[34] As pointed out in Balcerowicz and Gelb (1994), exchange rates that prevailed under central planning cannot be used to impute equilibrium values.

[35] See EBRD (1994) and IMF (1994). The common pattern was for revenues to decline during the first year of reforms but to rebound starting in the second year.

[36] This substitution was predicted by Bruno (1993b) and pointed out by EBRD (1994) and Coricelli (1994). In Hungary and Poland, increases in social security expenditures have

Table 8. *Levels and change in revenue, expenditures, and fiscal balance,*
1989-94

Country	CLI	Change in share as percentage of GDP			1994 levels as percentage of GDP		
		Rev-enue	Expen-diture	Bal-ance	Rev-enue	Expen-diture	Bal-ance
Advanced reformers							
Slovenia	4.16	4.6	5.8	- 1.2	46.6	47.5	- 0.9
Poland	4.14	6.5	1.5	5.0	47.9	50.4	- 2.5
Hungary	4.11	- 6.8	- 1.7	- 5.1	52.3	58.8	- 6.5
Czech Republic[a]	3.61	- 10.9	- 13.8	2.9	51.2	50.7	0.5
Slovak Republic[a]	3.47	- 11.6	- 11.5	- 0.1	50.5	53.0	- 2.5
Average	3.90	- 3.6	- 3.9	0.3	49.7	52.1	- 2.4
High intermediate reformers							
Estonia	2.93	- 8.0	- 7.5	- 0.5	35.0	35.0	0.0
Bulgaria	2.90	- 21.9	- 17.3	- 4.6	38.0	44.1	- 6.1
Lithuania	2.72	- 25.2	- 17.1	- 8.1	25.1	30.4	- 5.3
Latvia	2.45	- 15.1	- 12.3	- 2.8	36.7	38.7	- 2.0
Albania	2.30	- 20.3	- 16.0	- 4.3	27.7	41.0	- 13.3
Romania	2.29	- 18.5	- 7.1	- 11.4	32.6	35.6	- 3.0
Mongolia	2.27	- 12.4	- 17.3	5.0	36.2	48.0	- 11.8
Average	2.55	- 17.3	- 13.5	- 3.8	33.0	39.0	- 5.9
Low intermediate reformers							
Russia	1.92	- 4.5	- 4.4	- 0.1	36.3	45.1	- 8.8
Kyrgyz Republic	1.81	- 14.2	- 3.7	- 10.4	24.3	32.7	- 8.4
Moldova	1.62	- 18.2	- 7.8	- 7.1	17.1	25.9	- 8.8
Kazakstan	1.31	- 21.7	- 15.7	- 6.0	19.0	23.5	- 4.5
Average	1.67	- 14.6	- 7.9	- 5.9	24.2	31.8	- 7.6
Slow reformers							
Uzbekistan	1.11	7.8	9.2	- 1.4	43.0	45.0	- 2.0
Belarus	1.07	- 1.6	3.4	- 1.5	36.6	38.1	- 1.5
Ukraine	0.80	15.9	25.7	- 8.4	42.3	51.4	- 9.1
Turkmenistan	0.63	- 26.2	- 23.9	- 2.3	6.2	7.3	- 1.1
Average	0.90	- 1.0	3.6	- 3.4	32.0	35.5	- 3.4
Affected by regional tensions							
Croatia[b]	3.98	12.3	8.1	4.1	27.2	27.6	- 0.4
FYR Macedonia	3.92	6.6	5.6	1.1	42.8	45.4	- 2.6
Armenia	1.44	- 15.2	11.2	- 21.6	37.0	61.0	- 24.0
Georgia	1.32	- 16.5	- 6.6	- 8.1	15.0	24.0	- 9.0
Azerbaijan	1.03	10.2	24.7	- 11.5	36.0	49.0	- 13.0
Tajikistan	0.95	- 4.9	- 0.5	- 1.0	35.4	38.1	- 2.7
Average	2.11	- 1.2	7.1	- 6.2	32.2	40.9	- 8.6

Table 8 (*cont.*)

Country	CLI	Change in share as percentage of GDP			1994 levels as percentage of GDP		
		Rev-enue	Expen-diture	Bal-ance	Rev-enue	Expen-diture	Bal-ance
East Asia							
Vietnam	3.42	8.7	− 3.2	5.5	24.7	25.2	− 0.5
China	3.08	− 5.1	− 4.7	− 0.4	11.4	13.3	− 1.9
Average	3.25	1.8	− 2.2	2.5	18.1	19.3	− 1.2

a 1989 figures for Czechoslovakia.   *b* Change over 1991–94.

Fiscal deficits increased on average for all CEE and FSU groups except advanced reformers between 1989 and 1994. Deficits averaged 2% of GDP in advanced reformers and 7% of GDP in intermediate reformers. They were surprisingly modest in slow reformers still experiencing very high inflation. In general:

> *Fiscal revenues and expenditures have been maintained in advanced and slow reformers but have fallen dramatically in intermediate reformers. Open fiscal deficits have been moderate in most countries.*

Quasifiscal Deficits. Quasifiscal expenditures may include extrabudgetary financing for debt writeoffs, implicit subsidies in connection with foreign exchange guarantee schemes, and implicit subsidies resulting from the provision of credit to banks and firms at highly negative real interest rates. This last category, which reflects attempts to maintain production and employment in industry and agriculture, is shown in Table 9 for a range of countries. The subsidies shown are calculated as the difference between the central bank discount rate and the inflation rate, applied to gross monthly (or quarterly) central bank credit outstanding to the nongovernment sector.[37] Estimates of

been particularly large. In 1993, social spending amounted to 18% and 20% of GDP, respectively. Hungary and Poland have also experienced a steady rise in interest payments on debt, to around 4–5% of GDP. As a result, total expenditures reached close to 60% of GDP in Hungary and 50% in Poland, higher than the European Union average.

[37] Quasifiscal losses are computed on average balances by month or quarter, and are divided by estimated monthly (or quarterly) GDP to obtain a percentage subsidy flow. These are then averaged to obtain the annual average.

Table 9. *Fiscal deficits and quasifiscal expenditures for selected countries, 1992-94 (as percentage of GDP)*

	Fiscal deficits			CB implicit subsidy[a]			Total		
	1992	1993	1994	1992	1993	1994	1992	1993	1994
Advanced reformers									
Poland	6.8	2.9	2.9	0.0	0.0	0.0	6.8	2.9	2.9
Hungary	5.7	7.0	6.5	0.0	0.0	0.0	5.7	7.0	6.5
Czech Republic[b]	0.5	−0.6	−0.5	0.3	0.8	0.1	0.8	0.2	−0.4
Slovak Republic[b]	13.1	7.6	2.5	0.3	1.7	0.0	13.4	9.3	2.5
Intermediate reformers									
Estonia[c]	−0.5	1.4	0.0	—	0.2	0.3	—	1.6	0.3
Bulgaria	5.0	11.1	6.1	1.3	0.8	0.7	6.3	11.9	6.8
Romania	5.5	1.0	3.0	5.9	3.9	0.0	11.4	4.9	3.0
Russia[c]	3.4	8.1	8.8	11.3	1.7	0.0	14.7	9.8	8.8
Kazakstan	7.3	1.2	4.5	32.7	n/a	2.6	40.0	n/a	7.1
Slow reformers									
Belarus[c]	6.4	9.4	1.5	26.5	9.3	3.4	32.9	18.7	4.9
Turkmenistan[c]	10.1	3.6	1.1	12.5	21.2	6.4	22.6	24.8	7.5
Uzbekistan[c]	10.2	8.4	2.0	13.1	18.5	19.0	23.3	26.9	21.0

Note: n/a = not available.

[a] Implicit subsidy from the central bank to commercial banks and economy due to difference between the central bank refinancing rate and inflation. Annual figures are averages of monthly (or quarterly) figures.

[b] For 1992, the nominal federation subsidy is divided 2 to 1 in favor of the Czech Republic.

[c] Calculations performed on a quarterly basis.

other quasifiscal expenditures are more difficult to obtain on a comparable basis.[38]

In countries where reforms lag and structural change has been resisted, the consolidated deficits, also shown in Table 9, are much larger than open fiscal deficits.[39] Central bank subsidies in the slow reforming countries have been on the order of three times the fiscal

[38] Extrabudgetary debt writeoffs have been estimated at an additional 3.4% of GDP in 1992 and 3.8% of GDP in 1993 for Bulgaria. Such writeoffs are known to exist in other countries, such as Hungary and Kazakstan. The importance of such writeoffs would be expected to mount after real interest rates are increased to positive levels.

[39] For comparison, central bank subsidies to state enterprises in China have been substantial over the last five years, but this has not so far caused excessive inflation because of rapid growth in the demand for money. See "China: State Finances" in *Oxford Analytica* (March 9, 1995). See also Cardoso and Yusuf (1994) and McKinnon (1994).

deficit, and far exceed any plausible estimate of tax revenue recouped from subsidized firms. Only in more advanced reformers, where stabilization is more or less achieved and rapid structural change is in progress, have these losses been eliminated. Declines in the consolidated deficits in 1994 for several slow reformers are encouraging in this respect.

Quasifiscal losses have been the major inflationary force in the slower reformers.

Monetary Developments. Table 10 shows real money growth, real money balances, and real interest rates across countries.[40] Nominal growth of broad money during 1992–94 has been lowest in advanced reformers, and highest in slow reformers and in countries affected by regional tensions.[41] The relatively low money growth of the advanced reformers was accompanied by policies allowing real interest rates to rise to either positive or slightly negative levels. Only in these countries have real money balances actually increased on average.

Broad money grew rapidly in intermediate and slow reformers while real interest rates were substantially negative. Real money balances fell sharply in 1992. Thereafter, they stabilized in the high intermediate reformers but continued to decline in the slower reformers. The real discount rate on central bank credit seems to have risen in 1994, although there is substantial variation across the countries.

These patterns reflect the strong causal links between structural reforms and monetary developments. Restrictive monetary policies in advanced reformers not only allowed stabilization, they also facilitated currency convertibility and liberalization. Liberalization, in turn, was needed to render effective the hard budget constraints that allow restrictive macro policies to be sustained. Together, liberalization and stabilization have then impelled the reallocation of real resources. In intermediate and slow reformers, continued large subsidies to state-owned agriculture and industry have been financed by central bank resources, but loose monetary policies did not prevent continued drops in output through the end of 1994. Output recovery

[40] For a discussion of conceptual issues and detailed reviews of monetary policy issues during transition, see Bredenkamp (1993), Bruno (1993a), Citrin, Anderson, and Zettelmeyer (1995), Edwards (1992), Sachs (1994), and Sahay and Vegh (1995).

[41] For transition economies, Citrin et al. (1995) support the view that nominal money growth is the best indicator of policy stance – better than real money growth or real interest rates. See de Grauwe (1995) for a more general discussion of assessing the stance of monetary policy.

Table 10. *Money, interest rates, and real balances*

Country	CLI	Broad money growth[a]	Real money balances (1991 = 100)			Discount rate in real terms (average %)	
			1992	1993	1994	1992–94	end-1994
Advanced reformers							
Slovenia	4.16	5	92	127	164	– 3	– 1
Poland	4.14	3	98	101	104	1	3
Hungary	4.11	2	105	106	102	0	1
Czech Republic[b]	3.61	1	106	104	111	– 1	– 1
Slovak Republic[b]	3.47	1	95	84	86	– 1	– 1
Average	3.91	2	99	104	113	– 1	0
High intermediate reformers							
Estonia[c]	2.93	7	25	20	21	n/a	– 3
Bulgaria	2.90	4	91	76	68	– 3	0
Lithuania	2.72	9	30	17	20	n/a	n/a
Latvia	2.45	6	29	28	34	– 8	0
Albania[d]	2.30	5[e]	82	89	105	– 4	2
Romania	2.29	7	63	43	41	– 8	12
Mongolia[f]	2.27	6[e]	56	36	40	– 16	– 8
Average	2.55	6	54	44	47	– 8	1
Low intermediate reformers							
Russia	1.92	15	32	23	16	– 17	– 2
Kyrgyz Republic	1.81	11	36	16	8	– 19	9
Moldova	1.62	13	23	9	3	– 18	0
Kazakstan	1.31	19	21	14	8	– 31	4
Average	1.67	15	28	16	9	– 21	3
Slow reformers							
Uzbekistan	1.11	19	45	53	71	– 35	– 12
Belarus	1.07	20	35	33	17	– 34	– 5
Ukraine	0.80	22	40	26	13	– 29	– 40
Turkmenistan	0.63	23	63	73	9	– 45	– 48
Average	0.90	21	46	46	28	– 36	– 26
Affected by regional tensions							
Croatia[b]	3.98	16	68	60	76	– 9	2
FYR Macedonia	3.92	19[g]	89	91	89	– 1	1
Armenia	1.44	24	22	7	2	– 33	– 26
Georgia	1.32	29	29	24	6	n/a	n/a
Azerbaijan	1.03	17	40	40	19	– 40	– 52
Tajikistan	0.95	19	39	30	n/a	– 30	– 16
Average	2.11	21	48	42	39	– 23	– 18

Table 10 (*cont.*)

Country	CLI	Broad money growth[a]	Real money balances (1991 = 100)			Discount rate in real terms (average %)	
			1992	1993	1994	1992–94	end-1994
East Asia							
Vietnam[g]	3.42	n/a	97	107	n/a	1	0.6
China	3.08	2[g]	123	141	168	−5	−5
Average	3.25	n/a	110	124	n/a	−2	−2.2

Notes: The discount rates in real terms are calculated assuming quarterly compounding. All averages are simple averages.
CLI = cumulative liberalization index. n/a = not available.
[a] Average monthly change, 1992–94.
[b] Data for 1992 are for the federation.
[c] The NBE credit auction rate is used for end-1994.
[d] Average interest rate collected over different types of credit.
[e] Broad money growth rate is taken from a quarterly average made monthly by taking a cubic root.
[f] The discount rate used is the clearing and settlement account; a midpoint of range is used.
[g] The average discount rate is for 1992–93. For Vietnam, the lending rate for working capital is used.

appears to be related to the improved allocation of available resources rather than to more relaxed monetary policy. In general:

Monetary and interest-rate patterns are consistent with the progression of reforms.

7. LIBERALIZATION AND POLITICAL FREEDOM

The foregoing discussion highlights the central importance of liberalization in the transition process, and we close by asking the question: "What determines the pace of liberalization?" We explore the hypothesis that economic liberalization is associated with political change.[42]

Country rankings of the cumulative liberalization index are shown in Table 11 along with measures of political freedom provided in the comparative survey of freedom for 1994 (Karatnycky 1995). This survey has been published annually by Freedom House since 1973 and

[42] See de Melo et al. (1995) for further analysis of the determinants of economic liberalization.

Table 11. *Political freedom and degree of liberalization*

Country	Political freedom	CLI 1994
Advanced reformers		
Slovenia	6.50	4.16
Poland	6.00	4.14
Hungary	6.50	4.11
Czech Republic	6.50	3.61
Slovak Republic	5.50	3.47
Average	6.20	3.90
High intermediate reformers		
Estonia	5.50	2.93
Bulgaria	6.00	2.90
Lithuania	6.00	2.72
Latvia	5.50	2.45
Albania	4.50	2.30
Romania	4.50	2.29
Mongolia	5.50	2.27
Average	5.36	2.55
Low intermediate reformers		
Russia	4.50	1.92
Kyrgyz Republic	4.50	1.81
Moldova	4.00	1.62
Kazakstan	2.50	1.31
Average	3.88	1.67
Slow reformers		
Uzbekistan	1.00	1.11
Belarus	4.00	1.07
Ukraine	4.50	0.80
Turkmenistan	1.00	0.63
Average	2.63	0.90
Affected by regional tensions		
Croatia	4.00	3.98
FYR Macedonia	4.50	3.92
Armenia	4.50	1.44
Georgia	3.00	1.32
Azerbaijan	2.00	1.03
Tajikistan	1.00	0.95
Average	3.17	2.11
East Asia		
Vietnam	1.00	3.42
China	1.00	3.08
Average	1.00	3.25

Sources: See Appendix for CLI (cumulative liberalization index). See Karatnycky (1995) for index of political freedom, which has been reversed for ease of comparison.

is based on the traditional political rights and civil liberties of Western democracies. The two components of the index are highly correlated and in previous research gave very similar results when used separately (Helliwell 1994). Country rankings, based primarily on responses to a checklist of indicators, reflect the judgment of a project team that consults a vast array of published materials as well as regional experts and human rights specialists.

The survey is not a scorecard for governments, but rather an assessment of the effect on personal freedoms caused by both government and nongovernment (e.g., military or religious-group) factors. There is some evidence that the survey findings are robust (Inkeles 1990). Following a conference in 1988 on measuring democracy, Inkeles concludes that the underlying measures of political freedom are common to all rating systems, even if specific indicators vary, and that there is high agreement in the results of alternative classifications.

In Table 11, the Spearman and Pearson correlation coefficients for all 26 CEE and FSU countries are 0.8 and 0.75, respectively. Excluding the countries affected by regional tensions, the Spearman rank correlation coefficient is 0.91 – indicating a very close correspondence indeed. A nonlinear relationship fitted to the data of all 26 CEE/FSU countries, excluding China and Vietnam, is shown in Figure 10. It indicates accelerated economic liberalization at higher levels of political freedom, and in general supports the following proposition:

Economic liberalization is typically associated with a similar degree of political change.

One explanation for this high correlation between political freedom and liberalization could be that both variables are strongly associated with an unidentified latent variable such as income. But Pearson and Spearman correlations between each of these variables and PPP (purchasing power parity) estimates of per capita GDP in 1989 are lower (0.39 for both in the case of liberalization, and 0.47 and 0.48 respectively in the case of political freedom) than those between the two variables themselves. The lower correlations between political freedom and income levels are consistent with the failure of global cross-country research to establish a systematic relationship between political freedom and economic growth (Helliwell 1994). They also suggest a need to look more closely at the relationship between political change and reform at the individual country level to understand the particular circumstances of the transition economies.

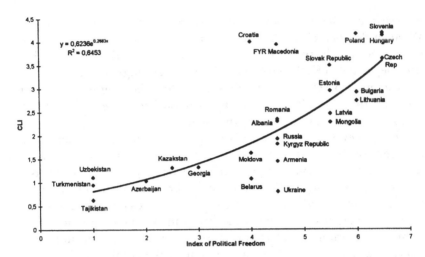

Figure 10. Political freedom and degree of economic liberalization.
Notes: Index of political freedom has been reversed for easier comparison with
the CLI (cumulative liberalization index); China and Vietnam excluded.
Sources: Freedom Review (January 1995); authors' calculations.

In CEE/FSU countries where former communist party leaders
have held power continuously (Uzbekistan, Turkmenistan, Kazakstan, and Ukraine), reforms have been slow and driven largely by
macroeconomic pressures arising from the breakup of the USSR and
attempts to maintain the status quo. In countries where there was a
clear break with the previous communist regime (Poland, Hungary,
Czech Republic, Albania, Lithuania, Estonia, and Latvia), liberalization has been most radical, as reflected in a rapid change in the
annual LI from near zero to close to unity during a phase of "extraordinary politics" (Balcerowicz 1993). So far, there has been little
reversal of such movements to liberalize, even where socialist political parties have regained control (as in Lithuania, Poland, Hungary,
and Estonia).[43]

Where power has been shared among a broad spectrum of political
interests (Russia, Bulgaria), or where local governments have opposed reforms initiated from the top (Russia), reforms have typically
been halting and sometimes inconsistent, placing such countries in
the intermediate category. In Bulgaria, for example, initial liberalization of internal and external markets, impelled by a particularly

---

[43] The lack of reversal is consistent with the view of Aslund (1994) that democratization checks
the power of the old elite.

difficult macroeconomic situation, was not matched by corresponding progress on private-sector entry. Moldova offers a similar experience. In contrast, unlike most non-Baltic FSU countries, Russia and the Kyrgyz Republic reforms in support of private-sector entry have moved almost as fast as other reforms. Mongolia has also moved quickly on private-sector entry, with the first comprehensive privatization program among intermediate reformers, even though its initial reforms of internal and external markets were halting.

The example of China and Vietnam appears to contradict the link between political and economic reform. China and Vietnam have liberalized economically while retaining strict controls on political rights and civil liberties, and the inclusion of China and Vietnam results in a drop in the rank correlation coefficient to 0.62. However, continuity in leadership at the center masks a substantial decentralization of political power to provincial and local governments. China experts would probably agree that this political decentralization has played a critical role in economic liberalization since the start of agricultural reforms in 1978. In Vietnam, the 1989 "renovation" reforms were followed by implicit decentralization of economic decision making through emphasis on initiative at the local level. In both cases, the East Asia model of gradual, decentralized, economic transition appears to have a political counterpart, even if it is not political freedom per se.

Although the preceding discussion focused on the effect of political freedom on economic reform, the direction of causality is actually two-way. Economic liberalization has strong political implications; it is an essential step in breaking the power of established structures, especially sector ministries that previously controlled industry and trade. This is true even where liberalization does not lead to replacement of the political and managerial elite.[44]

8. CONCLUSIONS AND IMPLICATIONS FOR POLICY DEBATES

Conclusions

Countries in CEE and the FSU differ in many respects, and their transitional experience also varies widely. Nevertheless, our analysis

---

[44] With the exception of East Germany (where loyalty and competency tests were imposed) and Czechoslovakia (where a process of ceremonial purification was applied), leading communists and managers have typically been able to take advantage of political connections

suggests strong common patterns for countries at similar stages of reform. The common legacy and the associated changes resulting from initial disruptions in the socialist economic coordinating mechanisms and subsequent liberalization measures go a long way toward explaining the transition experience.

Reform can be usefully thought of as encompassing the duration as well as the intensity of economic liberalization, as defined by the liberalization of internal and external markets and facilitation of private-sector entry. Analysis based on cumulative liberalization provides a useful insight into country experience with growth and inflation. Growth is positively associated with liberalization, and inflation is negatively associated with liberalization. Moreover, liberalization has been an important element of stabilization policy, even though its initial impact entails a spurt in prices, and even though liberalization is by no means a sufficient condition for regaining price stability.

The necessity, if not the inevitability, of liberalization derives from the weakening of governments that initiated a process of political *glasnost* as well as economic opening up. This precluded the application of direct controls that would have been needed to stabilize unreformed systems, where enterprises were not separated from government. The close relationship between economic liberalization and political freedom helps to explain why some countries moved more quickly on reforms and others did not.

An examination of the macroeconomic and sectoral patterns underlying this aggregate experience confirms the usefulness of classifying countries by stage of reform, and suggests that many developments are bidirectional in nature. In advanced reformers, liberalization has permitted the reallocation of capital and labor from industry toward services and an associated return to positive growth from the expansion of previously repressed sectors. While the severe macroeconomic imbalances that built up in the last years of the Soviet Union are a costly legacy, the main problem in stabilization is continuing monetization of the fiscal and quasifiscal deficits, associated with attempts to maintain employment under the old system.

Policy Implications

These findings have several implications for recent policy debates, as follows.

and technical expertise to redefine their role toward commerce and business management. See e.g. Rona-Tas (1994).

Stabilization as a Priority. The patterns revealed here shed light on a number of questions raised by other studies. Portes (1993) and others have argued that policies have overemphasized stabilization relative to structural reform. Although it is hard to respond to this view at a general level when the circumstances – say, between Ukraine and the Czech Republic – differ substantially at the country level, it seems to us that such arguments miss the strong complementarity between macro and micro policy and the high apparent costs of sustained inflation in the slow reforming countries.

The empirical analysis in this paper supports Balcerowicz and Gelb (1994) and Ickes and Ryterman (1994), who maintain that strong interactions between liberalization and stabilization are expected. It also supports the conclusions of Easterly and Bruno (1994), who have found evidence in other countries that neither effective functioning of markets nor renewed investment is possible with severe macroeconomic price instability; thus, stabilization becomes a priority for the resumption of growth. The analysis in this chapter suggests moreover that the output costs of stabilization have not been large. At the same time, it should be recognized that stabilization is rendered more difficult by severe output contractions during the early stages of liberalization; such contractions reduce potential tax revenues and raise claims on fiscal resources to cushion the effects. Stabilization is also rendered difficult by the absence of external financing and by the large depreciation in the exchange rate that accompanies early stages of liberalization.

Big-Bang versus Gradualist Approach. A continuing debate has been whether or not countries should follow a big-bang or gradualist approach to reform. Two points can be made. First, the close relationship between economic liberalization and political freedom suggests that it may be unrealistic to expect a given regime to perceive, or in fact to have, a very wide range of options. Second, the time profiles estimated here suggest that – to the extent that regimes do perceive or have options – rapid reform is preferable to slow reform, given the breakdown in the central planning apparatus. The status quo was not a viable option for CEE and FSU countries. Inflation and output losses in countries that have managed to postpone adjustment are now far larger than in the more advanced reformers, even though transfers from Russia cushioned the terms of trade shocks for several other non-Baltic FSU countries into 1993.

Fiscal Constraint on Reform. Many analysts have emphasized the need for tight and active fiscal policies in order to support stabilization and enterprise restructuring; they have also underlined the importance of quickly reforming the tax system.[45] At the same time, fiscal deficits are expected to increase. The "transitional recession" and lags associated with the development of a new tax system are expected to result in a fall in revenues in the short run. Furthermore, social expenditures are expected to increase as they are transferred from enterprises to the budget.

Some observers have in fact argued or implied that there is a "fiscal constraint" to rapid reform (Aghion and Blanchard 1994; Chadka and Coricelli 1994). These studies note that there are fiscal costs, associated with closing or restructuring state enterprises, that need to be offset by revenues generated from new private businesses. Otherwise, the budget balance deteriorates as reforms are implemented; revenues from state enterprises decline while unemployment benefits increase. These studies further note that tax rates on the private sector need to be low so as not to discourage growth. Meeting a target budget deficit may therefore require measures to sustain state enterprises, the traditional tax base.

The cross-country comparisons carried out here suggest a different conclusion. As we have documented, fiscal revenues and expenditures have tended to remain high (relative to GDP) in advanced reformers, and fiscal deficits have been noticeably smaller than in the slower reformers. Even if there are reasons – cultural, institutional, or structural – why the fiscal position is stronger in advanced reformers, there is no convincing evidence that a slower pace of reform has strengthened the fiscal position of intermediate reformers.[46] As suggested earlier, the lack of adjustment by state enterprises in the face of structural shifts in demand may result in negative value added for many of these enterprises, and therefore no taxable profits. The failure of slow reformers to maintain fiscal balance is highlighted by the fact that their consolidated fiscal and quasifiscal deficits are even worse than those of intermediate reformers.

Choice of Nominal Anchors in Stabilization Programs. Substantial debate surrounds the choice of nominal anchors in stabilization programs

---

[45] See Balcerowicz and Gelb (1994), Bruno (1993b), Fischer and Gelb (1991), Kopits (1991, 1993), Sachs (1994), and Tanzi (1991, 1993).

[46] It is certainly possible, for example, that the institutional infrastructure (tax code, tax administration, expenditure control) and general conditions of societal order and compliance are stronger in advanced reformers.

(Citrin et al. 1995; Sachs 1994; Sahay and Vegh 1995). The main choice has been between a money anchor and an exchange-rate anchor. Both have often been used in combination with restrictions on public-sector wages, and the debate has been primarily over whether greater reliance should be placed on the exchange-rate anchor. The uncertainty of changes in money demand, the adequacy of foreign reserves, and the role of the chosen anchor in signaling and establishing credibility are seen as choice factors. At the same time, it should be recognized that both money and exchange-rate anchors have proven to be effective in a variety of stabilization programs in transition countries. This is consistent with our evidence suggesting that the most critical factor for the success of stabilization in transition countries is likely to be the extent of economic liberalization, irrespective of nominal anchor choice. As discussed widely in the literature, what is critical for the success of stabilization programs is their credibility; in the context of transition, credibility does not come without extensive liberalization.

Unemployment as an Indicator of Reform. Unemployment is strongly associated here with the CLI. The higher levels of unemployment recorded in CEE as compared to FSU countries is consistent with the differences, pointed out by other researchers, in incentives to register for unemployment and the extent to which firms respond, through formal layoffs, to decreases in activity. The Kyrgyz Republic, one of the leading reformers in the FSU, also seems to be exhibiting similar employment patterns. Windell, Anker, and Sziraczki (1995) show that enterprise employment fell by a third between 1991 and 1994, which is consistent with rising unemployment data reported by the World Bank (1995).

APPENDIX

THE LIBERALIZATION INDEX AND HOW IT WAS DERIVED

Table A gives the cumulative liberalization index (CLI), as well as the annual liberalization index (LI) and its components, for the 28 countries included in this study. It also shows, in the last column, the CLI normalized to reflect the number of Poland-equivalent reform years; this normalized CLI is used in the regime-switching regressions of Section 5.

An extensive process of consultation was followed in assigning annual country rankings for each component of the LI. First, the authors proposed rankings on the basis of their own knowledge and country reports. Second,

Table A

Country	Index	1989	1990	1991	1992	1993	1994	Total	Normalized CLI
Group 1									
Slovenia	I	0.6	0.7	0.9	0.9	0.9	0.9	4.9	
	E	0.5	0.7	0.8	0.9	0.9	0.9	4.7	
	P	0.2	0.5	0.5	0.6	0.7	0.7	3.2	
	Weighted	0.41	0.62	0.71	0.78	0.82	0.82	4.16	5.02
Poland	I	0.2	0.7	0.7	0.9	0.9	0.9	4.3	
	E	0.2	0.9	0.9	0.9	0.9	0.9	4.7	
	P	0.3	0.5	0.6	0.7	0.7	0.8	3.6	
	Weighted	0.24	0.68	0.72	0.82	0.82	0.86	4.14	5.00
Hungary	I	0.5	0.8	0.9	0.9	0.9	0.9	4.9	
	E	0.5	0.7	0.9	0.9	0.9	0.9	4.8	
	P	0.1	0.3	0.5	0.6	0.7	0.8	3	
	Weighted	0.34	0.57	0.74	0.78	0.82	0.86	4.11	4.96
Croatia	I	0.6	0.7	0.7	0.8	0.9	0.9	4.6	
	E	0.5	0.7	0.7	0.8	0.8	0.9	4.4	
	P	0.2	0.5	0.5	0.6	0.7	0.7	3.2	
	Weighted	0.41	0.62	0.62	0.72	0.79	0.82	3.98	4.81
FYR Macedonia	I	0.6	0.7	0.7	0.8	0.9	0.9	4.6	
	E	0.5	0.7	0.8	0.8	0.9	0.9	4.6	
	P	0.2	0.5	0.5	0.5	0.6	0.6	2.9	
	Weighted	0.41	0.62	0.65	0.68	0.78	0.78	3.92	4.73
Czech Republic	I	0	0	0.9	0.9	0.9	0.9	3.6	
	E	0	0	0.8	0.9	0.9	0.9	3.5	
	P	0	0.4	0.7	0.8	0.9	0.9	3.7	
	Weighted	0	0.16	0.79	0.86	0.9	0.9	3.61	4.36
Slovak Republic	I	0	0	0.9	0.9	0.9	0.9	3.6	
	E	0	0	0.8	0.9	0.8	0.8	3.3	
	P	0	0.4	0.7	0.8	0.8	0.8	3.5	
	Weighted	0	0.16	0.79	0.86	0.83	0.83	3.47	4.19
Group 2									
Estonia	I	0.1	0.3	0.5	0.9	0.9	0.9	3.6	
	E	0	0.1	0.3	0.7	1	1	3.1	
	P	0.1	0.2	0.2	0.4	0.6	0.8	2.3	
	Weighted	0.07	0.2	0.32	0.64	0.81	0.89	2.93	3.54
Bulgaria	I	0	0	0.9	0.9	0.9	0.8	3.5	
	E	0.3	0.5	0.9	0.9	0.9	0.8	4.3	
	P	0.1	0.1	0.2	0.3	0.3	0.4	1.4	
	Weighted	0.13	0.19	0.62	0.86	0.66	0.64	2.9	3.50
Lithuania	I	0	0.3	0.5	0.8	0.9	0.9	3.4	
	E	0	0	0.2	0.5	0.9	1	2.6	
	P	0.1	0.1	0.3	0.4	0.6	0.8	2.3	
	Weighted	0.04	0.13	0.33	0.55	0.78	0.89	2.72	3.29

Table A (*cont.*)

Country	Index	1989	1990	1991	1992	1993	1994	Total	Normalized CLI
Latvia	I	0	0.3	0.5	0.8	0.9	0.9	3.4	
	E	0	0	0.2	0.5	0.8	1	2.5	
	P	0.1	0.1	0.2	0.3	0.4	0.6	1.7	
	Weighted	0.04	0.13	0.29	0.51	0.67	0.81	2.45	2.96
Albania	I	0	0	0.2	0.9	0.9	0.9	2.9	
	E	0	0	0.2	0.9	0.9	0.9	2.9	
	P	0	0	0.3	0.3	0.4	0.4	1.4	
	Weighted	0	0	0.24	0.66	0.7	0.7	2.3	2.78
Romania	I	0	0.5	0.5	0.5	0.7	0.8	3	
	E	0	0.1	0.3	0.6	0.7	0.8	2.5	
	P	0	0.1	0.3	0.3	0.4	0.5	1.6	
	Weighted	0	0.22	0.36	0.45	0.58	0.68	2.29	2.77
Mongolia	I	0	0	0.4	0.5	0.6	0.7	2.2	
	E	0	0	0.4	0.4	0.5	0.6	1.9	
	P	0	0	0.5	0.7	0.7	0.7	2.6	
	Weighted	0	0	0.44	0.55	0.61	0.67	2.27	2.74
Group 3									
Russia	I	0	0	0.1	0.6	0.7	0.7	2.1	
	E	0	0	0.1	0.5	0.6	0.7	1.9	
	P	0.1	0.1	0.1	0.4	0.5	0.6	1.8	
	Weighted	0.04	0.04	0.1	0.49	0.59	0.66	1.92	2.32
Kyrgyz Republic	I	0	0	0	0.3	0.6	0.8	1.7	
	E	0	0	0	0.4	0.6	0.8	1.8	
	P	0.1	0.1	0.1	0.3	0.6	0.7	1.9	
	Weighted	0.04	0.04	0.04	0.33	0.6	0.76	1.81	2.19
Moldova	I	0	0	0.1	0.5	0.7	0.7	2	
	E	0	0	0.1	0.5	0.6	0.6	1.8	
	P	0.1	0.1	0.1	0.2	0.3	0.4	1.2	
	Weighted	0.04	0.04	0.1	0.38	0.51	0.55	1.62	1.96
Armenia	I	0	0	0.2	0.5	0.6	0.6	1.9	
	E	0	0	0.1	0.4	0.4	0.4	1.3	
	P	0.1	0.1	0.1	0.3	0.3	0.3	1.2	
	Weighted	0.04	0.04	0.13	0.39	0.42	0.42	1.44	1.74
Georgia	I	0	0	0.3	0.5	0.6	0.6	2	
	E	0	0	0.3	0.3	0.3	0.3	1.2	
	P	0.1	0.1	0.1	0.2	0.2	0.2	0.9	
	Weighted	0.04	0.04	0.22	0.32	0.35	0.35	1.32	1.59
Kazakstan	I	0	0	0.1	0.5	0.5	0.5	1.6	
	E	0	0	0.1	0.4	0.4	0.4	1.3	
	P	0.1	0.1	0.2	0.2	0.2	0.3	1.1	
	Weighted	0.04	0.04	0.14	0.35	0.35	0.39	1.31	1.58

Table A (*cont.*)

Country	Index	1989	1990	1991	1992	1993	1994	Total	Normalized CLI
Group 4									
Uzbekistan	I	0	0	0	0.4	0.4	0.5	1.3	
	E	0	0	0	0.2	0.2	0.4	0.8	
	P	0.1	0.1	0.1	0.2	0.3	0.4	1.2	
	Weighted	0.04	0.04	0.04	0.26	0.3	0.43	1.11	1.34
Belarus	I	0	0	0.1	0.2	0.3	0.4	1	
	E	0	0	0.1	0.2	0.4	0.4	1.1	
	P	0.1	0.1	0.1	0.2	0.3	0.3	1.1	
	Weighted	0.04	0.04	0.1	0.2	0.33	0.36	1.07	1.29
Azerbaijan	I	0	0	0	0.5	0.7	0.7	1.9	
	E	0	0	0	0.2	0.2	0.2	0.6	
	P	0.1	0.1	0.1	0.1	0.1	0.2	0.7	
	Weighted	0.04	0.04	0.04	0.25	0.31	0.35	1.03	1.24
Tajikistan	I	0	0	0.1	0.4	0.5	0.5	1.5	
	E	0	0	0	0	0.1	0.1	0.2	
	P	0.1	0.1	0.2	0.2	0.2	0.3	1.1	
	Weighted	0.04	0.04	0.11	0.2	0.26	0.3	0.95	1.15
Ukraine	I	0	0	0.1	0.3	0.2	0.4	1	
	E	0	0	0.1	0.2	0.1	0.2	0.6	
	P	0.1	0.1	0.1	0.2	0.1	0.2	0.8	
	Weighted	0.04	0.04	0.1	0.23	0.13	0.26	0.8	0.97
Turkmenistan	I	0	0	0	0.2	0.3	0.4	0.9	
	E	0	0	0	0.1	0.1	0.2	0.4	
	P	0.1	0.1	0.1	0.1	0.1	0.1	0.6	
	Weighted	0.04	0.04	0.04	0.13	0.16	0.22	0.63	0.76
East Asia									
Vietnam	I	0.6	0.6	0.7	0.8	0.8	0.8	4.3	
	E	0.5	0.5	0.5	0.5	0.5	0.6	3.1	
	P	0.5	0.5	0.5	0.5	0.5	0.5	3	
	Weighted	0.53	0.53	0.56	0.59	0.59	0.62	3.42	4.13
China	I	0.5	0.6	0.6	0.6	0.7	0.7	3.7	
	E	0.5	0.5	0.5	0.5	0.5	0.6	3.1	
	P	0.4	0.4	0.4	0.4	0.5	0.5	2.6	
	Weighted	0.46	0.49	0.49	0.49	0.56	0.59	3.08	3.72

the authors consulted the World Bank and other country specialists on a country's pace of reforms over time and on its ranking relative to other transition countries known by the specialist. Third, revised rankings were submitted to a second round of comments from relatively senior experts who have a comparative perspective across a wider range of countries. And fourth, for the 26 countries in CEE and FSU, a further adjustment was

Table B. *Correspondence of the 1994 liberalization index components with EBRD report indicators*

	EBRD indicators				
LI components	Price liberal- ization and compe- tition	Trade and foreign exchange system	Large- scale privat- ization	Small- scale privat- ization	Banking reform
I (internal prices)	X[a]				
E (external markets)		X[b]			
P (private-sector entry)[c]			X	X	X

[a] I is further differentiated to reflect the status of state trading.
[b] E is further differentiated on the basis of Chapter 8 in the EBRD report.
[c] P is calculated as the sum of the indicator values, where banking reform is used as a proxy for a favorable environment for private-sector development.
Source: EBRD (1994).

made based on the transition indicators in the EBRD's 1994 *Transition Report* (table 2.1) and the accompanying text. This adjustment was designed to introduce further objectivity into the country rankings; Table B describes the correspondence between the transition indicators and the LI components.

In the final analysis, the rankings reflect the authors' judgment. Individual errors in judgment no doubt exist, but we believe that the general picture of economic liberalization suggested by the country rankings over time is reasonable.

REFERENCES

Aghion, Philippe, and Olivier Blanchard (1994), "On the Speed of Adjustment in Central Europe," in S. Fischer and J. Rotemberg (eds.), *NBER Macroeconomics Annual*, vol. 9. Cambridge, MA: MIT Press, pp. 284–320.

Aslund, Anders (1994), "Lessons of the First Four Years of Systemic Change in Eastern Europe," *Journal of Comparative Economics* 19(1): 22–39.

Balcerowicz, Leszek (1993), "Common Fallacies in the Debate on the Economic Transition in Central and Eastern Europe," Discussion Paper no. 11, EBRD, London.

Balcerowicz, Leszek, and Alan Gelb (1994), "Macropolicies in Transition to a Market Economy: A Three-Year Perspective," prepared for the World Bank Annual Conference on Development Economics (28–29 April, Washington, DC).

Berg, Andrew (1993), "Recession and Structural Adjustment in Poland," presented at IMF seminar on "Recession and Reform in Poland" (January, Washington, DC).

Berg, Andrew, and Jeffrey Sachs (1992), "Structural Adjustment and International Trade in Eastern Europe: The Case of Poland," *Economic Policy: An European Forum* 14: 117–73.

Brada, Joseph, I. J. Singh, and Adam Torok (1994), *Firms Afloat and Firms Adrift: Hungarian Industry and the Economic Transition.* London: M. E. Sharpe.

Bredenkamp, Hugh (1993), "Conducting Monetary and Credit Policy in Countries of the Former Soviet Union: Some Issues and Options," Working Paper no. 93/23, International Monetary Fund, Washington, DC.

Brown, Annette N., Barry W. Ickes, and Randy Ryterman (1994), "The Myth of Monopoly: A New View of Industrial Structure in Russia," Working Paper no. 1331, Policy Research Department, World Bank, Washington, DC.

Bruno, Michael (1993a), *Crisis, Stabilization and Economic Reform: Therapy by Consensus.* Oxford, UK: Oxford University Press.

Bruno, Michael (1993b), "Stabilization and the Macroeconomics of Transition: How Different is Eastern Europe?" *Economics of Transition* 1(1): 5–19.

Cardoso, Eliana, and Shahid Yusuf (1994), "Red Capitalism: Growth and Inflation in China," *Challenge* 37: 49–56.

Chadka, Bankim, and Fabrizio Coricelli (1994), "Fiscal Constraints and the Speed of Transition," Discussion Paper Series no. 993, Centre for Economic Policy Research, London.

Citrin, Daniel, J. Anderson, and J. Zettelmeyer (1995), "The IMF's Approach to Stabilization in the Baltics, Russia and the Other FSU Countries," *Economic Policy in Transition Economies (MOCT),* vol. 5, no. 2. Dordrecht: Kluwer.

Coricelli, Fabrizio (1994), "Fiscal Issues in Transition Economies," Department of Economics, University of Sienna, Italy.

Dabrowski, Marek (1995), *Western Aid Conditionality in Post Communist Transition.* Warsaw: Case Publishers.

de Grauwe, Paul (1995), "Monetary Policies in the EMS," in C. Bordes, E. Girardin, and J. Melitz (eds.), *European Currency Crises and After.* New York: Manchester University Press.

de Melo, Martha, Cevdet Denizer, Alan Gelb, and Stoyan Tenev (1995), "Explaining Transition: The Role of Initial Conditions in Reforming Socialist Countries," mimeo, Policy Research Department, World Bank, Washington, DC.

Easterly, William (1995), "When is Stabilization Expansionary?" Working Paper, Policy Research Department, World Bank, Washington, DC.

Easterly, William, and Michael Bruno (1994), "Inflation Crises and Long-

Run Growth," mimeo, Policy Research Department, World Bank, Washington, DC.

Edwards, Sebastian (1992), "Stabilization and Liberalization Policies for Economies in Transition: Latin American Lessons for Eastern Europe," in C. Clauge and Rausser (eds.), *The Emergence of Market Economies in Eastern Europe*. London: Basil Blackwell.

European Bank for Reconstruction and Development [EBRD] (1994), *Transition Report*. London: EBRD.

European Bank for Reconstruction and Development [EBRD] (1995), *Transition Report Update* (April). London: EBRD.

Fedorov, Boris (1995), "Macroeconomic Policy and Stabilization in Russia," in Anders Aslund (ed.), *Russian Economic Reform at Risk*. New York: Pinter.

Fischer, Stanley, and Alan Gelb (1991), "The Process of Economic Transformation," *Journal of Economic Perspectives* 5(1): 91–105.

Gelb, Alan, Gary Jefferson, and Inderjit Singh (1993), "Can Communist Economies Transform Incrementally? The Experience of China," in O. Blanchard and S. Fischer (eds.), *NBER Macroeconomics Annual*, vol. 8. Cambridge, MA: MIT Press, pp. 87–133.

Helliwell, John F. (1994), "Empirical Linkages between Democracy and Economic Growth," *British Journal of Political Science* 24(2): 225–48.

Ickes, Barry, and Randi Ryterman (1994), "From Enterprise to Firm: Notes for a Theory of the Enterprise in Transition," Chapter 5 in Robert Campbell (ed.), *The Postcommunist Economic Transformation*. Boulder, CO: Westview.

Inkeles, Alex (1990), "Introduction: On Measuring Democracy," *Studies in Comparative International Development* 25(1): 3–6.

International Monetary Fund [IMF] (1994), *World Economic Outlook: World Economic and Financial Surveys*. Washington, DC: IMF.

Karatnycky, Adrian (1995), "Democracies on the Rise, Democracies at Risk," *Freedom Review* 26(1): 5–22.

Kopits, George (1991), "Fiscal Reform in European Economies in Transition," Working Paper no. 91/43, International Monetary Fund, Washington, DC.

Kopits, George (1993), "Reforming Social Security Systems," *Finance and Development* 30: 21–3.

Kornai, János (1993a), "Transformational Recession: A General Phenomenon Examined through the Example of Hungary's Development," *Economie Applique* 46(2): 181–227.

Kornai, János (1993b), "The Evolution of Financial Discipline under the Postsocialist System," *Kyklos* 46(3): 315–36.

Kornai, János (1994), "Transformational Recession: The Main Causes," *Journal of Comparative Economics* 19: 39–63.

McKinnon, Ronald I. (1994), "Financial Growth and Macroeconomic Stability in China, 1978–1992: Implications for Russia and Other Transitional Economies," *Journal of Comparative Economics* 18(3): 438–70.

Milanovic, Branko (1995), "Poverty, Inequality and Social Policy in Transition Economies," Paper no. 9, Research Project on Income Distribution During the Transition, Policy Research Department, World Bank, Washington, DC.

Orazem, Peter F., and Milan Vodopivec (1994), "Winners and Losers in Transition: Returns to Education, Experience, and Gender in Slovenia," Working Paper no. 1342, Policy Research Department, World Bank, Washington, DC.

Portes, Richard (ed.) (1993), *Economic Transformation in Central Europe: A Progress Report*. London: Centre for Economic Policy Research.

Rona-Tas, Akos (1994), "The First Shall Be Last? Entrepreneurship and Communist Cadres in the Transition from Socialism," *American Journal of Sociology* 100(1): 40–69.

Sachs, Jeffrey (1994), "Russia's Struggle with Stabilization: Conceptual Issues and Evidence," presented at the World Bank Annual Conference on Development Economics (May, Washington, DC).

Sachs, Jeffrey, and Wing Thye Woo (1994), "Structural Factors in the Economic Reforms of China, Eastern Europe, and the Former Soviet Union," *Economic Policy* 18: 102–45.

Sahay, Ratna, and Carlos Vegh (1995), "Inflation and Stabilization in Transition Economies: A Comparison with Market Economies," Working Paper no. 95/8, International Monetary Fund, Washington, DC.

Sargent, Thomas (1992), "The Ends of Four Big Inflations," in Robert Hall (ed.), *Inflation, Causes and Effects*. University of Chicago Press and National Bureau of Economic Research.

Tanzi, Vito (ed.) (1992), *Fiscal Policies in Economies in Transition*. Washington, DC: International Monetary Fund.

Tanzi, Vito (1993), "The Budget Deficit in Transition: A Cautionary Note," *IMF Staff Papers* 40(3): 697–707.

Taylor, Lance (1994), "Market Met Its Match: Lessons for the Future from the Transition's Initial Years 1994," *Journal of Comparative Economics* 19: 64–87.

Thuyet, Van Pham (1995), "Legal Framework and Private Sector Development in Transitional Economies: The Case of Vietnam," mimeo, Policy Research Department, World Bank, Washington, DC.

Windell, James, Richard Anker, and Gyorgy Sziraczki (1995), "Kyrghzstan: Enterprise Restructuring and Labor Shedding in a Free-Fall Economy, 1991–1994," Labor Market Paper no. 5, Employment Department, International Labor Office, Geneva.

World Bank (1993), "Uzbekistan: An Agenda for Reform," World Bank, Washington, DC.

World Bank (1995), "Kyrgyz Republic Economic Report," World Bank, Washington, DC.

CHAPTER 2

The Great Contractions in Transition Economies

Robert A. Mundell

One of the most remarkable economic events of the twentieth century has been the tremendous contraction of output experienced by the economies of Eastern Europe and the former Soviet Union as they underwent the transition from communist to postcommunist or market economies. As with the Great Depression, economists will be debating the blunders that created this contraction long after it has become an artifact of history. For economists it will be a rich mine of data for testing alternative theories of great contraction.

1. MAGNITUDE OF THE CONTRACTIONS

How great was the collapse during the transition? Between the end of 1989 and the end of 1992, real GDP in the Eastern European (EE) countries – for present purposes, Poland, Hungary, the Czech Republic, the Slovak Republic, Romania, and Bulgaria – fell cumulatively by 22.1%, an enormous decline. The contraction was 7.6% in 1990, 11.6% in 1991, and 4.8% in 1992. It was reversed in the following year with positive growth of 0.7% in 1993, increasing to 2.1% in 1994.

If the contraction was large for the EE countries, it was enormous for the new countries that emerged from the collapse of the Soviet Union. Still falling in early 1995, real output in the countries of the former Soviet Union (FSU) had fallen by 48.4% by the end of 1994. This collapse was made up of successive declines in real GDP of 3.7% in 1990, 11.3% in 1991, 18.3% in 1992, 12.9% in 1993, and 15.0% in 1994.

Table 1 shows the changes in GDP for individual countries for the four years 1990 to 1993. The penultimate column presents the maximum contraction; the final column, 1994 output as a percentage of 1989 output. Table 1 suggests that the cumulative contractions were

Table 1. *Changes in GDP (%) for 21 countries, 1989–94*

Country	1990	1991	1992	1993	1994	Maximum contraction[a]	1994/1989
Uzbekistan	− 0.7	− 0.6	− 9.6	− 3.5	− 4	− 17.2	82.8
Hungary	− 4.3	− 11.9	− 4.5	− 2.3	+ 2.0	− 17.6	84.0
Poland	− 11.7	− 7.8	+ 1.5	+ 3.8	+ 4.7	− 18.6	89.8
Czech Republic	− 1.1	− 14.2	− 7.1	− 0.3	+ 2.7	− 21.4	80.7
Slovak Republic	− 1.1	− 15.96	− 7.1	− 4.1	+ 4.8	− 25.9	77.7
Estonia	− 3.6	+ 11.8	− 31.6	− 25	+ 4.0	− 30.6	69.4
Bulgaria	− 10.7	− 11.7	− 7.7	− 4.7	+ 0.2	− 32.7	67.7
Romania	− 7.9	− 13.7	− 15.4	+ 1.3	+ 3.4	− 32.8	70.5
Turkmenistan	+ 1.8	− 4.7	− 15	+ 7.8	− 25.0	− 33.3	67.7
Belarus	− 3	− 2	− 10	− 9	− 21.5	− 38.9	61.1
Russia	− 3.6	− 9	− 19	− 12	15.0	− 46.8	53.2
Kyrgyzstan	+ 4.8	− 5.2	− 16.4	− 13.4	− 26	− 46.8	53.2
Latvia	+ 2.7	− 8.3	− 32.9	− 20.0	+ 2.0	− 49.4	51.6
Kazakstan	− 0.4	− 13	− 13	− 13	− 25	− 50.8	49.2
Moldova	− 1.5	− 18.0	− 21.3	− 4.0	− 30.0	− 57.3	42.7
Ukraine	− 3.6	− 13.4	− 14.0	− 16.0	− 24.0	− 54.2	45.8
Tajikistan	+ 0.2	− 9.7	− 33.7	− 21	− 12	− 58.3	41.7
Armenia	− 7.2	− 8.8	− 48.2	− 9.9	+ 2.0	− 60.2	40.5
Azerbaijan	− 11.7	− 0.7	− 36.2	− 13.3	− 22.0	− 62.2	37.8
Lithuania	− 5.0	− 13.1	− 35.0	− 20.2	− 20.0	− 65.7	34.3
Georgia	− 12.4	− 20.6	− 43.4	− 35.0	− 30.0	− 82.1	17.9

[a] Maximum cumulative declines in output over the available years 1990–94 as long as they were positive.
Sources: Calculated from WEFA *Economic Outlook* (April 1993, April 1994, January 1995). The WEFA data for GDP in 1992 and 1993 are from the Statistical Committee of the Commonwealth of Independent States, *Statistical Bulletin* 2 (44), January 1994, pp. 3–4.

on a scale – outside of war – never before experienced in modern world history. One must go back to the Black Death in the middle of the fourteenth century to find a comparable output collapse.[1]

The economist can best appreciate the significance of the contraction by comparing it to the decline in output during the Great Depression of the 1930s. In that great contraction sixty years ago – which the older generation of economists considered the greatest economic calamity of its lifetime – real GDP fell by 20% in the United States, by 5% in the United Kingdom, by 11% in France, and by 39% in

---

[1] The contraction associated with the Black Death was due to the death of as many as 40% of Europe's population, and must have involved at least that large a contraction of output. On the other hand, the decline in per capita income was no doubt much smaller and may even have been negative.

Germany.[2] Except for the contraction in Germany – which brought the Nazis to power – the contractions in Eastern Europe and the former Soviet Union in recent years were in most cases on a larger scale than those of the Great Depression.

Comparison of the "great contraction" with the Great Depression may, of course, seem misleading. The Great Depression was associated with deflation;[3] the contraction in the countries of Eastern Europe and the former Soviet Union was accompanied by high inflation.

A number of questions immediately arise. Is the contraction over? Was it a necessary price of the transition from a planned to a market economy? Could the transition have been achieved without, or with a smaller, loss of output? What was the economic function of the contraction? Did it help to effect the transition from a planned to a market economy – and, if so, how?

This essay has a narrower scope, and will address two major types of questions. One is: What caused the contractions? The second is: Why did the contractions differ so widely between countries?

2. CAUSES OF THE CONTRACTIONS

Before attempting to explain the variations in cumulative contractions among the countries, it should be observed that a small contraction is not necessarily preferable to a large contraction. If the collapse of output represented production that did not produce utility or disposal value (e.g., unnecessary armaments that had no resale value on world markets), then the output contraction figures would not represent a loss of real income or consumption. Alternatively, if the contractions fulfilled a necessary economic function (e.g., imposed a shock that was, for some reason, indispensable to the transition), then a large contraction could be the promise of higher output in the future.[4] If the contraction were a necessary part of the transition adjustment process, low contractions might simply mean that the country had postponed a necessary adjustment and transferred the contraction to a later date – intertemporal smoothing of production.

---

[2] See e.g. Saint-Entienne (1984, pp. 5–9).

[3] The deflation was caused by a shortage of international reserves and tight money associated with the return to the gold standard in the 1920s at an undervalued gold price and overvalued currencies expressed in gold.

[4] As a general principle, countries should seek to maximize the present discounted value of the stream of future output, where the capitalization rate is the social rate of interest. Thus an "investment" in the transition from planned economy to market economy should yield a

In what follows we shall review six basic theories of the contraction. Three of these explanations are based on internal factors, and three on external factors.

2.1. Were the Contractions a Negative Mirage?

One influential view claims that the contractions never took place or, if they did, were on a far smaller scale than the statistics indicate. According to this view, the recorded contractions are a figment of flawed national statistics. Put another way: the statistics, like a mirage in reverse, fail to record production that has actually taken place. This theory is, not surprisingly, urged by many individuals and institutions who were closely involved in formulating the transition strategy.

There are at least three versions of this theory. The first version asserts that output was overstated under communist planning, because output reflected plans (not achievements) and managers overstated outputs. The second version asserts that output is understated in the transition economies; this is because the statistics accurately record the collapse of output in the state sector, but fail to record the output of small new firms in the private sector. The third version alleges that contractions in output were manifested mainly in a collapse of inefficient investment and that the contractions in output did not reflect contractions in consumption.

At the outset it should be acknowledged that it is common ground that aggregate output statistics leave much to be desired. If aggregate statistics are inadequate in western countries, they are much worse in the former communist countries of Eastern Europe and, again, even more deplorable in the new states that emerged or re-emerged out of the Soviet Union. A major problem is that the statistical authorities under communism measured state output but failed to measure private output. Difficulties exist with respect to data collection in the new states as well as with reconciling output data with incomes and expenditure data. Statistical discrepancies between alternative measures of GDP are often substantial.[5]

---

return at least equal to the social rate of interest. This means that the accumulated loss in the value of output during a contraction must be more than offset by the accumulated value of output during the expansion after discounting it by the social rate of interest. In practice, the criterion is more complicated because it involves weighing the welfare of different generations. Almost certainly, the oldest generation will lose by the contraction because its members will not be around to enjoy the higher living standard at the new plateau.

[5] See the discussion in the EBRD (1994, pp. 184–91). See also Starr (1995, p. 46). Starr argues that the *Goskomstat* (the Russian rump of what used to be Soviet Union's statistical monopo-

The negative mirage theory looked better a few years ago, when it was first suggested, than it does today. It is inevitable that the output of new private enterprises is neglected or underrecorded owing both to errors in statistical gathering and to underreporting for tax reasons. No doubt there is also a substantial underground economy in the new postcommunist states. But neither of these observations provide a satisfactory theory of the contractions.

To establish that incorrect statistics account for the contraction would require demonstrating (1) that the underground economy in the transition period is greater than that under communism, and (2) that the underreporting of new firms is on a scale sufficient to account for the enormous output collapse. Both these propositions are doubtful. Even if there was substantial underreporting of new firms in the private sector, in most of the countries this sector was much too small for even rapid growth to significantly alter the GDP contraction figures.

If the negative mirage theory is correct, its supporters should predict a rapid rebound in measured output as reporting improves, and a vast upward revision of earlier figures as data becomes recorded ex post. So far, neither has occurred on a scale large enough to account for the enormous contraction in some countries, even though the new governments have every incentive to put the best face on their transition experiments.

Let us turn now to the third version of the argument – the contention, based largely on anecdotal evidence, that output contractions did not reflect contractions in consumption. Reliable data for consumption in the FSU states are, unfortunately, not available, so it will be necessary to evaluate the contention using data for Eastern Europe alone. Table 2 shows changes in output and changes in consumption for six EE countries during the period 1990–94, in addition to the cumulative change in output between 1989 and 1993.

Even after allowing for weaknesses in the data, the claim that consumption did not decline, or did not decline by much, is clearly refuted by the data in the table. Except for Hungary, where the contraction in consumption was 19.5%, consumption in the EE countries

list) completely ignores output in the private sector, and that estimates of its undercounting of GDP ranges from 25% upward to 60%, with a consensus figure of about 45%. The extent to which a correctly revised measurement of output would affect the degree of output contraction would depend on the extent to which output was underestimated before as compared to after the transition – i.e., on the extent to which the underground economy is higher now than it was in the pretransition year.

Table 2. *Growth rates of GDP and consumption for selected countries*

	1990	1991	1992	1993	1994	Cumulative, 1989–93
Poland GDP	− 11.7	− 7.8	1.5	4.0	4.7	− 14.1
Poland Cons.	− 17.5	− 11.1	− 2.3	3.9	4.0	− 26.6
Hungary GDP	− 4.3	− 11.9	− 4.5	− 1.0	2.0	− 21.3
Hungary Cons.	− 5.8	− 13.2	− 1.6	0.7	1.5	− 19.5
Czech GDP	− 1.1	− 15.9	− 7.1	0.0	2.7	− 22
Czech Cons.	− 0.8	− 17.2	− 10.4	0.0	0.5	− 26.5
Slovak GDP	− 1.1	− 15.9	− 7.1	− 4.0	4.8	− 25.9
Slovak Cons.	− 0.8	− 17.2	− 10.4	0.0	0.5	− 26.5
Roman GDP	− 7.9	− 13.7	− 15.4	1.0	3.4	− 32.1
Roman Cons.	− 7.9	− 20.9	− 4.5	1.3	1.9	− 29.5
Bulgarian GDP	− 10.7	− 16.7	− 7.7	− 7.0	0.2	− 36.4
Bulgarian Cons.	− 3.8	− 19.5	− 8.3	− 6.0	0.0	− 33.5

Sources: WEFA *World Economic Outlook,* vol. 3: Developing and Planned Economies in Transition (April 1993); WEFA *Eurasia Outlook* (1994).

declined by more than 25%. In Poland, the contraction in consumption was 26.6%; in the Czech and Slovak Republics, 26.5%; in Romania, 29.5%; and in Bulgaria, 33.5%. Not only were the contractions in consumption large, they were of the same order of magnitude as the contractions in output. In three of the new republics, the contractions in consumption were greater than the contractions in output!

Five years after the transition began, the outputs of even the most successful countries are still substantially below recorded output of the pretransition economy. This is also true of consumption, which – from the evidence available for EE countries – fell just as much or more than output. It is true that current output in the transition economies is underrecorded (as in most countries), and it is probably also true that such output is underrecorded to a greater extent today than it was before the transitions. It is, however, patently not true that the contractions did not take place.

Denial of the evidence that the contractions took place is particularly unfortunate because it means that the theories and policies underlying the transition process will not be corrected. The danger is that the negative mirage theory will be used as a false alibi for mistakes in transition strategies.

2.2. Did Entrepreneurship Fail to Materialize?

A second theory attributes the contraction to the absence of a supply response on the part of the private sector. While the public sector released resources as it contracted, the private sector did not take advantage of the new available resources to expand private output.

There are two main types of explanations for the inadequate supply response. One is a sociological theory, that the necessary type of human capital was missing. The spirit of entrepreneurship had been killed by forty years of communism, entrepreneurial schools were locked, and the people were unwilling to accept the risks involved in setting up their own businesses.

The other theory is economic: the supply response in the private sector did not take place (or took place to a much lesser extent than was possible) because the private sector was still saddled with the legal and bureaucratic hangover from the communist era, and so experienced artificial impediments to its development. Growth of the private sector was inhibited by (a) laws, regulations, and prohibitions; (b) tax rates and quantitative restrictions; and (c) inadequate capital markets and state-owned banking systems.

The importance of the supply-side explanation is a subject for detailed microeconomic analysis of the individual countries to assess the impact of (a)–(c) on production. It is sometimes not realized just how detrimental to production are high or progressive tax rates and bureaucratic regulations. Nor is it always realized that a healthy private sector cannot function effectively in the context of a government-owned banking system; the banking system is first of all a data system, and banking confidentiality is ruled out in the government sector. Hence, an absolutely indispensable precondition of recovery from the output contraction is banking reform, which must mean conversion of state-owned banks to a privately owned and workably competitive banking system. It is also necessary that the regulatory system and the tax system encourage rather than inhibit free enterprise and growth in the private sector.

As time passes, the lack-of-entrepreneurship theory, like the statistical mirage theory, is a wasting asset; it seems less and less likely that a continued depression of output below pretransition levels can be accounted for by a failure of the entrepreneurial spirit. It remains true, however, that private enterprise in many of the transition economies is stifled by bureaucratic regulations, primitive tax rates, and a nationalized banking system. Until deregulation, tax reform, and privatization are achieved, output will remain below its potential. Thus, although its importance cannot yet be quantified, the supply-side factor cannot be entirely discounted.

2.3. Did Credit Restriction Cause the Contractions?

A third theory is that the contractions were caused by credit restriction. Because of high budget deficits and the incentive structure provided by IMF programs, authorities were forced to restrict credit and reduce the rate of monetary expansion. In socialist economies, many loss-making enterprises depended on infusions of credit to keep them in business. The "soft budget constraint" allowed firms to depend on credit from the central authorities rather than increasing efficiency to avert failure. As a result, when the requirements of the transition transformed the soft budget constraint to a hard budget constraint and credit was denied, enterprises failed and output contracted. In some cases also, it is argued, attempts at disinflation raised real interest rates and made it unprofitable for many firms to produce at all, let alone expand.

Let us consider these arguments in turn. It is true that, in many of the socialist countries, state firms were making losses and were propped up by credit. The economic issue is whether these state enterprises are, or were, potentially viable under private management, or at least under different management. If they are not, it is better that they go out of business or be sold for scrap value. In the meantime, it is necessary for new private firms to take up the slack and employ the resources set free from the failing state enterprises. Credit should therefore be shifted from the failing state firms to the new private firms. But if credit is withdrawn from state enterprises without being made available to the private sector, the contraction in state output will take place without any corresponding compensation in output growth in the private sector.

In order to test whether the contraction was due to a rise in real interest rates, it would be necessary to deflate nominal interest rates by the rate of expected inflation. Unfortunately, there are no data on expected inflation, and the actual inflation rate is often used to measure "real" interest rates. In some countries that undertook disinflation, the actual rate of inflation fell much more rapidly than the nominal rate of interest, leading to the conclusion that the real interest rate rose.

The argument seems at first to have some relevance for Poland, where sharp disinflation took place between 1990 and 1992. The rate of inflation was over 500% in 1990 but was quickly brought down to less than 80% in 1991, to less than 50% in 1992, and to less than 40% in 1993. Over the same period, interest rates changed by much less: the lending rate was 101.4% in 1990, 54.6% in 1991, and 39% in 1992.[6] There is hence a prima facie case for the hypothesis that real interest rates rose during the contraction. However, a closer look raises some doubts. The most important year for the contraction was 1990, when output fell by 11.7% and consumption by 17.5%. This was the year of the explosive inflation of 555.4%. In the following year, when the rate of inflation was brought down to 76.4%, output declined by "only" 7.1%; in 1992 and 1993, when the contraction ended and positive growth resumed, the rate of inflation continued to fall. We cannot be sure that this real interest–rate theory – based correctly on inflationary expectations – does *not* hold, because we do not have an independent index of expectations. However, if the theory is based on ex post real interest rates then it does not seem to hold in the case of Poland.

A fortiori, the theory does not hold in the other countries, where in all cases the rate of inflation increased between 1990 and 1991 and usually by more than tenfold.[7] Moreover, in all the FSU countries (but not in those of Eastern Europe), inflation was higher in 1992 than it was in 1991; leaving out the Baltic states and Russia itself, inflation in the FSU states also was more rapid in 1993 than in 1992. Given that output contraction was for the most part greatest in 1991 and 1992, it must be concluded that a theory based on evidence for high real interest rates collapses.[8]

2.4. Were Inside–Outside Factors to Blame?

What are inside–outside (or internal–external) factors when trade blocs disintegrate? The fall of communism was associated almost simultaneously with a collapse of the CMEA (Council for Mutual Economic Assistance) trade bloc and the disintegration of the Soviet customs union. Intrabloc trade suddenly became international trade, subject to the barriers that countries have always been fond of.

---

[6] See IMF (1994).

[7] See Table 13 in Section 3.

[8] Calvo and Coricelli (1993) examine the hypothesis that the output collapse was due to the "credit crunch." They argue that the decline in the stock of real credit, the taxation of capital gains on inventory, and the shifts from negative to positive interest rates in EE countries more than offset gains to firms from the revaluation of their inventories and the erosion of the

Table 3. *Total and interregional trade, 1990*

Country	Total	Intraregional	Share of intraregional
USSR			
Russian Federation	18.3	11.1	60.6
Ukraine	29.0	23.8	82.1
Belarus	47.3	41.0	86.8
Uzbekistan	28.5	25.5	89.4
Kazakstan	23.5	20.8	88.7
Georgia	28.9	24.8	85.9
Azerbaijan	33.9	29.8	87.7
Lithuania	45.5	40.9	89.7
Moldova	33.0	28.9	87.7
Latvia	41.4	36.7	88.6
Kyrgyz Republic	32.3	27.2	85.7
Tajikistan	35.9	31.0	86.5
Armenia	28.4	25.6	90.1
Turkmenistan	35.6	33.0	92.5
Estonia	32.9	30.2	91.6
Eastern Europe			
Bulgaria	30.1	16.1	53.4
Czechoslovakia	23.0	10.9	47.2
Hungary	34.1	13.7	40.3
Poland	19.6	8.4	43.1
Romania	17.6	3.7	21.0

Notes: Total trade is measured as the average of exports and imports as percentage of GNP; intraregional trade refers to trade within the USSR and the CMEA.
Source: Michalopoulos and Tarr (1994, p. 15).

The importance of external factors as an explanation of the contraction of the countries in transition involves both trade dependence and the direction of trade. Table 3 shows the 1990 ratio of the average of total exports and imports to both GNP and intrabloc trade. From Table 3 it may be seen that, within the FSU, total trade accounted for a low of 18.3% of GDP for Russia and a high of 47.3% for Belarus. In five countries in Eastern Europe, total trade ranged between

real value of their debt. For the period under study (1990 and 1991) they find a sharp contraction of credit associated with the contraction of output, consistent with a causal relationship. However, as pointed out in the discussions of the paper, the causation could have been reversed, with the output contractions causing the credit contraction.

Table 4. *Trade with the rest of the world as share of total trade, 1990 and 1993 (percent)*

Country	Exports		Imports	
	1990	1993	1990	1993
Armenia	1.8	19.2	12.6	54.2
Azerbaijan	6.5	35.8	16.4	34.3
Belarus	10.5	19.2	17.3	18.1
Estonia	4.5	57.5	11.1	65.5
Georgia	5.0	43.9	15.5	51.5
Kazakstan	11.0	32.8	11.8	26.2
Kyrgyz Republic	2.1	28.4	19.4	22.9
Latvia	3.4	43.9	17.1	34.3
Lithuania	5.7	42.8	12.3	30.4
Moldova	3.9	21.5	14.5	22.0
Russia	39.0	73.6	42.1	75.8
Tajikistan	13.1	69.0	10.3	65.4
Turkmenistan	4.5	40.0	9.5	46.1
Ukraine	17.1	52.6	19.4	33.9
Uzbekistan	9.1	41.3	9.9	36.5
FSU	24.6	62.0	27.5	56.8

Note: Trade is evaluated at implicit exchange rates, not official and commercial exchange rates.
Source: Michalopoulos and Tarr (1994, p. 6).

17.6% of GDP for Romania and 34.1% for Hungary. Of this total trade, the share of intraregional trade was exceptionally high in the FSU countries – ranging from 82.1% to 92.5% (except for Russia, at 60.6%). As might be expected, the share of intraregional trade was much smaller in the EE countries, ranging from 21.0% for Romania to 53.4% for Bulgaria.

How did these shares change after 1990? Table 4 shows the remarkable shift from intraregional to international trade between 1990 and 1993. However, the shift was accomplished primarily by a collapse of intraregional trade, rather than by a large increase in extraregional trade.

2.5. How Important Were Changes in the Terms of Trade?

Among the external shock theories, there has been considerable focus placed upon the effect of changes in the terms of trade. For example,

Kenen (1990) estimated the terms-of-trade effects of the transition to world market prices on the basis of data disaggregated by SITC and CMEA commodity groups.[9] Using national cross rates between the transferable ruble and the U.S. dollar, Kenen arrived at a deterioration of the terms of trade of five members – Poland, Hungary, Czechoslovakia, Romania, and Bulgaria – ranging from 24% to 37% based on 1989 trade flows. See also IMF et al. (1990, vol. I, apx. II-3).

Rodrik (1992) analyzed the shock due to the collapse of trade. He divided the shock from the collapse of CMEA trade for the years 1990 and 1991 into three components: (i) a terms-of-trade effect; (ii) an import-subsidy/export-tax removal effect; and (iii) a market-loss effect. After accounting for multiplier effects also, Rodrik concluded that the combined shock accounted for about 30% of the downturn in Poland, 60% in Czechoslovakia, and 100% in Hungary. However, even if we assume adequate methods and sufficient data to account for such a large share of the contractions in 1991 and 1992, what explains the contractions in subsequent years?

There seems little doubt that many of the countries in Eastern Europe suffered a worsening of their terms of trade. The theory is, however, incomplete at best. First, changes in the terms of trade would not be taken into account in measurement of output declines evaluated at constant price levels; terms-of-trade effects, far from explaining the statistical contractions, would have to be added to the contractions to estimate changes in real income. Second, even if real income effects associated with changes in the terms were included in the figures for the contractions, they would not have been sufficient to account for changes in output on the scale that materialized. For example, a 30% deterioration of the terms of trade would have an income effect equal to 30% of the initial value of imports; if imports accounted for (say) 40% of GDP, then the decline in real income would be only 12%. But the contractions in more than half the countries were over 30%, and in 18 of the countries were over 20%.

Third, the terms of trade in a closed area is to a large extent a zero-sum game: while five of the main CMEA countries may have experienced serious declines in the terms of trade over the period 1989–94, some of the other countries experienced corresponding improvements in their terms of trade. Table 5 shows the terms of trade for interstate trade among the FSU countries between 1990 and 1993.

[9] In 1990 the CMEA included Bulgaria, the (former) Czech and Slovak Federal Republic, Cuba, the (former) German Democratic Republic, Hungary, Mongolia, Poland, Romania, the USSR, and Vietnam.

Table 5. *Terms of interstate trade among FSU countries, 1990–93*

Country	1990	1991	1992	1993
Armenia	100	107	85.0	75.1
Azerbaijan	100	105.3	94.8	97.9
Belarus	100	103.2	87.7	83.4
Estonia	100	107.5	87.7	72.9
Georgia	100	105.9	75.4	72.9
Kazakstan	100	95.1	98.1	97.0
Kyrgyz Republic	100	104.0	87.3	81.5
Latvia	100	104.1	87.3	81.4
Lithuania	100	105.1	80.7	74.2
Moldova	100	106.1	66.4	65.0
Russia	100	97.4	113.6	120.1
Tajikistan	100	110.3	86.8	75.5
Turkmenistan	100	109.9	121.9	152.0
Ukraine	100	96.0	94.1	88.8
Uzbekistan	100	109.3	94.5	91.6

Source: Michalopoulos and Tarr (1994, p. 17).

From the table it is clear that the terms of trade of the largest country, Russia, improved between 1990 and 1993 (after a small dip in 1991). Yet Russia's output contracted by 38% from 1990 to 1993 and by an additional 14% the following year, a larger contraction than that experienced by the countries whose terms of trade improved.

Although terms-of-trade effects are significant, these considerations suggest that they are not sufficient to account for the magnitude of the contractions. Other, more important factors, were at work.

Where Did the Export Multiplier Go? Changes in exports and imports can affect income even if the terms of trade are constant. A collapse of foreign markets can bring about a foreign trade–multiplier effect on output. The multiplier effect can operate from either the demand side or the supply side. Let us consider each of these multipliers in turn.

The demand-side multiplier, familiar from Keynesian economics, occurs as a result of the feedback effects on aggregate demand. A billion-dollar loss of export markets results in a worsening of the trade balance and a reduction in supply of current output (and employment). The loss of income reduces spending on both home and foreign goods and services, bringing on a secondary contraction of income and a lessening of the fall in the trade balance (because imports have fallen). The cumulative contraction will continue until net savings (including any budget surplus) and imports together have fallen by $1 billion, which will require an income contraction of some multiple of the reduced export demand. If, for example, the sum of the marginal propensity to save and the marginal propensity to import were 1/3, the multiplier would be its reciprocal, 3, and the contraction of output would be $3 billion.[10]

To calculate the demand-side multiplier effects of a collapse of export markets, it is convenient to turn the multiplier formula, which relates the changes in exports to consequent changes in income, into an elasticity formula $\epsilon = \sigma\kappa$ that relates the percentage change in income with respect to exports, where σ is the share of exports in GDP and κ is the export multiplier. Suppose, for example, that the multiplier is 2 and the share of exports in GDP is 0.4. In this case the elasticity of income with respect to exports is 0.8. This means that a 10% fall in exports would induce an 8% fall in income; similarly, a 40% fall in exports would induce a 32% fall in income. Using the demand-side multiplier analysis, we can easily account for a substantial part of the output declines.

Table 6 shows the colossal fall in intra-FSU trade between 1990 and 1993, ranging from 42.4% to 89.2%. Apart from the steep declines for the quasiwarring Caucasian states – 89.2% in Georgia, 83.7% in Armenia, and 82.0% in Azerbaijan – the most remarkable declines occurred in the Baltic states: 85.4% in Latvia, 83.2% in Estonia, and 79.1% in Lithuania. The Baltic states were among the most vulnerable of the FSU, in terms both of their overall openness and of their high share of intraregional trade.

It is also necessary to consider changes in exports with the rest of the world. For the FSU countries, this is shown in Table 7. It can be seen from this table that, although the Baltic countries lost substantial trade with the rest of the world in the first years of the transition,

---

10 This argument ignores the government sector and the marginal propensity to tax, as well as a positive marginal propensity to invest and repercussion effects on exports. For example, suppose that: the marginal propensity to save, s, is 1/6; the marginal propensity to import, m, is 1/6; and the marginal tax rate, t, is 1/3. Then the multiplier $k = 1/(s + m + t) = 1.5$. If we also suppose that the marginal propensity to invest $i = 1/6$, then the multiplier becomes $k = 1/(s - i + m + t) = 2$. Account should also be taken of feedback effects on income in the rest of the world and of the matrix multiplier phenomenon when direct and indirect changes take place in many countries at the same time. For an elaboration of the mathematics of these multipliers see Mundell (1965).

Table 6. *Trade collapse among FSU countries, 1990–93*
(billions of U.S. dollars)

Country	1990	1991	1992	1993	Percentage change, 1993/1990
Armenia	3,509	1,882	1,335	583	– 83.7
Azerbaijan	6,105	4.575	2,318	1,124	– 82
Belarus	17,224	12,415	9,659	7,349	– 57.3
Estonia	2,468	1,928	732	414	– 83.2
Georgia	56,724	2,723	662	617	– 89.2
Kazakstan	8,443	7,231	6,928	4,610	– 45.4
Kyrgyz Republic	2,445	2,605	1,193	595	– 75.7
Latvia	5,028	3,116	2,479	734	– 85.4
Lithuania	6,575	4,741	2,287	1,372	– 79.1
Moldova	5,853	2,991	1,558	1,373	– 76.5
Russia	74,710	58,837	42,464	27,493	– 63.2
Tajikistan	2,377	1,621	423	245	– 89.7
Turkmenistan	2,469	2,614	2,496	1,425	– 42.3
Ukraine	38,319	27,342	17,722	10,878	– 71.6
Uzbekistan	8,169	6,642	2,989	2,874	– 64.8
FSU	189,337	141,216	95,204	61,657	– 67.4

Source: Michalopoulos and Tarr (1994, p. 4).

they quickly recovered: by 1993, their exports exceeded the exports at the beginning of the transition.

Is There a Supply-Side Import Multiplier? Traditional multiplier analysis assumes that output responds or contracts with aggregate demand, and that changes in investment induce an equal increase in saving. The implicit assumption is that there is excess capacity and hence there are no shortages or restrictions to choke off supply when demand increases. In a world of excess capacity, increments to capacity are not needed when demand and output expand. This approach is typically used to explain the international transmission of the business cycle, and doubtless supplies a partial explanation for the effect of the collapse of trade on output.

There is, however, another possibility. Even in a world of full employment, a collapse of exports could have a multiplier effect on output. This supply-side multiplier arises because a collapse of export markets reduces the capacity to import. If imports are essential

Table 7. *Trade of FSU countries with the rest of the world,*
1990–93 (billions of current U.S. dollars)

Country	1990	1991	1992	1993	Maximum decline (%)
Armenia	109	70	40	29	63.3
Azerbaijan	723	487	754	351	51.5
Belarus	3,438	1,661	1,061	737	78.6
Estonia	198	50	242	461	74.7
Georgia	515	30	161	222	94.2
Kazakstan	1,777	1,183	1,489	1,529	16.2
Kyrgyz Republic	89	23	77	112	74.2
Latvia	304	125	429	460	58.9
Lithuania	679	345	557	696	49.2
Moldova	405	180	157	174	55.5
Russia	80,900	53,100	41,600	43,900	48.6
Tajikistan	609	424	111	263	81.0
Turkmenistan	195	146	1,145	1,156	25.1
Ukraine	13,390	8,500	6,000	6,300	55.2
Uzbekistan	1,390	1,257	869	1,466	37.5
FSU	104,721	67,581	54,691	57,857	47.8

Source: Michalopoulos and Tarr (1994).

to maintain production, then a forced reduction in imports will create bottlenecks that reduce production capacity. Hence the relation between import reduction and output reduction also needs to be examined.

A complete analysis would require both an elaboration of the vertical structure of production and an input–output table of the economy, in order to account for (a) commodities and factors that are inputs into their own reproduction and into the production of other commodities and (b) acceleration effects arising from the need to adjust capacity to expected supply. For example, if there is a fixed relation between output and capital stock, then a given increase in output would require an equiproportionate increase in the stock of capital, which would create a disproportionate increase in investment[11] over the gestation period of the new capital equipment.

[11] The two most important pioneers in the analysis of investment fluctuations over the business cycle were Mikhail Tugan-Baranowski (1865–1919), a Ukrainian economist who became Minister of Finance in the Ukrainian Republic of 1918, and Arthur Aftalion (1874–1956), a Bulgarian economist who lived most of his life in France and is generally credited with the first enunciation (in 1913) of the acceleration principle.

More to the point, in the absence of new borrowing or increased use of reserves, a fall in exports would have to be matched by an equal fall in imports. If imports are capital goods needed for replacement of parts or growth, then the marginal efficiency of capital falls and complementary domestic investment is shut down, creating technological unemployment. Thus, even in the absence of a demand-side multiplier or terms-of-trade effects, reduced exports lead to unemployment and output contraction.

The model, in its extreme form, is as follows. Let $Y = \theta K$ express the relation between output Y and capital K. Suppose that trade must be balanced: $M = \pi X$, where M denotes imports; X, exports; and π, the terms of trade. Suppose also that investment, dK/dt, is equal to imports; hence $dK/dt = \pi X$. Then the growth rate λ of output is equal to $\theta \pi \sigma$, where σ is the share of exports in income. If θ and π remain constant then a given percentage reduction in the export share leads to an equal percentage reduction in the growth rate.

Of course, it would be inappropriate to assume that the terms of trade are constant. As we have seen from Table 3, the terms of trade changed substantially over the period in question. The decline in the value of exports is a composite of both price and quantity effects. According to the formula $\lambda = \theta \pi \sigma$, changes in output can be explained by a combination of changes in the export share and changes in the terms of trade (assuming the output/capital ratio θ is constant).

By a crude adjustment, Table 8 splits the changes in exports into price and quantity effects. To be precise, it takes the data on the changes in exports of each country and assumes that these data reflect both price and quantity effects. Table 8 then takes the numbers for changes in the interstate terms of trade, assumes that they are applicable to all exports, and finally subtracts them from the total change in the value of exports. It may be noted from Table 8 that the changes in the quantity of exports are of the same order of magnitude as the changes in output; that is, the dominant effects on income arose from changes in quantity rather than price.

The strong relation between changes in exports and changes in income suggests a major explanation for the contractions. However, it does not by itself determine whether demand or supply effects are more relevant. A general equilibrium analysis would be required to disentangle the effects of demand and supply. In particular, it would be necessary to distinguish between the effects of (a) the world recession of 1990–92 on export demand of the EE and FSU countries;

Table 8. *Export and output changes, 1990–93*

Country	Exports	Terms of trade	Export volume	Income
		Percentage change in		
Armenia	– 83.1	– 24.9	– 58.2	– 62
Azerbaijan	– 78.7	– 2.1	– 76.6	– 72
Belarus	– 58.6	– 16.6	– 42.0	– 42
Estonia	– 70.5	– 17.0	– 53.5	– 55
Georgia	– 86	– 27.1	– 58.9	– 79
Kazakstan	– 40.4	– 3.0	– 37.4	– 54
Kyrgyz Republic	– 72.3	– 18.5	– 53.8	– 48
Latvia	– 78.9	– 18.6	– 60.3	– 48
Lithuania	– 71.6	– 25.8	– 45.8	– 57
Moldova	– 74.4	– 35.0	– 39.4	– 53
Russia	– 56.3	+ 20.1	– 76.4	– 47
Tajikistan	– 83.5	– 24.5	– 59.0	– 70
Turkmenistan	– 18.9	+ 52.0	– 70.9	– 30
Ukraine	– 67.5	– 11.2	– 56.3	– 60
Uzbekistan	– 56.2	– 8.4	– 47.8	– 14

(b) the interaction between export supply and import demand in connection with the end of CMEA; and (c) the collapse of the Soviet Union customs union and free-trade area.

2.6. Was There Insufficient Foreign Aid?

Another theory concerns the role of foreign aid in reducing the contractions. A country that has access to foreign capital can increase output faster than a country that must rely on its own resources. If the rate of return on the invested capital exceeds the rate of interest on the loan, the country gains by borrowing. At the time the Cold War ended, many economists thought that a huge loan to the Soviet Union – $150 billion was the figure mentioned by a Harvard group – would be needed to effect the transition. If such a loan had been financed and delivered then the Soviet Union might possibly have held together. But would that have been a good thing?

Borrowing can be a mixed blessing. One danger is that borrowing goes into unproductive consumption, leaving the country saddled with a debt without the increase in capacity needed to service it. One of the weaknesses of intergovernmental lending is that only rarely can the lender impose enforceable conditions on its use. This holds

Table 9. *Debt levels and the contractions*

Country	Debt ($ billion)	Population (million)	Debt per capita ($)	Contraction (%)
Hungary	25	10.2	2,451	17.6
Poland	50	38.6	1,295	18.6
Czech Republic	6	10.3	583	21.4
Slovak Republic	4	5.4	759	25.9
Bulgaria	13	8.8	1,454	32.7
Romania	5	23.2	188	32.8

also for the international lending institutions. For example, on 11 April 1995, the IMF approved a standby loan of about $6.8 billion to Russia, designed to bring inflation under control and stabilize the ruble. But the budget deficit, magnified by Russia's war against Chechnya, makes it unlikely that stabilization will be achieved quickly.

It is not clear whether in the long run countries would gain more from borrowing than they would lose by the requirements of debt service and amortization. Yet countries have a great temptation to incur debt even if its rate of return does not justify it. There are two forms of externalities that lead to overborrowing. One is the possibility that debts will not have to be repaid in full; the debt decade has brought that bad lesson home to every would-be borrower. The second externality arises from political systems in which governments can court popularity at home by borrowing and leave their successors the burden of funding the repayment or, as the case may be, going into default.

Has borrowing helped countries through the transition? The evidence is mixed. Hungary and Poland, with high debt levels, had low contractions; on the other hand, Bulgaria, with a higher proportionate debt level than Poland, had a large contraction. Moreover, the Czech Republic had both a low contraction and a low debt rate, but Romania had a high contraction and a low debt level. There is no obvious relation between the contraction size and level of foreign debt (see Table 9).

3. WHY DID THE CONTRACTIONS DIFFER?

We now turn to the second problem, that of determining why the output contractions differed so widely in the various countries. In Table

Table 10. *Low and high contractions, 1990–93*

Low		Medium		High	
Uzbekistan	17.2	Estonia	30.6	Kazakstan	50.8
Hungary	17.6	Bulgaria	32.7	Ukraine	54.2
Poland	18.6	Romania	32.8	Moldova	57.3
Czech Republic	21.4	Turkmenistan	33.3	Tajikistan	58.3
Slovak Republic	25.9	Belarus	38.9	Armenia	60.2
		Russia	46.8	Azerbaijan	62.2
		Kyrgyzstan	46.8	Lithuania	65.7
		Latvia	49.4	Georgia	82.1

Source: Table 1.

10, the cumulative contractions are divided into three groups – low, medium, and high. The "low" countries experienced contractions up to 26%; the "medium" countries experienced contractions between 30% and 50%; and the "high" countries experienced contractions of more than 50%. The following observations can be made.

Of the EE countries, none are in the high contraction group and only Bulgaria and Romania are in the middle group.

Three of the countries in the high contraction group are affected by regional tensions: insurrectionism in Georgia, and the strife between Azerbaijan and Armenia over enclaves.

Tajikistan, in the high contraction group, has retained its communist government and faces increasing opposition from anticommunists and Islamic fundamentalists.

One of the Asiatic FSU states (Uzbekistan) is the lowest of the low contraction group, and two others (Turkmenistan and Kyrgyzstan) are in the middle group.

It is clear that different factors are at work in determining the degree of contraction. Four interrelated factors are the extent of industrialization, the level of human capital, openness of the economy, and urbanization. It is likely that the most open countries, which are also typically the smaller countries and the most specialized, will suffer more from the breakdown of the Soviet market than the less open, more agricultural countries. For the FSU republics in 1988, Table 11 depicts five indications of development: (1) industrialization, measured by the percentage of employment in industry; (2) urbanization, the percentage of the population living in urban areas; (3) "in-

Table 11. *Indexes of development for FSU republics, 1988*

Country	Percent- age of employ- ment in industry	Percent- age of urban popu- lation	Intra- Soviet trade as a per- centage of NMP	Doctor- ates and candi- dates per 10,000 of popu- lation	Scien- tific workers per 10,000 of popu- lation	Relative income per capita (USSR = 100)
USSR	38	66	29.3[a]	19	53	100
Russia	42	74	18.0	22	71	110
Ukraine	40	68	39.1	14	39	96
Belarus	40	67	69.6	13	38	102
Estonia	42	72	66.5	31	61	133
Latvia	40	71	64.1	23	51	123
Lithuania	41	68	60.9	21	44	114
Moldova	28	48	62.1	8	16	84
Georgia	29	57	53.7	32	67	108
Armenia	39	70	63.7	28	70	86
Azerbaijan	26	54	58.7	15	29	71
Kazakstan	31	58	30.9	10	23	93
Turkmenistan	21	46	50.7	7	13	71
Uzbekistan	24	40	43.2	7	14	62
Tajikistan	21	32	41.8	6	12	54
Kyrgyzstan	27	38	50.2	8	18	72

Notes: NMP = net material product.
[a] In 1988, NMP in the Soviet Union was 72.0% of GDP.
Source: IMF et al. (1990, vol. I, pp. 219–25, tables 19, 24, 26).

ward openness," measured by the ratio of intra-Soviet trade to the collective GDP of the Soviet bloc; (4) human capital, measured by the proportion of candidates or doctors[12] in the population as well as by the proportion of scientific workers; and (5) relative income per capita, with USSR = 100. By all criteria the Baltic countries were, before independence, among the most industrial, the most urbanized, the most open, and the best educated, and also had the highest standard of living. Because of their level of development they were the most specialized; because they were specialized they depended most on trade; and because they depended most on trade, they were vulnerable when trade collapsed. By contrast, the Asiatic FSU countries are rural, nonindustrial, and relatively closed. The percentage of industrial employment in Kazakstan, Turkmenistan, Uzbekistan,

---

[12] A Soviet rank of "candidate" is said to correspond to a North American Ph.D., while a Soviet doctorate is typically awarded only to senior scholars; see IMF et al. (1990, vol. I, p. 222).

Table 12. *Contraction, trade, and production*

Country	Con-traction (%)	Trade/GDP (%)	Intra-regional Trade/GDP (%)	Main products or exports
Uzbekistan	17	28.5	25.5	Natural gas, chemical industry, mining, cotton, fruit, grain, sheep, cattle
Hungary	18	34.1	13.7	Major exports: raw materials and semifinished goods, 35.1%; industrial consumer goods, 26.3%
Poland	19	19.6	8.4	Major export markets 1993Q2: Germany, 31.6%; FSU, 13.7%; Italy, 6.6%; U.K., 4.2%
Czech Republic	21	23.0	10.0	Major exports: manufacturing goods, 43.3%; machinery and transport equipment, 27.6%
Slovak Republic	26	23.0	10.9	Major exports: meth. products, chemical products, machinery, equipment
Estonia	31	32.9	30.2	Computers, electric motors, measuring instruments, textiles, fishing; cattle, pigs, dairy products, potatoes, flax, grain
Bulgaria	33	30.1	16.1	Major exports: industrial machines and equipment, 43.3%; processed food products, 11.8%; fuels and raw materials, 7.0%
Romania	33	17.6	3.7	Major exports: machinery and equipment, 37.6%; energy and raw materials, 23.2%; consumer goods, 17.1%
Turkmenistan	33	35.6	33.0	Natural gas and oil, chemicals, salt mining; cotton, fruits, vegetables, silkworms, sheep, goats
Russia	47	18.3	11.1	Oil and gas extraction, mining, metallurgy, machine building, chemicals, grain, potatoes
Kyrgyzstan	47	32.3	27.7	Metallurgy, textiles, hydroelectric power, livestock, potatoes, vegetables, sugar beets
Latvia	49	41.4	36.7	Electric industry, textiles, food, chemicals, paper, potatoes, grain, flax, dairy, beef cattle
Kazakstan	51	23.5	20.8	Metallurgy, chemicals, machinery; grain, beets, cotton, fruits, meat, wool

Table 12 (*cont.*)

Country	Con-traction (%)	Trade/GDP (%)	Intra-regional Trade/GDP (%)	Main products or exports
Ukraine	54	29.0	23.8	Mining, metallurgy, chemical, light and food industries; grain, sugar beets, sunflowers, vegetables, flax, beef, pigs, poultry
Moldova	57	33.0	28.9	Food production; grapes, vegetables, grain, sunflowers
Tajikistan	58	35.9	31.0	Food production, textiles, sheep, cattle, yaks, vegetables
Armenia	60	28.4	25.6	Mining, machine tools, chemicals, textiles, cereals, potatoes, vegetables, grapes
Azerbaijan	62	33.9	29.8	Oil and gas, chemicals, steel, winter wheat, rice, cotton, tea, citrus fruits
Belarus	65.7	47.3	41.0	Chemicals, automotive and agricultural machinery, machine tools, potatoes, barley, flax, pigs, cows
Lithuania	65.7	45.5	40.9	Electronics, high-precision mechanical tools, chemicals, wood, paper, textiles, food; grain, potatoes, sugar beets, vegetables, flax, beef cattle, hogs, poultry
Georgia	82.1	28.9	24.8	Food processing, grapes, citrus fruits, tea

Tajikistan, and the Kyrgyz Republic varies between 21% and 31%, compared to a 40–42% range in the Baltic states; levels of openness for the five countries listed vary from 30.9% to 50.7%, compared to 60.9–66.5% in the Baltic states.

Further evidence is provided by the composition of production, shown in Table 12. The three Baltic states suffered deeper contractions, on average, than the countries of Eastern Europe. These states were among the richest and most industrialized of the former Soviet Union republics. Estonia produces computers; Lithuania and Estonia produce electric motors and metal-cutting machines; Latvia and Lithuania produce equipment for livestock raising; and Latvia produces radios, tape recorders, refrigerators, electric irons, washing machines, and children's bicycles. In view of their high level of specialization, they were among the most vulnerable to the collapse of trade. The loss of Soviet and CMEA markets was not easily absorbed at home, and product quality is only recently proving to be competitive in international markets.

Among the three Baltic states, Lithuania's contraction was the greatest and longest; of the three states, only Lithuania was still contracting in 1994. Not surprisingly, in the pretransition years it was more trade-dependent in general and more intrabloc-trade-dependent in particular. Indeed, as Table 12 shows, the contractions in the three Baltic states were in direct proportion to both their openness and their openness with respect to intrabloc trade. There is no doubt that the collapse of trade was a major cause of the contraction among the more industrialized and trade-dependent states.

For many countries, the trade collapse is not a sufficient explanation. War, religious strife, and political unrest have been important factors explaining the severe contractions in the Caucasian republics. Armenia, Azerbaijan, and Georgia have been among the worst hit, with contractions of (respectively) 60.2%, 62.2%, and 82.1%. Armenia, however, seems to have hit bottom. Azerbaijan, despite an attempted coup in March 1995, has a chance to resume growth by 1996, particularly in view of the international competition (between Iran, Turkey, the United States, and Russia) over rights to its vast petroleum resources.

The commodity composition of output is also an important factor: whether a country's income derives from agriculture, raw materials, or industry. Countries such as Uzbekistan and Turkmenistan, which had relied on natural gas and/or oil exports, suffered relatively lower contractions. Partly for this reason, these countries may also have made less progress toward the transition to free-enterprise market structures. It could be argued that some low contraction countries have made so little progress toward the transition that they have merely postponed the contraction to a later date.

What about the inflation factor? Have countries with moderate or low inflation fared better than countries with high inflation or hyperinflation? Table 13 presents some of the relevant information. It is apparent that there is a positive relationship between the magnitude of the contraction and the average rate of inflation. Except for Uzbekistan, which was sustained by exports of natural gas, low contractions were associated with low inflation and high contractions were associated with high inflation.

Table 13. *Changes in price level (%) for 21 countries, 1990–95*

Country	1990	1991	1992	1993	1994	1995	Con-traction 1990–94
Uzbekistan	3.8	106.0	410.0	1,509.0	935.4	110.4	17.2
Hungary	29.0	34.2	21.6	21.1	21.2	28.3	17.6
Poland	555.4	76.7	44.3	37.6	29.5	21.6	18.6
Czech Republic	10.0	10.8	12.5	18.0	9.7	7.8	21.4
Slovak Republic	10.0	10.8	10.0	25.3	11.7	7.2	25.9
Estonia	17.0	210.6	1,069.3	35.0	41.7	28.9	30.6
Bulgaria	26.3	405.0	79.4	63.9	121.9	32.9	32.7
Romania	4.2	230.6	199.2	295.5	61.7	27.8	32.8
Turkmenistan	4.7	88.5	770.0	10,826	1,328	2,400.0	33.3
Belarus	4.5	94.1	1,060	1,996.5	1,959.9	240.0	38.9
Russia	5.6	92.7	1,570.0	840.0	203.0	130.0	46.8
Krygyzstan	4.1	107.4	1,090.0	1,366.0	87.2	31.9	46.8
Latvia	10.5	124.5	951.2	60.0	35.9	24.2	49.4
Kazakstan	4.1	94.9	1,669.0	2,165.0	1,060.3	60.3	50.8
Moldova	4.5	98.1	1,110.0	2,705.7	104.6	23.8	57.3
Ukraine	4.8	83.5	2,000.0	10,156	401.0	181.0	54.2
Tajikistan	4.9	84.8	910.0	7,325.5	240.0	1,200.0	58.3
Armenia	6.9	140.2	140.2	10,878	1,761.9	45.2	60.2
Azerbaijan	6.1	111.5	1,110.0	980.0	1,609.7	95.0	62.2
Lithuania	8.4	224.7	1,020.5	189.0	45.0	28.8	65.7
Georgia	3.3	78.5	913.4	5,000.0	7,380.0	57.4	82.1

Source: WEFA Group, *Eurasia Economic Outlook* (August 1996).

Association does not, of course, prove causality. Although it is generally agreed that low (high) inflation is conducive (detrimental) to efficiency and growth, it would be a mistake to conclude thereby that the cause of large contractions was inflation. On the contrary, without denying the feedback effects, it would be more accurate to conclude that sizable contractions, by reducing government revenues, created budget deficits that – through inflationary finance – caused the inflation. In turn, the monetary and fiscal chaos, initially an act of desperation, had feedback effects that exacerbated the contractions and delayed the recovery.

4. WHAT CONCLUSIONS CAN BE DRAWN?

The first and most obvious conclusion is that output contracted by a cumulative percentage never before experienced in the history of capitalist economies (at least in peacetime). Early denials that the contractions were occurring have proved to be incorrect. We observe that cumulative contractions over the 1990–94 period ranged widely, from a low of 18% to a high of more than 80%.

Contractions were distributed among the EE and FSU countries in distinct groups. High contractions were associated with the three Caucasian republics, due partly to war and civil strife and partly to their economic isolation. Another group of countries in Central Asia had mixed results depending importantly on two factors: their mineral dependence and the extent of their transition. Oil and gas exports have sustained the incomes of Uzbekistan and Turkmenistan, but this source of revenue may also have postponed the transition – and put the contractions farther into the future.

For the Baltic States and Belarus, increasing contractions were associated both with increasing trade dependence and the severity of deteriorations in the terms of trade. The two largest states, Russia and the Ukraine, were less trade-dependent than other FSU countries yet suffered substantial contractions (of 47% and 54%, respectively). Russia's terms of trade improved over the period whereas the Ukraine's worsened; this may explain the percentage difference in their contractions.

Countries where output contracted the least included four Eastern European countries (Poland, Hungary, the Czech Republic, and Slovakia) where preconditions for the transition were most advanced.

The collapse of trade was a partial but immediate cause of the overall contraction, operating through the international trade multiplier, supply bottlenecks, and the terms of trade. An important ancillary cause was the collapse of state-owned enterprise before private enterprise was ready to take its place. Obstructionism in government policy was a more important constraint on output than a failure of entrepreneurship.

The main cause of the slow (or nonexistent) supply response was the lack of infrastructure and appropriate government policies. Private enterprise was impeded by several factors: unfavorable tax rates compared to taxes on state-owned enterprises; laws and regulations restricting the number of workers in private enterprise; restrictions on firing; an unstable monetary system, which impeded the calculation of profit opportunities; restrictions on foreign exchange; the absence of credit facilities in an efficient capital market; and residual state control of banking. The contractions represented a bungle of economic policy on an unprecedented scale. However, with the harm already done, it would not serve the interests of any country to turn back the clock and undo the institutional progress that has been achieved.

When political realities make it possible to control the timing of the transition, countries should move rapidly toward creating the preconditions for an energetic supply response while phasing out and/or privatizing loss-making state-owned enterprises at a pace that is consistent with an expanding private sector. Countries (such as China) that want to proceed with the transition should learn from the mistakes of the EE and FSU countries and take an entirely different path.

REFERENCES

Blejer, M. I., G. A. Calvo, F. Coricelli, and A. H. Gelb (eds.) (1993), *Eastern Europe in Transition: From Recession to Growth?* (proceedings of a conference on the macroeconomic aspects of adjustment). Washington, DC: World Bank.

Calvo, Guillermo, and Fabrizio Coricelli (1993), "Output Collapse in Eastern Europe: The Role of Credit," in Blejer et al. (1993), pp. 92–106.

European Bank for Reconstruction and Development [EBRD] (1994), *Transition Report.* London: EBRD.

Kenen, Peter (1990), "Transitional Arrangements for Trade and Payments among the CMEA Countries," Working Paper no. 90/79, International Monetary Fund, Washington, DC.

International Monetary Fund [IMF] (1994), *International Financial Statistics.* Washington, DC: IMF.

IMF, IBRD, OECD, and EBRD (1990), *A Study of the Soviet Economy,* vols. I–III. Washington, DC: IMF.

Michalopoulos, C., and D. G. Tarr (eds.) (1994), *Trade in the New Independent States.* Washington, DC: World Bank/UNDP.

Mundell, Robert A. (1965), "The Significance of the Homogeneity Postulate for the Laws of Comparative Statics," *Econometrica* 33: 349–56.

Rodrik, Dani (1993), "Making Sense of the Soviet Trade Shock in Eastern Europe: A Framework and Some Estimates," in Blejer et al. (1993), pp. 64–85.

Saint-Entienne, Christian (1984), *The Great Depression 1929–38: Lessons for the 1980s.* Stanford, CA: Stanford University Press.

Starr, S. Frederick (1995), "The 'Glass is Half Full' Case for Russia," *The International Economy,* March–April.

CHAPTER 3

Enterprise Credit and Stabilization in Transition Economies: Experience with Enterprise Isolation Programs

Marcelo Selowsky and Matthew Vogel

Stabilization programs should incorporate budgetary allocations to assist downsizing large money-losing enterprises in which output has collapsed but where such enterprises remain the major provider of "public goods": artificial employment, social services, and public utilities to workers and dependent populations. This is particularly important where no overall GDP growth is expected in the short run and when labor markets are not integrated – that is, workers probably will not leave these enterprises voluntarily as part of overall labor mobility.

Budgetary allocations to assist directly in divesting such public goods may have to come early, and take priority over commercial bank recapitalizations and even over credit expansion to the rest of the economy. Otherwise, the pressures for subsidized credit and arrears financing for these enterprises will remain, some of it being used to artificially maintain output levels. This will threaten both the sustainability and the efficiency of the stabilization program.

By combining, under one institutional roof, both (a) the isolation of enterprises from banking system credit and (b) the provision of budget resources to divest public goods, *enterprise isolation programs* may be an efficient tool to achieve downsizing. Credit cuts may become more acceptable if labor and interested communities are assured that resources will be available for severance payments, labor redeployment assistance, and the transfer of social services. This assurance should become an important incentive when overall fiscal revenues are scarce.

The views presented here are the authors'; they do not necessarily represent those of the World Bank. We wish to thank colleagues at the World Bank for their helpful comments and suggestions.

Under this framework, the agency will disburse funds directly to workers through severance payments and redeployment assistance, and to local governments taking over social services. They will not be made available to enterprises for working capital to maintain or restructure output. Such use of funds would generate a moral hazard (enterprises seek entry into program), would push the agency into "industrial policy" debates with line ministries and enterprise managers, and may result in delaying downsizing and privatization. Unless isolation programs are strictly bound in their use of budgetary funds in the directions described here, they may do more harm than good.

1. INTRODUCTION

The collapse of central planning in Eastern Europe and the former Soviet Union (FSU) and the realignment of domestic relative prices caused enormous shifts in the economic and financial position of enterprises. The reduction in the demand for capital goods and military output, the collapse of COMECON and interrepublic Soviet trade, and the opening of the overall trade regime explain part of this realignment. Negative value–added sectors, protected through heavy underpricing of raw materials and energy, have felt the brunt of economic liberalization.

Under central planning, the economy was subject to a significant amount of cross-subsidization between enterprises and between enterprises and consumers. Price liberalization and a more open trade regime have sharply reduced such cross-subsidization. However, because political pressures remain to keep certain sectors alive, such cross-subsidization has simply been replaced by explicit subsidies from the fiscal budget, as well as less explicit assistance including forced credit allocation, credit arrears, interest subsidization from the banking sector, and tax arrears.

The substitution of "directed credit" (credit expansion to protect specific sectors) for cross-subsidization has been a major source of overall credit expansion and inflationary pressures at the start of the reform program. Even when aggregate credit has been reduced as part of successful stabilization programs, directed credit has resulted in a significant crowding out of credit to other sectors, particularly to the emerging private sector. In spite of stabilization, directed credit in many countries dominates the lending operations of banks. In addition, the existence of tax and interenterprise arrears and of forced rollover of bank debts threatens the sustainability of stabilization and the further reallocation of resources.

The conclusion is that progress in stabilization, as well as its quality and sustainability, will require structural reforms such as downsizing key sectors of the economy. Many times the enterprises in these sectors are quite large, overstaffed, located in isolated regions (company towns), and hence the major source of employment to the community. They are difficult to privatize unless there is initially a significant labor retrenchment and a divestiture of noncore functions, such as the provision of social services.

The purpose of this essay is to review some of the initiatives countries are taking to isolate key groups of such enterprises from the banking system while providing explicit budgetary resources to finance their working capital and assist in their downsizing – the so-called restructuring agencies (more irreverently called "jails" by some). There are significant tradeoffs in such a strategy, and experience from which lessons can be derived is very recent. Today this strategy has been implemented or initiated in several countries, ranging from Albania, FYR Macedonia, and Romania in Central Europe to the Kyrgyz Republic and Kazakstan in Central Asia. Other countries are seriously considering similar options.

In Sections 2–4 we review the initial conditions, that is, the importance of directed credit and subsidies to the enterprise sector. We attempt to assess the initial level of implicit oversubsidization – in many cases, with significant effects on inflation – that must be replaced by explicit conditional and temporary budget subsidization under the isolation exercise. In Sections 5 and 6 we discuss the theory and reality of the isolation option, under what circumstances it may be more relevant, and the experience so far. Section 7 derives some conclusions.

2. DIRECTED CREDIT TO THE ENTERPRISE SECTOR

Past allocation of credits and subsidies to enterprises has not only contributed to inflation and macroeconomic instability, but has also created disincentives for sectors that should have shed resources under the new constellation of relative prices.

Table 1 shows the aggregate effects of directed credit to the enterprise sector. It shows that directed credit expansion was significant as a share of total central bank credit expansion – the crowding-out

Table 1. *Directed credit expansion to
state enterprises*

	As a percentage of	
	Total credit expansion	Average base money[a]
Russia 1992	104	231
Romania 1993	94	282
FYR Macedonia 1992	100	65
Kazakstan 1993	26	170

[a] From previous year.
Sources: Government authorities, World Bank, and IMF staff estimates.

Table 2. *Income redistribution induced
by the inflation tax and negative interest
rates (as a percentage of GDP)*

	Loss	Gain	Net gain
Russia[a]			
Households	– 12	0	– 12
Enterprises	– 18	16	– 2
Financial sector	0	8	8
Budget	0	4	4
Other republics	0	2	2
Kazakstan[b]			
Households	– 14	0	– 14
Enterprises	0	14	14

[a] From February 1992 to January 1993.
[b] 1993.
Sources: For Russia, Easterly and Vieira da Cunha (1994); for Kazakstan, World Bank.

effect – and also contributed significantly to overall liquidity expansion and hence to inflation. In Russia and Romania, directed credit expansion accounted for more than a 200% increase of the money base, while in Kazakstan it reached 170%.

Table 2 shows the income redistribution induced by the changes in the financial asset position of households and firms in Russia and

Kazakstan during peak inflation periods. That redistribution in- cludes the inflation tax on households (as their real cash balances de- preciate with inflation) plus the gains accrued by the recipient of credit when that credit was priced below the rate of inflation. Enter- prises targeted for the bulk of subsidized credit received a subsidy equivalent to 16% of GDP. Those enterprises not receiving credit had a deterioration in their financial asset position (inflation tax) equal to 18% of GDP.

Of course, a heavy inflation tax was paid not only by households but also by those sectors that were crowded out in the allocation of credit. In the case of Kazakstan, we have data for the aggregate enter- prise sector only, which received a transfer from households equal to 14% of GDP.

Despite our efforts, we have not been able to break down further the direction of subsidized directed credit. Ideally, we would disag- gregate the subsidy at the level of individual (large) firms or groups of firms by activity. This would allow identification of extreme cases of subsidization – for example, by comparing the subsidy with the wage bill.

Let us try to compare the directed credit subsidy to enterprises in Russia in 1992 to a possible estimate of the wage bill in those enter- prises. From the national accounts, the cash wage bill of the indus- trial sector is estimated to be around 9% of GDP. If the directed credit went to a subset of industrial enterprises accounting for half of that wage bill (4.5% of GDP), then the credit subsidy of Table 2 would be equal to 3.5 times the wage bill. This is an underestimate, insofar as directed credit was probably even more concentrated. In other words, subsidization went far beyond the cash wage bill and fi- nanced overall working capital and probably some investment as well; the subsidy doubtless financed the maintenance of output levels in spite of heavy enterprise losses.

Fan and Shaffer (1994) examined the link between the cumulative reduction in employment in the 1991–92 period and (lagged) credit expansion in 1992. Figure 1 shows that the heavy industry sectors (e.g. machine building and metal working or MBMW), which had the strongest cumulative employment reduction, received in 1993 the highest percentage increase in bank credit. This suggests that credit policy followed and tried to compensate the employment decline, probably delaying the downsizing.

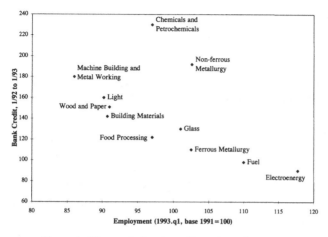

Figure 1. Change in bank credit and employment.

3. WHY IS ISOLATION NEEDED?

The first question that emerges is why isolation of a predetermined number of enterprises under a new agency is needed at all. One could argue that a government having the political will to tighten credit and depoliticize its allocation could directly impose a "universal hard budget constraint" by restricting credit expansion to the banking sector through a neutral vehicle, such as the auctioning of credit to banks. The banks themselves would then make decisions regarding credit allocation. They would judge the viability of enterprises and, if private or privatized firms look better, would automatically redirect credit out of the money-losing enterprises remaining in the state sector. This, of course, depends on the creation of an independent banking sector with enough incentives to protect and expand its capital.

In addition, the government could follow a universal policy of budgetary support to relieve enterprises from all noncommercial responsibilities. The government could implement a universal enhanced program of offering severance payments to fired workers, financing of retraining, and assisting in the transfer of social services (education and health) from enterprises to local government. Such a program would facilitate privatization and – by relieving enterprises from such noncommercial objectives – increase their potential viability and access to credit from the commercial banking sector.

In other words, why not implement a program of *generalized* tight credit plus *generalized* budgetary support?[1] Hasn't this been the experience of Estonia, Poland, Slovenia, and the Czech Republic, at least as far as universal tight credit is concerned? Several factors may be listed that differentiate these countries from those that today are considering the isolation option.

Market Economy Experience. Many countries in Central Europe and the Baltics had already been exposed to world markets and trading with the West. Simultaneously, many had inherited legal institutions capable of supporting markets and private-sector growth. In these countries, enterprise adjustment and factor reallocation have been easier.[2] Central planning was stronger in the countries of the former Soviet Union, and many of these countries had no experience with markets.

Market Incontestability. Many countries of Central Asia are geographically isolated from major world markets. Even after trade liberalization, many sectors remain "nontradeable" owing to extremely high transportation costs. Hence output price determination – in the absence of an outside price anchor – remains highly political. Because of the lack of domestic competition, bilateral monopoly situations are common, requiring some degree of covert intervention. Markets are not contestable.

Company Towns. Throughout Eastern Europe and the former Soviet Union, central planning left in place some very large enterprises that originally were the single producers of parts or assembly for the overall Soviet system. These firms were usually the main employers in the region. In Central Asia, many of these enterprises were quite isolated from overall labor markets and the network of public services (see Box 1); often, the town did not even exist before the creation of the enterprise. These enterprises therefore became the main providers of both employment and basic services. Labor mobility out of these enterprises is highly restricted.

---

[1] This neutral policy could be referred to as a "credit auction plus generalized pink slips" strategy.

[2] Hoekman and Pohl (1995) point to the successful restructuring of enterprises that were able to reorient and/or expand production to export markets.

Box 1. *The company town: Maili Sai and its electric lamp factory*

The town of Maili Sai, nestled at the northern end of the Maili Soo Valley in west-central Kyrgyz Republic, is the epitome of a company town. The town itself was essentially nonexistent before the discovery of uranium brought interest to the remote area in the Tien Shan mountain range, just above the border with Uzbekistan.

Maili Sai's isolation from the industrialized world came to an end as the arms race began just after the Second World War. Ethnic Russians, as well as Germans from western Ukraine, were brought to the site as part of Stalin's settlement plans for Central Asia. To this day, employment in the company is composed of these groups and not of ethnic Kyrgyz. In order to maintain employment after the mine was exhausted in 1965, an electric lamp factory was constructed on the old main mine site. There was no economic rationale for placing the factory in Maili Sai: the Maili Soo Valley's only exit is south through Uzbekistan, and all inputs and products must be transported across as many as five borders. (There are no material inputs located within 400 km, with most being more than 1,500 km away.)

Of the town's 29,000 inhabitants, 22,000 depend directly on the factory and the 5,500 jobs it offers. There is no other employment to speak of in Maili Sai. The town would die should the factory be liquidated. The company supplies the town with all of its electricity, heating, and water. The costs of providing basic utilities and social services ranging from housing to medical assistance represented more than 30% of total costs during production (halted in mid-1994), and now, at stoppage, represent more than 60%. Recent tremors and landslides have destroyed months of finished goods in inventory, as well as significant sections of the town, which the company must rebuild.

Although the cheap labor and generally decent condition of the plant allow some hope for the future, labor retrenchment of about 50% would be needed, aside from the divestiture of social assets. Other serious problems remain: landslides have pushed contaminated uranium sites closer to inhabited areas of the valley, and the cost of cleanup for this, as well as the possibility of future earthquakes, preclude the private sector from interest in the company. Furthermore, the governments of Russia and Germany have been active in promoting the welfare of their respective ethnic groups; a plant closure could be construed as a prejudicial act aimed at marginalizing these minorities.

Banking Institutions and the Legal Framework for Creditors. Throughout the FSU, the banking sector is at best incipient and subject to intense political pressures from line ministries. The legal framework necessary to ensure creditor rights is nonexistent or difficult to enforce.

There are significant constraints on the efficient intermediation of a decentralized banking system.

Obviously, a government that allows the banking system to be pressured by specific enterprise lobbies will be unable to prevent those very same pressures from being exerted on the isolation agency. However, one must recognize that governments are not monolithic. The central bank and the finance ministry are usually the main forces behind privatization and the imposition of a universal hard budget constraint. The pressures for subsidized directed credit to maintain output come from the line ministries in control of the enterprises. Isolating the most problematic enterprises reduces the control of line ministries and may help to create a new authority with more transparent and less politicized decision making.

Finally, one could argue that the isolation option may have some advantage over the "credit auction plus pink slips" strategy in the context of limited budgetary resources. Placing credit isolation and budgetary support *under one institutional roof* may facilitate those large enterprises to accept a "quid pro quo"; they may accept the credit cut if they are assured that budgetary resources for downsizing will be available. It is then crucial that such funds actually be used for downsizing and not for something else.

4. PARADIGM FOR AN ISOLATION PROGRAM

The purpose of an isolation program should be to rapidly bring the enterprise in question to privatization or closure while defusing political pressures and alleviating social concerns. The process should be transparent, with automatic rules, and should provide an opportunity for the firm to survive as a going concern under the new set of relative prices. Speed and automaticity minimize the amount of time that the enterprise remains in a state of "governance limbo."

In the ideal isolation program, the agency should not itself be in charge of decisions regarding the long-run viability of the firm or how to restructure output. All such decisions should be the result of the market test when enterprises are auctioned and transferred to private owners. Decisions regarding restructuring would then become endogenous, to be undertaken by the new owners. The purpose of the agency is to provide the optimal environment (or the optimal signals) so that the prospective new owners can make a full assessment of the *production* enterprise, not the social enterprise. If there are still no interested buyers through privatization, the enterprise would be liquidated. We now discuss what should be the main activities of the agency and how its budget should be used.

Helping the Transfer of Social Services Provided by Enterprises

As discussed earlier, many enterprises under isolation provide significant services such as education, health services, heat, and electricity to adjacent towns. Communities expect enterprises to continue providing these services if they remain in operation. One role of the agency should be to assist in transferring these responsibilities and their financing to local governments.

It could be argued that the provision of social services is automatically incorporated in lower cash wages, without influencing the cost of labor. A tax would emerge only if workers value these services below the cost to the firm of providing them. However, we believe that such responsibilities impair the flexibility of restructuring the firm by any new private owner. It is more difficult to reduce employment if the dismissed workers do not have access to social services after leaving the enterprise. The perception by adjacent communities – that these services are entitlements so long as the enterprise remains in operation – increases the probability of tension between the enterprise and the local population. This will impair the process of privatization and of attracting prospective buyers.

Helping in the Downsizing, Particularly Employment Reduction

Most enterprises are significantly overstaffed, so contracting employment will be a difficult process for the new private owners. One way to assist the process will be to assure and publicly announce a minimum package of severance payments and reallocation and training assistance, to be financed by the agency for any worker who will be separated by the restructuring of the firm *under the new owners*. Such a policy will then be incorporated in the ex ante restructuring plans of prospective buyers and their willingness to purchase the enterprise.

Under this framework, the agency is not involved in decisions regarding the optimal extent of downsizing. Such decisions would be made by potential buyers, supported by some subsidization on the part of the agency to divest social assets and artificial employment. In other words, the agency does not participate in any industrial policy decision.

Past Liabilities: Limiting the Use of Agency Resources

Most enterprises in the typical isolation exercise have significant liabilities: wage and tax arrears and debt to other enterprises and to banks. And many have environmental liabilities, since present sites may be contaminated owing to past industrial practices. Should the resolution of past liabilities be a responsibility of the agency? Should its budget be used for this purpose?

The clearance of liabilities is basically a redistributive problem. It should not be the responsibility of the agency or its budget – if its objective is forward-looking – to assist in enhancing the value of the firm out of its future productive activities. Obviously, at the macro level the distinction is less clear. There are obvious links across the economy: particular resolutions of past debts may have important moral hazard effects, decapitalized banks may impair new credit intermediation, and so forth.

Nevertheless, specific resolution or allocation of past liabilities may influence the chances of privatizing the enterprise as a going concern. By allowing the possibility of debt–equity swaps, the agency may be able to prevent premature liquidations. However, bringing creditors into an equity position can also jeopardize the future of the firm, particularly in those environments that were the main reason for the isolation exercise to start with. To the extent most creditors are public enterprises or public banks (i.e., highly politicized or subject to political pressures), the governance of the firm will not be improved by these creditors taking equity positions, which could also hamper the possibility of bringing in private investors.

The best policy is *not* to allow the redistributive issue – how much creditors should be compensated – to contaminate the future governance issue. Perhaps the best alternative is simply to write off the debt for the enterprise before privatization and then use parts of the proceeds of the selling price to compensate past creditors. The key is to prevent, in the process of solving the debt problem, the re-entry of public-sector equity holders who would repoliticize the firm and jeopardize its governance, particularly in the midst of its privatization.

Reality

Under the ideal isolation program, the firm will be quickly auctioned after social services responsibilities are removed and legal documents are drafted assuring new owners about the severance payment mechanism described previously. However, reality is messier. Given that most enterprises are significantly overstaffed, prospective private buyers will want to see some downsizing prior to purchase. This will reduce their risk of becoming involved in disruptive and politically sensitive labor conflicts, which would be particularly threatening to foreign investors.

But how does the agency assess the magnitude of the required downsizing to be undertaken prior to privatization? This requires some kind of a restructuring plan or staff analysis – something we would wish only the new private owners to do. In addition, the overall process will not be instantaneous; it may take months under the best circumstances. In the interim, the enterprise will continue to run losses. What rules, if any, should the agency follow to cover such losses?

It is clear that the process of labor reduction assisted by severance payments and other labor assistance programs will have to start immediately upon isolation. To assess and defend the required employment reduction, the agency will need to develop a business plan that is judged as independent and transparent. During this process, the maximum running losses to be covered by the agency should be only what is needed to pay wages. If the enterprise, in spite of the employment reduction supported by severance payments, cannot achieve an operating balance, then it should be immediately closed.

In summary, the budget of the agency should always have a "labor bias": severance payments should be offered directly to workers, not to the enterprise; losses to be covered cannot be larger than the wage bill and should be temporary. There should be a bias for direct labor assistance rather than production support. And one may even risk some overshooting on the severance payments side: workers could be offered benefits if they leave, independent of dismissal. This will generate a bias toward excessive labor downsizing, which is not a bad bias. If that is the case, future owners could always rehire workers and re-establish an optimal employment level. The only cost will be the fiscal cost of excess severance payments, that is, a rent earned by labor. But this is a cost worth incurring in order to achieve a deep downsizing of enterprises and to avoid financing operating losses, a major source of moral hazard.

5. THEORY AND REALITY: EXPERIENCES WITH ISOLATION PROGRAMS

How do the existing isolation programs match up with our so-called paradigm, and what do we know about their performance, having acknowledged the problems they face? These questions are not easily answered; data are not readily available on program performance, and the observation period is short. Only Albania and Romania have programs with more than a year of operation. Yet these questions are vital. The majority, not the minority, of the late reformers of Central Asia, the Caucasus, and western FSU are planning to institute similar programs.

The following section highlights the main features of existing programs, and provides a brief overview of the enterprise-sector context in which they were developed. Through these case studies, we hope to illustrate the types of programs being used under different macroeconomic and policy environments.

Romania's Directorate of Special Restructuring

Despite reform efforts that began in 1990, particularly trade and price liberalization, inflation has persisted in Romania. Continued operating losses in the enterprise sector, financed by the financial system and government budget, have been a major source of inflation. Quasifiscal losses amounted to 13% of GDP in 1992, due to a government policy of lending to enterprises at negative real interest rates. By 1994, the government had eliminated this form of subsidy, and commercial banks had developed sounder lending policies, greatly limiting lending operations to loss makers. Nevertheless, a significant number of state-owned enterprises (SOEs) were able to continue financing losses through the accumulation of supplier and tax arrears, totalling some 13% of GDP by mid-1994.

Strengthening of bank lending practices, the start of the privatization program, and the enforcement of sound payment mechanisms have helped Romania reduce the burden of state enterprises on the fiscal budget and financial system. In 1993, the government created an isolation program, the Directorate of Special Restructuring

(DSR), under the auspices of the State Ownership Fund (SOF), to restructure 30 loss makers (as part of a pilot program to be expanded later) that were judged to need downsizing before privatization. Overstaffed and laden with social assets and inviable production lines, these companies required assistance to sell peripheral assets, settle liabilities, and liquidate or privatize productive assets.[3] The companies were isolated from the banking system, and technical assistance was provided to assist enterprise managers to design financial recovery plans (FRPs) with the objective of achieving financial viability primarily through passive restructuring.

The approved FRPs had to be implemented on a tight schedule, given the limited resources available to cover losses. A budget of approximately $240 million (0.8% of GDP, raised from the SOF dividend tax on enterprises) was allocated to implement the FRPs. Nonperformance would be punishable by liquidation and/or the firing of managers. Failure to reach agreements with creditors (debt service was suspended under the program) also led to required assets sales. If financing was approved through the FRP, enterprises could apply for bank credit. This is one of the main features of the Romanian program that differs from others: enterprises could access financial markets prior to privatization, without privatization in the near or immediate future as a quid pro quo.

Satisfied with the results of the pilot program, the government extended the program to include an additional 120 enterprises, 70 of which are pig and poultry farms. This new set of 150 companies is by far the most expansive of its kind. Employment in the isolated industrial enterprises alone amounts to 750,000, more than 30% of industrial employment in mid-1994. Obviously, the expanded set now has a smaller budgetary allocation per enterprise (given the same resource envelope), but enterprises are not as isolated as the programs in other countries; bank credit is available, and interenterprise financing within the SOF is not transparent. The sheer size of the program threatens to jeopardize the ability of the DSR to monitor and control the restructuring plans of the 150 companies, and virtually ensures that resources will be dispersed rather than focused on the most problematic enterprises.

---

[3] The program also includes several public utilities (*regies autonomes*), which would remain as state holdings over the medium term. These companies would undergo cost-cutting measures and receive technical assistance to improve revenue collections; the government would raise prices for cost coverage.

Albania's Enterprise Restructuring Agency (ERA)

The first democratically elected government of Albania undertook an ambitious stabilization effort in 1992. Comprehensive trade and price liberalization induced an immediate supply response in the services and agriculture sectors, but led to a complete collapse in the industrial sector.[4] Industrial output fell by almost 80% over two years. Losses in the industrial sector mounted, which were financed by the newly created commercial bank and through direct subsidies from the budget. To deal with these growing problems, the government froze interenterprise financing through the payment system, and curtailed bank credit except to a core group of large SOEs.[5] In effect, a hard budget constraint was imposed on the enterprise sector by mid-1993, in a matter of months.

From 1992 on, labor retrenchment in the state enterprises accelerated. Alternative employment opportunities (in the services, agriculture, and construction sectors) fueled this massive shift in labor force, and a significant portion of the work force (more than 20%) found employment in Greece and Italy. The availability of alternative employment at significantly higher wages – the public-sector average wage was $45 per month in 1993, while wages in the new private construction firms were as high as $100 – was crucial to alleviating pressure on the government to sustain employment in the majority of state factories. In fact, labor retrenchment in the industrial sector almost matched the output decline. Despite the region's most severe collapse in industrial output and employment, and without the privatization of medium- and large-scale industries, Albania has achieved the region's highest rates of growth. None of this growth, or the prospects for growth in the medium term, could be credited to any reactivation of output from the state industrial sector.

With the imposition of the hard budget constraint, the government focused its energies on (a) privatization of state enterprises and (b) establishment of the Enterprise Restructuring Agency (ERA) in order to isolate politically sensitive loss makers and privatize (or liquidate) them. The ERA became fully operational in January of 1994.

---

[4] The Albanian industrial sector was composed of obsolete Russian and Chinese technology, primarily from the 1950s and 1960s.

[5] The Albanian government continues to provide financing through the investment budget for so-called strategic companies – i.e., the petroleum, copper, and chromium companies – as well as utilities. While not directed credit per se, there is pressure to lend the little available under the ceiling to these companies, which are the few state industries still operating.

Staffed with approximately ten local experts in finance, industry, and law, and with two part-time foreign consultants, the agency undertook diagnostic studies to develop business plans. As expected, ERA ran into a series of bureaucratic obstacles that have continued to plague operations. Although plans were designed for privatization and liquidation, ERA was forced to follow administrative procedures that have prevented quick implementation of these plans and have forced the agency to maintain output support for the enterprises.

Budget resources, intended primarily for severance payments and some fixed costs, have been used primarily for working capital. Financial and management control mechanisms, although well documented in the operational guidelines, are hard to implement. Many enterprise managers do not cooperate with ERA, since they see the agency as a threat to participation in insider privatization and pirating of assets. Furthermore, administrative procedures and approvals required from other government agencies have prevented ERA-sponsored management/employee buyouts (MEBOs) and joint ventures for the more promising companies. Agency staff is very competent; diagnostic studies and restructuring plans are typically of excellent quality, but implementation is slowed by the bureaucratic and legal system.

The Kyrgyz Republic's Enterprise Reform and Resolution Agency

One of the most isolated republics of the FSU, the Kyrgyz Republic confronted perhaps the most severe shock from the collapse of Soviet central planning. Originally, distorted prices and distribution systems created industrial facilities that filled niches in the FSU-wide production process. Once the interrepublic trade regime dissolved, and prices and trade were liberalized, the country turned to inflationary finance in an attempt to avoid a total collapse of industry. Nevertheless, it soon became apparent that no degree of financial support could maintain a significant portion of the country's industrial base under a new set of relative prices. Inflation rocketed as the government diverted resources to loss-making enterprises from potentially viable enterprises, the budget, and the banking system.

While reducing inflation by tightening credit policy and accelerating privatization, the government had not been able to prevent transfers from the banking system and from other enterprises through payment arrears to large loss makers. For this reason, the Enterprise

Reform and Resolution Agency (ERRA) was created in mid-1994 to isolate 28 SOEs from budgetary, financial-sector, and supplier finance. See Box 2.

Box 2. *The isolation exercise in the Kyrgyz Republic:*
the View of The Economist

"But low inflation will not last without underlying reform. The factories that used to rely on cheap credit need to be reorganized or shut down. Here the Kyrgyz have taken an innovative, but potentially dangerous, approach. With the help of the World Bank, they have set up something called the Enterprise Restructuring and Rehabilitation Agency [sic; Enterprise Reform and Resolution Agency]. Twenty-nine of the most indebted enterprises have been removed from the banking system; their wage bills and running costs are being paid from the government budget, which in turn receives money from the Bank.

This approach, the first of its kind in the former Soviet Union, seems a clever short-term solution. Bankrupt enterprises no longer sully the banking system, but nor are they simply shut down overnight, with the increase in unemployment that implies.

Yet there could be problems, largely because the Kyrgyz and their mentors see the agency's job very differently. World Bank officials talk about a "morgue" where inviable enterprises will gradually die. Mr. Akaev, though, sees the agency as a hospital where ailing enterprises will be nursed back to health. This vision, shared by many of the factories themselves, is dangerous: it implies a grand government industrial policy in a country that can ill afford it, particularly when the Bank money dries up. Having set up this agency, the Bank now needs to ensure this does not happen."

December 10, 1994

The ERRA essentially covers two groups of enterprises. The first group, composed of 11 enterprises, is under a "care and maintenance" program that shut down enterprise operations (some of which were already not operating) and placed workers on administrative leave with partial pay until a comprehensive viability study could be completed and a downsizing plan implemented. Such a policy prevents the further use of funds to cover operating costs – it is cheaper to pay workers not to go to work. If viable (on certain lines), financing may be provided for enterprise working capital; if inviable, then workers would be provided severance and social assets would be turned over to local authorities.

The second group of enterprises, under "partial stoppage," could use the ERRA budget for passive restructuring, including the release of workers, liquidation of assets, and divestiture of social assets. Enterprises are released from ERRA through either liquidation or privatization.

FYR Macedonia's Special Restructuring Program

The economy of the former Yugoslav Republic (FYR) of Macedonia has simultaneously faced the shock of the disintegration of Yugoslavia, the war in Bosnia, the trade embargo on Serbia, and the Greek embargo. The government has moved quickly to implement a forceful program of stabilization and structural reforms to get through this difficult period.

Many large industries, however, had traditionally been exclusive providers and clients within the Yugoslav system. These enterprises not only had to adjust to new market conditions, but lost significant sources of supplier finance and clientele. Enterprises have been forced to confront the temporal complications associated with the trade embargo as well as higher transportation costs, the result of not being able to ship out of Salonika. The political will to shut down or withhold financing to loss makers was considerably reduced as enterprise managers and workers demanded resources to cover what they considered "transitory" losses.

The government could not afford to cover the losses of industrial enterprises, and in May 1994, implemented the Special Restructuring Program (SRP) in order to isolate 23 industrial enterprises and two utilities from the banking system; the program aimed at downsizing and privatizing the enterprises by the end of 1995. The enterprises selected for the SRP represent some 60% of arrears and 80% of losses in the enterprise sector, the highest coverage ratio among isolation programs.

Although some of the selected enterprises were operating at a profit, political reasons dictated that they be included because significant labor shedding was required and the government wanted to focus its resources on labor assistance. A unique feature of the ownership structure in the former Yugoslavia is that the majority of companies are socially owned, not "state" owned. The ownership structure is not visible to all stakeholders. Therefore, enterprises entering the SRP may have less reason to restructure, as incentives are not in place to undertake the necessary labor shedding. For this reason, the

SRP was created with the power to remove the authority of the work-ers' council, establish a board of directors to approve passive restruc-turing plans, and create trusteeships to form a transitory governance until privatization.[6] For the utilities selected, the SRP would develop a strategy for the government to liberalize controlled prices while im-plementing cost-cutting programs.

Kazakstan's Rehabilitation Trust

In Kazakstan, the drastic changes in relative prices have not led to significant restructuring of the enterprise sector. Credit to loss-making enterprises has been the primary source of inflation, and the continued generation of losses has in turn fueled greater demand for additional financial flows. Many enterprises originally catering to the Soviet market have not adjusted to the collapse in demand. The continued control of farm output prices (until the fall of 1994), in spite of liberalization of input prices, forced the government to direct credit toward loss-making farms and agro industries. While credit has been tightened, interenterprise arrears have continued to be a significant problem, rising to as much as 7% of GDP in the third quarter of 1994.

The government is making additional efforts to impose a budget constraint on enterprises. They include development of the commer-cial banking system, further tightening of overall credit, acceleration of privatization, and isolation of the largest loss-making enterprises in a restructuring program.

Established in the spring of 1995, the Rehabilitation Trust (RT) will take financial and managerial control of 20 distressed industrial companies selected on the basis of arrears. The enterprises include a range of industries, but are dominated by metallurgy and machine-building industries. The objective of the RT is to prevent the further accrual of payment arrears (in the form of bank, supplier, and other liabilities) by becoming the only source of financing to these enter-prises, and to condition this financing on the implementation of restructuring plans designed by the enterprises. These plans will attempt to identify commercially viable activities and to sell off non-profitable units that could not be restructured. In the case of inviable enterprises, full liquidations will be undertaken.

---

[6] A government-appointed member of the board of directors was given a 51% voting share to ensure that management changes could be made if needed.

Financing for the RT will come from an initial capitalization from the budget, as well as some technical assistance from donors. Funds will be used to finance operating losses as enterprises are restructured. The budget for 1995 is equal to one third of the losses financed in 1994, thus imposing a significant financial constraint. Any new investment could be undertaken only after graduation from the program, financed by the commercial banks or private investors. To facilitate downsizing, the RT may provide resources for severance payments as prescribed by the enterprise business plan. Nonbank creditors would have to negotiate debt rescheduling.

6. COMPARATIVE REVIEW OF ISOLATION PROGRAMS

Table 3 presents some of the major design features of the different programs. No two are alike. All of the programs, except Romania's, have focused on a manageable number of industrial enterprises, with no program having more than 35 companies. The Romanian program includes 150 companies – some industrial, some agricultural, and some utilities – with an aggregate employment exceeding 750,000.[7] Many of the included enterprises are operating near capacity and could become viable with some relatively moderate restructuring, which immediate privatization should be able to achieve. The success of the program will depend heavily on the ability of the agency to focus its human and financial resources on the worst loss-making enterprises – those in need of major downsizing – rather than trying to share them among all enterprises.

On the other hand, programs in FYR Macedonia and the Kyrgyz Republic have focused at the outset on the worst loss-makers, including many enterprises in which production has been shut down. Especially for the Kyrgyz Republic, many of these enterprises are isolated in company towns and are candidates for liquidation; the government anticipates a high political cost for quick closure, and has given the program four years to downsize the companies. The Albanian authorities, when ERA was created, anticipated similar ramifications to quick downsizing. As it turned out, the program may not even have been needed, as market forces attracted labor out of the state enterprise sector and so alleviated most political pressure to

---

[7] This figure reflects employment in the industrial enterprises alone, and does not include employment in farming companies.

Table 3. *Isolation programs compared*

Country	Selection coverage[a]	Number of enterprises	Number of employees	Degree of isolation[b]	Program lifespan	Debt workout	Bank finance	Earmarked severance
Albania	Low	32	12,963	High	2 years	None	No	No
Romania	Low	150	>750,000	Low	n/a	Restructure	Yes	No
Kyrgyz Republic	Moderate	29	40,000	High	4 years	Cash	No	No
FYR Macedonia	High	23	43,044	Moderate	1 year	Swap	Yes	Yes
Kazakstan	n/a	20	n/a	Moderate	4 years	Restructure	Yes	No

Note: n/a = not available.
[a] An assessment of the quantity of losses and/or arrears captured by the selection of enterprises.
[b] An indicator of financial as well as administrative isolation.

maintain loss makers. In a nutshell, employees of the state industries in Albania had options and wanted to leave, whereas in a country like Kyrgyz, often the employees could not leave.

Debt–equity swaps can be a useful tool for alleviating debt service. Yet there is a danger of using debt–equity swaps when creditors are state entities (e.g. utilities or banks that may not be soon privatized), as these groups may do nothing to impose governance on the enterprises. Macedonia has resolved this issue by forcing state beneficiaries of swaps to sell their shares to the private sector within a year. They will want to maximize the value of these shares at the time of sale, and so have incentive to maintain or improve the value of the company in the interim.

Macedonia forestalls any polemic about the use of funds by explicitly earmarking agency resources for severance payments and labor retraining programs. Theirs is the only program that sets aside funding in this way. Technical assistance is also used to undertake enterprise staff analyses, which aim to set appropriate labor retrenchment targets and to devise labor assistance programs as well as a complementary general program for social assistance.

Although Macedonia's program has only recently begun, it seems to have the most coherent design of the ongoing programs. Budgetary funds are *explicitly* set aside for severance payments, and bank credit – though accessible – is limited to fill secured sales orders. The program does not impose the strictest degree of isolation, but it is evident that there is real will on the part of government to quickly divest these companies without killing them. The government of Macedonia has sent a clear message to all participants in the program: enterprises will be privatized withinin a year, and the program will provide a downsizing plan and labor assistance to facilitate this process.[8] The program itself will be eliminated in a year, so there is no hope of continuing state support to the companies as public entities.[9] Given this signaling, labor retrenchment has been higher than expected, and the government has been forced to increase the SRP budget for severance payments.

[8] The Macedonian government has undertaken a public information campaign to describe the rationale behind the downsizing of the country's largest companies.

[9] In their restructuring programs, Romania and FYR Macedonia have included utilities that will not be privatized in the short term. Agency objectives for these enterprises are to instruct the government on pricing policy while instituting a cost-cutting and revenue-generating restructuring plan.

7. CONCLUDING REMARKS

Redefining the Isolation Exercise

The clearest case for an isolation exercise with a special budgetary allocation is when enterprises are producing only a share of their historical output but still keep employment levels (employment responsibilities) and provide social services consistent with their previous levels of output. In other words, the enterprise has basically become a provider of public goods. It is here where a significant gap will emerge between social and private calculations in the process of privatization. In this situation, there is a need to transfer or significantly reduce such responsibilities prior to privatization.

The argument becomes stronger when workers have few alternatives in the short run – both in the region and in the rest of the economy – and where there is very little chance the enterprise could survive under the new relative prices. This conforms better to the situation of some former heavy/military industries in Central Asia. Many of these enterprises were the main (or the sole) producer of specific components in the military–industrial complex for the Soviet market. The basic purpose of the isolation exercise is (a) to prevent credit and subsidies being given to maintain output, and (b) to ensure that budgetary allocations are given for severance payments and the transfer of social services. Thus the agency should become not a *production maintenance* or *productive restructuring* agency but rather a *social adjustment* agency.

There are too many moral hazards and political pressures on the agency if it is expected to give the enterprise more time to restructure output prior to privatization. There is no obvious reason a specially created agency would have a comparative advantage in meeting such an objective. Enterprises should be privatized quickly as part of the overall transition process; the agency cannot be relied upon to impose governance. If actions taken under the isolation program in any way slow the privatization of an enterprise, the isolation program has failed.

This discussion may also have some relevance for the design of stabilization programs. Under the overall financial programming, a minimum allocation should be assured for a transparent program of severance payments and social services transfers for the least viable enterprises. This should be done early. Such assistance will reduce

Table 4. *Bank recapitalizations*

Country	Year(s)	Amount[a]	Share of GDP (%)
FCSR[b]	1991	5.0	14.6
Slovenia	1993	1.2	10.0
Poland total		9.5	2.8
	1991	5.5	7.2
	1993	0.8	0.9
	1991–94	2.0	0.6
	1994	1.2	1.3
Hungary	1991–94	3.0	2.0
Croatia	1994	0.6	4.4

[a] Billions of U.S. dollars.
[b] Former Czechoslovakia.
[c] Poland conducted four different bank recapitalization programs from 1991 to 1994.
Source: Barbone (1995).

pressures on obtaining credit to maintain output. It is better to face this issue candidly and early on, since doing so will facilitate the overall sustainability of the stabilization program. It will also serve to separate the public- and private-goods functions of the enterprise, an important and irreversible step once substantive downsizing has begun.

A related issue arises regarding the timing of commercial bank recapitalizations. Many such exercises have significant fiscal costs (see Table 4). If a large part of the bank's portfolio problem is nonperforming loans to a small number of large loss makers, then the issue is whether or not these recapitalizations were premature. A better sequence in the use of fiscal resources may be to finance the downsizing of these enterprises first. Recapitalization of banks without such downsizing may simply delay the required adjustment in the financial and enterprise sectors, while generating an important moral hazard.

The Political Economy of Implementation

It will not be easy to implement a policy where agency funds are explicitly earmarked for severance payments, labor redeployment assistance, and local government assistance – that is, circumventing enterprise managers and line ministries. The line ministries will resist the inclusion of their enterprises in isolation unless financing is available to sustain production and some form of active or neutral restructuring.

As long as some discretion is given to the agency to finance working capital under the restructuring plan (even if the plan is designed by an objective party), the pressure will be enormous to divert funds away from the social adjustment function. It will be difficult for agency staff – which in most cases are drawn from the line ministries – to resist such pressures, since they have only a temporary guarantee of employment (after which they must probably return to the line ministry or other government agency). Agency staff thus have little incentive to take the political heat for unpopular decisions and may, given the opportunity, perpetuate work by drafting pro-production plans or simply delaying actions.[10]

Obviously, the job can be made easier if the agency is given strong powers to implement its mandate. However, to the extent that in many economies output targets are still seen as a goal, politicians will probably want to distance themselves from the agency, or seek to modify its design and implementation. After all, a major objective of the program – isolation and limited access to funds – has been accomplished. How the reduced funds are actually spent may become a moot point for politicians.

Under this redefined role, the agency will have to look for other constituencies and partners in the government and the enterprises. It should work closely with the ministries of labor, social assistance, health, and education, and should include labor unions in negotiations. Special links should be made with the local authorities that will eventually bear the responsibility for the provision of social services.

REFERENCES

Barbone, Luca (1995), "Macroeconomics of Transition," unpublished manuscript.

Easterly, William, and Paulo Vieira da Cunha (1994), "Financing the Storm: Macroeconomic Crisis in Russia, 1992–1993," Working Paper no. 1240, Policy Research Department, World Bank, Washington, DC.

Fan, Qimiao, and Mark E. Schaffer (1994), "Government Financial Transfers and Enterprise Adjustments in Russia, with Comparisons to Cen-

---

10 Consultants may also have reason to propose active restructuring plans to justify their continued involvement in the project.

tral and Eastern Europe," Internal Discussion Paper, World Bank, Washington, DC.

Hoekman, Bernard, and Gerhard Pohl (1995), "Enterprise Restructuring in Eastern Europe: How Much? How Fast? Where? Preliminary Evidence from Trade Data," Working Paper no. 1433, Policy Research Department, World Bank, Washington, DC.

CHAPTER 4

Employeeism: Corporate Governance and Employee Share Ownership in Transitional Economies

D. Mario Nuti

A number of countries have embarked on a program of privatization using vouchers, establishing a form of people's capitalism. Here my advice is a word of caution, one that most of them have already taken to heart: *Beware of the corporate governance problem.*

Joseph Stiglitz[1]

What's happened so far is not privatization, it's collectivization, which puts the workers and managers in charge of enterprises. Their interest is in increasing wages, not investment. This is a new problem created by this style of privatization.

Grigory Yavlinsky[2]

I'm the man who makes the decisions.

Viktor Kozeny[3]

1. GENERAL ISSUES

Under the heading of "corporate governance" we include problems arising when an enterprise is owned by more than one owner and

Earlier versions of this paper were presented at a Conference on Corporate Governance, European Forum for Democracy and Solidarity (Bratislava, 2–3 June 1994); and at the BASEES Annual Conference, session on "Corporate governance in the transitional economies in Eastern Europe" (Fitzwilliam College, Cambridge, 25–27 March 1995). Useful comments and suggestions have been provided by conference participants and in particular by Alessandra Cusan, Martha de Melo, Michael Ellman, Saul Estrin, Tina Takla, and Marie Lavigne. Financial support from ACE project 92-0098-R on "Financial Intermediation during the Transition" is also gratefully acknowledged.

[1] Stiglitz (1994, p. 262); emphasis added.
[2] At the Davos Forum, March 1993. The quote is from de la Camara Arilla (1994).
[3] Founder, manager, and 25% owner of HC&C (Harvard Capital & Consulting Investment Fund, Prague); cf. George Soros's dictum, "A company is not a democracy" as quoted by Kozeny (*Financial Times*, 3 April 1995).

managed by a hired managerial group, and also the rules and incentives appropriate to make it function as efficiently and impartially as if it were owned and run by a single owner–entrepreneur. Throughout this essay we shall refer to co-owners as shareholders, thus implicitly referring to joint stock companies; unless otherwise stated, decisional (voting) powers are presumed to be distributed in proportion to ownership. Mutatis mutandis, identical considerations apply to any form of enterprise co-ownership and attribution of decisional powers.

Two basic classes of problems arise in joint stock companies: (i) establishing shareholder control over managerial discretion; (ii) avoiding or resolving conflicts between groups of shareholders that may occur when a controlling interest is vested in shareholders who also have a stake in company activity in another capacity. *Stakeholders* include employees, managers, suppliers (including creditors), customers (including debtors), competitors, local authorities, the state, or any economic subject otherwise exposed to external economies or diseconomies related to enterprise activity (including environmental effects).

In transitional economies, the direct privatization of small establishments – the so-called small privatization - has resulted in a large number of small (up to 50 employees) and indeed "micro" (up to five employees) enterprises that are directly managed by a single owner and therefore do not raise these kinds of problems. However, privatization of large state enterprises, which accounts for the bulk of privatized output and employment, typically has involved precisely the patterns of ownership and management associated with corporate governance problems: *multiple ownership* and *delegation of managerial functions* to professional executives.

We *exclude* from a strict definition of corporate governance those issues that arise not only in corporate structures but in any type of enterprise, that is, such issues as: competition;[4] hard budget constraints (i.e., depoliticization, market-assessed performance and incentives, credit discipline, bankruptcy and liquidation procedures); law and order and contract enforcement; minimum regulation of financial institutions; accounting and financial standards;[5] and minimum protection of stakeholders – or, more generally, the design of rules and incentives that might induce an enterprise to behave in the interest not only of ownership but of a broader group, possibly

---

[4] "I view competition as far more important than privatization" (Stiglitz 1994, p. 261).
[5] These have received much attention in Great Britain with the 1993 Cadbury Report, due for reassessment in 1995.

extending to the government or society as a whole. These issues are certainly relevant for corporate governance, especially in transitional economies (see Section 7), but only indirectly; they are essential components of a market environment and are therefore of more general interest for the whole systemic transition. We also exclude issues specifically arising in the run-up to privatization.[6]

This essay first outlines the general problems of corporate governance and their possible resolution in market economies, including transitional economies. It then concentrates on a particular form of intrashareholder conflict – namely, that which may arise when employees, whether individually or collectively, own enough shares to control company activities.

The interest of this particular case is threefold. First, contrary to intentions and expectations,[7] the sale, lease, or gift of state enterprises' capital to their employees has turned out to be an important channel of privatization in all transitional economies with the exception of the Czech Republic – indeed, the most important in many cases (e.g., Russia, Mongolia, Romania, and Poland). Hence the use of the label *employeeism*.[8]

Second, the implications of employee ownership have been grossly neglected, particularly in view of the inordinately massive literature devoted to employee self-management and value-added sharing from Ward (1958) and Vanek (1970) to date. Indeed, employee ownership lends itself to being confused, and often is, with self-management, which is fundamentally different. The employees of Ward's "Illyrian" firms (or of traditional cooperatives or Yugoslav enterprises) hold *ephemeral rights of use,* which are not transferable to others and moreover are *conditional on continued employment* (or on continued connection, as with e.g. an old-age or invalidity pensioner). Since there is no such thing as a nontransferable or conditional property right, the problems associated with Ward-type self-managed enterprises are, on the contrary, precisely those of employee *non*ownership.

On the one hand, when employee ownership is properly modeled, it is expected to produce beneficial effects on labor productivity – and therefore indirectly on employment also – through the exercise and

---

[6] These may range from concealment of profit to deliberate loss making or rapid disinvestment; see Aghion, Blanchard, and Burgess (1994) and Cornelli and Li (1994).

[7] Proposals for employee ownership in the transition, by Ellerman (1990) and Weitzman (1991), are notable exceptions.

[8] This term is borrowed from Miyazaki (1993), who used it – with much less reason – with reference to Japanese enterprises.

mutual monitoring of labor effort and the avoidance and resolution of conflicts.[9] On the other hand, when employees have a controlling property share they are automatically expected always to choose higher labor earnings and higher employment levels than prevailing in nonemployee-controlled enterprises (Blanchard et al. 1991). As we shall show, this argument needs strong qualifications.

Third, it turns out that when a conflict *does* arise between employee shareholders and other shareholders, the mechanisms that can usually be relied upon to resolve stakeholder–shareholder conflict are not applicable to this special case. Other safeguards must be introduced. Otherwise, the company is bound to suffer from biases (toward higher wages and higher employment than in otherwise equivalent companies) that are bound to prevent access to outside risk capital; moreover, the company is likely to become institutionally unstable. Yet, even economists who regard socialist ideology as officially dead (Stiglitz 1994, p. 279) still believe – with good reason – that "there remains scope for further experimentation. For instance, we need to study forms of economic organization involving more worker participation and ownership" (p. 277).

2. SHAREHOLDERS' CONTROL OVER MANAGERS

Traditionally, the study of corporate governance has emphasized the separation between enterprise ownership and control, that is, the delegation of managerial functions to a professional executive (or group of executives treated as a single unit).[10] Professional managers always have some discretion, which they may use to pursue their own interests instead of simply maximizing the market valuation of the enterprise as a going concern in the best interests of ownership. Thus managers will also be interested in other targets to which their earnings and other rewards (status, fulfillment, self-esteem) are frequently related – for instance, enterprise size (whether measured by employment, output, or capital) or growth. A principal–agent problem arises

---

[9] For instance, Alchian and Demsetz (1972) see employee ownership as a way to overcome the incompleteness of labor contract specifications and the difficulties of monitoring labor effort. See also Jensen and Meckling (1976), Conte and Svejnar (1990) and Hansmann (1990).

[10] See Berle and Means (1932). Some authors define corporate governance exclusively in terms of shareholder–manager relations: "Corporate governance is the arrangements by which shareholders hire and fire managers and monitor and reward them so that they optimally serve the shareholders' interests" (Bergstrom 1994, p. 19). Gray and Hanson define corporate governance as "shareholder monitoring [of] managerial behavior" (1993, p. 1).

of how to induce a manager to behave as if he or she were the enterprise owner.[11] However, in a single-owner enterprise the separation between control (delegated to a professional manager) and ownership does not in itself create significant problems. The single owner directly stipulates hiring conditions, hires and fires managers, and has both the opportunity and the incentive to closely monitor enterprise activities.[12]

The problem arising in this case, as well as its solution, has been known since time immemorial. For instance, in the parable of the unjust steward, the manager is threatened with loss of employment;[13] in the parable of the talents, the master switches assets from the zero-rate-of-return agent to the profit-maximizer.[14] As the old proverb goes, "L'occhio del padrone ingrassa il cavallo" [A horse flourishes under his master's eye].

Industrialization has made owner control over managers actually easier, by concentrating activities in a smaller space (the factory floor) than in such territorially diffused activities as agriculture. In the Soviet-type system, state enterprises seemed to suffer from the separation of ownership and control in spite of there nominally being a single owner – the state. However, their problems derived primarily from the lack of a market environment (i.e., *all* enterprises were state enterprises). Moreover, ownership in practice was not really vested with any particular state agency: often ownership belonged to all, and therefore nobody was owner.[15]

[11] A contrary view holds that governance by independent management is a necessary condition of enterprise success, especially in multinational companies and in capital-intensive sectors (see Chandler 1977, 1990). This view is backed neither by convincing theoretical arguments nor by specific empirical evidence.

[12] Indeed, we could argue that separation between ownership and control is neither sufficient nor necessary for corporate governance problems to arise. We can easily imagine a jointly owned enterprise managed directly by the owners (i.e., without such separation) and yet subject to possible conflicts of interest between owners if they are also stakeholders.

[13] "Once there was a rich man whose agent was reported to him to be mismanaging his property. So he summoned him and said, 'What's this that I hear about you? Give me an account of your stewardship – you are not fit to manage my household any longer.' At this the agent said to himself, 'What am I going to do now that my employer is taking away the management from me?'" (Luke 16: 1-4). Although the "rascally agent" who used his master's money to make friends for himself was actually praised for this by his master (Luke 16: 8-9), this attitude was clearly considered atypical: "the Pharisees, who were very fond of money, heard all this with a sneer" (Luke 16: 14-15). All references herein to the Gospels are from Phillips (1972).

[14] "And throw this useless servant into the darkness outside, where there will be tears and bitter regret" (Matthew 25). Another illustration can be found in the parable of the wicked husbandmen (Luke 20 or Matthew 21).

[15] Kornai (1992, pp. 110-30) investigates managerial motivation under the old system: political and moral conviction, identification with the job, power and promotion, prestige, material

In reality, issues of corporate governance are due not to separation between ownership and control per se but rather to *multiple* ownership. Compared to a single owner, multiple owners have lower incentives and lower opportunity to monitor and control managerial activities. Any individual part owner would appropriate only a part of the benefits of such monitoring while incurring all of its costs (otherwise, monitoring efforts might be duplicated); thus, free riding is encouraged. Such incentives and opportunities are all the lower, the higher is the degree of ownership fragmentation; this dilutes owners' potential control over managers: "wider ownership dispersion leads to greater shareholder passivity" (Gray and Hanson 1993, p. 7). This is a *principals–agent* problem.

Economic literature usually relies on two possible ways of resolving this question (see e.g. de Cecco 1989; Corbett and Mayer 1991; Gray and Hanson 1993; Jackson 1994). The so-called German–Japanese model of corporate governance relies on the *actual* presence of one or at most of a very few major shareholders (e.g., 80% of joint stock companies in Germany have at least one shareholder with at least 25% of the voting shares), and on a formal or informal role for banks and other financial institutions as shareholders and as depositories of shares (entitled to exercise the underlying voting powers on behalf of share depositors). Such concentration of share ownership and voting power establishes a degree of control over managerial discretion, as well as incentives to exercise such control, that is comparable to the case of a *single*-owner enterprise.

The Anglo–Saxon model relies on the discipline imposed by the *potential* emergence of a dominant shareholder: for well-functioning financial markets, an underperforming managerial team is always exposed to the challenge of hostile takeover bids, with successful bidders gaining from dismissing existing managers and raising enterprise performance, to the advantage also of all other shareholders (Marris 1966; Auerbach 1988; Jensen 1988; Lazonik 1992). The effectiveness of such challenges depends on the development and depth of the financial markets that provide capital for potential bidders; on legal or customary obstacles to successful bidding by outsiders; on

benefit, a quiet life, fear of punishment. "The official ideology suggested that every functionary would manage his activities 'like a proprietor', but there were no incentives that could inspire the managers to develop a truly proprietory motivation since the gains from doing better would not end up in their pockets. Risk taking was for the same reason avoided, since successes from new technology or other innovations never paid off" (Bergstrom 1994, p. 5).

possible limitations built into company statutes;[16] on other defense mechanisms set up against potential challengers (e.g. contingent liabilities placed upon successful bidders – so-called poison pills – or defensive cross-shareholding of and by other companies, as in the Japanese *keiretsu*). The takeover mechanism is far from perfect,[17] but the risk of takeover undoubtedly places some restraint on managerial discretion. (For a comparison of the two mechanisms, see Franks and Mayer 1990, 1992; on the specific problems of transitional economies, see Frydman, Phelps, and Rapaczynski 1993).

Some transitional economies have deliberately selected one of these models. Poland seems to have selected the German–Japanese model: financial restructuring of enterprises and banks has led to frequent debt-for-equity swaps that give banks a share in their debtor enterprises; in the Polish mass privatization program, each enterprise taking part in the scheme has a special relation with one particular national investment fund, which is supposed to hold no less than one third of the shares and play a significant part in enterprise fundraising and management. The Czech, Slovak, and Russian mass privatizations, on the contrary, impose maximum ceilings on any investment fund's holdings of any company's shares (as a proportion of both the fund's and the company's assets). Russian voucher investment funds, for instance, sell certificates for vouchers or for money which they use to buy shares, but are forbidden to invest more than 5% of their capital in any one firm, or to hold more than 10% of a given firm's shares (see Bornstein 1994). These provisos suggest a reliance on an Anglo–Saxon-style discipline of financial markets through potential takeovers.

The problem with investment funds, as with all holding companies, is still one of incentives – now, once-removed. As Stiglitz (1994, p. 189) puts it, "Who will monitor the monitors?" (An identical question is raised by Coffee 1994, p. 8). In Poland, as in the Czech Republic, the fees earned by investment fund managers are geared only to portfolio value and not to *changes* in that value (Coffee 1994, p. 75), thus grossly attenuating – if not altogether removing – incentives to raise portfolio performance.

---

16 For instance, some Dutch corporations are owned by foundations rather than shareholders, who are mostly holders of nonvoting stock. The bulk of voting shares in the Dutch company Phillips, for instance, is owned by a foundation that is effectively controlled by managers. One cannot buy voting shares in the Amsterdam market. As a result, managers do not necessarily behave in the interest of shareholders, although they are still bound by efficiency considerations because they must still make enough profit to pay interest on company loans.

17 See Stiglitz (1994) for a strong criticism.

For the Czech case, Coffee (1994, p. 60) recommends elimination of the 20% ceiling on the equity share of a single company that an investment privatization fund (IPF) may hold. However, such funds are often, in the Czech Republic, to a large extent owned by banks. In principle this could be beneficial:

Banks may exercise more effective control than do shareholders, or bond-holders for that matter, a point made long ago by Berle (1926). For banks the costs of intervention and the free-rider problems will be less severe than for shareholders. Because most bank lending is short term, banks can quickly withdraw their funds if they believe the firm is misbehaving. (Stiglitz 1994, p. 189)

However, "the relationship between Czech banks and their IPFs is obscure. . . . Whether IPFs will develop into active institutional investors or passive agents of their indirect banking parents remains unresolved" (Coffee 1994, pp. 94–5). Meanwhile, Czech banks are still largely in the hands of the state. The combination of company shares still held by the state property fund, those controlled by banks directly or indirectly (through their shares in investment funds), plus other cross-shareholdings, still give the state "at a minimum . . . a very substantial potential voice in corporate governance, even if the current administration (whose free market preferences are beyond dispute) declines to exercise that voice" (Coffee 1994, pp. 5–6). State failure to exercise such power simply allows other shareholders to yield a voice disproportionate to their holdings, and facilitates the kind of shareholder–stakeholder conflict discussed in the next section. More generally, banks in transitional economies are usually burdened with bad loans and – precisely as stakeholders – may have a vested interest in not precipitating a company crisis by calling their loans or initiating bankruptcy and liquidation procedures.

Notwithstanding government intentions, it would seem that in all transitional economies neither the German–Japanese nor the Anglo-Saxon mechanisms of corporate control are yet fully at work. Company ownership is mostly too fragmented to allow for a controlling interest to emerge and to restrain managers in the interest of all shareholders. Yet markets are too thin and undercapitalized to allow potential takeover bidders to come forward with a credible chance of success, especially since many shareholders (in particular, employees) are often subject to considerable restrictions on the immediate marketability of their shares. "The market does have some instruments – such as takeover mechanisms – which socialist economies do not have" (Stiglitz 1994, p. 195). Hence the widespread feeling that in spite of

the quick development of financial markets and of rapid privatization, including mass privatization, managers still enjoy discretionary
powers greater than would be compatible with the proper functioning
of a market economy. Transitional economies can expect, at the very
least, the same kind of problems experienced by the less developed
(e.g., Italian) European financial markets.[18]

3. SHAREHOLDING STAKEHOLDERS

Multi-owner enterprises – of which joint stock companies owned by
shareholders are the most general and diffused form – have voting
rules linking control rights to property; however, these rules are not
in themselves always sufficient to obtain the same results of single
ownership and entrepreneurship. Shareholders who are also stakeholders (as defined in Section 1) might acquire control and exercise
it to the undue detriment of other shareholders.[19]

Consider, for instance, a controlling interest held by a shareholder
or group supplying an input to the company. Suppose shareholding
suppliers were to force a higher quantity of, and/or a higher price for,
their sales to the company. All shareholders without exception would
suffer a loss, but those shareholders who happen to supply enterprise
inputs at the higher price will also have gains. Similar examples could
be easily constructed for other stakeholders: shareholding lenders
forcing a higher interest rate on their loans to the company; shareholding borrowers forcing a lower interest rate; shareholding buyers
forcing a lower output price; and so on, always with respect to market conditions.[20]

It would be wrong, however, to think that a controlling interest by
one group of stakeholders will necessarily lead to exploitation of other
shareholders. In all these cases, shareholding stakeholders may be losing more as shareholders than they gain as stakeholders (e.g., as suppliers or buyers) depending on their share in enterprise yield (divi-

[18] "In Italy the reallocation of ownership and the opportunity of access to enterprise control
meet with severe obstacles, which contribute to constrain enterprise growth and explain the
adjustment lags and restructuring jolts typical of our economic development" (Barca 1994,
p. 6).

[19] Pyramid control of companies (whereby company A controls a larger company B, which in
turn controls an even larger company C, and so on) provides an opportunity for leveraged
control (Berle and Means 1932), thus allowing control by shareholders directly owning
much less than a majority of shares. A similar result derives from cross-shareholding. Here
we refer to a "controlling interest" regardless of how this may be obtained.

[20] On the state as stakeholder, see Cusan (1994).

dends and capital gains, assumed here to fully reflect profits and be proportional to equity) *relative to* their share in total supplies or sales (or, in the case of other stakeholders, in their share of whatever transfer is being forced from the company to stakeholders). Thus an individual who holds an ownership stake such that his share of enterprise yield is lower than his share of enterprise purchases (or sales) will gain more as a stakeholder than lose as a shareholder from higher input prices (or lower output prices). If such shareholding stakeholders collectively happen to hold a controlling interest in the company, even without collusion they have an incentive to exercise their power to manipulate input and output prices to their own advantage. This is not a principal–agent problem but rather a *principals–principals* problem.

It should be noted that the root of the problem is not the presence of a concentrated controlling interest (as with the German–Japanese model), but rather an inequality among shareholders in the ratio between shareholding and stakeholding (appropriately defined). If 100% of the shares were owned by suppliers or buyers in exact proportion to their share of supply or purchase, then no problem would arise. Although concentration may facilitate the rise of a controlling interest, the conflict between stakeholders and other shareholders can arise through sheer pursuit of self-interest by group members, even for a dispersed ownership within the group and in the absence of collusion.

Consider, for instance, a company renting homogeneous land from a group of shareholders who, collectively, have a controlling interest in the company. Before rushing to conclude that those landowners have an interest in pressing for a high land rental to be paid by the company, it is essential to consider the relative distribution of shares and of the land leased to the company. Take the ith shareholding stakeholder supplying L_i of land out of a total quantity L leased to the company, and holding K_i shares out of a total of K. A price h that is higher than the market rental w will lead to a gain of $(h - w) \cdot L_i$ as supplier and a loss of $(h - w) \cdot L \cdot K_i / K$ as shareholder; that is, a net effect of

$$f = (h - w) \cdot (L_i - L \cdot K_i / K), \tag{1}$$

which, since $(h - w)$ is assumed to be positive, will be a net gain as long as

$$L_i / L > K_i / K. \tag{2}$$

In fact, any landowner who has a greater share in company equity than in the lease of land to the company will lose more as a shareholder – from an above-market rental of land to the company – than gain as a landowner.

A similar proposition may be put forward for a possible oversupply of a homogeneous input L sold to the enterprise by controlling stakeholders, over and above the quantity $\hat{L}$ at which the value of its marginal productivity equates supply price w. Call y' the value of the marginal product yielded on average in the company by excess units $(L - \hat{L})$, where $y' < w$ and c is the opportunity cost of L. Continued oversupply yields, to each stakeholder supplying a quantity L_i, a gross gain $(L - \hat{L}) \cdot (w - c) \cdot L_i/L$ and a gross loss $(L - \hat{L}) \cdot (w - y') \cdot K_i/K$. Let us assume (i) identical opportunity cost of the input inside and outside the enterprise (i.e., $c = y'$); (ii) identical probability of each unit of L being made redundant if supply is cut down to $\hat{L}$ and overuse ceases; and (iii) indifference to risk of redundancy for parity of expected earnings. The net effect g of L overuse is then

$$g = (L - \hat{L}) \cdot (w - c) \cdot L_i/L - K_i/K). \qquad (3)$$

For assumed positive overuse $(L - \hat{L})$ and excess price over and above opportunity cost $(w - c)$ – without which overuse is not damaging – g remains positive so long as (2) is satisfied. Again, those stakeholders who hold a smaller share of enterprise capital (K_i/K) than of supply (L_i/L) will have an interest in continued oversupply. Thus, the risk of intrashareholder exploitation, in the form of excess price and/or excess use of inputs supplied by shareholders, arises only when a controlling interest is exercised by stakeholders each of whom individually has a lower share of company equity than of input supply (or other relevant stake).

If we call a *balanced equity share* one that is equal to the share of input supplied to the company, then in general the shareholder–stakeholder conflict arises not from stakeholders' control, or even from stakeholders' majority holding of company shares, but more precisely from control being in the hands of stakeholders who individually own less than a balanced share. When this happens, there is no need for prior collusion on the part of less-than-balanced shareholders; they need only to be active and to exercise their vote in their self-interest. Therefore, the problem is not due to share ownership concentration, which on the contrary reduces the chances for collusion – another advantage of the German–Japanese model. The problem arises because of inequality between individual relative positions as shareholder and stakeholder (see the diagram in the Appendix).

All formal or informal limitations on the power of shareholders and/or managers that might survive during the transition are bound to interfere with standard mechanisms of corporate governance. In particular, the presence of nonvoting shares raises the probability that less-than-balanced shareholders might be able to exercise control. However, nonvoting shares must be included in K_i for the purpose of comparing K_i/K and L_i/L, duly weighted for the possible difference in the relative impact of an economic decision on the gain or loss of different categories of shares. (Nonvoting shares usually yield a more secure and less variable return.)

In turn, intrashareholder exploitation by stakeholders raises the profitability of mergers between the company in question and stakeholding enterprises, as well as the profitability of their joint takeovers by third parties. By eliminating such internal transfers, the new unit gains more than the shareholding stakeholders lose; the probability of intrashareholder exploitation can thereby be reduced or eliminated. Conglomerate mergers with output buyers or with input suppliers, or horizontal mergers with competitors, can fully internalize stakeholders' external effects and therefore ensure that noncontrolling shareholders do not suffer from inefficient company operations. In transitional economies, however, there seems to be no evidence of significant company mergers or of shareholder–stakeholder conflicts – except for extensive employee ownership.

4. EMPLOYEE OWNERSHIP AND CONTROL

In general, the acquisition of a noncontrolling interest by managers and employees in their own enterprises can be regarded as a positive development that promotes productivity, better labor relations, and economic democracy; the diffusion of employee ownership is encouraged in the European Community (see Uvalic 1991). The acquisition of a *controlling* interest by less-than-balanced shareholders, however, is associated with potentially adverse effects.

Employees constitute a special category of stakeholders: when they are controlling shareholders *and* potential net gainers from raising earnings above the market rate, they are not subject to the discipline of takeovers and mergers discussed previously. Labor is ultimately supplied by individuals, not by companies; even companies that specialize in hiring and reselling labor services cannot own or hire labor

as if it were machines or land. Employees (and managers) cannot
individually merge or be taken over; hence their possible exploitation
of other shareholders cannot be eliminated by the takeovers or mergers. If less-than-balanced employee shareholders have a controlling
interest, then there must be at least a strong temptation to pay higher
earnings and/or force overemployment; the only objective constraints
will be those of bankruptcy and of the minimum investment required
to maintain viability.

The first constraint does not prevent employees' appropriating
company present value, effectively expropriating and disenfranchising other shareholders. The investment constraint may ensure the
maintenance of some minimum positive capital without, however,
preventing capital consumption above that minimum. This is one of
the main reasons why worker ownership and control, while perfectly
legal in market economies, are the exception rather than the rule.
(There are other reasons: lack of capital and collateral, as well as
double exposure to risk both for income and capital and therefore
limited access to credit; see Nuti 1995).

In the case of employee shareholding, an essential distinction must
be made between employees and managers. First, the same problem
applies to managers when they can determine managerial rewards,
but they are unlikely to have a controlling interest on their own. Managers usually influence their own salaries collectively, across and not
within companies, by tacit collusion (*ruk ruka'* in Russian; *una mano
lava l'altra* in Italian). Otherwise shareholding managers, while still
pursuing their own objectives, behave more like a single owner as
their share holdings increase. Indeed, managerial ownership of shares
(and in particular of options) is extensively used precisely in order to
ensure that managers will behave in the interest of shareholders. This
aspect of managerial motivation may be particularly important in
transitional economies, where the imperfection of markets for managerial skills (Jones and Kato 1994) – and managers' resulting lack
of concern for their reputation – may encourage predatory behavior
(Cusan 1994).[21]

---

21 Recent disquiet in the United Kingdom about excessive payments to managers in the form
    of options is due to the fact that normally managers benefit from *any* growth trend in the
    stock exchange, and not just from the above-average performance of their shares. Equiva-
    lent disquiet over fast-rising managerial salaries in privatized state companies, especially
    former public utilities, is due to the fact that higher salaries have normally been granted to
    the same managers whose earlier lower salary was judged by them and the market as an
    equilibrium, and not to new managers who had been commanding such higher salaries in
    the marketplace. Britain's Greenbury Committee is attempting to establish a code of prac-
    tice on top executive pay.

Second, managerial salaries may be totally unrelated to wage levels within the enterprise, in which case managers would behave as outsiders (unless they had some control over their own salaries as a result of their managerial position and not of their shareholder status). Third, if a component of management salary were directly related to the company average wage by a formal or informal coefficient, then only that coefficient could be regarded as the managerial L_i/L for the purpose of comparison with managers' K_i/K. Managers are likely to be larger-than-average shareholders, and therefore likely to own a greater share of company equity than the share of their wage-related component in the total wage bill (including such components). It follows that any risk of overpay or overemployment depends not on a controlling interest vested jointly in managers and workers, but on a controlling interest vested in those workers who hold a less-than-balanced share.

However, there may also be an advantage in employee shareholding. Shareholding employees may be willing to accept less than the going wage – for different reasons, according to whether or not they are less-than-balanced shareholders. If condition (2) is not satisfied, then they may expect to recover their current lost revenue directly through higher future dividends and capital gains than would otherwise be the case. If condition (2) is satisfied and the enterprise is on the verge of bankruptcy, shareholding employees may expect to recover their lost current revenue indirectly through higher future earnings and/or employment – which they might be able to enforce if they have a controlling interest. Here employees choose to postpone the exercise of their power, thus enhancing short-term employment. The result may seem identical to flexibility of earnings (as suggested by Layard 1995), but there are differences. Here the result is enterprise-wide work sharing, with high countrywide dispersion of earnings. We have not wage flexibility but rather employment rigidity – an obstacle to labor redeployment and thus a potential inefficiency.

Hansmann (1990) attributes great importance to labor heterogeneity and to possible conflicts between employees due to heterogeneous skills, age, seniority, blue/white collar status, interests and abilities, and attitudes toward effort; he concludes that employee ownership would work better for small enterprises with homogeneous labor. Such labor heterogeneity may explain why some employee-owned enterprises are effectively controlled by managers. This is not a problem but instead the solution to the corporate governance problems associated with employee ownership – as long as managers are also shareholders to the extent of being motivated primarily by enterprise economic performance rather than the pursuit of their other individual interests.

However, when a conflict arises between shareholding employees and other shareholders, other instruments are needed for avoiding intrashareholder exploitation. One simple remedy may be the stipulation that, in order to be a shareholder, any employee must hold a share *at least as high* as his or her share in the total wage bill (defined as including all payments related to a basic or average wage, i.e., possibly also for managers). In other words, condition (2) must *not* be satisfied. A move in this direction is exemplified by the recent case of Rhône–Poulenc privatization, where senior managers were asked to buy at least a year's salary worth of company shares.[22]

This provision may not be sufficient to avoid overemployment if any of the following conditions obtain: aversion to risk of dismissal for unchanged expected average earnings; concentrated probability of dismissal in particular groups; and, in particular, higher opportunity cost of labor inside the enterprise than outside. A positive balance of these factors may lead to the maintenance of excess employment even when condition (2) is not satisfied. In that case, another stipulation is necessary – namely, that redundant workers enjoy a continued right to an income *supplement* that brings their income outside the enterprise (whether employed elsewhere or unemployed) to the same level they would have enjoyed had they remained in the enterprise.[23] In transitional economies, a major implication of this provision must be continued access of redundant workers to the exceptional welfare facilities (canteens, housing, holidays, health, education) traditionally provided by the enterprise to its employees. Such largesse may be costly, but so is continued overemployment. At least this provision will raise overall labor mobility and therefore contrib-

---

[22] Although the Rhône–Poulenc rule does not in principle guarantee that employee holdings are sufficiently large to rule out a conflict with other shareholders, the arithmetic of the relevant variables (company capital value per employee, managerial salary, proportion of wage-related component in managerial salary) is such as to induce one to expect that managers (almost certainly) and other employees (normally) would not clash with other shareholders.

[23] Income (instead of employment) protection is the solution proposed by Meade (1993) for his own version of a fully participatory enterprise, with complex alternative provisions for retired employees. However, in Meade's participatory enterprise, employee conflicts with other shareholders – which are likely to occur in view of Meade's proposed distribution to employees of an initial equity stake proportional to their initial share in value added – are resolved by arbitration.

ute to labor redeployment and reduced unemployment – if not immediately then in the long run.

Suppose that, despite these considerations, employee ownership of
a kind adverse to corporate governance prevails in a particular country. What then? There is a basic institutional instability in this kind
of employee-controlled enterprise, which could be regarded literally
as a transitional form of ownership that is bound to disappear fairly
quickly. *Either* less-than-balanced shareholding employees cease to
combine these prerogatives (i.e., they leave the enterprise, and/or
sell their shares to other employees, who thus cease to be less-than-
balanced holders, and/or sell their shares to nonemployees) in numbers sufficient for residual shareholding employees to collectively lose
a controlling interest; *or* the company loses all outside shareholders
and so reverts to a form of cooperative; *or* the company shrinks for
lack of new risk capital and of unsecured loans. Thus, *the employee-
owned enterprise, unless tamed, is bound to be literally a* transitional *form of
enterprise, whether in transitional economies or in standard market economies.*

5. EMPLOYEE OWNERSHIP IN THE TRANSITION

The last thing that the new postcommunist leaders – from Balcerowicz to Gaidar – wished to promote was the emergence of significant
forms of employee ownership. Yet employee ownership emerged almost everywhere. In part this was the result of public policy measures
forced on the new governments by the need to implement a quick and
smooth transition; in part it happened by default.

Employee ownership became necessary for a variety of reasons
(see Nuti 1994):

(1) to compensate employees for the loss of self-management (notably in Yugoslavia and Poland and to a smaller extent in Hungary);
(2) as a result of the transformation of former public-sector cooperatives into enterprises run by elected officials and independent
   from central organs – if the transformation was accompanied by
   the distribution of shares to employees; and
(3) to win employee support for the transition in spite of concern
   for its short-run adverse effects on real wages and large-scale
   unemployment.

Unintended employee ownership also happened by default, given the
following factors:

(1) the low and often negative value (at the ruling fixed wage rates but not for more flexible participatory earnings) of some state enterprises for which there could not have been other takers;

(2) the shortage of domestic capital, which placed employees (especially in view of their inside information) in a good position with respect to domestic outsiders, while alternative external buyers frequently evoked xenophobic reactions; and

(3) employees' and managers' natural inclination, in the absence of information about other enterprises and other localities, simply to automatically select the one which they knew best and was most important for their livelihood – the "balkanization of ownership."

In Poland, managerial and employee buyouts turned out to be the single fastest privatization track, with about 1,500 buyouts by mid-1994 via so-called liquidation privatization (applicable to viable enterprises, and not to be confused with liquidation of insolvent enterprises). Other state companies privatized through this channel were sold mostly to foreign buyers.

Buyouts were an important element of privatization in Ukraine and especially in Romania, where MEBOs (management and employee buyouts) accounted for about 98% of all the privatizations of state-owned companies to mid-1994. In Hungary, about 5% of the estimated value of socially owned capital stock is to be given to employees under the various schemes in operation.

Mass privatization – outside the Czech Republic – was instrumental in the promotion of employee ownership, either as a result of investment decisions by voucher holders (even in the absence of favorable terms for the purchase of employee shares) or as a result of government policy. In Mongolia, insiders ended up owning 45% of enterprises. In Russia, the mass privatization program gave every adult the chance to become a shareholder; under Option 2 of state enterprise privatization, up to 51% of the voting shares could be purchased by employees and by managers at a price corresponding to 1.7 times the enterprise book value, which – in view of rampant inflation – was usually a most generous concession despite often inappropriate productive capacity.[24] It is reported that this option was exer-

---

[24] Shares could be paid for partly in money and partly in vouchers (up to 50%, later raised to 80%). Option 1 was the concession of 25% free shares, nonvoting unless and until sold, plus an option of a further percentage of voting shares (10% for workers and 5% for administrative officers) at a 30% discount. Option 3 was only for medium-sized firms with more than 200 employees and fixed capital between 1 and 50 million rubles. Subject to the

cised in over 80% of Russian privatizations (Ash and Hare 1994) – prompting Grigory Yavlinsky's comment quoted at the start of this chapter.

The Russian Option 2, by granting over 50% equity to virtually all employees, was bound to create precisely the kind of stakeholder-shareholder conflict discussed here, owing to a controlling interest in the hands of less-than-balanced shareholders – unless managerial holdings plus additional acquisition of shares reduced the number of less-than-balanced shareholders below that required to exercise a controlling interest. It is no accident that the state property committee favored Options 1 and 3, fearing precisely that an employee majority of voting shares would lead to excessive wages and lower reinvestment while outsider investors would be reluctant to invest in an employee-controlled firm (Chubais and Vishnievskaia 1993). Apparently Option 2 was preferred by managers who expected workers would vote with them, and by workers who thought they would protect employment, fearing outside control. Option 1 was preferred by managers when they feared that workers would not support them, and by workers when the enterprise was relatively capital-intensive and/or unprofitable.

6. EMPIRICAL EVIDENCE

Empirical evidence on ownership and performance of enterprises in transitional economies is still scant but is steadily accumulating. Much of it reflects concern about relative economic performance of different types of enterprises, including employee-owned enterprises as compared to state, state-privatized, and private enterprises. For Poland, see Pinto, Belka, and Krajewski (1993); for Russia, see Boeva and Dolgopiatova (1993), KPMG-CERT (1993), and Bergstrom (1994). These are extremely valuable studies, often focusing on employee ownership in the transition (see e.g. Earle and Estrin 1995), but are not directly concerned with questions of corporate governance.

approval of at least two thirds of the workers' collective, a group of workers and managers would undertake, with the appropriate property fund, to restructure the enterprise in a year according to a plan specifying which level of employment would be preserved. If successful, the group would obtain 20% voting shares at book value, while all workers and managers could acquire a further 20% of the shares at a 30% discount. With all three options, the rest of the shares were to be sold at public auction to nationals and foreigners.

Data about ownership structure and in particular about employee share ownership tend to lump together employees and managers (e.g. Ash and Hare 1994 on Russia). In any case there is a tendency to look at the implications of a controlling interest by managers and/ or employees without checking whether a controlling interest is held by less-than-balanced holders on their own.[25]

The fact that data do not come in the form required to rigorously investigate issues of corporate governance is partly due to objective difficulties. It is hard enough to distinguish between employees and managers as shareholders, let alone to check and compare individual relative shares in enterprise capital yield and in wage-related payments. Moreover, whether a given total holding by less-than-balanced shareholders is or is not a "controlling interest" depends on share distribution among shareholders, degree of activity, perception of self-interest, and so on. There is no minimum threshold, since even a majority of shares may not be enough in the face of apathy by shareholding employees. The most we could realistically expect is a truthful answer by managers to the question of whether or not their decisions are constrained by employee shareholdings, in order to then perform a comparison between the performance of the two resulting classes of companies (with respect to employment, earnings, investment, restructuring, etc.). If even these data are not available, it is probably because of the typical but unhelpful classification of companies simply according to degree of employee ownership, rather than the necessary discrimination between a controlling interest by less-than-balanced shareholding employees versus all other cases. Thus, inferences that may be drawn from available data are very scant; unsuitable data is the likely cause of the often inconclusive nature of such inferences.

In Russia, "Closed subscription by employees followed by an open voucher system has given insider stakeholders – workers and managers – shares in newly privatized Russian firms. On average, . . . insiders gain 60–70% of a privatized enterprise's equity under alternative options" (Lieberman and Nellis 1994). Bergstrom (1994) reports that, according to official documents of the Russian state committee for management of state property (GKI), "on average insiders [employees and former employees] hold 56% of shares in the enterprises

---

25 For Russia, see Bergstrom (1994), Blasi (1994), Linz (1994), and Earle, Estrin, and Leshchenko (1995); for Hungary and Poland, see Takla (1995); for Hungary, Poland, the Czech Republic, Romania, and Russia, see Earle and Estrin (1995); for Mongolia, see Korsun and Murell (1994a,b).

studied"; 78% of total privatized enterprises chose Option 2, averaging 61% of the voting stock. (In only four cases did insiders not buy additional stock at voucher auctions, because they were outbid by outsiders.) In one case, the general director declared a holding of 38%; in other cases, management personnel held 5–23%; and in a number of cases the largest outsider investor did not hold more than 1–2% of total stock. The largest stake of a single outside investor was 31%. Voucher investment funds held 1–8% of total stock.

Pistor (1993; quoted in Earle et al. 1995) reported on a sample of 36 Russian companies privatized in late 1992 and early 1993, finding that employees received an average of 61.8% of all shares (57% of voting shares); outsiders had 19% on average, and the state property fund retained 19.1%. No data were provided on the distribution of ownership among insiders. Earle et al. (1995) also cite a World Bank survey from October of 1993. For 92 privatized firms in the Moscow and Vladimir oblasts, managers secured 17% and workers 61% of total shares (including nonvoting shares).

Blasi (1994) reported on a survey of 127 Russian privatized firms, of which 90% had majority employee ownership, corresponding to an average of 65% for all insiders (60% median; i.e., few firms had low insider ownership). Top managers had an average of 8.6% (5% median) of all shares, including nonvoting shares.

The Czech Republic is one country where employees and managers were given hardly any incentive to acquire shares in their own companies. In Hungary, opportunities for employee ownership were created by the June 1992 law on ESOPs (employee stock ownership plans; MRP in Hungarian) and by the "self-privatization" program. There were 184 MRP privatizations by the end of September 1994 (involving at least 40% of employees), and 187 enterprises out of 435 in the self-privatization program were estimated to have resulted in dominant employee stakes. However, it is believed that most of these MRPs and buyouts actually led to dominating managerial ownership or control.

In Poland, about three quarters of the enterprises privatized by "liquidation" were under employee control, with an average of 50.8% held by employees and managers (see Earle and Estrin 1995). Takla (1995) reported on a World Bank survey of 200 Hungarian and Polish firms. In (respectively) 2.6% and 5.7% of the cases, employees owned all the shares; in 8.4% and 5.7% of the cases, employees owned between half and all the shares; and in 23.9% and 8.3% of the cases, employees owned some shares but less than half the total.

However, ownership pattern did not appear to make a significant difference in enterprise performance.

In Romania, a program to accelerate MEBOs was launched in early 1993 by the Romanian state ownership fund; by mid-1994, nearly 600 companies had been privatized, most of them 100% to their employees. A CEU survey of 66 of these companies reported that, on average, the employees owned 96% of the shares in the 58 companies for which information was available, though ownership distribution among employees showed considerable variance. In MEBO privatized companies there are significant limitations on the tradeability of shares – but only until these have been fully paid (see Earle and Estrin 1995).

The maintenance of employment has been found to rank very high in privatized Russian enterprises: "Very few had so far made a reduction of the working force. . . . [E]mployees now have a considerable potential influence over the direction of the business through their ownership of shares. Privatization in this sense may simply have delayed rather than facilitated the restructuring of enterprises which needs to take place" (Ash and Hare 1994, p. 631). This may well be the case, but does not necessarily follow from the evidence provided by Ash and Hare, who take for granted that a controlling interest by employees – whom they lump together with managers – will always result in overemployment and above-market wages.

In Russia, both privatized and remaining state enterprises generally exhibit relatively high employment levels (as compared to necessary restructuring) accompanied by low average and marginal pay (although Linz 1994 reports higher provision of social services the higher is employees' total equity). It remains to be seen whether this particular employment–wage tradeoff is the consequence of a deliberate unconstrained choice by controlling employee owners or rather the result of controlling managers choosing this tradeoff in order to reduce social opposition to their actions. In either case, it may be a consequence of prevailing near-bankruptcy conditions (as suggested by generalized lack of investment; see Ash and Hare 1994).

Boeva and Dolgopiatova (1993) studied ten enterprises employing between 200 and 1,200 persons during the autumn of 1992; the sample included some state enterprises. The authors found that, in the majority of cases, managerial priority was given to the preservation of employment, money wages, and other benefits (housing, privileged loans, etc.), often financed through asset stripping. One of the managers was reported to have said: "One has to let people live."

7. CONCLUSIONS

We have defined corporate governance in terms of two issues arising in modern enterprises from the delegation of managerial functions to professional executives and from multi-ownership, features that are typical of joint stock companies (hence co-owners are labeled shareholders). The first issue is shareholder control over managerial discretion; the second is resolution of conflicts between shareholders who are also stakeholders (i.e., employees, managers, suppliers, buyers, borrowers, lenders, competitors, the environment, local communities, the state) and the rest of shareholders. These general problems have been reviewed from the perspective of transitional economies, concentrating on the stakeholder–shareholder conflict with special reference to employee share ownership.

In general, a conflict arises not from stakeholders' majority holding of company shares, or even stakeholder control, but more precisely from control being in the hands of stakeholders who individually own less than a "balanced share." This is defined as a share in company capital (or, strictly speaking, in company capital *yield,* i.e. dividends plus capital gain) equal to their share of explicit or implicit company transfers to that particular category of stakeholders (in the case of employees, their share of company wages and wage-related payments to employees). When this conflict arises, it may lead to above-market transfers from the company to controlling stakeholders. In the case of employees or of any other company supplier, the conflict is bound to take the form of overemployment and overpay beyond the levels dictated by profit-maximizing behavior at market prices. The stakeholders in question may thereby appropriate the entire present value of the company, or at any rate any excess over the minimum necessary to maintain its viability, effectively disenfranchising outsider shareholders. This very possibility is bound to preclude access to risk capital, or even to unsecured credit.

With employee shareholding, an essential distinction must be made between managers and other employees. First, managerial salaries may be totally unrelated to wage levels within the enterprise; in this case, higher managerial holdings imply greater incentives for managers to behave as outsiders (unless they have a significant say on their own salaries, in which case the reasoning must be repeated for managerial labor). Second, even if a component of their salary were directly related to the average company wage, managers are likely to hold considerably more equity than average shareholders, and therefore are likely to own a greater share of company equity than the share of their wage-related component in the total wage bill (including such components). For both reasons, when classifying enterprises according to the degree of employee ownership, it seems best to exclude managerial shares.

Typically, employee ownership creates a problem for corporate governance when employees (on their own, not counting managers) have a controlling interest that is diluted among a greater share of employment than of capital. The Russian Option 2, granting over 50% equity to virtually all employees, was bound to create precisely this setup – unless managerial holdings plus subsequent share transactions reduce the number of less-than-balanced shareholders to a level below that required to exercise a controlling interest. There is no need for prior collusion on the part of less-than-balanced shareholders; they only need to be active and to exercise their vote in their interest.

For shareholding stakeholders other than employees, the possible conflict with other shareholders is expected to be resolved through the profitability of merging the company in question with a company providing or taking over the function of those stakeholders. However, the personalized nature of labor services, unlike that of other intermediate inputs, prevents this kind of conflict resolution for shareholding employees.

There is a simple solution to this problem: namely, the stipulation that stakeholders who are also shareholders must hold a minimum share in company equity no smaller than the share of their stakeholder interest in the whole of that interest. For instance, employees should hold a share of company capital, if any, at least equal to their share in the company wage bill.

A company controlled by employees who are also less-than-balanced shareholders is subject to inherent institutional instability. Their control ceases as shareholding becomes more consolidated within the company – as shareholding employees cease to be employees (through retirement and voluntary or involuntary quits) and/or cease to be less-than-balanced shareholders (i.e., selling their holdings to nonemployees, or to other employees who thus acquire, or already hold, a more-than-balanced share). Alternatively, the enterprise, without access to risk capital, eventually is likely to enter into liquidation.

Besides ownership patterns, there are other major factors that affect corporate governance. Direct constraints on company decision making, inherited from the old system, may block shareholder power or managerial power over enterprise employees (see Takla 1995). There are frequent and large-scale fraudulent cases, such as pyramid banking (MMM in Russia, Charitas in Romania) and the disappearance of many Russian voucher investment funds, made easier by the lack of transparency and disclosure (see Bornstein 1994).

Among recent cases of gross – indeed, outlandish – malpractice by Russian company managers, widely reported by the financial press in 1995, are the following. The oil company Komineft secretly issued free shares to only some of its shareholders. The Krasnoyarsk aluminum company's managers simply deleted from its shareholders' registry a British shareholder of 20% of company equity. Managers of Primorsky, one of the largest Russian shipping companies, doubled the number of its shares outstanding and sold them to its subsidiary PriscoStocks, which was under their direct control, for 0.5% of market price. (The subsidiary bought the entire share issue – equivalent to a 50% stake in the company – for $90,000, while the firm's market value was $36 million). Apparently, "Unauthorized stock issues are a growing method among some directors to regain control of their newly privatized companies. So far, these share issues have been deemed legal" (*Wall Street Journal,* 4 April 1995).

These practices – much more blatant and spectacular than insider trading in standard market economies – are clearly lethal for the establishment of corporate governance. However, rather than a point of debate within the scope of corporate governance, such issues are part and parcel of a much wider problem for transitional economies: the establishment and maintenance of law and order, the protection of contracts, and the fight against organized crime.

APPENDIX

Here we offer a diagrammatic illustration of the possible conflict between stakeholding shareholders (who here are also suppliers of input L) and other shareholders. (See diagram, overleaf.)

If input L is not homogeneous then qualities are weighted by their prices, which are presumed to move all together. We set:

OA = percentage of L supplied by nonshareholders;
BZ = percentage of equity not held by suppliers of L;
K_i/K = individual share in company equity;
L_i/L = individual share in supply of input L;
"balanced share" if $K_i/K = L_i/L$;

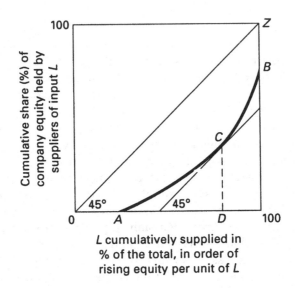

L cumulatively supplied in
% of the total, in order of
rising equity per unit of L

AD = percentage of L supplied by shareholders holding less than their balanced share (by construction); and

DC = percentage of equity capital held by suppliers of AD.

If DC turns out to be a *controlling* interest, then suppliers of AD have an incentive to exercise it and force the company to pay a higher price for L than the market rate, since they would lose less as shareholders than they would gain as suppliers. Hence the company will employ more L than is profitable. This may eliminate profits or actually induce losses, financed through capital consumption. All other shareholders are damaged (suppliers of L holding more than a balanced share will reduce their shareholdings down to a "balanced" level). There will be no incentive for risk capital to acquire shares. Restructuring will be held up.

If L stands for land, lathes, leather, or lorries, then suppliers may internalize potential efficiency gains by forming a company that would merge with the customer company to mutual advantage. However, if L stands for labor then this is not possible, because companies can neither own labor nor hire it on the same terms as machines.

REFERENCES

Aghion, Philippe, Olivier Blanchard, and Robin Burgess (1994), "The Behavior of State Firms in Eastern Europe: Pre-privatization," *European Economic Review* 38(6): 1327–49.

Alchian, Armer, and Harold Demsetz (1972), "Production, Information Costs and Economic Organization," *American Economic Review* 62(5): 777–95.

Ash, Timothy N., and Paul G. Hare (1994), "Privatization in the Russian Federation: Changing Enterprise Behavior in the Transition Period," *Cambridge Journal of Economics* 18: 619–34.

Aslund, Anders, and Richard Layard (1993), *Changing the Economic System in Russia*. London: Pinter.

Auerbach, A. J. (1988), *Corporate Takeovers: Causes and Consequences*. University of Chicago Press.

Barca, Fabrizio (1994), *Imprese in Cerca di Padrone: Proprieta' e Controllo nel Capitalismo Italiano*. Bari: Laterza.

Bergstrom, Lars (1994), "Corporate Governance in Newly Privatized Russian Enterprises: A Field Study," Working Paper no. 80, Stockholm Institute of East European Economics.

Berle, Adolphe (1926), "Non Voting Stock and 'Bankers' Control," *Harvard Law Review*.

Berle, Adolphe A., and Gardner C. Means (1932), *The Modern Corporation and Private Property*. New York: Macmillan.

Blanchard, Olivier, Rudiger Dornbusch, Paul Krugman, Richard Layard, and Larry Summers (1991), *Reforms in Eastern Europe*. Cambridge, MA: MIT Press.

Blasi, J. (1994), "Ownership, Governance and Restructuring," in Lieberman and Nellis (1994), pp. 125–40.

Blinder, S. (ed.) (1990), *Paying for Productivity: A Look at the Evidence*. Washington, DC: Brookings Institute.

Boeva, Irina, and T. G. Dolgopiatova (1993), "State Enterprises During Transition: The Formation of Strategies," Conference paper (June, Stockholm), Institute of East European Economics.

Bornstein, Morris (1994), "Russia's Mass Privatization Program," *Communist Economies and Economic Transformation* 6(4).

Cadbury [Sir Adrian] Committee (1993), *Report on the Financial Aspects of Corporate Governance*. London: HMSO.

Chandler, Alfred D., Jr. (1977), *The Visible Hand*. Cambridge, MA: Harvard University Press.

Chandler, Alfred D., Jr. (1990), *Scale and Scope*. Cambridge, MA: Harvard University Press.

Chubais, Anatoly, and Maria Vishnievskaia (1993), "Main Issues of Privatization in Russia," in Aslund and Layard (1993).

Coffee, John C. (1994), "Investment Privatization Funds: The Czech Experience," mimeo, Columbia University Law School, New York.

Conte, M. A., and Jan Svejnar (1990), "The Performance Effects of Employee Ownership Plans," in Blinder (1990), pp. 143–72.

Corbett, J., and C. Mayer (1991), "Financial Reform in Eastern Europe: Progress with the Wrong Model," *Oxford Review of Economic Policy* 7(4): 57–75.

Cornelli, Francesca, and David D. Li (1994), "Perverse Behavior of State Enterprises before Privatization," Seminar Paper, London Business School.

Cusan, Alessandra (1994), "Corporate Control in Eastern Europe," M.A. Dissertation, Birkbeck College, London.

de Cecco, Marcello (1989), "Alternative Modes of Financial Organization," in Kessides et al. (1989), p. 196-204.

de la Camara, Arilla Carmen (1994), "The Role of Managers in the Process of Privatization in Russia," unpublished manuscript, Barcelona University.

Earle, John S., and Saul Estrin (1995), "Employee Ownership in Transition," London Business School.

Earle, John S., Saul Estrin, and Larisa L. Leshchenko (1995), "The Effects of Ownership on Behavior: Is Privatization Working in Russia?" London Business School.

Ellerman, D. P. (1990), *The Democratic Worker-Owner Firm*. Boston: Unwin-Hyman.

Franks, J., and Colin P. Mayer (1990), "Capital Markets and Corporate Control: A Study of France, Germany and the UK," *Economic Policy* 5: 191-231.

Franks, J., and Colin P. Mayer (1992), "Corporate Control: A Synthesis of the International Evidence," mimeo, London Business School and City University Business School.

Frydman, Roman, Ed S. Phelps, and A. Rapaczynski (1993), "Needed Mechanisms of Corporate Governance and Finance in Eastern Europe," *Economics of Transition* 1(2): 171-208.

Gray, Cheryl W., and Rebecca J. Hanson (1993), "Corporate Governance in Central and Eastern Europe: Lessons from Advanced Market Economies," Working Paper, Policy Research Department, World Bank, Washington, DC.

Hansmann, H. (1990), "When Does Worker Ownership Work? ESOPs, Law, Firms, Codetermination and Economic Democracy," *Yale Law Journal* 99(8): 1751-1816.

Jackson, Marvin (1994), "Property Rights, Company Organization and Governance in the Transition," in Jackson and Bilsen (1994), pp. 1-34.

Jackson, Marvin, and Valentjin Bilsen (eds.) (1994), *Company Management and Capital Market Development in the Transition* (LICOS Studies on the Transitions in Central and Eastern Europe, vol. 2). Amsterdam: Avebury.

Jensen, M. C. (1988), "Takeovers: Their Causes and Consequences," *Journal of Economic Perspectives* 2(1).

Jensen, M., and W. Meckling (1976), "Theory of the Firm: Managerial Behavior, Agency Costs, and Ownership Structure," *Journal of Financial Economics* 3: 305-60.

Jones, Derek, and Takao Kato (1994), "The Determinants of Chief Executive Compensation in Transitional Economies: Evidence from Bulgaria," Working Paper no. 94/8, Hamilton College, Clinton, New York.

Kessides, Christine, Timothy King, D. Mario Nuti, and Kathy Sokil (eds.) (1989), *Financial Reforms in Socialist Economies*. Washington, DC: World Bank and Economic Development Institute.

Kornai, János (1992), *The Socialist System: The Political Economy of Communism*. Princeton, NJ: Princeton University Press.

Korsun, Georges, and Peter Murrell (1994a), "Ownership and Governance on the Morning After: The Initial Results of Privatization in Mongolia," ASSA Conference Paper (Boston), University of Maryland, College Park.

Korsun, Georges, and Peter Murrell (1994b), "The Politics and Economics of Mongolia's Privatization Program: A Brief History," mimeo, University of Maryland, College Park.

KPMG-CERT (1993), *A Study of the Russian Privatization Process: Changing Enterprise Behavior*. Moscow: Heriot–Watt University and SovEcon.

Layard, Richard (1995), "Unemployment Policy: Did Russia Do It Right?" ASSA Conference Paper (6–8 January, Washington, DC).

Lazonik, W. (1992), "Controlling the Market for Corporate Control: The Historical Significance of Managerial Capitalism," *Industrial and Corporate Change* 1(3).

Lieberman, Ira, and John Nellis (eds.) (1994), *Russia: Creating Private Enterprises and Efficient Markets*. Washington, DC: World Bank.

Linz, Susan (1994), "Production and Employment in Privatized Firms in Russia," *Comparative Economic Systems* 36(3): 105–14.

Marris, Robin (1966), *Managerial Capitalism*. London: Macmillan.

Meade, James E. (1993), *Liberty, Equality and Efficiency – Apologia pro Agathotopia Mea*. London: Macmillan.

Miyazaki, Hajime (1993), "Employeeism, Corporate Governance and the J-Firm," *Journal of Comparative Economics* 17(2).

Nuti, Domenico Mario (1994), "Mass Privatizations: Costs and Benefits of Instant Capitalism," CISME-LBS Working Paper no. 9, London Business School.

Nuti, Domenico Mario (1995), *The Economics of Participation*. Jeddah: IRTI-IDB.

Pinto, Brian, Marek Belka, and Stefan Krajewski (1993), "Transforming State Enterprises in Poland: Evidence on Adjustment by Manufacturing Firms," *Brookings Papers on Economic Activity* 1: 213–70.

Phillips, J. B. (1972), *The New Testament in Modern English*. New York: Collier.

Stiglitz, Joseph (1994), *Whither Socialism?* Cambridge, MA: Harvard University Press.

Takla, Lina (1995), "Issues of Corporate Governance in the Visegrad Countries," Conference Paper (March, Cambridge, UK), British Association for Slavik and East European Studies.

Uvalic, Milica (1991), "The PEPPER Report: Promotion of Employee Participation in Profits and Enterprise Results in the Member States of the European Community," *Social Europe* suppl. 3.

Vanek, Jaroslav (1970), *The General Theory of Labor-Managed Market Economies.*
    Ithaca, NY: Cornell University Press.
Ward, Benjamin M. (1958), "The Firm in Illyria: Market Syndicalism,"
    American Economic Review 48: 566–89.
Weitzman, Martin (1991), "How Not to Privatize," Conference Paper, Rome
    University, Torvergata.

PART II

Country Studies

CHAPTER 5

Inflation and Stabilization in Poland, 1990–95

Stanislaw Wellisz

The Polish liberalization and stabilization program that was put into effect on January 1, 1990, called for the removal of virtually all price controls[1] and for a sharp curtailment of production subsidies. These measures magnified the effects of pre-existing inflationary forces. Within one month, the retail price index rose by 79.6%. The inflation was, however, quickly brought under control by the stabilization measures adopted as a part of the reform package.[2] By August, the rate of price increase declined to 1.8% per month. Yet the goal of complete price stability by year's end proved to be elusive. In 1991, prices still rose by over 70%; inflation slowed down in subsequent years but remained at a two-digit level (Table 1).

To throw light on the causes of the persistence of inflation, let us briefly examine Poland's post-1990 monetary and exchange-rate policy. The history of Polish stabilization may be divided into three distinct periods: the fixed–exchange-rate period (1 January 1990 – 17 May 1991), which was followed by the periodic adjustment period (which lasted until 27 August 1993) and the crawling peg period.

1. INFLATION IN THE FIXED–EXCHANGE-RATE PERIOD

The Solidarity-led regime that was formed in autumn of 1989 inherited a partially liberalized and half-dismantled command system, and an economy hovering on the verge of hyperinflation.[3] During

---

[1] The reform reduced the extent of administered prices from 50% to 10%. On 1 January 1990, the administered price of domestic coal was raised by 600% and that of coal for industrial use by 400%. Railway freight charges and electric rates were raised by 200%. Periodic further upward adjustment in administered prices took place over the following years; coal prices were decontrolled in 1993.

[2] The fiscal deficit was to be reduced from 7.5% of GDP in 1989 to 1% in 1990. The January 1990 volume of real credit was to be 25% lower than in December 1989.

[3] See e.g. World Bank (1987).

Table 1. *Inflation and budget surplus (deficit)*
for Poland, 1990–94

Year	A Consumer price index (previous year = 100)	B Fiscal budget surplus or deficit as percentage of GDP
1990	717.8	+ 0.4
1991	171.1	− 7.0
1992	142.4	− 6.0
1993	135.3	− 2.7
1994	133.3	− 3.2

Sources: Column A: GUS (Central Statistical Office). Column B: Ministry of Finance and World Bank estimates, as reported in World Bank (1994). The fiscal deficit estimate for 1994 was reported in *Rzeczpospolita* no. 259 (3908) of November 7, 1994.

the last quarter of the year, the new government took measures to limit the rate of expansion of net domestic assets, and also to reduce the gap between the official exchange rate of the zloty and the free-market rate. These steps were preliminary to the 1 January 1990 introduction of a comprehensive stabilization and liberalization program known as the *Balcerowicz plan.*[4]

Among the key goals of the Balcerowicz plan was the restoration of a stable, convertible currency. Initially, the zloty was made internally convertible. The official exchange rate, which stood at 5,560 zl/$ during the last week of December 1989, was set at 9,500 zl/$ – somewhat below the then prevailing black-market rate. The government pledged to maintain the initial exchange rate for three months, after which it could be adjusted, if necessary. The zloty was deliberately undervalued to enable the government to adhere to its pledge in the face of the expected upward price adjustment induced by liberalization.

The adoption of the limited-horizon fixed–exchange-rate policy was motivated, on one hand, by the wish to "anchor" the zloty, and, on the other, by the desire to leave room for readjustment should the initial rate turn out to be inappropriate. Yet such a policy carried a high risk of encouraging destabilizing speculation.

[4] For a discussion of the 1989 mini-stabilization and of the Balcerowicz plan, see Wellisz, Kierzkowski, and Okólski (1993).

In order to restrict credit expansion, the National Bank of Poland (NBP) sought to maintain interest rates at a positive real level.[5] The NBP set the January discount rate based on a forecast that severely underestimated the increase in the price index, and the real return on zloty deposits was, in fact, negative, while in February and in March it barely exceeded zero. A holder of a dollar account (or of a dollar hoard) who switched to a zloty account at the beginning of January and then back to dollars at the end of the guaranteed fixed–exchange-rate period could have earned, in three months, a 70% return! Polish households' dollar holdings, estimated at $6 to $9 billion, exceeded official reserves by a factor of two or more. Even though Poland obtained a $1 billion stabilization loan, large-scale speculation could have precipitated a collapse of the exchange rate. However, the government's declaration that the rate would remain fixed for three months seemingly lacked credibility. Very little switching and re-switching took place. Thus, paradoxically, the lack of credibility facilitated the maintenance of the fixed exchange rate. As it turned out, no devaluation was necessary at the close of the three-month period.

The restrictive fiscal and monetary measures seemed to work "too well." Originally it was foreseen that, under the IMF-approved stabilization plan, the fiscal budget would be in deficit during the first half of the year; this deficit was to be balanced by a surplus in the second half of the year. Likewise, an initial balance-of-payments deficit was to be compensated by a later surplus, so that, for the year as a whole, both accounts would be in balance. In fact, however, at mid-year the fiscal budget was in surplus. So was the balance of payments, and foreign reserves accumulated at an unwonted rate.[6] There were signs of a forthcoming recession: the volume of credit (in real terms) declined more sharply than planned. Output was plummeting, and unemployment was beginning to rise. The excessive stringency resulted in an excessively rapid accumulation of reserves. Relaxation of monetary and fiscal policies seemed to be in order; the IMF goals could be met even in the face of fiscal and balance-of-payments deficits in the closing months of the year.

The immediate effects of fiscal and monetary relaxation were positive. The recession appeared to be stemmed, while inflation continued

---

[5] The NBP's discount rate for January, February, and March was set (respectively) at 36%, 20%, and 10% per month.

[6] In order to slow down the growth of reserves, the government put into effect temporary tariff reductions and suspensions. As a result, the unweighted average rate of protection declined from 11.65% to 5.82%; see Nogaj (1992, p. 65).

to abate. By September, however, prices began to rise again, while the positive effects of the monetary stimulus appeared to wear off. The government reverted to a contractionary policy, but – in view of a deepening recession – stopped short of drastic measures.

In 1991, the recession deepened. Profits of state-owned enterprises declined very sharply, depriving the government of a major source of revenue.[7] The fiscal budget was, once again, in deficit (see Table 1). In the face of a fixed exchange rate, rising prices led to a continuing real appreciation of the zloty – a highly undesirable development at a time of deepening recession. On 17 May 1991, the government reacted by reducing the nominal value of the zloty to 11,000 zl/$.

Did the dollar peg help stabilize Polish prices? The initial announcement that the zloty would remain internally convertible into dollars at a fixed exchange rate for a three-month period was meant to calm inflationary expectations. The announcement proved not to be credible, hence it did not accomplish its task. The dollar anchor was meant to stabilize Polish prices by providing a linkage with world prices. But, as long as the zloty was undervalued, the dollar link exercised an upward price pull. When, as a result of the rise of internal prices, the anchor began to hold, the zloty–dollar link was severed.

2. THE CRAWL-CUM-MINIDEVALUATIONS PERIOD

The May 1991 minidevaluation was accompanied by a switch from the dollar anchor to a trade-weighted foreign exchange basket.[8] This shift was not unjustified. Because of the fluctuations of the dollar-ECU exchange rate, the zloty–dollar linkage introduced an extraneous disturbing factor in the trade between Poland and Western Europe, Poland's main trading partner. But the linkage to a basket does not have the transparency, and does not carry the credibility, of a linkage to a single strong currency. The abandonment of the dollar standard looked like a signal of retreat from the fixed–exchange-rate policy.

On 1 October 1991, the fixed parity was replaced by a "crawling peg." The initial rate of crawl was set at 1.8% per month (about 24%

---

[7] In 1990, state-owned enterprises registered high profits, which reflected (1) lags in the revaluation of inventories and of depreciation allowances in the face of a rapid price rise, and (2) the increased zloty value of foreign exchange accounts held by enterprises. In 1991 and in 1992, state-owned enterprise as a whole recorded losses.

[8] The U.S. dollar was assigned a weight of 45%, the deutsche mark 35%, the pound sterling 10%, and the French and Swiss francs 5% each.

Table 2. *Index of consumer prices and of real
effective exchange rate (1990 = 100) and foreign
currency reserves ($ billion), 1991–94*

Year	Quarter	CPI	Real effective exchange rate	Foreign reserves
1991	1	153.6	145.5	4.305
	2	171.5	160.6	3.898
	3	181.9	154.9	4.373
	4	199.7	154.7	3.625
1992	1	225.6	154.6	3.637
	2	246.1	147.9	3.948
	3	264.6	148.8	4.180
	4	290.9	158.0	3.992
1993	1	319.0	165.7	3.467
	2	339.8	165.8	3.186
	3	357.2	160.6	3.539
	4	390.0	159.4	3.985
1994	1	422.7	164.2	4.786
	2	458.8	165.2	4.896
	3	479.6	164.1	5.741
	4	520.3	168.4	5.728

Source: International Monetary Fund.

per year). On 26 February 1992, the zloty was devalued by an additional 12%. Another devaluation (this time by 8%) came on 27 August 1993; however, at the same time, the rate of the crawl was cut to 1.6% per month.

Throughout the "crawl-cum-minidevaluations" period, the NBP closely followed what Dornbusch (1982) has called the "PPP-oriented exchange rate rule." Adherence to this rule tends, on the one hand "to maintain the exchange rate constant, thereby stabilizing demand." On the other hand, the "exchange rate affects costs and prices through the domestic cost of imported intermediate goods."[9] Between the second quarter of 1991 and the second quarter of 1993, foreign reserves remained at an approximately constant level, and so did the real exchange rate (Table 2). The exchange-rate adjustment system mimicked, as it were, a policy of flexible exchange, putting the entire responsibility for maintenance of price stability on the domestic fiscal and monetary authorities.

[9] Dornbusch (1982, p. 159).

3. THE 1991–93 POLISH INFLATION:
SOME STATISTICAL MEASURES

Let us now inquire into the sources of inflation in the crawl-cum-minidevaluations period. In 1991–93, the Polish economy was still in an early stage of transition. Given the fledgling banking system, there was some possibility of an atypical price response to fiscal and monetary stimuli. Possibly, too, exogenous shocks (changes in the tariff structure or in the internal tax structure, adjustments in the administered prices of transport and of energy) may have had a marked effect on the inflation rate. To throw light on these issues, we shall compare the behavior of the Polish economy with that of other countries.[10]

We first address the issues of the role of money and of banking in the Polish economy. Polish M2/GDP and credit/GDP ratios are lower than those in Western Europe, the United States, or Japan. However, cross-section regressions show that the degree of monetization, as measured by the M2/GDP ratio, is positively related to the GDP per capita.[11] The actual degree of monetization in Poland does not deviate in a statistically significant fashion from the degree of monetization predicted by the regression of M2/GDP on GDP per capita.[12]

---

[10] The following discussion is based on cross-section comparisons for the years 1991, 1992, and 1993. The analysis utilizes IMF data for all countries of the world, except for countries with fewer than two million inhabitants. The sample size varies, since not all data are available for all the IMF member countries for all three years. The differences in coverage are of minor importance since the estimates for the three years are highly consistent. It should also be pointed out that the IMF figures utilized in the analysis were obtained by converting national currencies into dollars at official exchange rates. This method of conversion introduces statistical "white noise." Summers and Heston (1991) also show that such figures are biased against the low-income countries.

[11] The relevant statistics of the regression of M2/GDP on GDP/capita (where GDP is measured in thousands of U.S. dollars) may be tabulated as follows.

Year	# of observ.	Adj. R^2	F value	Prob. $> F$	Regr. coeff.	T value	Prob. $> T$
1991	79	0.3665	46.127	0.0001	0.019807	6.792	0.0001
1992	70	0.3764	42.642	0.0001	0.017863	6.530	0.0001
1993	56	0.4553	46.977	0.0001	0.019499	6.854	0.0001

It should be noted that the inclusion of GDP in the denominator of the LHS and in the numerator of the RHS biases the results *against* the hypothesis that the "depth" of monetization increases with the level of development.

[12] The relevant statistics are tabulated as follows.

Year	Actual value	Predicted value	St. err. predict.	Residual	St. err. resid.
1991	0.3163	0.3760	0.028	−0.0597	0.219
1992	0.3576	0.3963	0.029	−0.0387	0.212
1993	0.3594	0.4124	0.031	−0.0530	0.265

Financial institutions play a greater role in economically advanced countries than in countries that are less developed. But in this respect, too, Poland does not deviate to any significant extent from the general pattern.[13]

Let us consider how adequate a purely monetary explanation of inflation would be – that is, how serious an error we shall commit if we fail to take into account the nonmonetary shocks. The simplest possible model expresses the annual rate of inflation as a function of the growth of M2 in the same year, while ignoring such important issues as the presence of adjustment lags, the nature of inflationary expectations, and the rate of GDP growth. Despite these simplifications, the model explains 60% of the intercountry variance in inflation.[14] The same relation holds for the economically leading countries and for all others.[15] For Poland, the actual and predicted rates of inflation are almost identical. We thus conclude that, as a first approximation, we may rely on a monetary explanation of the Polish inflation.

We now shift our attention to the sources of money creation. During the crawl-cum-minidevaluations period, the M1 multiplier remained constant while the M2 multiplier increased by about 15% (Table 3). However, this accounts for only a small fraction of the expansion of broad money and of the strength of the inflationary push.

Received economic doctrine points to fiscal deficits as the major cause of inflation. To quote Fischer and Easterly (1990, p. 139), "Rapid money growth is conceivable without an underlying fiscal imbalance, but it is unlikely. Thus rapid inflation is almost always a fiscal phenomenon." The theory underlying this statement has a venerable history going back to Keynes, who pointed out that "inflationary finance is the form of taxation which the public finds hardest to evade and even the weakest government can enforce, when it cannot enforce anything else."[16]

---

[13] A cross-section regression of the domestic credit/M2 ratio on GDP/capita using a sample of 80 countries yields an adjusted $R^2 = 0.54$ (significant at the 0.01 level) and a positive regression coefficient statistically significant on the 0.001 level. The actual value of the credit/M2 ratio for Poland does not deviate significantly from the value predicted by the regression.

[14] For 1991, the basic statistical results are as follows.

# of observ.	Adj. R^2	F value	Prob. $> F$	Regr. coeff.	T value	Prob. $> T$
75	0.6109	117.204	0.0001	0.850709	10.826	0.0001

[15] The coefficient of a dummy variable, inserted to distinguish between the economically leading countries and the rest of the world, is statistically insignificant.

[16] Keynes (1924, p. 46). For a recent discussion of the rationale of taxation through inflation, see Vegh (1989).

Table 3. *Money multipliers: Poland 1990–94*

Year	Quarter	M1/Reserves	M2/Reserves
1990	1	0.9	2.5
	2	1.1	2.4
	3	1.1	2.3
	4	1.1	2.2
1991	1	1.0	2.3
	2	1.1	2.6
	3	1.1	2.6
	4	1.0	2.4
1992	1	1.0	2.6
	2	1.0	2.7
	3	1.0	2.8
	4	1.0	2.8
1993	1	1.0	3.0
	2	1.0	3.0
	3	1.0	3.1
	4	1.2	3.5
1994	1	1.2	3.4
	2	1.1	3.4
	3	1.2	3.6
	4	1.4	3.9

Source: International Monetary Fund.

A crude rule of thumb is that the higher the proportion of the fiscal deficit (FD) to the GDP, the stronger the inflationary push. This "rule" turns out to be highly unsatisfactory. For our sample as a whole, the cross-section relation between the FD/GDP ratio and the rate of inflation is statistically insignificant. A division into a subsample consisting of 19 highly developed countries (group D) and a subsample including all the others (group L) reveals the following.

In group D there is a statistically weakly significant positive relation between the FD/GDP ratio and the inflation rate.[17]

As a group, the L countries are more inflation-prone than the D countries: in 34 of the 37 cases they have higher inflation rates than would be indicated by the statistical relation between the FD/GDP ratio and the inflation rate for the D group.[18] It is prob-

[17] The adjusted $R^2 = 0.115$; $F = 3.342$, significant at the 5% level.
[18] The difference between the two groups of countries is statistically significant. The F-test value equals 4.03. For an F-test value of 3.23, the null hypothesis is rejected at the 5% level and for $F = 5.18$ at the 1% level.

Table 4. *Actual and estimated inflation for Poland,*
1991–93 (previous year = 100)

Year	Consumer price index		Producer price index	
	Actual	Estimated	Actual	Estimated
1991	177	173	148	158
1992	145	143	128	138
1993	135	128	132	125

Source: International Monetary Fund.

able that L countries tend to monetize a higher proportion of their deficit than the D countries.

For L countries, the relation between the FD/GDP ratio and the rate of inflation is statistically insignificant. This means that the FD/GDP ratio cannot be used as a predictor of the rate of inflation in an L country.

A somewhat more sophisticated measure takes into account the degree of monetization of the deficit:

$$R/GDP(P + G) = FD/GDP,$$

where R = reserve money, P = inflation rate, G = rate of growth of output, and FD = fiscal deficit. It follows that

$$P = R/FD - G.$$

When applied to Polish data for the years 1991–93, this equation yields the results shown in Table 4.

The estimates are remarkably close to the actual figures. In four out of six cases, the estimates are marginally lower than the actual figures; in the two other cases they are marginally higher. The slight downward bias of the estimates may reflect the increase in the magnitude of the M2 multiplier (see Table 3).

Let us muster one more piece of evidence. As Table 5 shows, between the end of the second quarter of 1991 and the end of the third quarter of 1993, the claims of the NBP on general government (expressed in constant zlotys) rose by a factor of 7.5. During the same period, foreign assets of the NBP remained virtually constant. It is clear, therefore, that the monetization of the fiscal deficit acted as the "motor of inflation."

Table 5. *Claims on general government and*
foreign assets of the NBP, 1991–94
(billions of zlotys at 1990 prices)

Year	Quarter	Claims on GG	Foreign assets
1991	1	4,255	31,280
	2	5,966	30,787
	3	9,689	31,938
	4	21,860	25,188
1992	1	23,931	27,521
	2	23,848	27,667
	3	24,020	28,664
	4	41,835	27,199
1993	1	42,813	22,716
	2	44,793	21,036
	3	45,912	24,635
	4	40,331	25,935
1994	1	36,634	29,935
	2	37,350	27,970
	3	36,927	30,858
	4	36,358	29,370

Note: GG = general government.
Source: International Monetary Fund. Calculated by deflating the current zloty figures by the consumer price index (1990 = 100).

4. THE "PURE CRAWL" PERIOD

The "pure crawl" policy represents, in a sense, a continuation of the
PPP-oriented policy of the crawl-cum-minidevaluations period. Yet,
in the earlier period, changes in the official exchange rate tracked the
market equilibrium valuation of the zloty, whereas in the later period
the exchange rate was set in accordance with a sliding parity schedule. The rate of downward slide was periodically modified, but at all
times the zloty was undervalued in real terms. Such a policy of active
exchange management

has become increasingly prevalent among developing countries in recent
years. With a view toward preserving competitiveness these countries have
frequently adopted rules under which the nominal exchange rate is depreciated continuously to offset differences between domestic and foreign inflation rates. . . . [R]ules which effectively target the real exchange rate establish a feedback mechanism from domestic inflation to the nominal exchange
rate. (Montiel and Ostry 1991, pp. 58–9)

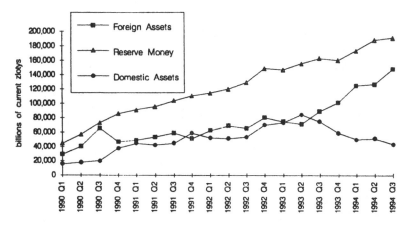

Figure 1. Money base in Poland, 1992Q1-1994Q3.

Starting in mid-1993, Poland's foreign reserves began to accumulate rapidly (Table 5; see also Figure 1). The influx of foreign exchange swelled the money base (Table 5). In order to slow down the foreign exchange inflow, the rate of crawl was cut in mid-1994 to 1.4% per month, and in January 1995 to 1.2% per month. Yet reserves continued to rise: by the end of the second quarter of 1993 they stood at $3.3 billion, and at $5.7 billion by the end of the fourth quarter of 1994. The rise continued during the first quarter of 1995, proof that the zloty was still undervalued.

Available statistics fail to reveal what caused the foreign exchange inflow. Preliminary figures indicate that - despite improvements in 1993 and 1994 - the balance of payments is still in deficit; hence the country should be losing (rather than gaining) reserves. But these figures do not take into account border trade with countries of the former Soviet Union. Possibly, too, there was an unrecorded influx of speculative capital. The Polish interest rates, in constant zloty terms, tend to be very low. For instance, during the last quarter of 1994, the NBP constant zloty discount rate was approximately zero (Table 6). However, given the 1.4% monthly crawl rate, the discount rate in terms of dollars amounted to 12.5% - a rate that was sufficiently high to perhaps attract speculative funds. How important such an influx may have been, and whether it actually occurred, are matters of conjecture.[19]

---

[19] According to Hanna Gronkiewicz-Waltz, the governor of the Bank of Poland, the inflow of short-term foreign capital accelerated during the first quarter of 1995, but even then it accounted for only 10% of the rise in reserves (Gronkiewicz-Waltz 1996, p. 18).

Table 6. *Central bank discount rates,*
rates of inflation, and real interest rates
in selected countries (1994Q4)

Country	A Discount rate (%)	B Inflation rate (%)	C Real interest rate (%)
United States	4.75	2.7	2.0
Belgium	4.50	2.0	2.5
Portugal	10.50	3.0	7.2
Colombia	44.90	23.2	17.6
Ecuador	44.88	24.6	16.2
Czech Republic	8.59	10.6	−1.8
Hungary	25.00	20.6	3.6
Poland	33.00	33.4	0.0

Notes: Column A, end of quarter; column B, 1994Q4/1993Q4.
Column C is calculated from columns A and B.

The policy of independent determination of the zloty's rate of slide
and of the nominal interest rate opened the NBP to conflicting pressures of interest groups. The undervaluation of the zloty was clearly
to the advantage of the export-oriented and import-substituting sectors of the economy. But undervaluation resulted in the accumulation of foreign exchange. To control inflation, the NBP attempted to
sterilize the growing foreign reserves. However, a tight money policy
ran counter to the interests of borrowers and in particular the government, which sought to issue new debt at the least possible cost.

These conflicts point to a fundamental flaw. As long as the rate of
slide is set so as to result in the continuing real overvaluation of the
zloty, international prices exercise an upward pull on domestic prices.
The policy of a sliding undervalued currency leads to a vicious circle
of devaluations and price increases (see Calvo, Reinhart, and Vegh
1994). Thus, even if the 1994 influx of reserves had been completely
sterilized, the 1.4% monthly slide rate of the zloty would have resulted in a 15% annual inflation. In fact, the NBP's nominal interest
rate was too low to achieve full sterilization. Yet according to NBP
critics, this rate was so high (in dollar terms) that it attracted specul-
ators and (in zloty terms) that it hindered recovery. Clearly, however, a lower nominal interest structure would have led to an even
faster rise in prices. The only solution to the dilemma is to eliminate
undervaluation, and to make a clear choice: either select an exchange

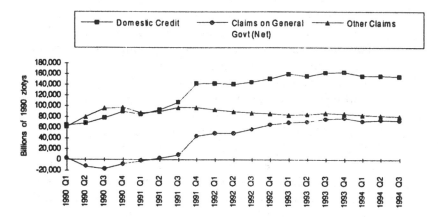

Figure 2. Polish real domestic credit as calculated by deflating nominal credit by the CPI, 1990Q1–1994Q3. *Source:* International Monetary Fund.

anchor and adopt a passive fiscal and monetary policy, or assume fiscal and monetary responsibility for the rate of money supply and let the market determine the exchange rate.

It would thus seem that (except for pressuring the NBP to reduce nominal interest rates) the fiscal authorities are to be exonerated from contributing to the inflation during the pure crawl period. Indeed, though the government failed to achieve a budgetary balance, the fiscal deficits did not feed inflation. In fact, the real value of NBP loans to the government declined (see Tables 1 and 5 and Figure 1). This does not mean that the deficits were harmless. The government borrowed from commercial banks, who cut back on lending for industrial and commercial purposes (Figure 2) to remain within credit limits. Government borrowing added to the demand for loanable funds; real interest rates rose and productive investment was crowded out. Hence fiscal policy, rather than NBP policy, is at the root of the credit tightness decried by borrowers.

5. SOME CONCLUSIONS

A review of the Polish experience reopens some important stabilization policy issues. The first concerns the new orthodoxy that calls for a "heterodox" (a multiple-anchor) approach. The success achieved by the Polish government in bringing inflation under control in the course of the first six months of 1990 can be ascribed to the stringent fiscal and monetary measures. It is, however, open to doubt whether the foreign-currency anchor contributed to the restoration of price stability. The linkage of the zloty to the dollar does not seem to have calmed inflationary expectations. Moreover, as long as the zloty was undervalued, the "anchor" exerted an upward price pull. When, in 1991, the anchor began to hold down the prices, it was hoisted.

The second question concerns the engine driving the persistence of the inflation. As the transition-triggered recession deepened, the government found itself incapable of balancing the budget. Monetization of the fiscal deficit explains the rise in prices from 1991 to mid-1993. Since that time, however, the real value of the general government's debt held by the National Bank of Poland declined while the rate of inflation continued to surpass 30% per year. The culprit, the data indicate, is the crawling peg – or, to be more precise, a crawling peg policy under which the zloty was consistently undervalued. Undervaluation exerted an upward pressure on prices through two channels: directly, through the pricing of products that entered foreign trade; and indirectly, via foreign reserve accumulation and growth of high power money. The crawl mechanism provided a backward linkage from prices to the exchange rate and so perpetuated the inflationary cycle.

The third question concerns the wisdom of covering the fiscal deficit through commercial placement of government securities. This method of deficit financing is noninflationary and thus avoids imposing a tax on cash balances. However, the commercial placement of government loans raises the total demand for loanable funds, raising the real interest rate; this is tantamount to imposition of an investment tax. The ills accompanying inflation are well known, yet the ills resulting from commercial bank financing of deficits are no less real. In Poland, banks have been funneling resources to the government and away from productive sectors of the economy. A government eager to promote investment should not, therefore, finance its fiscal deficit by borrowing from commercial banks. The best way to avoid inflation is to balance the budget by trimming inessential expenditures and by levying explicit taxes that do not excessively distort the economy.

REFERENCES

Calvo, Guillermo A., Carmen Reinhart, and Carlos A. Vegh (1994), "Targeting the Real Exchange Rate – Theory and Evidence," unpublished manuscript.

Dornbusch, Rudiger (1982), "PPP Exchange-Rate Rules and Macroeconomic Stability," *Journal of Political Economy* 90(1): 158–65.

Fischer, Stanley, and William Easterly (1990), "The Economics of the Government Budget Constraint," *World Bank Research Observer* 5(2): 127–42.

Gronkiewicz-Waltz, Hanna (1996), "Jak należało prowadzić politykę pieniężną," *Rzeczpospolita* 236(4450): 18.

Keynes, John Maynard (1924), *Monetary Reform.* New York: Harcourt, Brace.

Montiel, Peter, and Jonathan Ostry (1991), "Macroeconomic Implications of Real Exchange Rate Targeting in Developing Countries," *IMF Staff Papers* 38(4): 872–900.

Nogaj, Mieczysław (1992), "Cele i Założenia Nowej Polityki Celnej," *Kontrola Panstwowa* 1: 128–45; reprinted in Instytut Koniunktur i Cen Handlu Zagranicznego (1994), *Polska Polityka Handlu Zagranicznego 1993–1994.* Warszawa: Instytut Koniunktur.

Summers, Robert, and Alan Heston (1991), "The Penn World Table (Mark 5): An Expanded Set of International Comparisons 1950-1988," *Quarterly Journal of Economics* 106(2): 328–68.

Vegh, Carlos A. (1989), "Government Spending and Inflationary Finance: A Public Finance Approach," *IMF Staff Papers* 36(3): 657–77.

Wellisz, Stanislaw, Henryk Kierzkowski, and Marek Okólski (1993), "The Polish Economy 1989–1991," in H. Kierzkowski, M. Okólski, and S. Wellisz (eds.), *Stabilization and Structural Adjustment in Poland.* London: Routledge, pp. 123–39.

World Bank (1987), *Poland Reform, Adjustment, and Growth.* Washington, DC: World Bank.

World Bank (1994), *Poland Policies for Growth with Equity.* Washington, DC: World Bank.

CHAPTER 6

The Political Economy of the Hungarian Stabilization and Austerity Program

János Kornai

1. THE HISTORICAL BACKGROUND

In this study I would like to place the current problems of the Hungarian economic policy in a wider historical and political economy perspective. For that purpose a brief outline of Hungarian development in the last three decades is needed.

The Hungarian economy's road from a centralized, planned economy to a market economy displays a number of features that distinguish it from other postsocialist countries, despite the underlying similarities. Four main characteristics can be emphasized, as follows.

(1) In economic policy priorities, much greater weight was placed in Hungary than elsewhere in the region on raising present-day material welfare and – in the subsequent period of mounting economic problems and stagnating or declining production – on curbing the fall in living standards. Conditions in Hungary had earlier been christened "goulash communism." The policy for several years after the change of political system continued the previous one in this respect, and can aptly be called "goulash postcommunism."

This new economic policy orientation had a golden age, between 1966 and 1975, without recession or stagnation and with consumption rising by an annual average of 5.3% (see Table 1). Yet it could not be continued forever, even though production at that time was still

The research underlying the paper was supported by the World Bank and by the Hungarian National Research Foundation (OTKA). I am most grateful to Mária Kovács for her help in gathering the data and clarifying the problems discussed in the study. I express my gratitude to Brian McLean for his translation of the Hungarian text. Among those with whom I consulted during the research were László Akar, Zsolt Ámon, Rudolf Andorka, Francis Bator, Lajos Bokros, Michael Bruno, Richard Cooper, Zsuzsa Dániel, Tibor Erdős, Endre Gács, Stanley Fischer, Eszter Hamza, George Kopits, Álmos Kovács, Judit Neményi, Robert Solow, György Surányi, Márton Tardos, and László Urbán, all of whom I thank for their valuable advice. Naturally I alone am responsible for the ideas expressed.

Table 1. *Absorption of GDP in Hungary, 1960-93*

Period	GDP	Final consumption		Gross investment	
		Household	Total	Accumu-lation of fixed assets	Total
1961–65	4.4	3.4	3.7	5.1	5.2
1966–75	6.3	5.3	5.3	9.1	8.5
1976–87	2.7	2.1	2.3	0.8	0.1
1988–91	− 4.0	− 2.9	− 2.5	− 5.1	− 7.3
1988–93[a]	− 3.3	− 1.7	− 0.7	− 3.7	− 4.1

Annual average growth rate, %

[a] The 1993 figure for total final consumption includes arms imports from Russia received as debt repayment.
Source: Central Statistical Office (1995c, p. 2).

growing fast – faster than consumption. However, under Stalinist economic policy the gap between the growth rates of production and consumption would have been much higher. The leadership would have used the upswing of growth to achieve a higher investment rate, and thus a much higher growth rate of GDP, and would have been contented with a much more modest improvement of consumption. One more remark (which will be discussed later in the chapter): the growth in production, and with it consumption, began in the 1970s to occur partly at the price of accumulating foreign debt. Moreover, the proportions of the domestic utilization of GDP reversed after 1975, with consumption's share rising and investment's falling. The growth in production slowed down steadily, remaining near stagnation for a long time, and then started to fall seriously in 1991. This is just the sort of situation that tests what weight consumption has in the priorities of economic policy. The consumption-oriented economic policy persisted against a stagnating and even shrinking economy. This it did before, during, and after the change of political system (although by then in a defensive manner). "If a fall in consumption is inevitable, let it fall as slowly and as little as possible," was the attitude. (See Table 2.) This aim was plainly apparent in the period 1988–93, when GDP fell by an average of 3.7% a year while the fall in consumption averaged only 1.5% a year (see Table 1).

Table 2. *Trends in GDP, consumption, real income,*
and real wages in Hungary, 1988–94

Year	GDP[a]	Per-capita consumption	Per-capita real income	Real wages per earner[b]
1988	100	100	99	95
1989	101	106	102	96
1990	97	100	101	92
1991	85	91	99	86
1992	83	91	95	85
1993	82	93	91	81
1994	85	—	95	87

Note: 1987 = 100.
[a] The GDP figure is not for GDP per capita.
[b] Through 1990, the figures refer only to the category of workers and
employees, excluding workers in agricultural cooperatives; from 1991,
they are included.
Source: Central Statistical Office (1995c, pp. 2, 11).

(2) A paternalist welfare state covering the entire population was
developed over several decades. Hungary can vie with the most developed Scandinavian countries in the range of codified entitlements
to benefits and in the proportion of GDP laid out on social spending,
even though per-capita production is only a small fraction of the level
in Scandinavia. Similar tendencies arose at the time in all Eastern
European countries, but Hungary went furthest by far and in this respect stands alone in the region.

(3) The process of transformation in Hungary has extended over
several decades; the initial steps were taken back in the 1960s. Although a few milestones can be mentioned (especially 1968, the elimination of mandatory plan instructions), the process as a whole has
been notable for its gradualism. Similarly gradual development in
this respect has occurred only in Slovenia.[1] In the eyes of those who
distinguish "shock therapy" ("big-bang" strategy) from a "gradualist"
strategy, Hungary represents one extreme of the latter, and in many
ways a special case of it: "gradualism Hungarian style."

[1] Yugoslavia set about dismantling the planning command system before Hungary did, and in
this sense the reform process has a longer history there. Slovenia is the only successor state
of former Yugoslavia where the change of political system has been uninterrupted. Ruptures
have occurred in all the others due to conflicts and wars between successor states or ethnic
groups.

(4) Hungary has been marked for decades by relative political calm. Whereas the transformation in some countries has been accompanied by civil warfare, here not a shot has been fired. While the change of political system in some countries took place at lightning speed amidst spectacular circumstances (collapse of the Berlin Wall, mass demonstrations on the streets of Prague, execution of the Romanian dictator), Hungary featured restrained negotiations over an extended period, with the ruling politicians of the old order and the hitherto repressed opposition reaching agreement on free elections and a new constitution. For decades there were hardly any strikes or street demonstrations. Though the economic problems have worsened, successive governments have preferred to muddle through rather than to enact measures that would rouse strong opposition and entail a risk of political destabilization.

These four characteristics form the "specific difference" of the Hungarian transformation. The four features are closely related. It is remarkable that, in spite of the political turnaround of 1989–90 (i.e., the shift from communist political power to parliamentary democracy), these four characteristics show great persistence and continuity – until more recent events: a stabilization and austerity program announced on 12 March 1995.

The need for a radical change (or intention of change) of macro policy was created by the negative side effects of the policies of goulash communism, goulash postcommunism, and overspending in paternalistic redistributive transfers and services.

This presents a special case of the well-known time preference problem of "now or later." The main aim of Hungarian economic policy for at least two decades could be described as seeking at any time to maximize consumption in the present and immediate future, at the expense of social debt that would devolve on later periods.

Here I use the concept of *debt* in its broadest sense. This comprehensive interpretation has already been employed by several authors;[2] let us examine its main components.

(1) Debt in the literal sense is what the country owes abroad. With this kind of debt, the connection is obvious: consumption today is being financed abroad, but this must be repaid tomorrow at the expense of tomorrow's consumption. This kind of debt is oppressively

---

[2] See Kornai (1972) and Krugman (1994). The latter uses the expression "hidden deficit" on pp. 161-9.

Table 3. *Indices of Hungary's convertible-currency foreign debt and debt servicing*

| Year | Gross debt[a] | Debt service | | Net interest payments as percentage of exports of goods |
		As percentage of exports of goods	As percentage of exports of goods and services	
1973	—	27.6	—	5.8
1974	—	23.4	—	5.6
1975	3.9	25.3	—	8.2
1976	4.5	22.3	—	4.5
1977	5.2	23.3	—	6.2
1978	7.6	34.8	—	7.9
1979	8.3	39.1	—	11.3
1980	9.1	41.4	—	17.7
1981	8.7	51.0	—	19.8
1982	10.2	47.9	39.6	23.1
1983	10.7	46.9	39.6	15.7
1984	11.0	53.1	45.7	16.6
1985	14.0	85.6	70.1	19.9
1986	16.9	97.0	75.1	23.0
1987	19.6	71.8	55.3	19.5
1988	19.6	61.4	46.7	19.6
1989	20.4	52.9	38.5	21.5
1990	21.3	62.7	45.5	22.3
1991	22.7	41.3	32.0	14.4
1992	21.4	43.9	31.9	12.1
1993	24.6	44.5	33.0	14.0
1994	28.5	—	—	—

[a] In billions of U.S. dollars.
Sources: Column 2—for 1975–81, UNECE (1993, p. 130); for 1982–93, National Bank of Hungary (1994, p. 137); for 1994, National Bank of Hungary (1995, p. 108). Columns 3–5—National Bank of Hungary (1994, p. 269).

large in Hungary's case (see Table 3). The defensive policy of curbing the reduction of consumption has been implemented primarily at the expense of foreign debt.

Among other factors contributing to the buildup of foreign debt is that the exchange-rate policy has tended to overvalue the currency, which weakened the incentive to export and allowed excessive import demand to develop. It was apparent in several periods, most recently from 1993 through 12 March 1995, that the financial authorities were postponing an increasingly inevitable devaluation.[3] This fitted in well with the economic policy of always postponing unpopular measures to the last minute. Devaluation, especially when coupled with a tighter wage policy, is known for cutting deep into living standards, which can be counted on to elicit unfavorable reactions from wage and salary earners. Postponement of devaluation is also a kind of "arrears," since an unpopular task is thereby left for a later government.

(2) Let us start by assuming that it is possible to determine what proportion of GDP must be invested to ensure (i) the maintenance and a modest but acceptable expansion of national wealth and (ii) a modest but acceptable expansion of production. If the proportion is less, some tasks that should be done now will be omitted and left for later. The "arrears" formed by the postponed acts of investment are a form of debt, which a later generation will have to pay instead of the present one. Hence these arrears can be considered as part of the social debt.

Table 4 compares the trend of persistently high investment proportions in some medium-developed, fast-growing countries with the declining trend over time in Hungary's investment proportion. I am not saying that Hungary should necessarily have maintained its high earlier proportion of investment, but the very great extent of the decrease demonstrates the line of thinking just described: an accumulation of investment arrears.

Expenditure in Hungary on the maintenance and renovation of housing and infrastructure (roads, railways, bridges, etc.) has fallen sharply. For example, housing construction has been falling dramatically for two decades, and in recent years the volume of housing constructed has plunged. This is offset in part by the fact that far fewer dwellings than before are being removed from the housing stock, as dwellings ready for demolition are being retained. See Table 5.

Especially menacing is the drop in long-term, slow-return, yet essential investment. Infrastructure investment can be grouped here. An increase in human capital can be classed as a long-term investment, along with development of higher education and scientific research. Neglect of such tasks does not cause immediate, tangible harm. The damage is long delayed and mostly takes indirect forms,

---

[3] In periods when a populist government ruled in certain Latin American countries, a tendency for the exchange rate to appreciate was apparent in every case.

Table 4. *Trends in gross domestic investment in fast-growing developing countries and in Hungary, 1980–93*

	Gross domestic investment as a percentage of GDP					
Year	Hungary	Indonesia	South Korea	China	Malaysia	Thailand
1980	30.7	24.3	32.0	30.1	30.4	29.1
1981	29.7	29.6	29.8	27.0	35.0	29.7
1982	28.5	27.5	28.9	28.9	37.3	26.5
1983	26.5	28.7	29.1	29.8	37.8	30.0
1984	25.7	26.2	29.8	31.4	33.6	29.5
1985	25.0	28.0	29.6	38.6	27.6	28.2
1986	26.9	28.3	28.7	38.9	26.0	25.9
1987	26.7	31.4	29.8	37.3	23.2	27.9
1988	25.3	31.5	31.1	38.1	26.0	32.6
1989	26.6	35.2	33.6	36.8	28.6	35.1
1990	25.4	30.1	36.9	33.2	31.5	41.1
1991	20.4	29.4	38.9	32.7	37.0	42.2
1992	15.2	28.7	36.6	34.4	33.8	39.6
1993	19.7	28.3	34.3	41.2	33.2	40.0

Source: World Bank (1995c, pp. 58–61).

so that "short-termism" easily leads to further postponement. This is just the case in Hungary: insufficient resources have been devoted to these important development tasks.[4]

(3) Another component of social debt is formed by legislative commitments to future consumption. These include promises of legally guaranteed pensions, family allowances, maternity benefits, sick pay, and all other welfare payments. These are promissory notes from the present generation, which the next generation will have to redeem. When these are eventually redeemed, they too will compete for resources with the investment required for economic development, and so it is justified to consider them as a component of debt.

I will use a single piece of data to exemplify the vast scale of such postponed commitments: the calculation made by the World Bank on the size of Hungary's "pension debt." This is the name given to the discounted present value of all pensions to be paid in the future under

---

[4] To give a single example, the sum spent on research and development in 1993, at constant prices, was less than a third of the maximum level of such spending in 1987. As a proportion of GDP, the sum fell from 2.65% to 1.01% (Central Statistical Office 1989, p. 13; 1994d, p. 13).

Table 5. *Housing construction and termination in Hungary, 1976-93*

| Period | Housing built | | Housing terminated |
	Thousands of m^2	Thousands of units	Thousands of units
1976-80[a]	5,976	90.5	19.8
1981-85[a]	5.472	73.9	15.2
1986-90[a]	4,631	54.5	11.4
1991	2,984	33.2	5.5
1992	2,400	25.8	4.5
1993	1,987	20.9	4.5

[a] Annual average.
Source: Central Statistical Office (1994c, pp. 16-17, 19, 25).

the laws and regulations that currently apply.[5] It emerged that the pension debt was equivalent to 263% of 1994 GDP. Similar calculations were made recently for seven OECD countries, of which Italy had the highest pension debt; the Hungarian figure is close to the Italian one.[6]

The accumulation of all components of social debt made a rigorous program of deep structural changes inevitable. In addition, certain short-term tensions became more critical as well; I will come back to this aspect later. The 12 March 1995 stabilization and austerity program was a brave action to face today's troubling macroeconomic difficulties, and also a first step in a long-lasting series of measures to change course and depart from the route followed for thirty years.

2. MAIN FEATURES OF THE PROGRAM

The program – or the "Bokros package" as it was called by the press, referring to the Minister of Finance, Lajos Bokros – consists of three main elements.[7]

(1) The forint was radically devalued with immediate effect, followed by the introduction of the system of a *preannounced crawling peg.*

---

[5] A discount rate of 2% was used for the calculation.
[6] See World Bank (1995a, p. 36; 1995b, p. 127).
[7] Hungary's present macroeconomic situation is analyzed in Csaba (1995), Erdős (1994), Kornai (1995b), Köves (1995), and World Bank (1995b).

In addition, a significant import surcharge (supplementary tariff) was introduced.

(2) A substantial cut in budgetary spending was laid down. This covered numerous appropriations, including several items of welfare spending, and some entitlements enshrined in law were reduced or withdrawn. A sizeable reduction in staffing levels at public offices was prescribed. The alterations were designed to reduce the budget deficit in 1995 and exert their effect even more in 1996.

(3) The government sought to achieve a sharp reduction in real wages and earnings, placing strict limits on the personal incomes derived in the public sector and on wage increases in firms in majority state ownership. It was assumed that this would curb wage increases in the private sector as well.

The stabilization program marks a clean break with the four main features described in Section 1, which typify the Hungarian road of systemic change.

(1) Consumption is replaced as a priority by the aim of restoring the seriously upset macroeconomic balance, so as to establish conditions for lasting growth and, at a later stage, for growing consumption. Defensive action to ward off the decline in consumption has been suspended. A sudden change has been made in the time preference of economic policy. In the dilemma of present consumption versus debt accumulation, the relative weights have been reversed. Heretofore, the future had been sacrificed to the present; now, sacrifices are being demanded of the present for the sake of the future. The accumulation of social debt had previously been accepted for the sake of present consumption (slowing of the fall in consumption, or possibly stagnation or a slight rise in consumption). Now a reduction in present consumption has been undertaken to prevent a further buildup of social debt.

(2) The paternalist welfare entitlements and transfers by the state were unassailable until 12 March 1995; there was no political force ready to recommend a well-specified and concrete reduction in them. Now, a turn has occurred. It has been shown to be possible not only to grant entitlements but, where justified, to revoke them as well.

(3) In sharp contrast to the gradualism, hesitancy, and piecemeal policies characteristic of recent decades, a package of measures with traumatic effects has been introduced with dramatic suddenness. True, this is a far less comprehensive program than the earlier shock

therapy in Poland or Russia, but that is partly justified by the difference in Hungary's situation in 1995. Yet a degree of similarity remains: the break with continuity, the sudden turn, and the trauma.

(4) The stabilization package brought the political calm to an immediate end. No one could believe that the March 12 measures had a consensus behind them. On the contrary, they have been greeted – by a wide variety of interest groups and political forces – with doubts and criticisms at best and at worst with vehement protests.

3. IMPROVING THE EXTERNAL BALANCE

I turn now to detailing some features of the stabilization package. Let us start with the problems of the country's external balance – that is, the situation with the trade balance, the current account, and the foreign debt. I am convinced that, under the present conditions, improving Hungary's external balances should receive top priority both now and in the near future. The situation worsened in the last period.

The main figures appear in Table 6, which shows exports growing strongly again in 1994 after a sharp setback in 1993. Unfortunately, the growth in imports hardly slackened, so that the balance of trade in both 1993 and 1994 was strongly negative. This was the main reason why the current-account deficit in two successive years attained and then exceeded 9% of GDP. This figure is unfavorable to an almost unprecedented extent, and it means that the country has entered the danger zone. It was primarily this signal, along with the postponement of devaluation and other corrective measures, that was behind the deterioration in Hungary's credit rating in the eyes of international finance. Although Hungary has so far met all its financial commitments in full, potential lenders see this as proof of goodwill, not of real solvency. If a country overspends to such an extent over a lengthy period, potential creditors start to worry.

This brings us to the first dilemma of the present Hungarian economic policy. Every statement that can be made about Hungary's payments position is provisional and conditional. Luckily, there has not yet been a catastrophe to prove conclusively that the lack of external equilibrium really is the primary problem today. Those less concerned by it may argue that export performance has improved and Hungary has sizeable foreign exchange reserves. So they still question whether it would not be more expedient to allow the debt

Table 6. *Hungary's foreign trade, 1990–94*

Indices	1990	1991	1992	1993	1994[a]
Exports					
Billions of U.S. dollars	9.6	10.2	10.7	8.9	10.7
Change over previous year:					
Volume index (%)	− 4.1	− 4.9	1.0	− 13.1	16.6
Value index (%)	5.7	24.3	10.4	− 2.8	20.1
Imports					
Billions of U.S. dollars	8.7	11.4	11.1	12.5	14.6
Change over previous year:					
Volume index (%)	− 5.2	5.5	− 7.6	20.9	14.5
Value index (%)	4.1	53.9	1.6	32.3	21.5
Balance of foreign trade					
Billions of U.S. dollars	0.9	− 1.2	− 0.4	− 3.6	− 3.9
Percentage of GDP	2.7	− 3.8	− 1.1	− 9.4	− 9.5

Notes: The figures include foreign trade on both the convertible and nonconvertible accounts. The 1993 figures also include the arms imports from Russia delivered as repayment of earlier debt.
[a] Preliminary figures.
Sources: For 1990–93 foreign trade, National Bank of Hungary (1994, pp. 207–8); for 1990–93 GDP, National Bank of Hungary (1993, p. 60), Central Statistical Office (1991, p. 60), Central Statistical Office (1994a, p. 103), and Central Statistical Office (1994b, p. 107); for 1994 foreign trade and GDP, preliminary estimates by Hungarian Ministry of Finance on the basis of customs statistics.

burden to remain at its present level, or even accept some further deterioration, and to stimulate production by drawing in outside resources to a greater extent.

This argument cannot be refuted directly with facts from Hungary's experience. No one can say precisely how far Hungary could go with its earlier practice of handling the balance of payments. But in any case we should remain mindful that the international financial world has always been subject to unexpected and unpredictable events. For instance, there may be a sudden, hysterical turn away from some country or other, a lightning loss of confidence, a panic capital flight, or a speculative attack on the country's currency. The destructive effects of such chains of events are apparent from the debt crises in Latin America.[8] Suddenly the channels of credit are blocked

[8] On the Latin American debt crises, see Larrain and Selowsky (1991), Sachs (1989), Sunkel (1993), and Williamson (1990).

and foreign direct investment stops, so that the reserves swiftly run out and the country becomes unable to meet its payments; this gives it a worse name still and plunges it further into the payments crisis. There is a grave fall in imports, which drags production and exports down as well. The recession may even reach 10–15% and last one or two years, which rapidly drives up unemployment.

The prime task for the stabilization package is to avert a grave upheaval of this kind. Although it will be some time before anything certain can be reported, the chances of avoiding a debt crisis can already be said to have substantially improved. Let us sum up the measures that will tend to make a substantial improvement in Hungary's external balances.

(1) The radical devaluation and prior announcement of the future course of nominal devaluation will stimulate Hungarian exporters and curb imports.

(2) Domestic and foreign experts debate strongly the advantages and drawbacks of various exchange-rate regimes. The regime now chosen by Hungary's financial authorities – the preannounced crawling peg – has certain advantages, above all that it makes the intentions of the policy makers plain and clear. It makes a prior commitment to keep the actual exchange rate within a designated band. This tends to take the edge off speculation and forestall the extra imports engendered by devaluation expectations. To this extent, if successfully applied, it will contribute to improving the trade and current-account balances. But such an exchange-rate regime entails dangers and risks as well. It ties the hands of the monetary authorities, reducing their room for maneuver. It stands or falls on whether events that are largely independent of the monetary authorities, notably the speed of inflation, remain consistent with the exchange-rate trend announced in advance. (I will return to this later.)

(3) A fall in imports is being encouraged not only by the exchange-rate alteration, but also by the customs surcharge on imports and a few other measures as well. This concurrently improves the competitive position of Hungarian production compared with imports. Let me note here that the question of which factors are causing the substantial growth in import intensity in every area of domestic absorption has not yet been sufficiently analyzed. The exchange-rate adjustment and customs surcharge will presumably not suffice in themselves to halt (much less reverse) this trend.

(4) By restricting domestic demand, the stabilization package induces (in fact, almost obliges) producers to exhibit export-oriented behavior.

(5) The curb placed on wage increases (and the levies proportionate to them) will improve the competitiveness of Hungarian products on the home market relative to imports, and on foreign markets relative to rival countries.

(6) The opportunities of convertibility have grown in the corporate sphere. This change encourages enterprises more strongly than before to keep their money in Hungary and not feel constantly induced to part with their forints, since now they can be easily converted into foreign currency at any time. Hence the holders of money are less tempted to convert it into foreign exchange and/or keep it abroad.

(7) It is now easier for banks and firms to raise foreign loans independently and directly. This decentralization will improve the composition of Hungarian debt and ease the problems of the government and the central bank.

(8) Exports are receiving stimuli and assistance in numerous forms. For instance, financial institutions specializing in foreign trade credit have been formed.

International experience shows that devaluations and other measures affecting foreign trade normally exert their influence only after a lag of several months. It can be hoped that the March 12 package will benefit the external equilibrium by the second half of the year. If it should turn out that the change is not strong enough then there should be no hesitation, in my view, about taking further measures. Ultimately it will be a year or two before the kind of profound structural change in Hungarian production, investment, consumption, and foreign trade is completed that can permanently improve the position of the trade and payments balances. I would not set numerical macroeconomic threshold values beyond which the country's external equilibrium situation could be called reassuring; instead, qualitative criteria should be designated.

The debt crisis must be given a wide berth, not just narrowly avoided. Full confidence in the country's creditworthiness must be restored. The country's credit rating, along with the assessment of the business prospects for investments in Hungary and of the risk entailed in loans to this country, must be restored at least to the level enjoyed in its best years from this point of view in the last decade.

4. INTERNAL FINANCIAL EQUILIBRIUM

The price to be paid for improving the external equilibrium will be a deterioration in other extremely important macro variables. The devaluation and import surcharge will hitch up the price level. It is too early to measure the effect, but dearer imports must certainly be expected to raise costs and thence prices. The first dilemma that arises here is to assess the relative importance of the tasks. Is a likely improvement in the external equilibrium worth the burden placed on the economy by a likely rise in the price level? The answer, in my view, must be affirmative: the former serves to avert a grave catastrophe, while the inflation rate, even if it rises somewhat, will still fall far short of catastrophic hyperinflation. The answer is affirmative even though some acceleration of inflation clearly will cause losses to many citizens, and will weigh heaviest on those least able to defend themselves. Of course, the assessment depends also on how great the inflationary thrust will be, and still more on whether the *acceleration* (i.e., the increase in the speed of inflation) continues or not. That would be a serious problem. A view of the course of inflation so far is given in Table 7. It would be desirable if the rate of inflation were to slow down after the initial push delivered by the devaluation.

Under prevailing conditions in Hungary, the permissible measure of inflation is limited by the commitments made by the government and the central bank concerning the exchange rate. The financial authorities announced in advance precisely what the forint exchange rate was going to be until 31 December 1995. This exchange-rate policy will achieve its purpose only if the buyers and sellers on the Hungarian foreign exchange market, which is fairly open and free, acquiesce to it not just verbally but also in the exchange-rate terms appearing in their transactions. Without going into the technical details, I would like to emphasize the implications for inflation. The planned trend in the exchange rate is based on a forecast concerning the widening of the gap between Hungarian inflation and inflation in the foreign currencies playing the main part in Hungarian foreign trade. According to the calculations of the finance ministry and the National Bank of Hungary, the preannounced exchange-rate course leaves room for the following normative limit on inflation, measured in terms of the consumer price index: the consumer price level at the end of the year may exceed the price level at a similar point in time

Table 7. *Consumer price indices*
in Hungary, 1988–95

Year	Average annual change (%)
1988	15.5
1989	17.0
1990	28.9
1991	35.0
1992	23.0
1993	22.5
1994	18.8
1995	
Jan.–March[a]	24.5
April[a]	29.2
May[a]	30.8
June[a]	31.0

[a] Compared with same period of previous year.
Sources: For 1988–94, Central Statistical Office (1995a, p. 40); for 1995, Central Statistical Office (1995b, pp. 31, 37) and information from the Central Statistical Office of Hungary.

last year by a maximum of 28–29%. This sum constitutes a normative requirement, not a forecast. It is an upper limit that must not be exceeded if the preannounced exchange rate is to be maintained.

Should Hungarian inflation turn out to be faster than this implicit inflation, a real appreciation of the Hungarian forint would take place: the National Bank of Hungary would have to give more dollars or marks for forints than they were really worth. When the currency market sensed the real appreciation, it would start expecting a devaluation sooner or later, a greater devaluation than was previously announced. So devaluation expectations would revive, which is just what prior announcement of the exchange-rate trend was supposed to avoid. One of the key issues in Hungarian economic policy is not to allow inflation to overstep the permissible limit. (If inflation should be *less* than the upper limit set by the exchange rate then that, of course, would have a favorable effect.) Whether inflation can be retained within this band depends mainly on two factors: wages and the budget deficit.

Wages. For many years, Hungary has experienced an inertial inflation in which expectations of price rises have fueled wage increases, and the increase in wages and other cost factors (or expectations of such an increase) have induced price rises. The question is whether the increase in the price of imports will filter through fully (or to a large extent) to wages. Devaluation usually meets with success when this effect is successfully impeded, at least for a while.[9] For this it is normally necessary to have a formal agreement between the government and the employers' and employees' organizations, but no such agreement has been reached in Hungary. Can this requirement be met without a formal agreement? Can it be forced by a narrowing of domestic demand, fear of higher unemployment, and recognition of the difficulties of the economic situation? It seems the answer differs from sector to sector. The wage pressure is far lower where the firm is close to the market – that is, in the competitive sphere of making tradable goods. The wage pressure is stronger, however, in the branches where there are no rivals competing, and where the wage rise need not be endorsed by the market but simply demanded from the government. Among cases that can be listed here are the monopoly or near-monopoly branches currently in state ownership, such as railways and electricity generation.

If wages start to swing, the devaluation will become almost ineffectual, and this country, like others, may be caught up in a destructive vortex: a vicious circle of devaluation, inflationary surge, and further devaluation.

The Budget. A budget deficit normally fuels inflation. There are exceptions to this – combinations of internal and external circumstances that allow a lasting budget deficit to coincide with a very low rate of inflation. Hungary is not one of the exceptions: there is strong connection in this country between the budget deficit and inflation.

One possible connection arises when the budget deficit is covered directly by the central bank in the form of credits. This is customarily called financing the deficit by "printing money." Hungarian legislation sets an upper limit to this form of financing, although to some extent the limit can be treated flexibly since it can be temporarily raised by passing occasional legislation.

---

[9] This was one of the reasons for the success of the Israeli stabilization in 1984. On the stabilization in Israel, see Bruno (1993), Fischer (1987), and Razin and Sadka (1993).

Table 8. *Indices of public debt*

Indices	1991	1992	1993	1994
Increase in gross public debt[a]				
(current prices, billions of Hungarian forints)	415.3	244.1	1,040.0	641.3
To domestic creditors	63.4	217.7	467.3	202.2
To foreign creditors	351.9	26.4	572.7	439.1
Increase in monetary base				
(current prices, billions of Hungarian forints)	179.9	188.3	172.1	178.6
Deficit financed by increasing public debt as				
percentage of total deficit financing	69.8	56.5	85.8	78.2
Deficit financed by broadening of monetary				
base as percentage of total deficit financing	30.2	43.5	14.2	21.8
Total domestic debt of consolidated public				
finance[b] as percentage of GDP	71.1	74.9	84.5	83.2

[a] Stated debt calculated by adding the gross debt of the budget and the National Bank of Hungary.
[b] Including devaluation debt. For an explanation of the devaluation debt, see Borbély and Neményi (1995).
Sources: Borbély and Neményi (1995, pp. 139, 145), and further calculations by Neményi.

The deficit can also be financed by issuing government securities for sale to investors at home and abroad.[10] This has increasingly become the main source of financing the deficit in recent years. (See Table 8, which presents the size of the budget deficit and the sources for financing it.)[11] It differs from printing money by *not* directly increasing the money supply (or more precisely the monetary base, which is the main force behind expansion and contraction of the money supply), but it has several other effects that can contribute indirectly to maintaining and even accelerating inflation. Let us ignore here the foreign loans, which were mentioned earlier. The domestic public debt has also grown to a threatening extent in recent years, which in itself deserves special attention. When the budget makes a very large demand on the domestic credit market, the price of credit (interest) is pushed up. The high nominal rate of interest will then be built into the inflationary expectations and so keep inflation high (or even speed it up in the case of a mounting deficit).

[10] From the macroeconomic point of view, a precisely equivalent procedure is when a loan is taken up directly by the central bank from a foreign creditor and lent on as credit to the budget.
[11] Pioneering work with retrospective processing, classification, and analysis of the data on Hungarian public debt was done by Borbély and Neményi (1994, 1995).

Another dangerous vicious circle has arisen. The high rate of interest raises the interest burden on the public debt, which comes to form a growing proportion of the budget deficit. The growing deficit, on the other hand, encourages the raising of new loans, and promises of still higher interest to satisfy the mounting demand. This again pushes the interest rate up, with an effect on the deficit, and so on.

There is nothing alarming in itself about a country having a sizeable public debt. This is customary not only at lower or medium levels of development, but in many mature market economies. What must be avoided is a mounting rate of increase in the public debt – a vortex of debt. This will ensue if the increase in the ratio of debt to GDP is accelerating. In this case it is obvious that tax revenues will sooner or later be unable to cover judicial, public-order, defense, and welfare spending, since the tax revenue will all go to financing debt repayments and interest; moreover, beyond a certain point, tax revenue will not even suffice for those. Hungary has not reached that stage, but several simulation calculations have shown that if the trend before March 1995 had continued, the country would have entered such a debt vortex in the foreseeable future and careered on toward financial ruin.[12]

We cannot resign ourselves to a vicious circle of budget deficits, high interest rates, and mounting state debt. But slowing it down and eventually halting it will require a whole range of measures. The credit demand from the budget is not the only factor affecting the interest rate, of course. A lot depends on the interest policy of the central bank and the commercial banks, on the efficiency of the banking sector, on institutional reforms to encourage personal savings (such as developing a system of voluntary pension and health-care funds), and on several other circumstances. I will not go on to these now. What can be said in any case is that reduction of the large budget deficit is a necessary condition for easing the demand pressure on the credit market. This will entail a great many changes on both sides of the budget.

On the expenditure side, the March 12 package can be considered a forceful *initial step*. As such it was a brave deed for the government and the majority in Parliament to take this first step in the face of so many kinds of opposition. There was a need for the radicalism and

---

[12] Long before the present stabilization program, the theoretical connections and numerical simulation of these processes were dealt with by Oblath and Valentinyi (1993). More recent calculations can be found in World Bank (1995b).

Table 9. *General government expenditure*
as a percentage of GDP: an
international comparison

Country	General government expenditure as percentage of GDP		
	1991	1992	1993
Bulgaria[a]	50.7	43.9	41.7
Czech Republic	54.2	52.8	48.5
Hungary	58.3	63.4	60.5
Poland[a]	48.0	50.7	48.4
Romania	40.4	42.2	31.0

Notes: The figures for general government expenditure
include central and local government expenditure and
expenditure of extrabudgetary funds. The figures reflect the consolidated budget; expenditure includes
interest payments, but not debt repayments.
[a] Spending does not include interest payments due but
not yet paid.
Source: Tyrie (1995, pp. 138–42).

forcefulness of the initial moves, to show that the government and the
majority in Parliament had ceased their hesitation and postponement of hard tasks and had committed themselves to action.

Unfortunately, when choosing the measures of the first package,
the following selection criterion was *not* applied: how to achieve the
necessary savings with the minimum sacrifice and consequently the
least public resistance. The stabilization program was published in a
way that failed to explain sufficiently clearly and convincingly what
its motives and likely results were.

Let us hope that the part of the stabilization package dealing with
the budget is only the start of reforming the whole system of public
finance. Although at this stage in the discussion I have only raised the
question of government expenditure in relation to inflation and the
budget deficit, in fact there is a deeper dilemma involved: How great
should the role of the state be in the economy and sociey? Before the
March 12 package, Hungary was devoting a higher proportion of its
GDP to budgetary expenditure than any country in the postsocialist
region (see Table 9). Although I would not join those taking an extreme libertarian view, seeking to reduce the state's role to the mini-

mum, I consider the role the state performs today (and still more yesterday) to be strongly out of proportion. A less centralized and more efficient administration is required.

This need for a smaller, cheaper, but more efficient state that can be supported on less tax should be the guiding idea behind the reform of public finance, in my view. One constituent of the reform is an overhaul of the welfare system. I would not recommend a complete withdrawal by the state, and I certainly do not subscribe to any agenda of demolishing the welfare state. The development of the welfare state is one of modern civilization's great achievements that must be preserved, but it would be worthwhile reducing its sphere and adding other mechanisms of provision.[13] I take the view that the role of centralized state participation in the welfare sphere financed by compulsory taxation should be reduced to more modest proportions. Welfare redistribution by the state needs augmenting to a far greater extent by nonprofit insurance and welfare service institutions based on voluntary employer and employee contributions. For those prepared to pay for them, there should be wider and more closely monitored services and insurance schemes available on a commercial basis. There is no room here to treat the reform of the welfare system in detail. I just wanted to point to the macroeconomic aspect of it, for this great and difficult social policy problem has a strong bearing on the question of overcoming the budget deficit.

For subsequent measures, it would be worth preparing much more thoroughly by paying close attention to the experts and representative organizations in specific fields and choosing much more carefully which spending items to reduce. Each cut raises a whole succession of specific dilemmas; it will take many tough decisions to outline the sphere of the direct losers and winners. When the regulations are being drawn up and a timetable decided for introducing them, it is not enough simply to aim at cutting the budget deficit. The prime consideration must be how best to dovetail the alterations into the overall reform of the welfare sector. The reduction in the state's obligations, the drop in taxes and compulsory contributions to finance them, and the establishment of new organizations based on voluntary payments should all take place concurrently, complementing each other in a

---

[13] This is also emphasized by Swedish economists critical of the excessive dimensions of the welfare system in the country that epitomizes the welfare state. They propose reforming the system – a considered reduction in the state's welfare spending along with other measures to make up for it – not a merciless elimination of it. See Lindbeck et al. (1994).

coordinated way. The greatest care must be taken to minimize the sacrifice accompanying the process and to ensure that it takes place as tactfully and humanely as possible. Citizens need to feel that in the longer term, even though the range of entitlements guaranteed by the state is narrowing, the tax burdens will also be less, so that the sovereignty of the individual and family grows and a higher proportion of income is at their disposal instead of the state's. It must be explained with great patience, compassion, and understanding that the reform of the welfare system will do a great service to the long-term interests of the whole of Hungarian society. Regrettably, these requirements were not met when the first group of measures to alter the welfare system were devised and announced. The omission contributed to the outcry and widespread opposition they encountered.

On the other side of the budget, tax revenues must rise. Development of the fiscal system has been one of the weakest points in Hungary's postsocialist transformation. In the struggle between tax evaders and tax officials, the former have proved much the sharper and more resourceful. For every change by the tax authorities, new loopholes have opened and new tricks been found by citizens intent on avoiding tax. The sections of the stabilization program dealing with taxation contained too much improvisation and sabre rattling and too many empty promises. I would recommend first and foremost broadening the tax base. The sphere of tax exemptions and concessions must be reduced and tax must be gathered from those intent on avoiding it. Here at last a "beneficial" circle can emerge. If tax morality improves and the tax base widens, tax rates can be lowered. For it is, above all, the almost insupportably high rates that have prompted people to evade tax and lurk in the "grey" economy. Hence rate cuts will broaden the tax base.

The question is often put as to what division of labor there should be between fiscal versus monetary policy when dealing with inflation. Some say the monetary policy should be far more restrictive, to make sure inflation is kept down even with an unchanged deficit. In my view this procedure is too costly and, if I may use the expression, too brutal. A draconian cut in the aggregate money supply and – as one of the main methods of doing this – a radical rise in the prime interest rates set by the central bank would have a detrimental effect on production and investment. It would weigh not only on loss-making, inefficient, nonviable enterprises, but on profitable, efficient, viable ones as well. In my view, the course of dramatically restricting the credit supply should be treated as an emergency brake, reserved for cases where inflation suddenly speeds up inordinately or a process of this kind threatens to get out of control. This leads to the next subject, the prospects for real production.

5. RECESSION VERSUS RECOVERY AND LASTING GROWTH

There has been widespread debate in recent years, in Hungary and internationally, about the causes of the recession that has developed during the postsocialist transition and about the conditions required for short-term recovery and for lasting growth.[14] In 1992–93 I hoped that the time for recovery had come, but it was too early. The government of the day confined itself to popular acts that would stimulate the economy – for instance, expanding the credit supply and aggregate domestic demand in general – while failing to take necessary but unpopular measures. For example, it did not carry out the currency devaluation many economists (including myself) were recommending, and actually continued a policy of real appreciation of the exchange rate. This was among the factors behind the appearance of ambivalent phenomena in the economy in 1994. Although the factors tending toward recovery strengthened, and there really was growth for the first time in many years, the equilibrium tensions heightened as well.

The debate over the question of contracting or expanding real production continues. Two extreme views can be found. One is to see a need for drastic contraction of production as the only way of curbing the "import hunger" and setting the trade and current-account balances to rights. Its adherents consider the contraction of production not as a negative, possibly inescapable side effect of a combined therapy but rather as the therapy itself. The view at the opposite end of the spectrum can be heard as well – that the present (or even higher) level of budget deficit must be accepted along with a further deterioration in the current account, for the sake of speeding up (rather than throttling) the recovery of production.

The March 12 stabilization program, or at least the published quantitative projections, eschew both these extremes. It does not

---

[14] For the debate in Hungary see Balassa (1994), Békesi (1995), Csaba (1995), Erdős (1994), Kopits (1994), Kornai (1993, 1995a), and Köves (1995). Of the foreign writings I would pick the following: Berg (1994), Calvo and Coricelli (1993), Holzmann, Gács, and Winckler (1995), Kolodko (1993), and Saunders (1995).

Table 10. *Utilization of gross domestic product*

Indices[a]	1991	1992	1993	1994[b]	1995[c]
1. Household consumption	68.6	72.8	74.0	73.6	71.2
2. Collective consumption[d]	9.4	12.0	14.4	11.7	10.4
3. Total final consumption $(1 + 2)^{d, e}$	80.6	84.8	88.4	85.3	81.6
4. Total investment	20.4	15.5	19.9	21.5	22.1
5. Domestic absorption $(3 + 4)$	101.1	100.3	108.2	106.8	103.7
6. Balance of foreign trade	-1.1	-0.3	-8.2	-6.8	-3.7
Exports	$-$	31.5	26.5	28.7	32.7
Imports	$-$	31.8	34.7	35.5	36.4

[a] All values given as a percentage of GDP.
[b] Preliminary data.
[c] Forecast.
[d] Including arms imports from Russia in repayment of earlier debt.
[e] The sum of total final consumption in 1991 includes the bank dividend not distributed between households and the state budget, for lack of a source of data (HUF 64.4 billion, or 2.6% of GDP).
Sources: For 1991, Central Statistical Office (1994b, pp. 72, 73); for 1992–93, Central Statistical Office (1995a, pp. 107, 108); for 1994–95, based on data and estimates by Hungarian Ministry of Finance.

contain immediate measures to promote directly an upswing of production. For the time being, the program is instead content (owing to the gravity of financial and foreign trade tensions) with far more modest production goals than could have been undertaken if the macroeconomic policy of the last two or three years had been more balanced. It aims at *no fall* in GDP and even, if possible, a continuation of 1994's growth at a lower level of 1–2%. At this production level, the program envisages a *restructuring* in the utilization of production, with the shares of exports and investment rising and that of consumption – especially collective, budget-financed consumption – falling. As far as the origin of total domestic absorption is concerned, there should be a growth in the share of domestically produced products and services and a fall in the share of imports.[15] (See Table 10.) The speed and depth of restructuring depends on several factors, among them the measures presented in the study so far. Experience will show how

[15] The requirement of rapid restructuring within a growth target already set at a more modest level was one of the fundamental ideas running through an article I published in 1994 in Hungarian (Kornai 1995a). So far as I can judge, the March 12 program is very close in this respect to the proposal I made then. Another idea in the article also found a place in the program's rationale: the need for "parallel concurrence" of moves to improve the equilibrium and measures to support growth.

fast the restructuring can take place. I do not wish to disguise the fact that I have many worries and uncertainties about this. Will the measures not overshoot the target, causing a sudden, excessive fall in aggregate demand? Will this not be accompanied by a bigger contraction in production than expected? If this happens, will it not lead to a fall in tax revenues that undermines the original objective of reducing the budget deficit?

Another cause for serious concern connected with the contraction of production is the conflict between short-term and long-term thinking. Hungary must today navigate under extremely difficult conditions, steering between several Scyllas and Charybdises at once. The danger is that the leaders responsible for the economy will be almost entirely taken up with short-term problems. This is a practice that cannot be accepted, if for no other reason than because constant postponement of the long-term tasks is what led to the present accumulation of troubles. There is a range of tasks that must be done *now* so that they can contribute to lasting growth after a longish gestation period. It is most important to assess every urgent task today not simply from the "fire fighting" point of view of averting catastrophe, but in terms of deeper, systemic, transformation-oriented reforms and lasting growth, so that decisions are reached after consciously weighing short-term–long-term dilemmas. A few examples may be listed as follows.

Present-day budget revenue is a major factor in reaching decisions on privatization, but it cannot be the sole criterion. No less important are the commitments a potential new owner will make to increasing capital, accomplishing investment projects, and bringing in new technologies.

In developing the financial sector, it is worth bearing in mind how the banks can contribute to resolving today's problems of external and internal equilibrium. But it is no less important to establish institutions for long-term lending and expand the credit available for production and housing investment. This involves establishing the conditions required for long-term deposits to become widespread, building up a network of voluntary pension and health funds, and developing more active investment activities by these funds and private insurance companies.

Overall state spending must be reduced, but it would be worth increasing the proportion within such spending of the sums devoted to investment.

However tough the measures required for reducing the budget deficit, the lessons of modern growth theory must not be forgotten: among the most important factors behind growth are research designed to assist production, enhancement of the skills of the work force, and modernization of professional knowledge. The development of these factors requires constant finances, and these must not be constricted even temporarily.

More stress on such long-term considerations can also help to win political acceptance for the stabilization program. Although the radicalism of these measures and their speed of introduction arose mainly out of a need to avert short-term difficulties and still greater trauma in the future, this argument alone is incapable of persuading millions to accept sacrifices that cause woe and suffering over a long period. If they are willing to accept this at all, it will be in the hope of a better future. Yet any convincing presentation of such a future has been almost wholly absent from the arguments in favor of the stabilization program. This leads to the last problem area covered in the study, the relationship between the economy and politics.

6. ECONOMIC AND POLITICAL STABILITY

The sections of the study so far have dealt with dilemmas over conflicts between different economic requirements. They covered trade-offs of a kind where the more one economic criterion is satisfied, the greater the concession that has to be made on another. There is, however, a still graver dilemma: conflicting requirements of economic and political stability.

What does past international experience show about the political requirements for stabilization programs? Strict and tough programs have been implemented successfully by strict and tough military dictatorships or other autocratic political regimes, such as Pinochet's Chile or South Korea before democratization. Restrictive measures have also been successfully applied by democratically elected governments, like Margaret Thatcher's Conservatives, but in that case the government had received a mandate especially for this task from an electorate fed up with the economic disarray under previous Labor governments. Also successful with a draconian program was Poland's Solidarity government in the early 1990s, which took advantage of its mass support at a unique historical moment when there was initial euphoria over the change of system.

Today's Hungarian coalition government is committed to maintaining parliamentary democracy. This rules out the autocratic type of solution. On the other hand, there is an absence of the kind of strong mass support (long-term or temporary) enjoyed by Thatcher or Balcerowicz.

So what kind of rearguard political defense can the program expect? To some extent it can rely on technocratic groups, as well as on some sections of the liberal intelligentsia with influence over public opinion. Entrepreneurs more or less agree with the program, with many reservations and criticisms, and can be expected to support it so long as it opens up the road to growth, from which they expect greater and safer earnings. It can hope for tolerance, if not support, from employees in expanding branches and firms and at workplaces where surplus labor has already been shed – in other words, from employees who do not feel their direct interests are infringed. Will this level of support (or passive endurance) suffice?

The initial reactions were mixed. Relatively few Socialist Party members in government and Parliament came out against the March 12 program, and those who did rejected it only in part. Party solidarity and cohesion, and the desire to remain in government, more or less prevailed in the Socialist Party. Even those who are against the program in their hearts, or by sensing the mood of their constituents, realized that defeat for the government would mean losing power, which they feared to risk. In the end the stabilization bill was passed by a big majority in Parliament, with relatively little amendment.

The parliamentary opposition came out strongly against the program, accusing the government of needlessly torturing the people. The popularity of the opposition party that used the strongest rhetoric to attack the stabilization program rose by several percentage points in a matter of weeks. A curious reversal of roles has taken place in Hungary. The Socialist Party, having won the elections by emphasizing its social sensitivity, is carrying out an almost "Thatcherite" program. Meanwhile, politicians who describe themselves as a conservative, center-right force are espousing social democratic arguments for the overblown welfare state and employees' wage demands.

As mentioned before, Hungary's model political peacefulness is over. Various forms of extraparliamentary protest have appeared with great intensity. Many strata and interest groups have already lodged protests, or at least criticized the program harshly. In a matter of months there were examples of all sorts of mass protest, from public

condemnations on television and in the press to street demonstrations and deputations to Parliament, and from strike threats to the
first actual strikes. The extreme right wing outside Parliament called
for civil disobedience and a tax boycott. All this may be only the beginning, as little of the effect of implementing the program has yet
been felt, and the March 12 package is not the end of the story in any
case. More restrictive measures will certainly be needed in the future
to cut the budget deficit further. If the foreign trade situation does not
improve sufficiently, the government may be forced to take further
painful measures for that reason as well.

7. THREE SCENARIOS

At the time of this writing there is no way to predict which way Hungary is bound. Several eventualities can be envisaged. I will confine
myself here to outlining three clearly defined scenarios.

7.1. Return to the Policy of "Muddling Through"

After a time, the present government or a reshuffled version of it returns to the well-trodden Hungarian road. Substantial concessions
are made to mass pressure, the stabilization program is toned down,
and the pace of implementation slowed. Actions classed as urgent
from the economic point of view are further delayed. The reduction
of state paternalism stalls at its present level. The government resigns
itself to a slow rate of growth or even stagnation. With luck, the policy does not end in catastrophe. (The bounds of this scenario are exceeded if it does.) It is not impossible to imagine that the policy of
muddling through could be continued for a good while after 1995,
although it will lose the country its chance of achieving rapid and
lasting growth.

There are many forces working to persuade those in power to abandon the course taken in the spring of 1995 and return to the old. Apart
from the ingrained Hungarian habits of decades, parliamentary democracy entices politicians to behave in this way – watching the public opinion polls and adjusting their policies to suit the requirements
of popularity.

The experience of several countries shows that the more fragmented is the political scene and the less institutionalized is the long-

term rule of some political grouping, the less inclined is the prevailing government to take unpopular actions with slow political return. Anticipation of political defeat in the foreseeable future is no incentive to embark on "altruistic" reforms with long-term prospects that entail thinking ahead over decades. Politicians are even more inclined than the general public to think in terms of the well-known Keynesian formula: "In the long run, we are all dead."

7.2. Perseverance and Political Downfall

The assumption in this case is that the present government perseveres with the strict principles of the stabilization program and is ready to carry it out consistently, but fails to obtain the political support for doing so. The resistance steadily grows, perhaps manifesting itself in a wave of strikes that paralyzes the economy or in mass protest of other kinds. This further damages the economic situation, making even stricter measures necessary, so that society enters a self-destructive spiral of restriction and resistance. On reaching a critical point, the process leads to the political downfall of the present government and its policies.

It is not worthwhile in this study to speculate at length on when and how this might happen. Would it come in 1998, at the next general elections? Or could it occur earlier, when the government party's own members desert them on a critical vote? I do not even include the possibility that the upheaval might bring down parliamentary democracy as well as the government, because I do not think there is a realistic danger of this happening in present-day Hungary.

If the government, adhering to the stabilization program, succumbs politically, its successor is quite likely (though not sure) to take up a different policy. It may return to the old Hungarian road of muddling through, for instance, or embark on a yet more perilous populist, adventurist policy, but this again points beyond the second scenario.[16]

---

[16] I do not want to hide my feeling that many foreign observers take too little account in their calculations of this political risk. I consider this especially dangerous and maybe damaging in the case of those whose positions may give them influence over events in Hungary, for instance, those who participate in decisions relating to Hungary in foreign governments or international organizations. It depends also on them whether the threat to Hungary described in the second scenario passes. A breakdown of political stability would pull the rug from under economic stabilization, not to mention the direct economic harm done by radical forms of mass protest.

7.3. Success After Delay

It is not unrealistic, given our knowledge of Hungarian conditions, to hope for a relatively favorable succession of events. The government may manage to do a better job of explaining why and how the stabilization program serves the public's interests. The resistance may not be so vehement. The storm of initial protest may blow itself out and patience come to prevail. The foreseeable future may bring favorable trends in the living standards of broad groups in the population, so that the atmosphere improves. The word "may" makes the uncertainty plain. I must add that much depends on how the stabilization program's active participants behave – the government, Parliament, political parties, interest groups, employers, and employees.

I do not see it as my task to weigh the chances for the three scenarios and the various intermediate and mixed cases, or to put subjective odds on the alternatives. I would like to hope the third scenario prevails, but I am ready to support the stabilization program even if the second scenario threatens. I am convinced that the good of present and future Hungarian generations requires us to find a new road that ensures lasting development.

REFERENCES

Balassa, Ákos (1994), "Van-e válság, és ha igen, miféle?" [Is There a Crisis, and If So, What Kind?], *Népszabadság*, October 29, pp. 17, 21.

Békesi, László (1995), "Mást választhatunk, de 'jobbat' aligha" [A Different Program Can Be Chosen, But a 'Better' One Hardly], *Népszabadság*, July 8, pp. 17–18.

Berg, Andrew (1994), "Supply and Demand Factors in the Output Decline in East and Central Europe," *Empirica* 21(1): 3–36.

Borbély, László András, and Judit Neményi (1994), "Az államadósság növekedésének összetevői 1990–1992-ben" [The Factors behind the Growth of the Public Debt, 1990–92], *Közgazdasági Szemle* 41(2): 110–26.

Borbély, László András, and Judit Neményi (1995), "Eladósodás, a külső és belső államadósság alakulása az átmenet gazdaságában (1990–93)" [Indebtedness, the Development of External and Internal Public Debt in the Economy of Transition, 1990–93], in Tamás Mellár (ed.), *Rendszerváltás és stabilizáció. A piacgazdasági átmenet első évei* [Change of System and Stabilization. The First Years of Transition to a Market Economy]. Budapest: Magyar Trendkutató Központ, pp. 123–66.

Bruno, Michael (1993), *Crisis, Stabilization and Economic Reform: Therapy by Consensus.* Oxford, UK: Oxford University Press.

Calvo, Guillermo, and Fabrizio Coricelli (1993), "Output Collapse in Eastern Europe," *IMF Staff Papers* 40(1): 32–52.

Central Statistical Office (Központi Statisztikai Hivatal) (1989), *Tudományos kutatás és kísérleti fejlesztés 1988* [Scientific Research and Experimental Development 1988]. Budapest.

Central Statistical Office (Központi Statisztikai Hivatal) (1991), *Hungarian Statistical Yearbook 1991.* Budapest.

Central Statistical Office (Központi Statisztikai Hivatal) (1994a), *Magyar statisztikai zsebkönyv 1993* [Hungarian Statistical Pocket Book 1993]. Budapest.

Central Statistical Office (Központi Statisztikai Hivatal) (1994b), *Magyar statisztikai évkönyv 1993* [Hungarian Statistical Yearbook 1993]. Budapest.

Central Statistical Office (Központi Statisztikai Hivatal) (1994c), *Lakásstatisztikai évkönyv 1993* [Yearbook of Housing Statistics 1993]. Budapest.

Central Statistical Office (Központi Statisztikai Hivatal) (1994d), *Tudományos kutatás és kísérleti fejlesztés 1993* [Scientific Research and Experimental Development 1993]. Budapest.

Central Statistical Office (Központi Statisztikai Hivatal) (1995a), *Magyar statisztikai zsebkönyv 1994* [Hungarian Statistical Pocket Book 1994]. Budapest.

Central Statistical Office (Központi Statisztikai Hivatal) (1995b), *Tájékoztató*, No. 1. Budapest.

Central Statistical Office (Központi Statisztikai Hivatal) (1995c), *Magyar statisztikai évkönyv 1994* [Hungarian Statistical Yearbook 1994]. Budapest.

Csaba, László (1995), "Gazdaságstratégia helyett konjunktúra-politika" [Trade-Cycle Policy Instead of Economic Strategy], *Külgazdaság* 39(3): 36–46.

Erdős, Tibor (1994), "A tartós gazdasági növekedés realitásai és akadályai" [The Realities of Lasting Economic Growth and Obstacles to It], *Közgazdasági Szemle* 41(6): 463–77.

Fischer, Stanley (1987), "The Israeli Stabilization Program, 1985–1986," *American Economic Review* 77(2): 275–8.

Holzmann, Robert, János Gács, and Georg Winckler (eds.) (1995), *Output Decline in Eastern Europe: Unavoidable, External Influence or Homemade?* (International Studies in Economics and Econometrics, vol. 34). Dordrecht: Kluwer.

Kolodko, Grzegorz W. (1993), "From Output Collapse to Sustainable Growth in Transition Economies. The Fiscal Implications," Working Paper no. 35, Institute of Finance, Warsaw.

Kopits, György (1994), "Félúton az átmenetben" [Halfway through the Transition], *Közgazdasági Szemle* 41(6): 478–97.

Kornai, János (1972), *Rush versus Harmonic Growth*. Amsterdam: North-Holland.

Kornai, János (1993), "Transformational Recession: A General Phenomenon Examined through the Example of Hungary's Development," *Economie Appliquée* 46(2): 181–227.

Kornai, János (1995a), "Lasting Growth as the Top Priority. Macroeconomic Tensions and Government Economic Policy in Hungary," *Acta Oeconomica* 47(1–2): 1–38.

Kornai, János (1995b), "Dilemmas of the Hungarian Economic Policy," *Acta Oeconomica* 47(3–4): 227–48.

Köves, András (1995), "Egy alternatív gazdaságpolitika szükségessége és lehetösége" [The Necessity and Scope for an Alternative Economic Policy], *Külgazdaság* 39(6): 4–17.

Krugman, Paul (1994), *Peddling Prosperity. Economic Sense and Nonsense in the Age of Diminished Expectations*. New York: Norton.

Larrain, Felipe, and Marcelo Selowsky (eds.) (1991), *The Public Sector and the Latin American Crisis*. San Francisco: ICS Press and International Center for Economic Growth.

Lindbeck, Assar, Per Molander, Torsten Persson, Olof Petersson, Agnar Sandmo, Birgitta Swedenborg, and Niels Thygesen (1994), *Turning Sweden Around*. Cambridge, MA: MIT Press.

National Bank of Hungary (1993), *Monthly Report* no. 1 (January). Budapest.

National Bank of Hungary (1994), *Annual Report 1993*. Budapest.

National Bank of Hungary (1995), *Monthly Report* no. 3 (March). Budapest.

Oblath, Gábor, and Ákos Valentinyi (1993), "Seigniorage és inflációs adó – néhány makroökonómiai összefüggés magyarországi alkalmazása. I. A pénzteremtésböl eredö állami bevétel és az államadósság. II. Az államháztartás, a jegybank és az államadósság dinamikája" [Seigniorage and Inflationary Tax – Application to Hungary of a Few Macroeconomic Relations. I. State Revenue from Money Creation and Public Debt. II. The Budget, the Bank of Issue and the Dynamics of Public Debt], *Közgazdasági Szemle* 40(10): 825–47; 40(11): 939–74.

Razin, Assaf, and Efraim Sadka (1993), *The Economy of Modern Israel: Malaise and Promise*. University of Chicago Press.

Sachs, Jeffrey (ed.) (1989), *Developing Country Debt and Economic Performance*. University of Chicago Press / National Bureau of Economic Research.

Saunders, Christopher T. (ed.) (1995), *Eastern Europe in Crisis and the Way Out*. Houndmills and London: Vienna Institute for Comparative Studies and Macmillan.

Sunkel, Osvaldo (ed.) (1993), *Development from Within. Toward a Neostructuralist Approach for Latin America*. Boulder: Lynne Rienner.

Tyrie, Andrew (1995), "Statistical Review. Recent Macroeconomic Developments," *Economics of Transition* 3(1): 129–48.

United Nations Economic Commission for Europe [UNECE] (1993), *Economic Bulletin for Europe 1992*, vol. 44. New York: United Nations.

Williamson, John (ed.) (1990), *Latin American Adjustment. How Much Has Happened?* Washington, DC: Institute for International Economics.

World Bank (1995a), "Hungary: Structural Reforms for Sustainable Growth," Report no. 13577-HU (first draft, 10 February), Country Operations Division, Central Europe Department, World Bank, Washington, DC.

World Bank (1995b), "Hungary: Structural Reforms for Sustainable Growth," Report no. 13577-HU (12 June), Country Operations Division, Central Europe Department, World Bank, Washington, DC.

World Bank (1995c), *World Tables 1995.* Washington, DC: World Bank.

CHAPTER 7

Preparation and Implementation of a Credible Stabilization Program in the Republic of Croatia

Nikica Valentić

1. POLITICAL FRAMEWORK

Croatia fought for and achieved its political independence in the early nineties, at a time of major changes in Eastern Europe. The process evolving in Croatia has since its beginning been democratically oriented and was triggered by democratic elections. Two principles formed the basis of our national credo: market economy and high democratic social standards.

However, the Yugoslav leadership of that period, under dominating Serbian influence, decided to wage a war against Croatia – exploiting all resources of the former state, especially the military. Croatia found itself in the position of facing radical sociopolitical structural changes while at the same time being exposed to the brutal aggression triggered by Serbian ambitions.

With the exception of a few individuals and states, the world did not understand our situation, so that Croatia faced dramatic moments for its existence. We were exposed to international pressure after being unjustly labeled as a state that does not respect human rights and freedom of the press. At that time, however, Croatia experienced the massive political support of its population in forming the state and implementing a program for independence and international affirmation of state interest.

In spite of adverse circumstances, Croatia continues to abide by the ideals of a democratic society, a state of law, and a market economy. Even in the most critical moments of the war, Croatia persevered in the implementation of its privatization and reconstruction program. This was made more difficult because Croatia lacked the support of the international community and so had to survive in an unfavorable political and economic environment. International monetary and other institutions were waiting for the crisis to end, so the expected inflow of foreign capital was frozen due to high risk.

I should mention that war damages were climbing to tens of billions of dollars, industrial production was stagnating, and one of the key economic branches – tourism – had almost ceased to exist. The number of refugees and displaced persons was increasing every day. As a result, high inflation set in. Nevertheless, Croatia decided to establish its monetary authority and issued its national currency, first the "Croatian dinar" and then the "kuna." It was an exceptionally audacious step, evoking amazement even in international circles. We realized that a national currency would be a symbol of independence and, more importantly, the foundation of our stabilization program and hence of the rehabilitation and development of the Croatian economy. We carried out our monetary reform without any foreign exchange reserves, and today such reserves exceed $2.5 billion in the entire banking system.

Croatia was forced to arm itself, so that expenses for defense and security rose continuously. Since Croatia is by constitutional definition a social state, the government is responsible for solving many serious problems: unemployment, providing for the considerable number of retired persons, and the consequences of numerous casualties from the war imposed on the country.

Internationally recognized, the Republic of Croatia is gaining friends in the world who support its pacifist policy, and is becoming a factor of stability and peace in this region of the world. Nevertheless, Croatia had to free its occupied territories and accomplished this with strengthened military power. The areas in the very south of Croatia (around Dubrovnik), then Maslenica, Western Slavonia, the plateau of Miljevac, and the pocket of Medak have been freed. All of this confirms the fact that Croatia is a respectable state, apt for international partnership.

The government relies on a stable political majority in the Parliament, a strong political party (the Croatian Democratic Union), and the personal support of president Tudman, as well as the backing of the population. Even the other political parties, regardless of their oppositional position, accept the fundamental principles of our political and economic program. All these factors allow the government to execute its duty within the framework of its authorization and its considerable reputation. When I assumed office in the spring of 1993, the government faced many open issues. Society was willing to make sacrifices, but required a decisive program and courageous decisions.

2. PREPARATION OF THE PROGRAM

Since the very beginning of my government's mandate in April 1993, we have been aware that the success of our economic policy would depend on its credibility – that is to say, the logical harmony of measures and instruments. On this credibility depended our ability to mobilize all resources within the government for a program that would be understood and supported both by ministers and administrative apparatus. On this credibility depended also our ability to provide convincing answers to the critique of oppositional parties, experts, and the general public (including the suspicions of international economic and financial circles), as well as our ability to enable the majority of citizens to understand and identify with the objectives of our stabilization program. On this credibility, finally, depended our ability to resist the pressures of interest groups and lobbies.

The message we sent out every day to the public before the announcement of our October program can be summarized in one sentence: *Inflation is an evil that distorts market activity and burdens the poorer social classes,* so inflation must be reduced. I pointed out publicly that our entire government, and especially myself, was prepared to take full political responsibility if we failed to reduce inflation by the end of 1993. We consciously announced a deadline, led by the belief that one should always promise less than what can objectively be achieved. During that period, however, we had no precise economic information at our disposal on how much and by when inflation could actually be reduced, so that the estimated relationship between our promises and objective possibilities was based on our intuition. Later it turned out that we had been correct in our assessment.

Prior to October 1993, we gradually built and maintained a reputation as an anti-inflation government, and succeeded in convincing the population that they had a compact and competent government. For instance, we fulfilled our promise to solve the acute energy problem in Dalmatia and strengthened our fiscal administration, which led to a significant reduction of our budget deficit as early as 1993.

The elaboration of program strategy was placed in the hands of a team of young Croatian economists. In choosing the team members, we discounted the factor of experience, because we felt that someone who had participated in forming the old socialist system would not be able to efficiently and quickly design a new system. At the same time, we began to analyze the behavior of political groups that, according to our assessment, were powerful enough to influence the fate of our program.

Above all, this applies to the *debtors' lobby*. Decades of high inflation and negative real interest rates have redistributed wealth from currency holders to debtors. Prior to the announcement we had expected that real interest rates would rise after inflation was reduced, and likewise we had expected strong political reactions from those affected by higher interest rates.

The second interest group, closely connected with the first one, is that of *structural lobbies*. These lobbies are composed of formal and informal affiliates expressing the interests of various enterprises that had been privileged by the socialist industrial policy. In the first post-socialist years, owing to the leadership's preoccupation with political and military events, these enterprises continued to enjoy fiscal and other selective preferences. Because we planned to stimulate the *market* economy (by reducing inflation) in order to provide equal opportunities for all, we expected significant opposition by exactly these lobbies.

The third kind of lobby consists of *regional lobbies*. Debtors' and structural lobbies could express their interests through local authorities in the regions where local enterprises suffered heavy losses (Istra, Slavonia, Dalmatia). Since regional lobbies seem to find easy channels of influence through the state's vertical political structures, we expected that such regional interests would be articulated up to the level of the Parliament of the Republic of Croatia.

Trade unions constitute another powerful political influence. Experience shows that Croatian trade unions react more strongly to changes in nominal wages than to changes in real wages. Because the growth rate of nominal wages was publicly slowed by means of an enactment, we anticipated this reaction. Moreover, trade unions are easily influenced by the other lobbies mentioned and may form strong (formal or informal) coalitions with them.

When we announced our program, we had not devised specific strategies to fight individual lobbies and organizations. We believed we had a strong anti-inflation reputation, a professionally developed program, strong political support, and a united government. For this reason we were confident of easily securing a majority in government

or Parliament. We also had at our disposal *decree laws,* a very powerful
temporary means of regulation with legal force. We knew that, because of the war, a strong national cohesion had been reached and
that aspirations were lower than usual, but we also knew that the Croatian people were nevertheless hoping for optimistic forecasts in the
economic areas of life. We therefore focused the announcement of
our program to achieve the strongest possible effect of surprise.

3. ANNOUNCEMENT OF THE PROGRAM

On Sunday night, 3 October 1993, I announced the program on Croatian television and achieved the desired effect. No businessman or
banker had anticipated our program, and so had not speculated on
the foreign exchange market. (Until Saturday morning, October 2,
except for Vice Prime Minister Borislav Škegro and myself, only four
persons from the narrowest informal counseling team had precise
information on the program.) Our program was simple, convincing,
and comprehensible: it contained precisely projected figures on the
growth of nominal wages and the nominal monetary base, on the
discount rate, and on the weakest level of the exchange rate that the
central bank was willing to accept. This part of the program was explained as the first stabilization stage, aimed at reducing inflation.
The program contained, furthermore, a second and third stage with
the objectives of maintaining low inflation and leading the country
into lasting growth. In addition to mechanisms for maintaining fiscal
balance, these stages incorporate measures for the privatization and
microeconomic reconstruction of banks and enterprises as well as
further liberalization and social policy. Such a program was easy to
explain, defend, and believe in. It was also compact, and represented
a long-term concept.

What followed was intense media exposure. In the first few days
after the announcement of the program, we visited all Croatian coun-
ties. Daily, we held four or five major meetings, inviting hundreds
of businessmen and politicians; this meant facing 400–500 influential
people every day. By the end of October we had directly encountered
about 5,000 decision makers.

The communication strategy for all meetings was simple. Aware
of the advantage of having achieved a surprise effect, we insisted on
openness and avoidance of hierarchical formalism. After briefly pre-
senting the program, we invited the participants to express their views

and ask questions. We also asked them to make concrete proposals, which allowed us to learn a great deal from their reactions. At the same time, people started to feel themselves a significant part of the process, which greatly facilitated their acceptance of the objectives and measures of the stabilization program.

The stage of program presentation was already slowing down when, just at the right time, something happened that justified our vision: around October 20, the national currency started to increase in value. This was a first concrete result, enhancing the surprise effect, because the majority of the population had never in their lifetime seen the national currency appreciate on foreign exchange markets and indeed many ministers had believed it never would happen. We used our informal contacts with the black market (which was expiring at that moment) every two hours in order to determine the differential. In spite of the fact that a high inflation rate – by which price growth was measured between September 20 and October 20 – had recently been published, this information did not excite anyone. Around November 1, all ad hoc information and the steady appreciation of the exchange rate indicated that the battle against inflation had been won.

However, the final victory was not declared even after official figures for November had been published, showing an inflation of 1.4% in retail prices and a producer price deflation of 4.6%. We still abide by our golden rule of promising less than can objectively be achieved. Although we did not hide our satisfaction, we emphasized publicly that two stabilization stages were yet to come.

At the time we did not witness any serious opposition to the program, owing to its spectacular success. Even opposition parties turned into allies, tacitly or openly supporting the program thanks to their belief in the program itself and the people implementing it. We were nevertheless conscious of the fact that political and lobbyist resistance would arise.

4. CURRENT SITUATION

Nineteen months after the program's announcement, the period of stable prices is persisting. Very low inflation, still among the lowest in Europe, reflects our fiscal stability. According to very conservative estimates, GDP increased in 1994 by 0.8%. Real wages are growing, while control of public enterprises – which in the meantime have stopped suffering losses – has been tightened. Nonetheless, public enterprises have considerable potential for increased effectiveness. We have begun with their reconstruction and preparation for privatization. Meanwhile, we plan to rehabilitate two major regional banks, after which we project the recovery of the largest bank according to a special plan. The legal framework for establishing a market economy is now being defined, and we are close to passing some very important laws: the new privatization law, the law on protection of market competition, and the law on investment funds.

Government is facing two major problems. The first is connected with the unrealistically high expectations of the population. The period of high inflation is long forgotten, and as fast a rise in prosperity as first appeared cannot be repeated. For this reason, the government must "cool down" the public and renew promises below objective possibilities, but today this is a difficult task. We face cheap political populism from both the opposition and the leading party, in that certain MPs do not refrain from unrealistic promises. The public is led to believe in fanciful scenarios, such as a cut in taxes and a simultaneous growth of pensions and public-sector wages. This is why we must make every effort to thwart unrealistic aspirations.

The second problem is connected with the establishment of a new lobby – the *manager lobby*. Owing to the intensified process of reconstruction and privatization, managers of banks or large enterprises that are still (mostly or completely) owned by the state have slipped into an unfavorable position. Nevertheless, we must continue to cooperate with these people, since there are not enough alternative teams of managers who could take over. Hence we are forced to proceed at a slower pace, because we must balance the external pressures on enterprises with their inner ability to change and adapt.

5. CONCLUSION

In 1981, the regime of that time filed charges against me because, among other reasons, the company I was managing made too much profit; I was accused of being a manager "of the Western kind." Many of my former colleagues have not faced such adversities, yet now must embrace the fundamental principles of business effectiveness: how to cut expenses and increase profit. I would therefore like to convey to Croatian managers that we are building a system without soft budget constraints, and without cheap redemption for their mistakes. I believe in market competition, and believe that it is the perfect social mechanism for preserving the vitality of a society that offers everyone a chance to succeed. There may be different types of market-oriented systems, but for all types I hold that *stability* is the vital prerequisite for the development of a sound market and democratic society. This was my firm conviction when I became Prime Minister, and today I know I was right.

Inflation was reduced in the Republic of Croatia in times between war and peace, with the number of refugees and displaced persons amounting to 8% of the total population, in conditions where great parts of the country were without normally priced electricity, in the face of international indifference, and without a dollar of help from international monetary institutions. If inflation can be conquered in such conditions, is there any justification for its existence? I firmly believe that the answer is: No.

In concluding, allow me to point out that Croatia has become a member of international organizations and a partner of international monetary institutions. It holds a clear position in Europe, so that eventual access to European institutions is expected as well. Croatia has become a significant political player and an increasingly desirable economic partner.

We truly believe in our program: striving for a stable national currency, production growth, entrepreneurship, social stability, and general economic progress. These objectives are not only pursued by the government, they are based on a general national consensus as well.

CHAPTER 8

Exchange Rate and Prices in a
Stabilization Program: The Case of Croatia

Velimir Šonje and Marko Škreb

INTRODUCTION

Croatia has achieved remarkable results in stopping high inflation
and maintaining price stability. After the average monthly rate of
inflation for January–October 1993 had reached almost 28%, November inflation was negligible and deflation occurred during 1994. Price
stability was achieved without direct price controls, mainly by using
the exchange rate: both nominal and real exchange rate appreciated
immediately after announcement of the program. Real money supply has recorded significant rates of growth since November 1993,
and real output showed signs of the recovery during 1994. The aim
of this essay is to explain the link between the exchange rate and
prices during this particular stabilization episode.

Standard explanations of exchange-rate and price dynamics assume integrated financial markets that ensure arbitrage conditions,
as well as a stable money demand function (see e.g. Dornbusch 1976).
Neither of these assumptions seems plausible for a country like Croatia. Money and capital markets are underdeveloped, regional risk
contributes to imperfect capital mobility, and real money declined
during high inflation (mostly as a result of currency substitution). In
order to analyze the interplay between the exchange rates and prices
we use an aggregate-demand–aggregate-supply model with the exchange rate as a cost–push factor.

In the first section we describe some basic facts about the Croatian
economy, and explain the first obstacle to the direct transmission of
exchange-rate fluctuations into aggregate prices: an increase in the
relative price of nontradables. In the second section we discuss the
second obstacle: a change in the exchange-rate regime. In the third
section we summarize findings by showing the importance of the exchange rate as a cost–push factor in an aggregate-demand–aggregate-

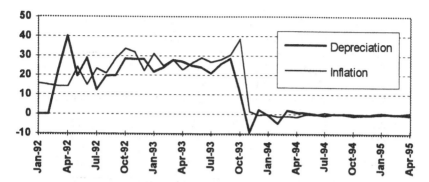

Figure 1. Monthly inflation and the rate of depreciation versus the
deutsche mark, 1992Q1–1995Q4.

supply model. In the last section we derive some policy prescriptions
and discuss the general importance of the results for economies in
transition.

1. THE CROATIAN ECONOMY 1992–95

Exchange Rate and Aggregate Prices

High inflation in Croatia ended in November 1993, after the announcement of the stabilization program in October.[1] The exchange
rate was the main tool of the stabilization project.

In Figure 1, the depreciation line goes below the inflation line starting in mid-1992, meaning that the real bilateral exchange rate[2] was
appreciating before price stabilization. The two lines remain close
after stabilization, indicating that the real bilateral exchange rate did
not change significantly during 1994 and 1995. However, there is no
doubt that the announcement of stabilization gave additional impulse
to real appreciation, although it did not change the historical sign
of the change. This can be verified by yearly data. Annual averages
of the real bilateral exchange-rate index are displayed in Table 1,
together with the main balance-of-payments data.

Croatia accumulated substantial international reserves during
the period of real exchange-rate appreciation, which started before

---

[1] For more details about the program, see Section 2 as well as Anušić et al. (1995).

[2] We use the German mark in our exchange-rate calculations because Germany is Croatia's
main trading partner and because the German mark was customarily used for transactions
in the shadow economy and was also a significant part of portfolio assets. Moreover, a large
portion of domestic assets is indexed to an exchange rate based on the German mark.

Table 1. *Real exchange rate and the balance of payments*
(millions of U.S. dollars)

Period	Real exchange rate	Current account	Capital account	Reserves	Errors and omissions
1992	100.0	329	– 220	– 167	58
1993	73.7	104	270	– 446	72
1994	54.4	103	584	– 793	106
1995[a]	52.9[b]	– 222	80	– 73	215

[a] First two quarters only.
[b] All four quarters.

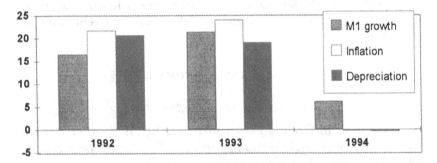

Figure 2. Annual averages of monthly rates of money growth, inflation,
and exchange-rate depreciation, 1992–94.

the announcement.[3] Reserves accumulation had significant impact
upon money supply. Indeed, average monthly rates of growth of M1
were 16.5% in 1992, 21.4% in 1993, and 6.2% in 1994. The last figure
is striking. The reader should bear in mind that the average monthly
rate of inflation was 21.7% in 1992, 24% in 1993, and – 0.25% in
1994; average monthly rates of depreciation (HRK/DM) were 20.7%
in 1992, 19.1% in 1993, and – 0.4% in 1994 (see Figure 2).

Although correlations in the rates of growth obviously exist, they
are far from what is expected. Rates of growth of nominal money supply in 1994 are surprisingly high when compared to the (negative)
rates of inflation and depreciation. The full effect is displayed in

---

[3] The increase in the central bank's international reserves during 1992–94 was $1.406 million
(U.S.), equivalent to approximately 10% of GDP.

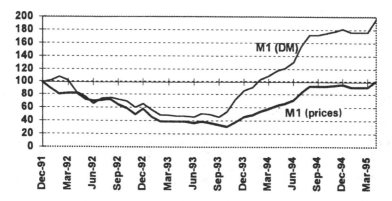

Figure 3. Indices of real money with exchange rate and retail prices as deflators.

Figure 3, which shows the monthly real money index measured in two ways – by using retail prices and the exchange rate as deflators.

These data show a significant increase in real money during the poststabilization period, as well as a difference between the behavior of the exchange rate and aggregate prices from 1992 to 1995. There are two reasons for the divergent paths of prices and the exchange rate: (1) an increase in the relative price of nontradables; and (2) a change in the exchange-rate regime that occurred at the very beginning of the stabilization program. The rest of this section is devoted to the first reason; the second reason is elaborated in Section 2.

Relative Price of Nontradables and Real Money

A proxy for the relative price of nontradables is displayed in Figure 4.[4] It shows a dramatic decline in 1992, and stable growth since the appointment of the new cabinet in April 1993. There are two reasons for growth: price liberalization in the public-services sector, and growth in domestic demand after the aggregate price stabilization.

The relative price of public services increased, owing to the government's price policy aimed at cutting the off-budgetary public deficit. The central government advanced that price policy by pushing up the relative price of electricity a few months before the announcement of the stabilization program. Other government agencies and off-budgetary funds followed suit by adjusting prices under

---

[4] The relative price of nontradables is approximated as a ratio between the prices of services that enter the cost-of-living index and the prices of goods that enter the retail price index.

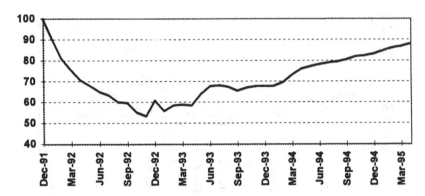

Figure 4. Index of the relative price of nontradables, 1992Q1–1995Q4.

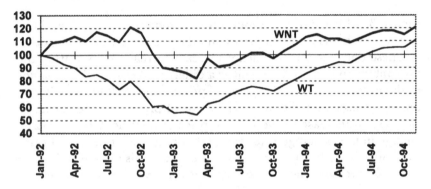

Figure 5. Indices of real average wage deflated by prices of tradables (WT)
and nontradables (WNT).

their control, such as those charged for local public utilities, health
and child care, and so forth.[5]

On the other hand, private suppliers of nontradables increased
their prices in response to demand.[6] The relevance of demand factors
is shown in Figure 5, which depicts the real average wage index measured in terms of tradables and nontradables.[7] The upper line shows
that from October 1993 to October 1994, the real average wage increased 19.3% in terms of nontradables but 45.9% in terms of tradables. When comparing the latest data with the trough in March of

---

[5] In most cases the price policy was simple: peg the price to the exchange rate after the initial
adjustment (Anušić et al. 1995).

[6] Demand-side explanations have begun to dominate traditional explanations that rest upon
differences in productivity (De Gregorio, Giovannini, and Wolf 1994).

[7] The series ends in November 1994 because of statistical inconsistencies: from December
onward, some cash fringe benefits were included in the calculation of net wage.

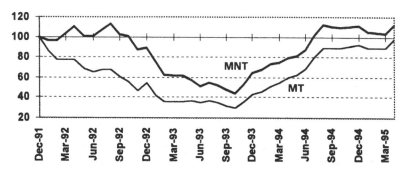

Figure 6. Indices of real money deflated by prices of tradables (MT)
and nontradables (MNT).

1993, the real average wage increased 40.6% in terms of nontradables and 95.6% in terms of tradables. The data indicate greater correlation between prices of nontradables and nominal wages than between prices of tradables and nominal wages, which is why real wage in terms of nontradables fluctuates less than real wage in terms of tradables.[8]

Real wage developments reflect fundamental change that has happened on the demand side – an increase in the demand for money. Figure 6 displays the behavior of the real money (M1) index measured in terms of tradables and nontradables. The difference in the two measures is due to observed changes in relative price, but both point to the beginning of the stabilization program (October–November 1993) as being the crucial moment for the jump in the demand for the stock of money.

The announcement of a credible stabilization program changed demand for real money via reduction in expected inflation (assuming a money demand function of Cagan's type: $m = f(\Pi^e)$). This was followed by an increase in real aggregate expenditures, which were directed mostly toward nontradable goods and so led to an increase in their relative price. Our conclusion holds regardless of the price elasticities of supply and demand in the two sectors, because a relative demand shift toward nontradables is a sufficient condition for growth in the relative price of nontradables. However, supply elasticities do matter when the overall output effect is also taken into consideration.

---

[8] Recorded differences reflect great differences in public perception of changes in the standard of living. Obviously, those who consume relatively more nontradables (generally, lower income groups) perceive much smaller improvements in their living standards than those who consume relatively more tradable goods (generally, higher income groups).

Relative Price of Nontradables and the Effect of Stabilization on Output

The effect of stabilization on real output depends on the simultaneous interplay of at least four factors, none of which are easy to assess. These factors include:

(1) demand shifts between tradables and nontradables, and a propensity to import;
(2) change in money velocity (which, together with real money, determines aggregate real expenditures);
(3) supply elasticity in the tradables sector; and
(4) supply elasticity in the nontradables sector.

Notice the importance of supply-side factors. Roldos (1995) pointed to supply-side "rigidities" that arise after stopping high inflation and real appreciation, stressing their link to the increase in relative price of nontradables. The argument rests upon Latin American experiences and goes as follows. Increases in real domestic demand that follow reduced inflation are mostly directed toward nontradables and imports, because productivity in the tradables sector is below the world level after real appreciation. That is why the relative price of nontradables rises when high inflation is curbed. Although real appreciation of the exchange rate makes the tradables sector inferior in comparison to competition from abroad, it enables the importing of cheaper and superior equipment, which raises productivity and attracts both domestic and foreign demand. However, increases in productivity take time, and this is why supply-side rigidities matter. Therefore, a current-account deficit that is generated mostly by imports of equipment would be a natural balance-of-payments position for a country that has just escaped the high inflation trap.

The supply-side argument is appealing when considered in light of Croatian experience. Table 2 presents data on real exchange rate, real output, and merchandise exports and imports for Croatia. Note that real GDP and the manufacturing production index both show signs of recovery despite continuing appreciation. Also note that the merchandise trade deficit is widening, and that imports of equipment are growing substantially. For the first four months of 1995, imports of equipment reached almost half of the previous year's amount, indicating that the growth impulse will likely continue.

Of course, one may fear for the stability of prices and the exchange rate, given the rapid growth of merchandise imports. However,

Table 2. *Real exchange rate, real output, and merchandise*
exports and imports

| | Real exchange rate | GDP index (1990 = 100) | Manu-facturing index (1990 = 100) | Merchandise[a] | | | |
| | | | | Total | | Equipment | |
				Exports	Imports	Exports	Imports
1992	100.0	71.42	61.12	4,597	4,461	674	468
1993	73.7	68.77	57.41	3,904	4,666	351	748
1994	54.4	69.34	55.91	4,260	5,229	528	898
1995	52.9	n/a	57.28	1,456	2,354	153	412

Note: n/a = not available.
[a] Millions of U.S. dollars.

growth in international reserves indicates that Croatia has enough room for increasing merchandise imports. Croatia is a net exporter of services, and receives additional capital inflows due to transfers from Croatian workers abroad. Moreover, foreign exchange deposits increased after price stabilization, a consequence of increases in overall confidence and optimistic expectations.

Therefore, the primary reason for the different paths taken by the exchange rate and prices is found in the growth of the relative price of nontradables. This in turn is due to the lagging supply response of the tradables sector, which works below world productivity at the beginning of the period of price stability. It follows that exchange-rate stability is the crucial factor for the hard budget constraint – which gives incentives for "restructuring" (i.e., raising productivity in the tradables sector) – to be binding. Otherwise, rising prices of tradables would jeopardize stabilization achievements.

However, nontradables cannot explain the different paths of exchange rates and prices before mid-1993, during high inflation. For this we must examine the effects of the exchange-rate regime.

2. CHANGES IN THE EXCHANGE-RATE REGIME

Reasons for High Inflation

Changes in the exchange-rate regime are closely linked to high inflation and stabilization. It is hard to explain average monthly inflation of 28% in 1993 by any standard textbook model. Probably that is why most people think of high inflation as a "bubble" or self-fulfilling phenomenon. Although this may be true for extreme cases (Germany after WWI, Greece after WWII, or the recent Serbian experience), the majority of inflation episodes do not display typical bubble behavior. Indeed, average monthly inflation in Croatia did not change much from mid-1992 to October 1993. Likewise, recent empirical findings suggest that bubble behavior is less common than previously supposed (see Scacciavillani 1994).

Theories of high inflation of the Croatian type are typically given in terms of monetization of the fiscal deficit. Deficits do give the prime impulse, but they cannot serve as explanations of the actual inflation rates. The "equilibrium inflation" needed for financing the deficit is generally lower than actual inflation in high-inflation episodes. An explanation for this phenomenon has been offered in the form of an *inflation tax curve*, which shows that the same deficit can be financed by either low or high inflation rates. Economies converge toward high-inflation ("bad") equilibrium because "good" (low-inflation) equilibrium is unstable.

Empirical work on Croatian inflation has confirmed this hypothesis. It was found that, even at the beginning of 1992, some 60% of actual inflation could not be explained by the fiscal deficit alone. In October 1993, the entire inflation was driven by other causes (Anušić et al. 1995).[9] The reason was the exchange-rate regime.

Old Exchange-Rate Regime

At the moment of monetary independence (end of 1991), Croatia inherited a fixed (pegged) exchange-rate regime. From the beginning of 1992, the National Bank of Croatia (NBC) started to form its own exchange rate. It kept the rate constant in January and February. In March and April the exchange rate was devalued.

At the end of April 1992, the government decided that banks licensed for operations in foreign exchange were free to determine the exchange rate according to supply and demand at the foreign exchange market. At the same time, the NBC board of governors decided that the NBC rate would be the average rate of the largest com-

[9] Approximations for deficit share of GDP showed a 6% share in 1992 and 1% in 1993; see Anušić et al. (1995, p. 20, table 1.2.1).

mercial banks. One could therefore argue that the rate has floated since May 1992.

In practice, the rate was set by the NBC, which tried to maintain a constant real effective exchange rate. In the highly inflationary environment, this meant constant depreciations that were pushing prices upward and fueling expected inflation. In general, depreciations fueled higher inflation, leading to real appreciation. To make a long story short, despite the legality of licensed commercial banks setting their own exchange rates, this did not happen. Commercial banks obediently followed unwritten rules of the NBC, and waited for fax messages from monetary authorities to see what exchange rate they should apply.

At the time of monetary independence, NBC international reserves were virtually zero. Consequently, in 1992 the NBC introduced regulations that commercial banks must surrender 25% of their total foreign exchange inflow.[10] Restrictions always create black-market premiums. The "street" premium on the exchange rate for cash in 1992 was 10–20%; the same was true for transactions (not considered legal) between enterprises. This system worked until mid-October 1993, when the stabilization program was announced and a new foreign exchange law became effective.

October (1993) Changes in the Exchange-Rate Regime

Initial pegging of the exchange rate to the deutsche mark (DM) was one of the main anchors of the stabilization program. An upper intervention point on the exchange-rate market was announced. Ceilings were: 4,444 HRD (4.4 kunas) for 1 DM in October, 4,600 HRD (4.6 kunas) in November, and 4,750 HRD (4.8 kunas) in December. This meant that the NBC promised to satisfy all demand for transactions in foreign exchange at the predetermined rate if the market rate were above the ceiling.[11] This regime lasted only two weeks, as its role was only to break forward-looking inflationary expectations. A new foreign exchange law was adopted in the Parliament on 7 October 1993, and enacted on 19 October. Under the new law, banks are

---

[10] Later on, this regulation was altered and banks had to sell 35% of transactions at the exchange offices, but finally this regulation was abolished. The NBC was buying all foreign exchange that commercial banks supplied over and above the required amounts (the 35% quota).

[11] Here, the upper intervention point or "ceiling" denotes the *weakest* level of the exchange rate that the NBC was willing to accept.

Table 3. *Commercial banks' net purchases of foreign exchange (millions of DM)*

	NBC	Individuals	Legal entities	Overall net
1993				
November	– 144	85	– 70	– 129
December	– 65	104	– 100	– 61
1994				
January	– 15	99	– 34	50
February	– 77	72	– 24	– 29
March	– 55	117	– 31	31
April	– 104	147	– 22	21
May	– 24	83	– 85	– 26
June	– 78	216	– 81	57
July	– 168	320	– 6	146
August	– 167	388	– 115	106
September	– 99	224	– 142	– 17
October	– 144	164	– 123	– 103
November	– 2	129	– 179	– 52
December	– 40	146	– 141	– 35
1995				
January	– 9	110	– 142	– 41
February	2	122	– 145	– 22
March	0	160	– 69	91
Total	– 2,379	5,371	– 3,019	– 27

Source: National Bank of Croatia.

free to set their exchange rates, current-account convertibility has been introduced, and exporters need not surrender their foreign exchange earnings to the banks.

A monetary anchor (base money) was one of the anchors announced at the beginning of the program. However, the monetary anchor was not obeyed. As a consequence of the sharp increase in demand for real money balances (see Section 1) and of the new exchange rate regime, the nominal exchange rate started to appreciate and households started to replace their foreign exchange savings with domestic currency. Something of a self-supportive spiral of increasing confidence occurred. Banks eager to attract domestic currency from households (and to deter them from replacing foreign exchange with domestic currency) started to raise the exchange rate.[12]

---

[12] It must be recalled that maintaining low liquidity in domestic currency was one of the techniques used by banks as a hedge against hyperinflation.

Table 4.   *Concentration of net foreign exchange reserves of commercial banks*

	9/30/93	10/31/94	4/28/95
Total amount[a]	748	952	1,054
Concentration ratio (CR4)	60%	52%	50%
Herfindahl index	0.135	0.116	0.121

[a] Millions of U.S. dollars.
Source: Computed from NBC data.

This nominal appreciation was completely unexpected in light of a decades-long history of constant depreciation and devaluations; that foreign exchange would suddenly become less valuable was an unexpected shock. Monetary policy supported the growth of the confidence spiral by strong restriction in the first days of the program, and all agents suddenly realized that they could lose if they did *not* hold domestic currency. Holding foreign exchange suddenly had high opportunity and transaction costs. The latter occurred when larger banks, unwilling to appreciate to the equilibrium level, started to ration domestic currency.

Nominal and real money growth based upon interventions (on auction principles) at the foreign exchange market started on 3 November 1993. Flows in the foreign exchange market can be seen in Table 3. Banks were net sellers (negative purchasers) of the foreign exchange not only to the NBC, but to legal entities as well. Natural persons were net sellers to banks (or banks were net purchasers) from the program's inception.

Part of the reason for nominal appreciation can be found in the structure of the foreign exchange market (see Table 4). This market is concentrated, but with a certain number of medium-sized and small players. Although these banks do not constitute a significant part of the foreign exchange market (the share of the two largest banks is 40–50% of all transactions), the exchange rate set by smaller banks played a crucial "signaling" role at the beginning of the program. They were first to raise exchange rates, and larger banks simply could not ignore them. The rate would have appreciated anyway, but the tremendous speed of reaction (which was later transmitted to disinflation) was induced by smaller banks.[13]

[13] Two banks have branches located 30 meters apart in the central city square of Zagreb. One is a large commercial bank, the other, a small one. The small bank was the first to raise the

Even though the exchange rate and aggregate prices were not perfectly linked, we can safely conclude that the exchange rate was the major determinant of aggregate price dynamics. The nature and magnitude of the influence changed in time owing to changes in economic policy, but transmission mechanisms can be roughly grouped under two headings: (a) direct influence (indexation and cost of imported goods); and (b) indirect influence (signaling effect, input–output effect, "potential competition" effect).

Direct and Indirect Transmission of Exchange-Rate Changes on Prices

Direct Transmission. Prices were most often indexed to the deutsche mark and to a lesser extent to other foreign exchange (e.g., natural gas prices were linked to U.S. dollars). With appreciation, prices started to decline. This time indexation worked in favor of disinflation. Furthermore, imported goods became cheaper with appreciation, and this became an important influence on the general price level. In both 1993 and 1994, imported goods and nonfactor services represented about 40–45% of estimated GDP.

Indirect Transmission. As already emphasized, exchange-rate depreciation was considered as the overall signal for inflationary expectations. The strong signaling effect of the exchange-rate changes was an important element in diminishing inflationary expectations in October 1993. The second indirect influence was due to the spread of cheaper imported components through the input–output system. Such links are hard to measure, but they obviously played a role in deflation. The third mechanism, labeled as potential competition, had effects on domestic tradable goods. As prices of imported goods remained the same or even fell at the beginning of the program, the prices of domestic substitutes could not be raised without impunity. This was true not only for imported goods, but for all tradables (as pointed out in Section 1). The potential competition of cheap imports is a real threat, and a genuine deterrent to any tradables increasing their prices.

exchange rate, and long queues of people formed at the entrance to each bank: people were selling foreign exchange to the big bank, and then buying it from the small bank. The transactions were relatively small, but the publicity of the affair supplied additional motivation for the large bank to raise rates only a few working days later.

3. THE EXCHANGE RATE AS A COST-PUSH FACTOR

Links between the exchange rate and prices suggest that the importance of exchange-rate movements is much greater than is usually assumed. Influence on the domestic price level and the demand for money can occur in the short run because expected inflation depends upon changes in the exchange rate. It is therefore legitimate to test the hypothesis that the exchange rate actually works as a cost-push factor in the Croatian economy.

The Model

Aggregate supply depends on aggregate prices and other supply shocks. Since we want to test for the role of the exchange rate as the supply shock, we isolate exchange-rate–driven supply shocks by taking the exchange rate as an explanatory variable (shifter) in the aggregate supply function:

$$Y^s = aP + bE + u^s. \tag{1}$$

The first term on the right-hand side is the aggregate price level, and the second term is the exchange rate. The third term is an error term that encompasses other supply shocks; this term is assumed to be normally distributed, with zero mean and constant variance.

Aggregate demand depends on prices P and nominal money supply M as follows:

$$Y^d = \alpha P + \beta M + u^d. \tag{2}$$

It is important to note that theory and considerations from the first two sections provide us with clear predictions for signs of the parameters: $a > 0$, $\alpha < 0$, $b < 0$, and $\beta > 0$. It will be of special importance here to estimate the size of parameter b, which describes the magnitude of the negative supply shock of exchange-rate depreciation (i.e., the positive supply shock of appreciation).

The model can be estimated in its reduced form, and the inverse least squares method can be used to derive parameters of the structural form. After equalizing (1) and (2) by the equilibrium condition and rearranging, the reduced-form equation for the aggregate price level is

$$P = -[b/(a + \alpha)]E + \beta/(a - \alpha)M + \epsilon, \tag{3}$$

where $\epsilon = [1/(a - \alpha)](u^d - u^s)$. Substituting (3) into (2) yields the second reduced-form equation for real output level:

$$Y = -[\alpha b/(a - \alpha)]E + \beta[1 + \alpha/(a - \alpha)]M + \epsilon', \qquad (4)$$

where $\epsilon' = \alpha\epsilon + u^d$. Equations (3) and (4) can then be estimated by ordinary least squares (OLS), and estimated parameters from the reduced form can be used to compute parameters of the structural form of the model.

Data and the Problem of Stationarity

We used quarterly data from the third quarter of 1980 through the last quarter of 1994 – 58 observations. Since there is no reliable GDP series for the entire period, we constrained our analysis to the Croatian manufacturing sector. Therefore, Y is the manufacturing production base index, P is producers' prices base index, money is M1, and the nominal exchange rate is a trade-weighted nondimensional index for exchange rates with seven developed countries. Data for quarters are three-month averages.[14]

A serious nonstationarity problem obviously exists, because we are dealing with an economy with a constant tendency toward high inflation. Variables are time-dependent. Since our main objective was to test for the sign and significance of the exchange-rate parameter b, nonstationarity might seriously endanger our results.[15] Hence we used the Sargan–Bhargava (1983) test as suggested in Holden, Peel, and Thompson (1990) in order to use series in their stationary form. The results of the tests are presented in Table 5. It follows that $\ln Y$, $\ln P$, $\ln M$, and $\ln E$ are $I(1)$ and should be taken in the form of the first difference in order to be stationary – $I(0)$. The variables used in regressions are of the following form: $x_t = (\ln X_t - \ln X_{t-1}) = d\ln X_t/dt$ for $X = Y, P, M, E$.

Regression results for the reduced form equations are:

$$p = 0.527e + 0.533m + \epsilon, \quad R^2_{adj} = 0.857, \quad DW = 2.19, \quad F = 336.36;$$
$$\quad (7.96) \quad\ (7.11)$$

$$y = -0.093e + 0.061m + \epsilon', \quad R^2_{adj} = 0.118, \quad DW = 1.56, \quad F = 8.46;$$
$$\quad (-2.93) \quad (1.69)$$

where t-statistics are given in parentheses.

[14] Special thanks to Danijel Nestic for providing the data.
[15] Our conclusions will depend heavily upon the t-test of the parameter b. However, Phillips (1987) has shown that the t-test is practically meaningless for regressions of nonstationary time series.

Table 5. *Results of the Sargan–Bhargava test*[a]

Variable	Constant	*t*-test	DW	H_0 = variable $I(1)$
ln Y	7.643	3.482	0.508	accepted[b]
ln P	5.555	8.460	0.006	accepted[c]
ln M	4.607	8.134	0.006	accepted[c]
ln E	– 2.863	– 4.437	0.006	accepted[c]

[a] Sargan and Bhargava (1983, p. 157, table 1).
[b] Accepted at 1% bound where theoretical value is 0.705.
[c] Accepted at 5% bound where theoretical value is 0.493.

All parameters are significant at the 0.01 level of the two-tailed *t*-test except for the money parameter in the output equation, which is significant at the 0.1 level. The value of the *d*-statistic[16] in the price equation suggests that there is no serial correlation, while the *d*-statistic in the output equation is in the "indecision zone." Statistical properties of the output equation are generally not convincing, but what matters is the sign and significance of the reduced-form parameters used for computation of the parameters in the structural form of the model.[17] Therefore, we used these estimates together with the parameter formulas from (3) and (4) to compute parameters of the structural form of the model as follows:

$$y^s = 0.11304p - 0.152084e,$$

$$y^d = -0.1756p + 0.153977m.$$

Note that this is a dynamic supply–demand model, with well-defined equilibria in rates of growth but not in levels. Both price

[16] Empirical *d*-statistics are computed in regressions with the intercept term. (DW denotes Durbin–Watson.)

[17] Signs of the parameters are stable. For example, an autoregressive form of the model takes the following form:

$$Y_t = 0.999Y_{t-1} - 0.099e_t + 0.076m_t, \quad R^2_{adj} = 0.968, \quad Dh = 1.69, \quad F = 858.39.$$
$$\quad (399) \quad\quad (-2.984) \quad (1.752)$$

(Dh denotes Durbin's h-test.) Notice the same sign and similar values of these parameters as in the reduced-form output equation in the text. Moreover, interval estimates from the OLS estimated reduced-form output equation at the $\alpha = 0.05$ level are $(-0.15625, -0.02881)$ for the depreciation parameter and $(-0.01198, 0.13257)$ for the money growth parameter. Parameters from the autoregression model lie within these bounds. The sign of the depreciation parameter does not change inside the interval, whereas the sign of the money growth parameter changes only in the negative extreme. These results seemed convincing enough to proceed with the inverse least squares method by using parameter estimates from the reduced form.

VELIMIR ŠONJE AND MARKO ŠKREB

elasticity parameters have the expected sign and are very low, meaning that both inverse aggregate supply and demand functions are very steep – the expected result.[18] Furthermore, the exchange-rate depreciation parameter is negative, which means that depreciation shifts the supply curve up and monetary expansion shifts the demand curve out.

Although the model is not designed to give accurate numerical predictions, it can successfully explain inflation and recession as well as disinflation and expansion. The rate of depreciation was determined exogenously prior to October 1993 (see Section 2), and the aggregate supply curve was constantly shifting upward. Nominal money supply was also growing rapidly, but the rates were insufficient to offset the negative impact of depreciation because real money demand was declining owing to lack of credibility and constant exogenous depreciations. Simultaneous emergence of inflation and recession was the inevitable outcome. The model also explains deceleration of inflation and output recovery under conditions of exchange-rate appreciation due to changes in economic policy. Appreciation shifts the aggregate supply curve downward along the demand curve, leading to deceleration of inflation and acceleration of growth of output (or slowing down the declining output trend if curves move in the negative output growth zone).

We believe that these results prove our hypothesis about the exchange rate acting as a cost–push factor in the Croatian economy. They also shed more light on reasons for the remarkable success in stopping high inflation in Croatia. Finally, these results explain the different paths of the exchange rate and prices as follows. In an economy that does not have well-defined equilibria in levels of GDP but only in the rates of growth, simultaneous movements of the exchange rate and prices depend on at least three factors:

(1) price elasticity of aggregate supply;
(2) price elasticity of aggregate demand; and
(3) demand for real money, which depends upon the overall credibility of economic policy, which in turn determines expectations.

---

[18] Theoretical expectation of the steep inverse aggregate demand curve can be based upon the traditional IS–LM model. Large price changes and/or nominal money changes imply large shifts of the LM curve. If the IS curve is steep – and this is what we expect for an economy like Croatia's – then these shifts will lead to less than proportional changes in real output. Theoretical expectation of the steep inverse aggregate supply curve is due to the role of expectations: inflation has no real effects if expectations and price contracts adjust in the short run.

It is important to note that relative shifts in real expenditures on tradables and nontradables, as well as relative price elasticities of supply and demand in the tradables and nontradables sectors, also influence the link between prices and the exchange rate. This was shown in Section 1.

Although the first two factors can be viewed as purely economic, the third factor encompasses more than economics. It includes significant problems of institutional change, behavioral rigidities, and policy-making mechanisms and regimes, which together are the crux of the transition problem. Therefore, the link between the exchange rate and prices, as well as real bilateral or effective exchange rates, arise as consequences of the complex interplay among both economic and noneconomic factors.

4. OPEN QUESTIONS

There are three questions looking for answers in these pages. First, if the link between the exchange rate and prices depends on numerous and complex factors, then how can its level be judged – that is, how can we tell whether the exchange rate is misaligned? Second, what policy prescriptions arise from the analysis? And third, do Croatian results have any general importance for other economies in transition?

Is the Exchange Rate Misaligned (Overvalued)?

Exchange-rate overvaluation can have dangerous economic consequences (see e.g. Dornbusch 1988). There are a couple of indicators that can be used in judgments on misalignment: (i) an index of the real effective exchange rate, and (ii) a general balance-of-payments position (see e.g. Fisher 1988). There are also "fundamentals" involved, and one should consider all pieces of information when making judgments about possible misalignment. With respect to the first criterion, our analysis indicates that the bulk of real appreciation occurred before the stabilization program. Thus it can be argued that the program did stabilize the *real* exchange rate.

The second criterion is the balance of payments: if a country has a large and widening current-account deficit, this is a strong indication that its currency is overvalued. In Croatia, current-account data and merchandise export and import data for 1994 show exactly the opposite. The current-account surplus is the same as in 1993 (see Table 1), and exports are higher in 1994 and 1993. Estimates of the export demand function revealed that manufacturing production in Croatia's main trading partners has the strongest influence on merchandise exports, while price elasticity of exports is relatively low[19] (Mervar 1994; Anušić et al. 1995). Thus, real exchange-rate appreciation has not affected exports. By the same token, exporters' claim that depreciation (or devaluation) would be an export-promoting policy is not valid.

Overvaluation is usually followed by a rapid decrease in international reserves, which is obviously not the case in Croatia: international reserves of the NBC have a very clear upward trend (see Table 1). The present situation of foreign debt and changes in arrears does not necessarily indicate that the exchange rate is overvalued, although a rise in the foreign debt is an ambiguous signal for a country with unresolved problems of foreign debt (with the London Club) and unallocated debt.

Moreover, Croatia's economic structure has changed substantially in the last several years. Because of transition, dissolution of the former Yugoslavia, and Serbian aggression, it goes without saying that the Croatian equilibrium exchange rate is significantly stronger than the rate in former Yugoslavia.[20] If we bear in mind that the exchange rate in Croatia is market-determined, existing data simply do not show that the exchange rate has been misaligned.

Policy Prescriptions

Our analysis reveals two crucial facts upon which policy prescriptions should be based: (1) the exchange rate is not misaligned; and (2) exchange-rate depreciation or devaluation is primarily a cost-push factor, not a demand–pull factor. The implications may be summarized as follows.

(1) Exchange-rate stability (giving up devaluations) is a neccessary, but not sufficient, condition for the budget constraint to be binding and for overall macroeconomic stability.

(2) The aim of stability is to create an environment where probability of bailouts at all levels of economic life would be sufficiently

---

[19] Note that this result is completely in accordance with the econometric results from Section 3.
[20] Productivity in Slovenia and Croatia was above the ex-Yugoslav average, and Slovenia has experienced real exchange-rate appreciation since 1991.

low to induce changes in behavior that lead to growth in productivity.

These facts and implications lead to the following policy prescriptions, which we present in the form of a behavioral algorithm. If there is convincing evidence that the exchange rate acts primarily as a cost-push factor, and if the structure of the banking sector exhibits at least some degree of competition, then:

(1) liberalize the foreign exchange market and introduce transparent auction routines;
(2) do not set a target nominal or real exchange rate – let it find its own equilibrium;[21] and
(3) do not fear nominal appreciation – increase the money supply only as long as costs of sterilization are not prohibitively high or as long as it is posible to sterilize without significant cost to the central bank.[22]

However, economic policy algorithms cannot always be applied in their pure form because history matters and circumstances differ. We conclude this chapter by addressing the potential transnational significance of our findings.

Conclusion: General Importance of the Result

Our main message concerns exchange-rate appreciation and its link to price reaction. Most stabilization programs relied on some form of fixing the exchange rate, and it is widely held that such a regime enhances program credibility. However, inflation inertia occurred even during successful episodes with the fixed rate. The Croatian program demonstrates that, by allowing appreciation, credibility is not only enhanced but is actually maximized, because this kind of program takes advantage of indexation and other exchange rate–prices transmission mechanisms that have developed during high inflation. Therefore, inflation inertia can be successfully eliminated in the extremely short run (a few days or weeks), and real exchange-rate appreciation (toward an equilibrium level) happens in the very short

---

[21] Announcement of the nominal target at the very beginning makes sense if policy makers fear a lack of credibility.
[22] The options for Croatia are: (a) generating a cash-flow fiscal surplus in the treasury account at the central bank, or (b) increasing the rate of the foreign exchange deposits that commercial banks must keep in foreign banks (60% at the moment).

run too, leaving much more time for policy makers to undertake such fundamental supply-side reforms as privatization and restructuring. Of course, conditions crucial for this story to be repeated in some other country are: (a) the stock of money must be lower than the desired stock of money at the beginning of appreciation; (b) the country must accumulate reserves; and (c) fiscal stabilization must already be on its way.

The specific role of the exchange rate has been stressed by other economists from Central and Eastern Europe. We do not claim that the exchange rate *in general* acts primarily as a cost–push factor, but we firmly believe that devaluation cannot be a meaningful policy for a country in transition. The mission and purpose of macroeconomic policy in Central and Eastern Europe is not (as is commonly believed in developed market economies) to react to shocks, but rather to create an environment with incentive mechanisms that can enforce behavioral change directed toward growth of productivity at the microeconomic level. The Croatian program was by all accounts successful in this regard. The final result, however, depends upon a much more complex set of policies that lie beyond the scope of our essay.

REFERENCES

Anušić, Z., Ž. Rohatinski, and V. Šonje (eds.) (1995), *A Road to Low Inflation: Croatia 1993/1994.* Zagreb: Government of the Republic of Croatia.

De Gregorio, J., A. Giovannini, and H. C. Wolf (1994), "International Evidence on Tradables and Nontradables Inflation," Working Paper no. 94/33, International Monetary Fund, Washington, DC.

Dornbusch, R. (1976), "Expectations and Exchange Rate Dynamics," *Journal of Political Economy* 84(6): 1161–76.

Dornbusch, R. (1988), "Overvaluation and Trade Balance," in R. Dornbusch and F. C. H. Helmers (eds.), *The Open Economy.* Oxford, UK: Oxford University Press (EDI series for the World Bank).

Fisher, S. (1988), "Devaluation and Inflation," in R. Dornbusch and F. C. H. Helmers (eds.), *The Open Economy.* Oxford, UK: Oxford University Press (EDI series for the World Bank).

Holden, K., D. A. Peel, and J. L. Thompson (1990), *Economic Forecasting: An Introduction.* Cambridge, UK: Cambridge University Press.

Mervar, A. (1994), "Estimates of the Traditional Export and Import Demand Functions in the Case of Croatia," *Croatian Economic Survey* 1: 79–94.

Phillips, P. C. B. (1987), "Time Series Regressions with Unit Roots," *Econometrica* 55: 277–302.

Roldos, J. E. (1995), "Supply-Side Effects of Disinflation Programs," *IMF Staff Papers* 42(1): 158–83.

Sargan, J. D., and A. Bhargava (1983), "Testing Residuals from Least Squares Regression for Being Generated by the Gaussian Random Walk," *Econometrica* 51: 153–74.

Scacciavillani, F. (1994), "Long Memory Processes and Chronic Inflation: Detecting Homogenous Components in a Linear Rational Expectations Model," Working Paper no. 94/2, International Monetary Fund, Washington, DC.

CHAPTER 9

Stabilization in Slovenia: From High Inflation to Excessive Inflow of Foreign Capital

Velimir Bole

1. INTRODUCTION

Immediately before Slovenia introduced its new currency in October 1991, the country faced huge internal and external disequilibrium as well as complete monetary disorder. Inflation was running about 20% per month, while production was plummeting 12% per year. The collapse of the Yugoslav market cut total sales by over 15%, while political risks blocked access to foreign credits. Hence, before "standard" steps toward transition to a private market economy could be taken, macroeconomic stabilization measures were badly needed to stop runaway inflation and mitigate effects of the collapse of Slovenian markets.

Macroeconomic stabilization is usually given the highest priority in the context of sequencing considerations (see Fischer and Gelb 1990). In the case of Slovenia, the paramount role of price stabilization was reinforced by the fact that creation of a new currency was the very process of establishing the credibility of a new state. Nevertheless, price stabilization was only one of two basic objectives of the monetary reform and foreign exchange–regime changes adopted in October 1991.

After the Yugoslav market fell apart, the Slovenian economy became highly open. Its foreign trade ratio climbed over 1.15, and imports of raw material alone exceeded 25% of GDP! In September 1991, with foreign exchange reserves (net of short-term debt) for only four days of imports, production was on the brink of collapse. It was essential to build up foreign exchange reserves and facilitate external liquidity of the economy as rapidly as possible. This was the second objective of the policy adjustments launched in October 1991.

This research was supported by the Commission of the European Communities, Market Access Europe ACE Programme Management, under contract ACE-92-0522-R.

Galloping inflation, almost negligible foreign exchange reserves, and restricted access to foreign credit made standard stabilization – either orthodox or heterodox – impossible. It was necessary to proceed on two tracks simultaneously: building foreign exchange liquidity and reducing inflation.

This essay presents an overview of policy adjustments and economic performances at the time of (and subsequent to) the new currency creation. Only basic policy adjustments for the financial stabilization[1] of the economy are given. That is, the only adjustments analyzed are those essential to building up foreign exchange reserves and reducing inflation. Different policies were synchronized (to support the two basic objectives) in steps. Therefore, the whole period of stabilization is divided into three phases according to when and how the various policies were inaugurated or started to support the stabilization.

The structure of this chapter is as follows: in Section 2, a brief overview of the stabilization strategy is given. Adjustments of the basic institutional setting underlying the foreign exchange market, made at the beginning of the stabilization, are described in Section 3. The first phase of the stabilization, in which money was squeezed in nominal terms, is presented in Section 4. The second phase is presented in Section 5, where the effects of switching the monetary policy to smooth cutting of real money supply are described. Bleak adjustment of income policy and the pricing of public-sector utilities is also tackled in Section 5. The third (and ongoing) phase of the stabilization is analyzed in Section 6; an overall summary is given in Section 7.

2. STRATEGY OF THE STABILIZATION

When the new currency was created it was not yet clear what monetary policy to set or how to stabilize the economy given the chaotic environment the Slovenian economy was facing. It appeared very difficult to adopt a (technically rather sophisticated) heterodox stabilization program, with fine tuning of all components of economic policy and credible consensus of the main social partners over its most important short-term goals of economic policy – particularly since most segments of economic policy (e.g. income policy, price

---

[1] Although the standard term "stabilization" will be used, "financial stabilization" would perhaps be more appropriate.

Table 1. *Indicators of economic policy (monthly indexes)*

	Base money	Narrow money	Direct taxes and contribution	Total net wage bill	Foreign exchange rate	Retail prices
1991						
November	100.0	100.0	100.0	100.0	100.0	100.0
December	127.0	106.9	130.6	119.5	107.8	115.4
1992						
January	110.5	109.8	118.5	117.3	107.8	132.9
February	110.7	114.1	123.8	136.9	138.5	147.6
March	142.3	116.1	152.6	152.9	145.8	164.6
April	147.6	138.2	187.8	176.6	147.6	173.0
May	168.7	133.2	189.3	187.8	148.6	184.2
June	188.1	143.3	231.0	210.8	146.3	195.1
July	207.6	153.6	235.0	23.2	149.5	198.9
August	219.8	169.7	244.6	231.1	158.8	201.7
September	242.7	179.7	238.9	237.3	166.1	207.2
October	254.9	189.2	247.5	256.5	169.3	214.3
November	255.4	194.8	261.2	262.1	173.8	220.2
December	270.3	227.4	333.9	308.8	176.5	222.7
1993						
January	277.9	221.4	271.1	269.4	177.5	230.9
February	287.1	224.4	283.1	316.2	179.3	234.6
March	292.7	231.4	326.9	309.4	184.7	237.9
April	301.5	236.8	292.4	305.2	191.5	240.3
May	308.5	243.6	295.2	293.5	198.1	243.6
June	324.5	267.2	296.0	293.4	202.0	247.3
July	338.0	276.1	308.5	304.3	202.3	249.3
August	343.3	277.5	303.7	308.2	203.0	253.5
September	350.5	285.5	298.3	316.9	206.0	257.8
October	361.9	298.0	306.6	332.6	211.4	265.3
November	361.5	298.9	321.5	323.9	216.5	269.5
December	381.4	323.5	376.3	391.7	220.9	273.6
1994						
January	383.2	308.9	305.9	332.6	223.0	277.7
February	391.5	321.8	314.5	355.2	224.8	281.3
March	402.6	321.7	378.9	372.9	226.7	284.4
April	421.2	344.5	347.3	392.4	228.2	290.3
May	444.4	342.8	361.3	339.3	229.3	293.2
June	465.9	351.7	353.5	387.2	229.7	297.9
July	492.4	361.9	365.5	388.9	230.0	301.2
August	508.4	367.8	375.3	386.7	230.6	304.6
September	522.3	367.9	376.3	398.9	231.9	309.1
October	541.5	386.6	382.5	418.6	233.2	315.3
November	589.3	399.5	413.5	424.9	234.4	320.0
December	635.9	459.6	478.4	468.9	235.8	323.5
1995						
January	639.2	421.2	377.8	421.5	236.7	327.1
February	632.8	424.9	398.4	441.1	236.4	330.0
March		438.2		453.8	235.6	331.7

Sources: Monthly Bulletin, Bank of Slovenia; *Statistical Bulletin*, Agency of the Republic of Slovenia for the payment system.

policy in the public utilities) were technically unable to support a heterodox stabilization program. When the new currency was launched, privatization had not even started, so only liquidity squeezing could be relied upon to contain wages. Furthemore, there were available only negligible foreign exchange reserves, not to mention reserves that would be necessary to support a price and foreign exchange–rate freeze. Therefore, exogenous money and a floating exchange rate were pinpointed as the basic principles of monetary policy, with restrictiveness as its main characteristic.

In October 1991, the new currency (the *tolar*) was launched; for details, see Mencinger (1993). Reshaping of the foreign exchange market was adopted in the same month, and adjustments of other policies were made through subsequent phases of stabilization.

The stabilization can be divided into three phases. In the first, pure "monetary" phase of the stabilization policy, excess liquidity of the banking system was wiped out. This phase lasted from October 1991 to February 1992. Inflation dropped from over 21% to 11% per month. In the second phase, the monetary policy adjusted money supply more smoothly. However, not all fundamentals were in place yet; the weakest segments were income policy and pricing of the public utilities. The second phase lasted through the end of 1992, when inflation fell to a moderate level (about 1.5–2% per month). In the third phase, money supply was neutrally adjusted to changes in real demand for money, while income policy, fiscal policy, and control of prices in the public sector began to support the price stabilization. As of April 1995, the third phase was not yet complete, although inflation started to drop toward single digits. Some indicators of changes in economic policy in the course of the stabilization are presented in Table 1.

3. RESHAPING THE FOREIGN EXCHANGE MARKET

Because a floating foreign exchange rate was one of the pillars of the stabilization policy, the institutional setting underlying the foreign exchange market was reshaped to enable a new (floating) foreign exchange regime. Changes were adopted in the same month that the new currency was launched. Boosting the foreign exchange-rate elasticity to shocks in demand was the main reason for these changes. Slow adjustments of the foreign exchange rate to changes in demanded quantities, or a severe lack of foreign exchange, could well have endangered foreign liquidity. Besides, the foreign exchange

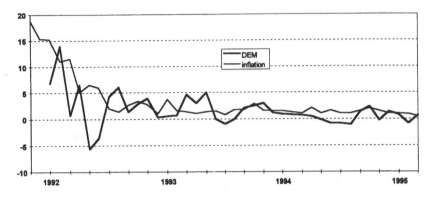

Figure 1. Growth rates of the exchange rate (DEM) in foreign exchange offices and inflation. *Source: Monthly Bulletin,* Bank of Slovenia.

market was highly monopolized at the end of 1991. One bank controlled over 60% of the transactions between Slovenia and the rest of the world. As a result, other inefficiencies of the highly monopolized foreign exchange market might also appear, increasing uncertainty and so endangering the stabilization. Reshaping the institutional setting of the foreign exchange market was intended to expedite the clearing of that market; presumably, this would mitigate the possibility of foreign exchange "attacks" and other potential monopoly effects.

The basic characteristics of the foreign exchange market did not change until 1995. On the market for foreign exchange, banks, enterprises, and households can take part (nonresident participation is restricted). Banks are completely free to trade in foreign exchange. Enterprises can sell foreign exchange to any economic unit (bank or enterprise) operating on the market. However, this must occur within 48 hours after foreign exchange inflow. The official exchange rate (mostly used for fiscal and bookkeeping purposes) is the two-month weighted average of daily averages of spot foreign exchange rates. On October 8, this rate was set at 32 tolars to 1 deutsche mark.

Free selling and buying of foreign exchange to households could trigger a speculative attack on Slovenia's limited foreign exchange reserves. For example, in October 1991 the total wage bill exceeded $145 million (U.S.), while over $26 million (net) was sold in foreign exchange offices. To increase exchange-rate elasticity on the demanded quantity, the central bank adopted "time segmentation" of the foreign exchange market (accessed by households) by determining, in advance, the length of the time interval in which net cumulative purchases in foreign exchange offices had to be at least zero. At first, time intervals of "positive netting" were set at one week. Through such time segmentation requirements, the central bank enforced even more severe foreign exchange liquidity constraints than were current whenever the demanded quantity jumped suddenly. Implementing time segmentation drastically increased the elasticity of the foreign exchange rate with respect to shocks in demanded quantity. Hence the possibility of speculative attacks was reduced significantly, as documented by three quasispeculative attacks in January 1992, March 1992, and February–March 1993 (see Figure 1). As the building up of foreign exchange reserves diminished the possibility of speculative attacks, time segmentation of the foreign exchange market was abandoned in April 1992.

4. SOFT MONETARY LANDING (PHASE 1)

At the end of September 1991, banks in Slovenia were "super" liquid, with their accounts (vault money and reserve requirements included) holding three times more liquidity than at the end of August. Hence, the period from 8 October 1991 to February 1992 was supposed to be a period of "soft landing" of base money (the first phase of the stabilization); the stance of monetary policy was not changed during this period. The base money was shrinking (in nominal terms) toward a target value that had been estimated in advance (at the very launching of the tolar) using equations of demand for real balances. Two assumptions behind this estimate were: (i) the fall in economic activity would correspond to 100% of the effects of the complete blockade of markets in the former Yugoslavia; and (ii) inflation in February 1992 would be 5% per month. Credits of the Bank of Slovenia to banks were actually shrinking until February 1992. Stretched and smoothed squeezing of credits to banks – rather than cutting credits in one move – were used to enable banks to reduce their credit exposure (with respect to enterprises) in a less harmful way.

Bank credits were frozen until the end of October 1991. After October, the ban on new credits was lifted because the squeeze on banks' liquidity was already severe enough to decelerate their credit activity. The discount rate was set at 24% per year. Through such a discount rate, inflation of 2% per month was the explicitly set target. Moreover, the central bank enforced linear rescaling of (nominal) interest rates on (old) dinar bank credits to enterprises to the much lower

Table 2. *Dynamics of economic performance (quarterly figures)*

	GDP (rates of growth)[a]	Unem- ployment	Interest rates[b] (real)	Inflation[c]	Current account ÷ GDP (%)
1992					
Q1	– 8.0	6.8	23.6	48.5	13.2
Q2	– 9.9	7.1	23.6	24.1	5.6
Q3	– 4.3	7.3	23.8	10.1	9.4
Q4	– 1.3	7.6	24.2	8.1	2.3
1993					
Q1	– 3.6	7.9	24.5	7.0	– 1.3
Q2	– 3.0	8.1	19.0	3.9	– 0.3
Q3	2.9	8.3	19.0	4.0	4.3
Q4	1.7	8.5	18.7	6.3	0.1
1994					
Q1	4.8	9.3	17.7	4.3	4.1
Q2	6.2	9.0	16.9	4.5	1.9
Q3	4.5	8.9	16.6	3.8	4.5
Q4	4.5	8.3	16.4	4.8	2.9

[a] Quarterly rates of growth on the yearly level.
[b] Real interest rates for short-term credit.
[c] Quarterly rates of growth.
Sources: Monthly Bulletin, Bank of Slovenia; author calculations.

level. The nominal part of interest rates was set to the targeted inflation rate of 2% per month, while the real part stayed approximately
equal to the actual (contracted) level.

Harmful effects of increasing real interest rates due to falling inflation were mitigated by rescaling interest rates. It was anticipated
that the expected capital gains of banks in the (coming) period of falling inflation would thereby be neutralized in advance by immediate
(mandatory) capital losses of the same dimension. For enterprises,
the effect of rescaling would have to be the opposite: it would have to
be just big enough to compensate for the increase in real interest rate
costs (because of effects of the lagged indexation) in the period of
(planned) falling inflation to the targeted level. This linear rescaling
of the interest rates was similar to the *tablita* of Latin American stabilization episodes, although there was no price freeze in Slovenia
and the rescaling was not applied to all (old) contracts. Rather, it was
applied only to existing bank credits denominated in old currency.
Rescaling of interest rates accelerated conversion (made only on a

Table 3. *Macroeconomic indicators*

	1992	1993	1994
Growth of real GDP (% change)	-5.4	1.3	5.0
Domestic private consumption (% of GDP)	52.9	55.2	54.0
Gross capital formation (% of GDP)	17.6	18.1	19.8
General government fiscal balance (% of GDP)	0.3	0.3	-0.2
Inflation (Dec. to Dec.)	92.9	22.9	18.3
Total external debt to exports (ratio)	21.7	24.5	25.7
Reserves[a] to imports (ratio)	16.8	21.6	33.2
Imports to GDP (ratio)	54.5	55.7	53.9
Exports to GDP (ratio)	63.7	58.7	57.7
GDP per capita (U.S. dollars)	6,195.0	6,366.0	6,957.0

[a] International reserves plus foreign exchange deposits of banks at year's end.
Source: Monthly Bulletin, Bank of Slovenia.

contractual basis) of old credits – denominated in dinars – into the new currency, and also made it possible to smoothly (stretched over five months) compress bank credits to enterprises. In sum, rescaling of interest rates made liquidity squeezing (to the "normal" volume) far less harmful – in terms of economic activity and appreciation of the foreign exchange rate – than it would have been in the case of a straightforward contraction of the money supply.

In the first phase there was no special adjustment of fiscal or income policy toward supporting a deflation-oriented monetary policy. In fact, some rather weak brakes for the highest wages were enacted in November and lifted in February 1992. It seems that the wage freeze was superficial in the first phase. As a result of previous cuts, the level of real wages was low enough not to endanger future stabilization. The threat of war, and the presence of horrors in nearby Croatia, reduced public pressure to increase wages. In any case, liquidity squeezing was tight enough, and recession was high enough, to prevent any significant real wage increase.

To illustrate the performance of the Slovenian economy in the soft monetary landing phase and afterwards, Tables 2, 3, and 4 list some basic economic indicators for the period after the launch of the tolar. The impact of monetary reform (introduction of new currency) on the economy was immediate. Economic performance went from bad to worse in the same month that the tolar was introduced. By destroying the common settlements system, transactions with other parts of

Table 4. *Balance of payments as percentage of GDP*

	1992	1993	1994
Balance on current account[a]	7.0	1.2	2.7
Change in reserves	− 5.1	− 0.9	− 4.6
NET external financing	1.7	1.7	3.0
Direct investment and official transfers	1.2	1.4	1.2
NET external borrowing	0.5	0.3	1.8
Memorandum items			
Currency and deposits of households	0.1	0.7	2.6
Deposits (rest of the world)	0.2	− 0.4	0.2

[a] Excluding official transfers.
Sources: Monthly Bulletin, Bank of Slovenia; author calculations.

former Yugoslavia were cut further, by more than 50% (about 15% of total sales) within one month of the introduction of the new currency. An additional increase in the political uncertainty, triggered by introduction of the tolar, made access to foreign credits more difficult than before. Even old trade credits, previously renewed regularly, were frozen. Therefore, imports of necessary raw materials were possible only on a cash basis. As a result, demand for foreign exchange increased tremendously, and inflation likewise received an additional push. The significant reduction of competing imported goods from former Yugoslavia and other countries – as well as speculative buying of consumer goods – accelerated inflation, which exceeded 21% per month in October 1991. At the end of the year, economic activity plunged even more than in the third quarter of 1991 (see Figure 2), while falling employment did not change the dynamics.

Two promising results achieved in the first phase are worth mentioning: a rapid increase in foreign exchange reserves, and reduced inflation. The high level of the starting exchange rate, as well as vigorous dynamics of the spot exchange rate in the first two months after October 8, promoted considerable export growth. Because recession and (previous) foreign exchange scarcity also prevented a rise in imports, net foreign exchange reserves rocketed. At the end of the first phase (in February 1992), the net foreign exchange reserves (including those of banks) already exceeded the volume of 15 days

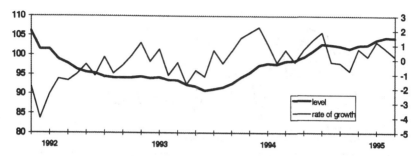

Figure 2. Industrial production, seasonally adjusted. Left scale:
index (December 1991 = 100); right scale: monthly rate of growth (%).
Source: Gospodarska Gibanja, Ekonomski Institut Pravne Fakultete.

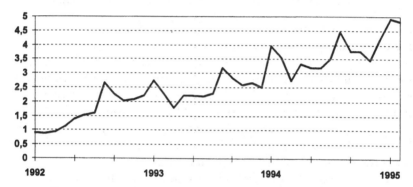

Figure 3. Foreign exchange reserves per unit of monthly imports
(includes international reserves and foreign exchange deposits of banks).
Source: Monthly Bulletin, Bank of Slovenia.

of imports; see Figure 3. Inflation started to retreat as well: falling
continuously, by February 1992 it had dropped to 11% per month.

5. SQUEEZING REAL MONEY SUPPLY (PHASE 2)

The second phase of the stabilization lasted from February to December of 1992. The basic principles of monetary policy – namely,
exogenous money and a floating exchange rate – remained the same
in the second phase. However, the stance of the monetary policy
changed. In the second phase, the supply of money was partially
adjusted to real demand for money[2] (base money and M1). Specifi-

[2] The target supply of money for every month was adjusted according to the estimated real demand for money in the previous month. Real demand for money was estimated as described

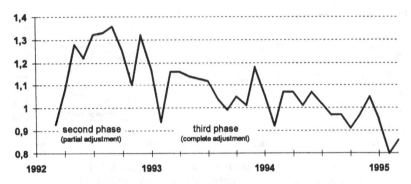

Figure 4. Target demand for money per unit of actual M1.
Sources: Monthly Bulletin, Bank of Slovenia; author calculations.

cally, the target base money for the next month was changed according to actual changes in inflation, interest rates, and economic activity in the previous month. However, planned saturation of demand
for real balances was increased slightly every month.[3] Needless to
say, other criteria (especially volume of interenterprise indebtedness)
influenced the perceived need for additional money supply (base
money) adjustments. Such guidelines for the money supply were to
be used until attainment of the fixed inflation target (2% per month)
set at the beginning of the stabilization in October 1991; see Figure 4.

Policy switching at the beginning of the second phase also included
new reserve requirement rates. In order to reduce high nominal interest rates paid by banks on sight deposits and to mitigate indexation, reserve requirements on sight deposits were significantly increased (to 13%), while reserve requirement rates on other deposits
(of longer maturity) were cut (to under 3%). In the second phase,
after second quarter 1992, the Bank of Slovenia started to sterilize the
increasing inflow of foreign exchange in order to prevent significant
real appreciation of the exchange rate. It did this mainly through
offering bonds bought and redeemed in foreign currency in addition
to bonds bought in tolars and redeemed half in tolars and half in foreign currency. The central bank also limited the access to liquidity
to only those banks absorbing greater-than-average excess foreign

---

in footnote 3. Seasonality of volume of transactions, as well as seasonal shocks in prices (in
March and September), was taken into account.

[3] Estimates for parameters in the equations for money demand were rather robust with respect
to both period of estimation and performance of the economy, so values of the latest available
estimates were used (see Bole 1992). Parameters were roughly 0.5 for transaction elasticity,
1.5 for price semi-elasticity, and 0.8 for interest-rate elasticity.

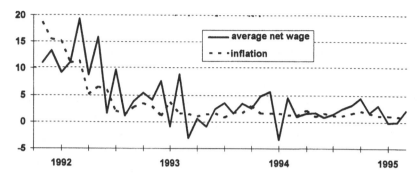

Figure 5. Growth rates for net wages and inflation.
Source: Monthly Bulletin, Bank of Slovenia.

exchange inflow (see Bole 1994). This was facilitated by swaps of foreign exchange, repos of the Bank of Slovenia foreign exchange bills, and credits collateralized by its foreign exchange bills.

In the second phase, the fundamentals were still not all in place. The government supported a restrictive monetary policy by running a slight surplus of the overall balance of government in 1992, whereas badly needed income policy measures were completely absent. Moreover, wages started to accelerate significantly in real terms (see Figure 5). The policy of public-sector pricing (e.g., gasoline, natural gas, communications) was not synchronized with other stabilization efforts; price corrections of the public utilities were made erratically and in big leaps. Apart from increasing the costs of inputs to other sectors, big leaps in controlled prices also had a significant "demonstration" effect on prices of other products. Only since May 1992 has the new government adjusted public-sector prices more smoothly and in accordance with the increasing average costs of public utilities.

New collective wage agreements became effective in the second phase. Collective wage agreements were not adjusted to actual economic performance. The average level of contracted wages was significantly higher (over 20%) than corresponding actual wages at the end of February 1992, when new wage agreements had to be enacted. Moreover, wage agreements were prepared without any sectoral coordination. Consequently, differences between minimum wages in different sectors of manufacturing, as well as between manufacturing and the public sector, were enormous. According to the new wage agreements, the contracted wages in the public sector had to increase the most. Their increase triggered, through the spillover effect, strong pressure on wages in the business sector. The slackness of economic activity, along with the rather restrictive monetary policy, made any significant adjustment of actual wages to newly contracted wages in the business sector difficult. Therefore, the probability of major social unrest in the second half of 1992 increased significantly. To prevent such disastrous events, policy makers prepared a law for freezing wages in the public sector. The law did not pass through parliament, so the government tried – unsuccessfully – to renegotiate wages for the public sector.

Until the end of 1992, the most outstanding characteristics of the Slovenian economy were further reduction of inflation, an increase in foreign exchange reserves, minor fluctuations in the exchange rate, and strong acceleration of wages. Inflation was falling continuously, due in part to restrictiveness of the monetary policy, real appreciation of the tolar, and calming of public-sector price increases. Although uninterrupted, inflation's fall occurred in steps. After every significant drop, in the next two months the drops were smaller. The target inflation of 2% per month was reached in July of 1992, nine months after monetary reform began. Relative prices started to change significantly in the second phase.

Because transfers were pegged to wages, acceleration of wages also pushed up social transfers. Increasing wages and transfers gave a significant boost to domestic final demand. Boosting domestic demand had two important effects: a severely repressed economy picked up and relative prices of nontradables started to accelerate. (Each effect has been demonstrated in the literature on contractionary devaluation.) Wage-driven increases of domestic demand halted the plummeting of economic activity. In the last quarter 1992, economic activity even started to grow. The relative prices of nontradables began sustainable growth in the same quarter of 1992.

Acceleration of exports and sluggish imports boosted current account surpluses to about 10% of GDP in the first half of 1992 (see Table 2). The successful performance of foreign exchange reserves in the first months of 1992 continued to the end of the year, when net foreign exchange reserves (including bank foreign exchange deposits) reached 9.2% of GDP ($1,124 million). Because the central bank did not completely saturate the demand for real balances in the second phase, the room it had for monetization of surpluses in the current account became so narrow that its support of the exchange rate

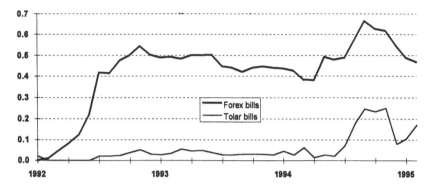

Figure 6. Bills of the Bank of Slovenia per unit of M1.
Sources: Monthly Bulletin, Bank of Slovenia; author calculations.

was too weak to prevent real appreciation of the exchange rate (see Table 1).[4]

6. MODERATE INFLATION (PHASE 3)

The third phase of the stabilization policy started in 1993. The monetary policy was reshaped only slightly, and the stance of the fiscal policy did not change at all. After December 1992, money supply was adjusted fully to the demand for real balances in the previous months. In fact, the track of three to four months' averages of supply was kept as close as possible to the track of the same averages of the targeted demand for money. The general government fiscal balance ran a slight surplus in 1993 and an almost negligible deficit in 1994 (see Table 3); the share (about 47%) of general government expenditure in GDP changed very little during the same period. Income policy stood in need of serious revision, yet important deficiencies were not removed. Although several attempts were made to contain wages and social transfers, they were only partially successful. Prices in the public sector were adjusted more smoothly, as changing costs of only the main inputs were taken into account. The central bank intensified its efforts to sterilize the huge inflow of foreign exchange (see Figure 6).

Income policy in the third phase remained the weakest link in the stabilization efforts (see Figure 5). Real wages had already started to

---

[4] During March–June 1992 the exchange rate was almost constant, even in nominal terms, although prices increased by over 18%!

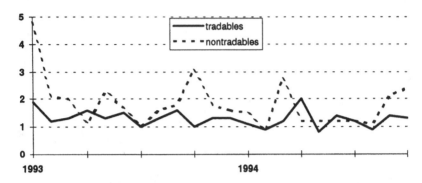

Figure 7. Monthly growth rate for prices of tradables and nontradables.
Source: Bole (1995).

grow in the second phase of the stabilization. Although various social
pacts were in preparation before 1994, none received the approval of
all parties taking part. Hence, the wage freeze in the first half of 1993
was the only period during which real wages dropped at least slightly
(by 1.4%). In the third phase (after 1992), the real costs of gross wages
increased on average by over 0.5% per month. Not until 1995, three
years after the start of stabilization, was the first credible social contract signed between workers and employers. It would have had to be
the first serious constraint on the fast growth of real wages.

Unsatisfactory income policy promoted two crucial effects, partly
noticed already in the first two phases: a huge inflow of foreign capital, and further increase in the prices of nontradables. Strong domestic demand and a foreign exchange glut set in motion a process of increasing distortions between the tradable and nontradable sectors.

Moderate inflation was the most visible characteristic of the period
following 1992. For more than two years, inflation remained in the
interval between 1% and 2.5%, and greater swings resulted only from
seasonal effects. It took two years to reduce inflation from 2% per
month to about 1.2%. (After that, disinflation accelerated, and inflation lessened over half to about 0.5% per month!) For the entire period after 1992, prices of nontradables led the game (see Figure 7).
The relative prices of nontradables continued to grow, as did their
relative variability. The relative prices of services climbed more than
15% over ten-year average values, while the relative prices of manufactured goods dropped about 5% under long-term average values
(see Figure 8).

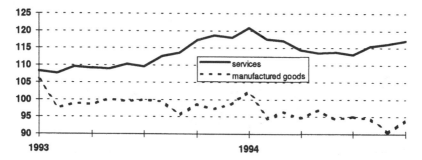

Figure 8. Relative prices of services and manufactured goods, where ten-year averages are set equal to 100. *Source:* Bole (1995).

There were three sources of the increase in relative prices of nontradables in that period (see Bole 1994). The first could be identified as a well-known effect of contractionary devaluation. The short-run impact of higher real wages gave a boost to output, notably in the nontradable sector, and so also to the relative prices of nontradables. The policy of changing controlled prices was the second cause of rising relative prices in nontradables. However, changes to controlled prices were significantly smoother in the third phase than in the first phase. Moreover, prices of other (controlled) products became crucial; that is, changing the prices of highly protected agricultural products was highly questionable.

There is strong empirical evidence for a third, longer-term cause of rising relative prices in nontradables. A slight modification of the Bhagwati–Kravis–Lipsey explanation (Bhagwati 1984; Kravis, Heston, and Summers 1983) of higher relative prices of nontradables in more developed countries can be applied to economies in transition (see Bole 1994). The argument is as follows: Before transition, the more capital-intensive sectors (mainly tradables) had a higher rate of hidden unemployment. After transition began, enterprises started to fire excess workers. Because the rate of hidden unemployment had been higher in the capital-intensive sectors before transition, those sectors reduced employment relatively more than the labor-intensive (chiefly nontradable) sectors. After the transition began, therefore, the growth of labor's marginal productivity in capital-intensive (mainly tradable) sectors exceeded its growth in labor-intensive sectors – and likewise for wages. Yet the "demonstration" effect induced wages in the labor-intensive sectors (e.g. services) to

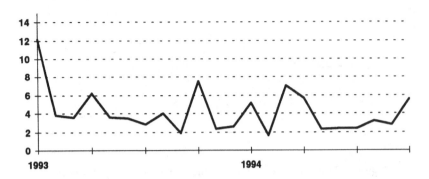

Figure 9. Variability of relative prices in cross-section variances.
Source: Bole (1995).

Figure 10. Variability of the relative prices of tradables
per unit of variability of all relative prices.
Source: Bole (1995).

accelerate also, which further increased the relative prices of non-tradables.

Not only the growth rate, but also the variability of relative prices of nontradables were greater. On average, variability of the relative prices in tradable sectors was more than 25% lower than the variability of all relative prices (see Figures 9 and 10). Such differences in variability of the relative prices (between tradables and nontradables) could result from erratic corrections of regulated prices in the nontradable sector. Namely, in the theory, changes in regulated prices are an important factor in the variability of relative prices (see e.g. Fischer 1981; Cukierman 1983; and Driffil, Mizon, and Ulph 1990).

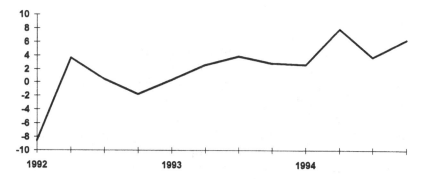

Figure 11. Inflow of foreign capital as percentage of GDP.
Sources: Monthly Bulletin, Bank of Slovenia; author calculations.

Changes in regulated prices are also a factor in the "dominant-sector" model used to explain rising inflation (Cukierman 1983). However, Granger testing fails to confirm a dominant-sector cause of prevailing inflation in Slovenia during the third phase of transition (see Bole 1995).

Although current-account surpluses were high, inflow of foreign capital started to grow in 1993. High nominal interest rates and a reduced exchange-rate risk premium pushed inflow of capital on average to over 4% of GDP (see Figure 11). As a result, foreign exchange reserves (including bank foreign exchange deposits) increased rapidly, by over 6% of GDP per year. Increases in reserves in the third phase were also extremely high compared to the recent episodes of increases of foreign exchange reserves in Latin America and Asia (Calvo, Leiderman, and Reinhart 1993a,b; Schadler et al. 1993). In 1992, current-account items (net of official transfers) contributed the most to the leap in foreign exchange reserves; in 1993 and especially 1994, relative contributions to the reserve increases changed significantly. Net external financing increased on average by over 2.8% of GDP, while the current-account surplus decreased on average to 2.1% of GDP (see Tables 2 and 4). Credibility of the country increased, so falling sovereign risk pushed up (normalized) trade credits. The reduced "currency" risk premium, as well as increased differences between interest rates on foreign exchange deposits in Slovenian banks and interest rates on (otherwise similar) deposits abroad, accelerated capital inflows through the household sector. External borrowing also increased in the third phase.

The floating–exchange-rate system, combined with a nonaccommodating monetary policy and the considerable magnitude of foreign exchange inflows, resulted in increased pressures on the real (as well as nominal) appreciation of exchange rates. Real appreciation of domestic currency started to skyrocket in 1994 (second year of the moderate inflation phase), to over 10% in December; in 1995, foreign exchange rates started to appreciate even in nominal terms. As the competitiveness of exporters in the world market plummeted, the strategic export segment of "new" exporters (enterprises no longer exporting to the collapsed Yugoslav market) started to fall into loss, accumulating much more than average indebtedness. In the period after 1993 (until the first quarter of 1995), only booming demand in foreign markets enabled exporters to endure the significant real appreciation of the tolar (over 13% in cumulative terms).

In the second phase of the stabilization (in 1992), bleak growth in economic activity demonstrated the fragility of domestic demand-driven growth of the Slovenian economy. Although gross wages shot up by over 19% (yearly), in real terms industrial production merely leveled off. On the other hand, increased demand in foreign markets after the first half of 1993 immediately gave a decisive and long-lasting boost to the economy. An extremely high foreign trade ratio (over 1.15) and strong growth of foreign markets enabled fast growth after the first half of 1993. In the second half of 1993, the growth rate of GDP reached on average 2.3% yearly, whereas in 1994 GDP increased by 5% (according to bulletins from the Bank of Slovenia). The unemployment rate also started to fall slowly, dropping to 8.3% in 1994. Obviously, strong growth of foreign markets enabled the economy to overcome the concurrent rise in the real costs of gross wages, which increased by 11.2% in 1993 and 1994.

Although "monetary" biased, the stabilization in Slovenia proved that monetary restrictiveness in the stabilization period can be significantly less harmful for economic activity – if the economy is highly open! However, the timing of stabilization must be chosen according to the growth in the world economy. It seems that a high openness in the economy coupled with growth in foreign markets enables policy makers to buy a little more time to put the fundamentals in place. Specifically, policy makers can then make the necessary adjustments to income (wage) policy more smoothly. Nevertheless, fundamentals must be set in place before the world economy levels off. Otherwise, stabilization would no longer be sustainable when foreign markets fall into recession.

7. CONCLUSIONS

When its new currency was launched in October 1991, the Slovenian economy was in significant external and internal disequilibrium. It faced high inflation (over 20% per month) and negligible foreign exchange reserves (only four days' worth of imports). Building reserves and reducing inflation were hence the basic objectives of the stabilization that followed. When it launched the new currency, the central bank declared a floating exchange rate and exogenous money as the basic principles of its policy.

Reshaping the foreign exchange market and applying a restrictive monetary policy were the basic pillars of stabilization. The budget was also set in order from the very beginning: the general government balance was in slight surplus in the period after the stabilization started. Of the fundamentals, wage policy and pricing of the public sector were not on the stabilization track at the outset.

The stabilization proceeded in three phases. In the first phase, pure squeezing of nominal money contained inflation to about 11% per month. The supply of money was partially adjusted to actual demand for money in the second phase. Income policy and pricing of the public sector were still not adjusted to the stabilization efforts. Moreover, real wages in the second phase started to grow quickly from their low level at the beginning of stabilization. At the end of the second phase, monthly inflation dropped to under 2%. In the third (and still ongoing) phase, a fixed monetary rule was adopted that incorporated unchanged values of transaction elasticity, interest-rate elasticity, and inflation semi-elasticity. Pricing of public utilities was adjusted to support the stabilization. As of April 1995, income policy had not yet been put on the stabilization track, although rates of growth in real wages had calmed considerably. Inflation was falling gradually but continuously, running at less than 1% per month in 1995.

The floating exchange rate and the strong recovery of foreign markets contributed to a dramatic increase in exports. Since stabilization, the current account has run a continual surplus; on average, it exceeds 3.5% of GDP. A falling foreign exchange–rate risk and real appreciation of the tolar triggered considerable inflow of foreign capital:

over 4% of GDP. Even though sterilized intervention measures were adopted, foreign exchange rates appreciated in real terms, and also (by 1995) in nominal terms. Appreciation of the exchange rate recently helped reduce inflation to only 0.4% monthly.

Throughout the stabilization period, relative prices of nontradables increased significantly. The increase in real wages and pricing of the public sector are presumable short-term reasons, whereas increased layoffs in the capital-intensive (mainly tradable) sectors are probable long-term causes. Variability of the relative prices of nontradables was also significantly greater than those of tradables. Falling inflation reduced changes in the relative prices and variability of the relative prices.

The foreign trade ratio of the Slovenian economy is over 1.15. Its high degree of openness considerably mitigated the harmful effects of the stabilization on economic activity and employment. The recovery of foreign markets immediately triggered strong growth of the economy, although fast real growth of the cost of wages was not contained. It seems that high openness and strong growth in the world economy enabled policy makers to adjust wages more smoothly and more slowly than would otherwise have been feasible. However, sustaining stabilization in the face of a fluctuating world economy requires that the fundamentals be set in place as soon as possible.

REFERENCES

Bhagwati, J. N. (1984), "Why are Services Cheaper in the Poor Countries?" *Economic Journal* 94: 279–86.

Bole, V. (1992), "What Happened with the Prices of Services?" [in Slovene], *Gospodarska Gibanja* (March 1994), pp. 19–38.

Bole, V. (1994), "Sterilization in a Small Open Economy; the Case of Slovenia," Working Paper no. 1994/1, presented at the international conference on alternative perspectives on finance (Bled).

Bole, V. (1995), "Unbalanced and Unanticipated Inflation" [in Slovene], *Gospodarska Gibanja* (January 1995), pp. 24–39.

Calvo, G. A., L. Leiderman, and C. M. Reinhart (1993a), "The Capital Inflows Problem: Concepts and Issues," IMF Paper on Policy Analysis and Assessment, International Monetary Fund, Washington, DC.

Calvo, G. A., L. Leiderman, and C. M. Reinhart (1993b), "Capital Inflows and Real Exchange Rate Appreciation in Latin America," *IMF Staff Papers* 40: 108–51.

Cukierman, A. (1983),"Relative Price Variability and Inflation: A Survey and Further Results," in *Variability in Employment, Prices and Money*

(Carnegie–Rochester Conference Series on Public Policy, no. 19). Amsterdam: North-Holland, pp. 103–58.

Driffill, J., G. E. Mizon, and A. Ulph (1990), "Costs of Inflation," in B. M. Friedman and F. H. Hahn (eds.), *Handbook of Monetary Economics,* vol. II. Amsterdam: North-Holland, pp. 1013–66.

Fischer, S. (1981), "Towards an Understanding of the Costs of Inflation: II," in K. Brunner and A. Meltzer (eds.), *The Costs and Consequences of Inflation* (Carnegie–Rochester Conference Series on Public Policy, no. 15). Amsterdam: North-Holland, pp. 5–42.

Fischer, S., and A. Gelb (1990), "Issues in Socialist Economy Reform," Working Paper no. 565, World Bank, Washington, DC.

Kravis, I., A. Heston, and R. Summers (1983), "The Share of Services in Economic Growth," in F. G. Adams and B. G. Hickman (eds.), *Global Econometrics: Essays in Honour of Lawrence R. Klein.* Cambridge, MA: MIT Press, pp. 188–218.

Mencinger, J. (1993), "How to Create a Currency? – The Experience of Slovenia," *Weltwirtschaftliches Archiv* 129(2): 418–31.

Schadler, S., M. Carkovic, A. Bennett, and R. Kahn (1993), "Recent Experiences with Surges in Capital Inflows," *Occasional Paper* no. 108, International Monetary Fund, Washington, DC.

CHAPTER 10

Macroeconomic Stabilization in the Baltic States

Ardo H. Hansson

1. INTRODUCTION

After years of concerted effort, most Central and Eastern European (CEE) countries have succeeded in bringing high inflation under control. Yet, only Croatia has been able to bring its rate of inflation near Western European levels (see Table 1). Excepting Croatia and ex-Czechoslovakia, inflation in even the most successful CEE countries remains in the range of 18–30% per year, with little hope of much reduction in 1995. Even the relatively lower inflation in Czechia and Slovakia has stayed above the levels that their authorities had hoped to achieve.

The same pattern of controlled but stubborn inflation is also seen in Estonia, Latvia, and Lithuania. The annual rates of CPI (consumer price index) increase in these countries fell from 953–1,163% in 1992 to 26–45% in 1994, but are expected to remain above 20% in 1995.

What are the main factors behind this qualitatively similar inflationary performance of many postcommunist economies? Which factors best explain the remaining cross-country differences? The Baltic states are in several senses the best context in which to begin answering these questions, providing the closest we have to a controlled experiment for determining the impact of various factors on inflation. First, these three countries are undergoing the same transformation as all of CEE, meaning that similar qualitative factors will be at work. Second, they resemble each other in size, general location, and inheritance from the Soviet era (with respect to both economic

This paper was prepared for the "First Dubrovnik Conference on Transition Economies" (8–9 June 1995) sponsored by the National Bank of Croatia. The author would like to thank Michael Connolly, Pekka Sutela, and conference participants for helpful comments. All remaining errors are mine alone.

Table 1. *CPI inflation in Eastern Europe,*
December 1993 – December 1994

Croatia	– 2.9
Czech Republic	10.2
Slovakia	11.7
Slovenia	18.3
Hungary	21.2
Latvia	26.3
Poland	29.5
Estonia	41.7
Lithuania	45.1
Romania	61.7
Bulgaria	121.9

Source: National statistical authorities.

structure and macroeconomic conditions). At the same time, they have enacted different enough policies and institutional arrangements (particularly exchange-rate regimes), and have received different enough external impulses, to allow identification of the main reasons for remaining cross-country differences.

Some factors still complicate such comparisons. To the extent that country size influences stabilization outcomes (e.g., through a stronger impact of the exchange rate on price levels), the performance of the Baltic states may not be quantitatively comparable to that of large countries like Poland and Russia. Second, if physical location near western markets matters – for example, by promoting trade expansion and foreign direct investment (FDI) – then comparisons with more remote states like Bulgaria or Romania will be hampered. Thus, comparisons of the Baltic states with the CEE countries must be largely qualitative.

Other factors complicate intra-Baltic comparisons. First, the three states began concerted stabilization at different times: Estonia in June 1992, Latvia in October 1992, and Lithuania in April–May 1993 (Saavalainen 1995). To the extent that the money stock and prices can move differently at various phases of stabilization (e.g., money demand rebounds sharply at first but then stabilizes), comparisons over a given time period become trickier. Second, these countries differ in the degree to which they had completed other reforms when stabilization began, especially in the extent to which subsidies had been reduced and prices freed. Third, their economies still had some structural differences. Estonia produces a significant share of its primary energy, whereas Latvia and Lithuania do not; also, Latvia was more industrialized than the others. Fourth, minor differences in location may have affected these states' ability to reorient trade to western markets and to attract FDI, with Estonia the most favorably placed. Finally, weak official statistics – often at different stages of transformation to a market economy basis – complicate the comparison of seemingly analogous figures.

Understanding the Baltic experience can be especially useful for the commonwealth of independent states (CIS) that are now starting to pursue serious stabilization (e.g. Ukraine and Moldova), and where some of the key initial conditions (direction of trade, dollar wage levels, etc.) resemble those in the Baltic states in 1992. This can help predict the future price paths of these states, and point to pitfalls on their road to controlled inflation.

The rest of the essay proceeds as follows. Section 2 describes the background and general characteristics of the stabilization performance of the Baltic states. Section 3 discusses the main factors contributing to the control of near-hyperinflation; Section 4 then explores the reasons why inflation stubbornly remains above Western European levels. Section 5 discusses the reasons for the different inflation experiences of the three Baltic states. Section 6 then explores the important link between the credibility and cost of disinflationary policies, and the possible resulting impact on longer-term inflation rates. Finally, Section 7 presents conclusions and areas for further study.

2. BACKGROUND AND GENERAL DEVELOPMENTS

The Baltic states stabilized their economies under much less favorable conditions than those of most CEE states and Russia. First, they experienced larger terms-of-trade shocks, due both to a high dependence on energy imports and to the relatively lower energy prices that prevailed in the FSU (former Soviet Union) as compared to CEE.[1] Second, as small countries, they were more affected by the collapse of trade that hit all economies in transition (again, Russia

---

[1] Saavalainen (1995) reports that in 1992, these terms-of-trade shocks were on the order of 10–15% in the Baltic states, as compared to 3–5.5% in Poland, Hungary, and Czechoslovakia. Conversely, Russia – as a net energy exporter – faced a positive terms-of-trade shock.

Table 2. *Change in real GDP in the Baltic states,*
1991–94

	1991	1992	1993	1994[a]	1994[b]
Estonia	– 12.6	– 14.2	– 8.6	– 3.2	+ 6
Latvia	– 10.4	– 34.9	– 14.9	+ 0.6	+ 2
Lithuania	– 13.1	– 37.7	– 27.1	+ 0.6	+ 1.5

[a] Official.   [b] IMF.
Sources: National statistical authorities; IMF.

would have been least affected). Third, in spite of having been relatively reformist and within the FSU, they probably inherited more
distorted economies than, say, Poland or Hungary, which had introduced some market elements during previous decades. Almost the
only sense in which the Baltics had better initial conditions was their
start from a position of zero foreign debt, as Russia took over all of
the foreign assets and liabilities of the FSU.

The recent macroeconomic performance of the Baltic states can be
described by six general indicators. First, poor starting conditions
led to *greater falls in output than in most CEE states* (see Table 2). The
cumulative fall in measured GDP from 1991 to 1994 was about 35%
in Estonia, 49% in Latvia, and 58% in Lithuania. Declines in agricultural and industrial output have been even greater. This contrasts
with a cumulative GDP increase of 3.3% in Poland, and declines of
15% in Hungary and 18% in Czechia.[2] At least by IMF estimates, all
of the Baltic states had restored growth in 1994 (Table 2), with
Estonia's higher growth rate partly reflecting the fact that it was the
first to experience an economic rebound.[3]

Second, *falling GDP has not led to high unemployment.* At the end of
1994, official unemployment ranged from 4.5% in Lithuania to 6.5%
in Latvia. The true level is somewhat higher, but joblessness has yet

[2] The increase in Poland reflects our choice of measurement period, which omits 1990, a year in
which Polish GDP declined. Dobozi and Pohl (1995) argue that official statistics may strongly
overestimate the declines in output in the western FSU states, but be far more accurate in
Eastern Europe. This claim is based on the assumption that electricity consumption is a reasonable proxy for the level of economic activity. In the Baltic states, electricity consumption
has fallen by far less than measured GDP, suggesting that the gap between the Baltics and
CEE is smaller than it appears.
[3] Figures from national statistical authorities show a decline of 3.2% in Estonia, and increases
of 0.6% in Latvia and Lithuania. However, owing to their poor coverage of the private sector, these estimates are less reliable than IMF data.

Table 3. *Consumer price inflation* *in the Baltic*
states, 1991–95

	1991	1992	1993	1994	June 1992 – June 1995
Estonia	303	953	35.7	41.7	326
Latvia	262	959	34.7	26.3	338
Lithuania	350	1,163	188.6	45.1	1,697

ª Percent, measured from December to December.
Source: National statistical authorities.

to become a serious political issue. The main reason for low unemployment is a sharp drop in labor force participation. Other factors include initial exchange-rate undervaluation (which helped to maintain average enterprise profit rates), relatively flexible labor markets, low unemployment benefits, and net emigration to the FSU.[4]

Third, *inflation has been brought down* from near-hyperinflation in 1992 (annual rates of 953% in Estonia, 959% in Latvia, and 1,163% in Lithuania) to under 50% in 1994 (41.7%, 26.3%, and 45.1%, respectively). See Table 3. This is in contrast to the CIS, where inflation remains much higher. The relative inflationary performance of Estonia and Latvia differs according to measurement period. From June 1992 (when Estonia left the ruble zone) to June 1995, they did about equally well: the CPI rose by a factor of 4.3 in Estonia and by 4.4 in Latvia. During 1993 and 1994, when both countries were pursuing concerted stabilization, Latvia did better, with cumulative inflation of 70% compared to 92% in Estonia. This was also true during the most recent 12-month period (June 1994 – June 1995), when Estonian and Latvian inflation rates were 29.2% and 23.6%, respectively.

Lithuania's performance has been consistently poorer. Its CPI rose by a factor of 18 from June 1992 to June 1995. Inflation during 1993–94 was a cumulative 319%. From June 1994 to June 1995, prices rose by 38.1%. As the 1995 rate is likely to be near 30%, Lithuanian inflation appears to be converging toward levels in the other Baltic states. The best characterization of overall performance is that, after beginning serious stabilization, Latvia has had the lowest inflation rates and Lithuania the highest.

---

[4] For instance, the population of Estonia has decreased by over 1% per year since 1992, which is due partly to negative natural increase. For more on labor market developments, see Saavalainen (1995).

Fourth, the Baltics are characterized by the *extreme convertibility of their new currencies*.[5] In 1994, they became the first three economies in transition to accept IMF Article VIII. Estonia and Latvia have abolished all limits on capital movement and foreign exchange accounts, while Lithuania has full current-account and high capital-account convertibility. The political and economic reasons for high convertibility relative to CEE remain unclear.

Fifth, the Baltic currencies have undergone *significant real appreciation* since the start of monetary reforms in June 1992. Measured in U.S. dollars, the level of the CPI had by June 1995 grown 4.5 times in Estonia, 5.6 times in Latvia, and 5.8 times in Lithuania. This translates into average annual increases in dollar prices of 65% in Estonia, 78% in Latvia, and 80% in Lithuania. Yet, in spite of massive real appreciation, exports have expanded rapidly. Relative to 1992, the dollar value of recorded 1994 exports was up 184% in Estonia, 21% in Latvia, and 212% in Lithuania. By 1994, trade had also sharply shifted away from FSU markets (including the other Baltic states). The FSU share of total trade fell from about 90% in all three states in 1991 to 32% in Estonia, 45–50% in Latvia, and 55% in Lithuania.[6]

Finally, the Baltic states had by 1994 developed a pattern of large trade and current-account deficits, even larger net capital inflows, and thus *a healthy growth of foreign reserves*. Current-account deficits have widened over time. In 1994, these amounted to 7.3% of GDP in Estonia, 3.5% in Latvia, and 2.2% in Lithuania. The corresponding growth in central bank gross reserves as a share of GDP was 2%, 3.3%, and 4%, respectively (see Table 4). This suggests net capital inflows in 1994 of about 9.3%, 6.8%, and 6.2% of GDP, respectively.[7]

3. HOW WAS HIGH INFLATION BROUGHT UNDER CONTROL?

To maintain focus, we will concentrate in the rest of our study on examining the comparative inflationary performance of the three Baltic states. We begin by exploring the two key reasons for the common Baltic pattern of sharply reduced inflation, both of which are very traditional.

---

[5] The monetary reforms in these countries have been widely described elsewhere. See Hansson (1994a), Lainela and Sutela (1994), and Repse (1994).

[6] The approximate figure for Latvia reflects the lack of a country-by-country breakdown of its mineral fuels imports, the bulk of which presumably come from Lithuania and the CIS.

[7] The calculation is inexact owing to "errors and omissions" in the balance of payments, and by the revaluation effects of exchange-rate changes on foreign reserves.

Table 4. *Indicators of the balance of payments in the Baltic states, 1992–94*

	1992	1993	1994
Current account balance (% of GDP)			
Estonia	+13.4	+2.4	-7.3
Latvia	+1.4	+6.8	-3.5
Lithuania	+19.1	-3.2	-2.2
Growth of foreign exchange reserves (% of GDP)			
Estonia		+11.9	+2.0
Latvia		+18.8	+3.2
Lithuania		+12.0	+4.0
Growth of foreign exchange reserves (% of initial base money)			
Estonia			7.24
Latvia			29.9
Lithuania			69.1

Sources: National statistical authorities; central banks.

Table 5. *Central government budget surplus[a] in the Baltic states, 1991–94*

	1991	1992	1993	1994
Estonia	5.1	1.5	1.0	0.5
Latvia	8.0	-3.0	-0.1	-1.9
Lithuania	1.6	-1.1	-1.0	-2.1

[a] Measured as a share of GDP.
Source: National statistical authorities.

First, all three states have so far kept *government budgets remarkably near balance* (Table 5). From 1991 to 1994, the largest annual central government deficit represented 3.0% of GDP in Latvia (in 1992). In 1994, Lithuania had the largest deficit of 2.1% of GDP. Estonia's state budget has been in slight surplus throughout. These budgets are tight by any standard, and far tighter than in most economies in transition (Table 6). The cross-country differences are too small to explain much of the variance in inflation experienced by the Baltic states, especially since Latvia has often combined marginally larger deficits with marginally lower inflation.

Table 6. *Central government budget surpluses*[a]
in transition economies, 1993-94

	1993	1994	1993-94[b]
Estonia	1.0	0.5	0.75
Czechia	0.1	1.0	0.55
Croatia	0.2	0.7	0.45
Slovenia	0.5	-1.0	-0.25
Latvia	-0.1	-1.9	-1.0
Lithuania	-1.0	-2.1	-1.55
Poland	-2.8	-2.8	-2.8
Romania	-1.8	-4.4	-3.1
Slovakia	-6.8	-5.7	-6.25
Hungary	-5.7	-7.5	-6.6
Bulgaria	-11.4	-6.8	-9.1
Russia	-10	-10	-10

[a] Measured as a share of GDP.
[b] Simple average.
Source: National statistical authorities.

The reasons for this common fiscal stringency remain unclear. Most proposed explanations are unconvincing, as there are always several counterexamples where the same factors go hand in hand with large deficits.[8] First, the positive 1991 terms-of-trade shock, due to faster price liberalization in the Baltics than in the rest of the FSU, was largely reversed in 1992 as the latter states freed prices, but did not lead to large deficits in the Baltics.[9] In fact, Russia has for several years had the most favorable terms-of-trade development yet still runs large deficits, casting further doubt on the role of this link. Second, the argument that the Baltics benefitted from starting with low tax/GDP ratios could as well be reversed; that is, one could argue that countries with larger state sectors had more room to cut expenditures and thus to balance the budget.[10] Third, an early shift toward indirect taxes (Estonia had already introduced a broad-based VAT by 1991) may help to explain the relative buoyancy of tax collection from one year to the next. However, since Baltic government revenue/GDP ratios are well below the levels of many countries running large

[8] Saavalainen (1995) enumerates most of these arguments.
[9] The 1992 shocks were some of the least favorable experienced by any economy in transition.
[10] However, if social programs are particularly difficult to cut, and if large expenditure/GDP ratios come mainly from these programs, such an argument becomes more plausible. For more, see Aslund (1994) and Sachs (1995).

deficits, this theory fails to explain why they have had more success in balancing budgets. Fourth, the apparent ease of implementing cash rationing as a way of controlling expenditures leaves open the question of why this did not simply lead to open arrears – as in, for example, Russia and Ukraine. Fifth, a lack of a foreign debt burden characterized *every* non-Russian FSU state, most of which have nonetheless run large budget deficits. Sixth, the existence of currency-board rules in Estonia and later in Lithuania (which ruled out central bank financing of the government) still leaves unanswered why budgetary pressures led to fiscal adjustment rather than to a repeal of these arrangements. Seventh, large fiscal deficits in, for example, Slovakia and Moldova (EBRD 1994) rule out any simple "small country" effect.

In the end, the real answers are likely to have a political economy basis rather than a technical basis. This could include the depth of the desire to escape the Soviet sphere, and the resulting willingness to accept IMF and other conditions on macroeconomic policy.[11] The role of such political economy factors deserves much further study.

The second factor behind controlled inflation has been relatively *tight monetary policies*. By moving to a modified currency-board arrangement (Estonia in June 1992, Lithuania in April 1994), the central banks of these two states largely ceased issuing domestic credits.[12] In 1994, the growth of central bank net domestic assets (NDA) as a percent of initial base money was only 4.4% in Estonia and – 7.7% in Lithuania. The analogous figure for Latvia was a still low 10.5%; this means that, although the Bank of Latvia does not strictly act like a currency board, Latvian longer-term money growth has also come largely from the balance of payments.[13]

This does not mean that monetary aggregates have remained stable. As theory would suggest, real money demand grew sharply once stabilization gained credibility and interest rates began to de-

---

[11] Some have claimed that the relative success of Czechia, Estonia, Slovenia, and Croatia in balancing state budgets (Table 6) reflects a "Germanic" desire to pursue sound policies, a theme that ventures well beyond the purview of this essay; in any case, such a theory is hard to substantiate. For more on the political economy of Estonian macroeconomic policy, see Hansson (1994b).

[12] The laws in these countries allow some exceptions to a pure currency-board rule. For instance, the Bank of Estonia can undertake limited bank rescue operations in the case of a banking crisis, provided that its net foreign reserves do not fall below the volume of base money.

[13] By law, the Bank of Latvia can provide the government with only seasonal credits of no more than 1/12 of the current budget year revenues.

cline. In 1993, Estonian base money grew by 113% while consumer prices rose by 35.7%, and Latvian base money grew by 107% while the CPI rose 34.7%. In 1994, once Lithuania was pursuing concerted stabilization, its base money rose by 61.4% while prices rose by 45.1%. With little growth of NDA, this came via the balance of payments – that is, via inflows of foreign reserves.

For this reason, and because minimum reserve requirements can also be changed (as in Lithuania in May 1993), the growth of total base money is not a good indicator of the thrust of monetary policy, at least not for periods when real money demand grows rapidly. Interpreting changes in broad money (e.g. M2) is even more difficult.[14] Separating out the shifts in money supply and demand would require formal statistical analysis, which is impossible until more data become available. Until then, the best (but still very imperfect) single indicator of the thrust of monetary policy is the growth of NDA, and this growth has been negligible.

4. WHY HAS FURTHER REDUCTION OF INFLATION PROVED DIFFICULT?

The common pattern of inflation staying above both Western European and expected levels is explained by four interrelated factors. First, phased *increases in key administered prices* (especially for home heating, rent and communal services, and public transport) produced a series of one-time price increases as subsidies were cut and/or prices freed. More generally, the move from Soviet to Western price structures required significant changes in relative prices. As long as prices are sticky downwards, these can translate into absolute price increases.[15] Such one-time shocks have had quite visible effects on monthly inflation rates, but their longer-run impact remains less clear. If cuts in subsidies allow a simultaneous cut in tax rates, this should have a deflationary effect elsewhere in the economy.

Second, and in a related fashion, *a general shift from direct taxes toward indirect taxes* in all three states created one-time jumps in the price

---

[14] For instance, the ratio of cash to deposits will depend both on interest rates and on the level of confidence in the banking system. The reserve/deposit ratio will depend on interest rates and on the menu of alternative ways of placing excess reserves. All of these factors influence the money multiplier and the relationship between money supply and demand in uncertain ways.

[15] For a discussion of the impact of such relative price increases in the Baltic states, see Ross (1994) and Richards and Tersman (1995).

level when VAT and excise tax rates were raised. For example, the November 1993 increase of Latvia's general VAT rate from 12% to 18% explains much of the sharp 8.8% jump in Latvian consumer prices that month.

Third, all three countries have experienced *significant capital inflows* (see Section 2). In Estonia, this largely took the form of FDI, which represented 10.6% of GDP in 1993 and 9.3% in 1994 – the highest rates in CEE and the FSU. Lithuania has attracted little FDI (0.76% of GDP in 1994), but used significant amounts of official loan financing. Latvia has used an intermediary mix of FDI and loan capital. All countries also appear to have experienced some reverse capital flight, as tight financial constraints and growing confidence in stabilization caused residents to repatriate some funds. To the extent that these inflows were not immediately and fully matched by imports, they led to a growth in foreign exchange reserves (Table 4). This increased the supply of base money, presumably more than the growth in nominal money demand, putting upward pressure on inflation.

Fourth, all three states began their stabilizations at greatly *"undervalued" exchange rates.* This must also have contributed to the inflows of foreign capital; the resulting low cost levels attracted FDI, and the small probability of depreciation raised the expected return in dollars from placing funds in the Baltics. This does not mean that exchange rates were too low at the time, but rather that they were below levels that would prevail in the medium term once productivity had begun to rebound.

The level of the exchange rate is best seen in the dollar value of average monthly wages. In June 1992, when Estonia began its stabilization, this value was $41 in Estonia, $31 in Latvia, and $45 in Lithuania. When Latvia began serious stabilization in October 1992, its average monthly wage was $36. When Lithuania tightened its monetary policy in May 1993, its average wage was $33. In other words, average wages were about $30–$40 when serious stabilization began. This contrasts to levels of $77 in Poland in the first quarter of 1990, and $129 in Czechoslovakian industry in January 1991. On the presumption that the long-run potential of the Baltic economies is at least as high as that of Poland (most prereform estimates placed Baltic per-capita GDP above Polish levels), this left significant room for growth of dollar wages.

The low initial wage levels were mandated by the similar levels prevailing in Russia, which at the time was the key trading partner of all three states. Setting the exchange rate to bring dollar wages close to, say, Polish levels (which by June 1992 had grown further to $204 per month) was not a serious option, as it would have destroyed the competitiveness of the unreformed industrial and agricultural sectors, which were still geared to FSU markets. Russia's average monthly wage remained in the $30-$40 range until mid-1993, when a fairly stable ruble–dollar exchange rate (combined with high inflation) brought it to $114 by December 1993. The resulting real depreciation of the Baltic currencies versus the ruble created new undervaluation, giving room for the additional price and wage increases that had been precluded until then.[16]

Although Latvia and Lithuania began with floating exchange rates and had periods of nominal appreciation (since September 1992 in Latvia), all three countries eventually "locked in" much of their undervaluation by *fixing or pegging their exchange rates*. Estonia fixed the kroon to the deutsche mark (DM) from June of 1992. Latvia informally pegged the lats to the IMF's Special Drawing Right (SDR) in February 1994, when the average monthly wage was still $109. Lithuania fixed the litas to the dollar in April 1994, when its average wage was only $82.[17] At these levels, there was still much room for further wage and price increases as productivity improved. Undervaluation, along with tight financial policies, also explains the ability of the Baltics to sustain these pegs, often in the face of large negative shocks (rumors of imminent devaluation in Estonia and Lithuania, a banking crisis in Latvia, early-1995 appreciation of the DM and voter backlash against reforms in Estonia, etc.).

There are several indirect signs that, after sharp drops at the start of reforms, the productivity of Baltic tradables producers has rebounded sharply. First, the Baltics have maintained huge growth rates of exports in the face of massive real appreciation (from June 1992 to June 1995, average annual increases in the dollar level of consumer prices have ranged from 65% in Estonia to 80% in Lithuania). Second, a common subjective view (based, for example, on the appearance of shops) is that the average quality of Baltic consumer goods and services increased markedly once firms were exposed to

---

[16] This factor could explain part of the surprisingly high inflation of late 1993 and early 1994. For example, from the third to the fourth quarter of 1993, CPI inflation (end-period to end-period) grew from 6.4% to 11% in Estonia, from 1.0% to 18.7% in Latvia, and from 8.2% to 21.7% in Lithuania.

[17] In the Latvian and Lithuanian cases, this fixing had been preceded by several months of nearly stable exchange rates brought about by central bank intervention.

competition from Western and other producers. This increased the competitiveness of local goods and services, allowing producers to sell them for higher dollar prices.[18]

An analogous effect is visible in the case of Japan. In 1970, the average yen–dollar exchange rate was 360 yen/dollar. If subsequent exchange-rate developments had reflected only measured inflation differentials between Japan and the United States, the rate in June 1995 would have stood at about 300 yen/dollar. Instead, it stood at 84 yen/dollar, while Japan continued to maintain a strong trade surplus. This can only be explained by sharp increases in the productivity of Japanese tradables producers, which are hard to measure yet important to consumers of Japanese products. Starting from the extremely poor quality levels of the FSU, the room for such productivity increases (and thus real exchange-rate appreciation) could be far greater in the Baltics.

Put differently, some of the recent inflation in the Baltic states might well be illusory, in the sense that higher prices partly reflect the better quality of available goods and services. Determining the true extent of such factors would require the estimation of hedonic price indices, which take into account the attributes of various goods. Since this is nearly impossible in practice, the true extent of such factors will remain speculative.

Viewed ex post and in this fashion, the Japanese-style pursuit of stable prices via gradual nominal appreciation was never a serious option in the Baltics (however, it could still damp some price increases). High capital mobility, as in the Baltics, means that interest rates should not deviate much from the "uncovered interest parity" condition. This states that the domestic currency interest rate should equal the rate on analogous dollar assets, plus the expected rate of depreciation of the domestic currency versus the dollar. A differential in the perceived riskiness of holding the two currencies could, of course, add a small risk premium or discount. If the public had believed that the actual average real rates of appreciation versus the dollar (at least 59% per year) could be achieved via nominal appreciation,[19] then nominal domestic interest rates would have had to fall

---

[18] At the beginning of reforms, most Baltic goods were of such low quality that they could be sold only at knockdown prices. This meant that even minor improvements in quality (e.g., better labels and packaging of food products) could greatly increase, if not the export potential of Baltic producers, then at least their ability to compete with imports domestically.

[19] If the dollar CPI increased by an average of 65% in Estonia, and if U.S. inflation was about 4%, then this translates into a change in the real exchange rate of $(1.65/1.04 - 1) \times 100$, or 58.7%. The change in the real rates in Latvia and Lithuania was even greater.

far below zero (possibly past −50%), which is inconceivable. For this reason, most of the needed real appreciation had to come via domestic inflation.

Finally, the Baltic states did not pursue serious wage controls or other incomes policies. Tax-based policies to limit state-sector wage increases were envisioned in the first IMF agreements, but never really implemented (less formal attempts to limit wage increases in the state sector were made). As the longer-term effect of such policies on inflation remains disputed, their positive or negative impact is hard to judge.

5. WHAT EXPLAINS INTRA-BALTIC DIFFERENCES IN INFLATION?

The common Baltic pattern of controlled but stubborn inflation includes three cross-country differences that need to be explained.

(1) Why has Lithuania's overall inflationary performance been worse than that of Estonia or Latvia?
(2) Why has Lithuania's inflation remained higher even after the introduction of a currency-board rule in April 1994?
(3) Why has Latvia had better inflationary performance than Estonia since the beginning of 1993?

Definitive explanations will require more detailed analysis, but some likely causes are discernible. Because government budgets have been tight in all three countries, the answers will not lie in different fiscal policies.

First, most of Lithuania's higher inflation occurred before late April of 1993, when an increase in reserve requirements signaled a tightening of monetary policy (Saavalainen 1995). Until late September of 1992, when Lithuania left the ruble zone, it did not have an independent monetary policy. During this period, its high inflation is explained by loose Russian financial policies.

The standard explanation for the continued high inflation during the first seven months of monetary independence, at an average rate of 20% per month, has been loose monetary policy (Lainela and Sutela 1994; Saavalainen 1995). A closer look presents a more complex picture. Data for the whole litas period are not available, but base money grew by only 0.1% in the first four months of 1993. More importantly, net domestic assets of the Bank of Lithuania (BoL) actually *fell* by 47.3% of base money during this period. In other words, the BoL was massively sterilizing inflows of reserves, which is normally an indication of tight monetary policy.

The actual source of inflation, suggested in conversations with some officials, appears to have been *low and falling money demand* (one indication is the extensive dollarization of the economy). In spite of its tightness, monetary policy was seen by the public as being loose, either at that time or in the future. Such perceptions may have arisen simply from the lack of a clear commitment to stringent policies by the BoL. By this interpretation, the appointment of a new BoL governor, who backed tight money rhetoric with increased reserve requirements, created enough confidence for money demand to begin growing, finally putting downward pressure on prices.

This experience confirms that monetary aggregates provide little if any evidence of the perceived thrust of monetary policy in the early stages of transition, when the public expectations that affect money demand are very volatile. More importantly, it shows that macroeconomic policy is not only about getting technical parameters right, but also about signaling a clear commitment to stringent policies. This can be done either by concrete actions and clear statements, or by creating institutions – such as currency boards – that lock in sound policies (Hansson and Sachs 1994). The role of such factors has received insufficient attention in the analysis and design of stabilization programs.

Lithuania's relatively higher inflation (from June 1994 to June 1995) is hardly the result of fiscal and monetary variables, the objective indicators of which point to tightness (Section 3). Three other explanations stand out. First, the "hand-tying" effect of Lithuania's currency board was smaller than that of Estonia's. Whereas Estonian law allows only parliament (rather than the central bank) to devalue, Lithuanian law gave this right first to the government and later to the BoL. The public's knowledge that a single institution capable of operating secretly might devalue the litas may have created uncertainty about the sustainability of the prevailing parity, keeping money demand low. An early challenge by opposition parliamentarians to the constitutionality of the currency-board law further eroded confidence that it would be sustained.

Second, the litas was more "undervalued" than the kroon or lats in June 1994, giving Lithuania more room for inflation as its economy restructured and adjusted to world prices. Average monthly wages were then $146 in Estonia and $140 in Latvia, but only $87 in Lithuania.

Third, but less tangibly, Lithuania appears to exert the weakest financial discipline over enterprises of all the Baltic states. One indication is the proper functioning of the bankruptcy system, which has so far been most effective in Estonia.[20] If firms can respond to tight financial policies by crediting themselves via accumulation of interenterprise debts, by forcing banks to roll over debts, or by lobbying the government for subsidies or other support, the true level of financial stringency will be lower than suggested by monetary and fiscal variables alone.

Finally, Latvia's better inflationary performance relative to Estonia since the beginning of 1993 can largely if not fully be explained by differences in nominal exchange-rate movements. During 1993–94, Estonia's CPI grew by 12.9% more than Latvia's. At the same time, the kroon appreciated relative to the dollar by 0.8% and to the lats by 34.5%. Put differently, the kroon depreciated versus the lats by 51.5%. Given that tradable goods – the prices of which are strongly linked to the exchange rate – represent more than half of the CPI basket, a 12.9% Latvian inflation advantage is consistent with such nominal exchange-rate differentials. In this sense, Latvia's policy of cutting inflation via deliberate but gradual appreciation of the lats (Repse 1994) was a success.[21]

6. POLICY CREDIBILITY AND THE COST OF DISINFLATION

Although we have focused on inflation, macroeconomic performance cannot be evaluated on the basis of this indicator alone. The most obvious other consideration (e.g., from Phillips curve methodology) is the output cost of disinflation. Put differently, sharp cuts in inflation may not be deemed a success if they lead to excessively high losses in output, especially if these losses make disinflation politically unsustainable.

It is now widely agreed that the cost of disinflation will depend on the information available to (and expectations of) the population regarding the policies being followed. If prices and wages were flexible then a well-understood and fully credible disinflationary policy

---

[20] According to EBRD (1994), some 200–300 bankruptcy procedures had been initiated in Estonia (compared to 1,045 in Poland, a much larger country), "only a few cases" in Latvia, and 8 cases in Lithuania.

[21] As noted in Section 4, it could never have been a recipe for price stability, because the required rate of nominal appreciation could hardly have been sustained by borrowers' paying positive nominal interest rates on lats-denominated loans.

would, in theory, have no output cost. Conversely, a poorly understood or not credible policy will lead to output losses as the public learns about the true policy stance. Credibility or its absence will play an especially great role in countries like the Baltic states, where the initial belief in the will or ability of new monetary authorities to pursue disinflation must have been low.

The mechanisms through which credibility affects macroeconomic outcomes are several.[22] The simplest and most relevant for the Baltic states works through the uncovered interest parity condition (see Section 4). Again, this states that if capital is fully mobile and domestic and foreign currency assets are seen as perfect substitutes (implying no risk premium), then the domestic interest rate should equal the foreign interest rate plus the expected rate of depreciation of the domestic currency relative to the foreign currency. This can be written as:

$$i = i^* + (E_e - E)/E,$$

where i is the domestic interest rate, i^* is the foreign interest rate, E_e is the expected exchange rate in the next period, and E is the exchange rate in the current period.[23]

Under this condition, if the exchange rate were expected to stay constant, then interest rates on domestic- and foreign-currency-denominated assets of a maturity equal to the time period in question (e.g. one month) would be the same. If, however, domestic currency were expected to depreciate during this period, then investors or lenders would require a higher interest rate in order to hold assets denominated in domestic currency.

Let us take the example of two countries, A and B, that are both pursuing the same actual policy of maintaining a stable exchange rate. The sole difference is that the public believes that country A really is pursuing such a policy (i.e., A is credible) but that country B's actual policy will lead to a devaluation of its currency during the period (i.e., B is not fully credible). To compensate for the expected devaluation of country B's currency, the nominal interest rate on assets denominated in country-B currency must exceed the interest on like assets in currency A. If, ex post, country B does succeed in maintaining its exchange rate, then the real interest rate (measured

---

[22] For a short discussion of these in a Baltic context, see Hansson and Sachs (1994).
[23] This is a convenient approximation to the exact form of the parity condition, which is $(1 + i) = E_e(1 + i^*)/E$.

in dollars) that country B borrowers must in fact repay will turn out to be higher than in A, and also higher than they had anticipated.[24] Unexpectedly high real interest rates in country B will have several effects on its enterprises and banks. First, some borrowers will no longer be able to earn sufficient rates of return to repay loans on the agreed terms, leading to more financial difficulties in country-B firms and more bad loans in country-B banks. Second, the high cost of standard trade credits will hamper economic activity, also cutting output. Finally, greater uncertainty about the stability of the exchange rate and the overall economy will reduce FDI into country B, worsening its long-run growth prospects.[25] In other words, a successful disinflation in both countries will come with more lost output, slower growth, and greater banking problems in country B.

The relevance of these factors in the Baltics is suggested by the very different nominal interest rates across space and time. This is shown in several examples, the most important being a comparison of Estonia and Latvia. In Estonia, the interest rates on low-risk assets have been very low. Rates on 28-day Bank of Estonia certificates of deposit (CDs) have long stayed in the range of 5–6% per year. Average interest rates on interbank loans have fallen from an already low 6.1% in January 1994 to 5.43% in December 1994 and then to 5.11% in May 1995.

In contrast, rates on 28-day Latvian government T-bills have generally hovered around 24–26% per year, with occasional larger fluctuations between 18% and 32%. The average rate for 1- to 3-month interbank loans fell from 42% in January 1994 to 33% in December. Given Latvia's better inflationary performance in 1994 (26.3% vs. 41.7% in Estonia), these higher nominal rates create the basis for much higher real interest rates.

A comparison of the 28-day rates alone would suggest a market expectation of depreciation of the lats versus the kroon of about 17.5% ($(1.24/1.055 - 1) \times 100$) on an annual basis, or about 1.25% over 28 days. Such a comparison *across* countries and types of securities (i.e. government vs. central bank) may be inaccurate because of differential country and default risk. A more appropriate comparison would be between similar domestic- and foreign-currency deposit (or loan)

---

[24] If purchasing power parity is assumed to hold in the long run, the same story could be told via domestic inflation rates. If these are expected to be different ex ante, but turn out to be identical ex post, then different nominal interest rates will translate into different real interest rates.

[25] The recent Mexican crisis is one good example.

Table 7. *Average interest rates[a] on 3–6-month lats-denominated loans and deposits in Latvian banks*

| | Loan rate | | Deposit rate | | Lats premium | |
Period	Lats	Forex	Lats	Forex	Loans	Deposits
Oct. 1993	75.5	78.9	50.1	25.4	– 1.2	19.7
Dec. 1993	88.6	74.4	43.1	24.9	8.1	14.6
Mar. 1994	63.1	58.5	39.9	21.4	2.9	15.2
Jun. 1994	68.3	61.8	34.6	26.0	4.0	6.8
Sep. 1994	57.2	40.4	30.5	19.4	12.0	9.3
Dec. 1994	34.2	23.7	17.6	17.8	8.5	0.0
Average[b]	64.5	56.3	36.0	22.5	5.6	10.9

[a] Percent per year.   [b] Arithmetic average.
Source: *Bank of Latvia Monetary Review* (1994:4).

interest rates *within* a country; this controls for country, transfer, and most commercial risk. Table 7 compares the average 3–6-month interest rates on both deposits and loans in Latvian banks for selected months between October 1993 and December 1994. Because a single large loan can at times affect the average, the calculated premium of lats interest rates relative to foreign-currency interest rates $((1 + i)/(1 + i^*) - 1) \times 100)$ can also fluctuate. For this reason, we calculate a simple arithmetic average of the six presented figures. These suggest still positive but somewhat lower premia than did the comparison of 28-day securities. The implied expected annual rate of depreciation of the lats relative to foreign currency is 5.6% based on loans and 10.9% based on deposits.[26]

One explanation (argued in Hansson and Sachs 1994) is that Estonia's currency-board rule, especially the stipulation that only parliament can devalue, created confidence in the stability of the exchange rate and brought Estonian interest rates down to near-German levels. Conversely, in spite of Latvia's good disinflation record, pro-

[26] Comparisons over different maturities produce quite similar estimates. As data for individual categories (e.g. 3–6 months) in given months can be affected by one or a handful of single transactions at atypical rates, single observations can show both large premia and discounts for the lats. However, if one takes the average of the twelve premia reported in Table 7 (i.e., six observations each for loan and deposit rates), then one finds higher lats interest rates over all reported horizons. A similar comparison in Estonia is made difficult by the fact that Estonian banks generally have been allowed to accept new foreign-currency deposits only since March 1994; the market for such deposits has remained small and thus volatile.

tracted nominal appreciation of the lats, and the clear personal commitment to tight policies by Bank of Latvia governor Einars Repse, the public may have continued to expect some depreciation of the lats, which had to be compensated by higher lats interest rates.

A second example is Lithuania before and after its switch to a quasi-currency board on 1 April 1994. In December 1993, the average interest rate on 1–3-month litas loans had been 91%. By March 1994 this had fallen to only 86%. Yet, as the BoL developed its track record and the credibility of the currency board grew, interest rates fell sharply. By May 1995, this average lending rate had fallen to 32%.[27]

Third, one could argue that the same phenomenon is also evident in Latvia, which switched from a managed float to tracking the SDR starting in February 1994. "Tracking" means that the Bank of Latvia did not promise to maintain this rate at all costs, as in Estonia. In spite of this weak commitment, such a peg may well have created enough short-run confidence to bring about a long-awaited drop in nominal interest rates (Table 7).

If the credibility of policies is actually at play, Latvia's most recent experiences provide a graphic example both of the costs of lower credibility and of the way in which expectations could become self-fulfilling.[28] Since September 1994, several medium- and large-scale Latvian commercial banks began encountering difficulties. In time, this led to suspension of their licenses and sometimes to the initiation of bankruptcy proceedings. The crisis culminated on 22 May 1995, when Baltija Bank – by far the largest in the Baltics – could no longer withstand a run on deposits and so induced intervention by the central bank (Kaminski 1995). Initial estimates of the size of the resulting losses range up to $400 million, or nearly 10% of Latvia's projected 1995 GDP (Thornhill and Kaminski 1995). Since then, several other major banks have failed (Kahar 1995).

The reasons most often given for these developments include lax supervision, unwise lending to major bank shareholders, and corruption. An additional if not alternative explanation is the macroeconomic one given previously – namely, that borrowers were simply

---

[27] The corresponding fall in the average rate on time deposits was from 80% in December 1993 to 66% in March 1994 to 21% in May 1995.

[28] The cumulative measured GDP decline from 1991 to 1994 was 35% in Estonia and 49% in Latvia, which also suggests that the cost of stabilization has been higher in Latvia. However, this conclusion is made less certain by possible differences in GDP statistics, and by the less favorable initial conditions under which Latvia began its stabilization.

unable to earn the real rates of return needed to repay the loans on the agreed terms, leaving banks with large portfolios of bad loans.[29] In other words, the decrease in nominal and real interest rates may have come too late.

As of July 1995, the crisis had yet to be resolved. All options available to the Latvian authorities were unpalatable. Disinflation would be maintained by choosing a harsh solution, but the resulting credit squeeze and temporary freezing of deposits could hamper economic activity. This would also lead to a withdrawal of other nonresident deposits from Latvia as owners began to fear that their value would not be maintained, thus reducing banks' income. Put differently, the cost of lower credibility would take the form of further bankruptcies and losses of output and services income.

If, at the other extreme, the authorities were to fully bail out depositors and recapitalize the failed banks, the resulting increases in government budget deficits and central bank credit would rekindle inflation and possibly lead to a devaluation of the lats. This inflation would in turn ease the burden on indebted firms by lowering the ex post real interest rates that they face. If Latvian authorities were to tread a middle path, allowing some real income loss and also some reflation and depreciation, then initial expectations could turn out to be self-fulfilling; that is, the public's initial belief – that the exchange rate could not be maintained in the face of the high output cost of deflation – would be confirmed.

The true importance of these effects will become evident only after several years, when stable, well-supervised banking systems and functioning bankruptcy systems have come into operation, and when improved national income accounts allow us to better assess the size of output decline. After all, until the recent Latvian crisis, Estonia had had both the lowest interest rates and the most severe open banking problems. This may simply reflect that events are still far from having run their full course in all three countries – financial problems can have long gestation lags. Put differently, the track record is still too short for making very strong conclusions about comparative inflation, growth, and banking performance.

---

[29] Another simultaneous factor appears to have been the falling profitability of the transit trade, which absorbed many of the resources of Latvian banks once Russia began to move its low domestic prices of raw materials closer to world market levels. The role of a relatively weak bankruptcy system (EBRD 1994) in allowing the accumulation or rolling over of bad debts should also be considered.

7. CONCLUSIONS AND FUTURE RESEARCH

Preliminary examination of the recent Baltic stabilization experience suggests that the move from high to controlled inflation was due to conventional macroeconomic policies. Once budgets were brought near balance and monetary policy tightened, inflation fell sharply. In the short run, however, tightness was reflected not so much in the settings of policy instruments (especially the growth of central bank net domestic assets), but rather in the creation of a public perception that the authorities were committed to lower inflation. With money demand being highly volatile, the exchange rate appears to have been a better nominal anchor than the money supply.

Explanations for the Baltic failure to bring inflation down to near Western European levels (a phenomenon also seen in other countries emerging from hyperinflation) are not specific to economies in transition, but are certainly much more pronounced there. Required relative price adjustments were larger than in most other less developed countries. The sudden opening up of small countries located near larger, high-cost neighbors created the potential for huge capital inflows (as a share of GDP), which in turn hampered the control of money supply and inflation.[30]

Most importantly, the opening of distorted planned economies that had been highly integrated with "the East" led to a sharp initial drop in productivity measured in foreign currency, and thus to a very depreciated initial exchange rate.[31] For this reason, undervaluation appears to have been unavoidable. Had these countries started from a more appreciated exchange rate, the export stimulus and FDI that stands behind much of their subsequent productivity growth may never have occurred.[32] Yet, when reforms began to produce a rebound in productivity, and thus an appreciation of the equilibrium real exchange rate, they created much room for inflation. Countries (like Ukraine) that are starting to stabilize from wage levels of around $30 per month (as in the Baltics in 1992) may therefore begin to follow similar inflation paths. This would be a vast improvement

---

[30] Such factors may also be important in Hungary and to a lesser extent in Czechia.

[31] This depreciation was also linked to loose financial policies and the resulting higher asset demand for foreign currencies.

[32] As Saavalainen (1995) notes, "undervaluation" would be more of a problem in countries starting with a more balanced macroeconomy, where fine tuning the inflation rate was an option. Starting from hyperinflation, it was possible to cut inflation even from an extremely "undervalued" exchange rate.

over past performance, but makes the achievement of "1% per month" medium-term inflation targets (standard to IMF agreements) a bit problematic.

The Baltic experience reinforces the importance of policy credibility and the way in which laws and institutions can bring this about. Lithuania brought inflation down only when its authorities were able to signal their commitment to stabilization, first by pronouncements and concrete actions, and later by moving to a quasi–currency board. Second, moving to a fixed or pegged exchange rate, even with little commitment to maintain this in the long run, appears to have created enough short-term confidence to begin reducing interest rates and with them the real costs of stabilization.[33] Third, the more the credibility of this fixed rate was enhanced by institutional bulwarks such as a currency board, the lower were nominal and real interest rates. Estonia tied its hands the most and had the best performance in this regard, while Latvia tied its hands the least and experienced the highest real interest rates.

Finally, the Latvian experience with floating exchange rates (more precisely, a managed float) shows that a policy of gradual appreciation can help to damp inflation, but also that the lower credibility of such a regime relative to fixed exchange rates may exact a higher cost in lost output. The relative costs of inflation and output loss are qualitative, meaning that one policy is not unambiguously better than another. Yet, the recent Latvian banking crisis – which may have some of its roots in this lower credibility, and which could now lead either to severe output loss or a reflation of the economy (the latter dissipating the benefits of past belt tightening) – at least hints that the costs of less credible policies will be high. A final evaluation of various strategies will be possible only after several years, when all three states have restructured their banking and financial sectors.

Several areas for future research appear to be especially promising. First, sorting out the shifts and effects of money supply and demand will require more formal statistical analysis. A growing track record will soon make this possible. Second, the role of capital inflows in promoting inflation needs to be more carefully assessed. When do these come from an accommodation of growing money demand, and when are they exogenous and thus possible promoters of inflation?

---

[33] Of course, supporting the fixed rate with appropriate monetary and fiscal policies was also a crucial element of success.

Third, what role do enterprise financial discipline and the strength of (and trust in) the banking system play in curbing or promoting inflation?

Finally, what has been the role of wage and incomes policies in promoting or hampering Baltic stabilization? What has been the impact of wage and price flexibility on the cost of stabilization? After all, the initial move to a market economy had the effect of a negative supply shock, which is usually thought to be more remediable by wage policy than by traditional demand management.

REFERENCES

Aslund, Anders (1994), "Why Goulash-Communism is a Liability Now," *Transition* 5(5): 6.

Dobozi, Istvan, and Gerhard Pohl (1995), "Real Output Decline in Transition Economies – Forget GDP, Try Power Consumption Data!" *Transition* 6(1/2): 17–18.

European Bank for Reconstruction and Development [EBRD] (1994), *Transition Report* (October). London: EBRD.

Hansson, Ardo H. (1994a), "The Estonian Kroon: Experiences of the First Year," in *The Economics of New Currencies*. London: Centre for Economic Policy Research, pp. 85–107.

Hansson, Ardo H. (1994b), "The Political-Economy of Macroeconomic and Foreign Trade Policy in Estonia," in Constantine Michalopoulos and David G. Tarr (eds.), *Trade in the New Independent States*. Washington, DC: World Bank, pp. 133–40.

Hansson, Ardo H., and Jeffrey D. Sachs (1994), "Monetary Institutions and Credible Stabilization: A Comparison of Experiences in the Baltics," presented at the conference on "Central Banks in Eastern Europe and the Newly Independent States" (22–23 April, University of Chicago Law School).

Kahar, Andres (1995), "Banks Dropping Like Flies," *Baltic Independent* (14–20 July), p. B1.

Kaminski, Matthew (1995), "Closure of Latvian Bank Raises Fears for Sector," *Financial Times* (24 May), p. 2.

Lainela, Seija, and Pekka Sutela (1994), *The Baltic Economies in Transition*. Helsinki: Bank of Finland.

Repse, Einars (1994), "The Experiences with the Latvian Ruble and the Lats," in *The Economics of New Currencies*. London: Centre for Economic Policy Research, pp. 197–210.

Richards, Anthony, and Gunnar Tersman (1995), "Growth, Nontradeables and Price Convergence in the Baltics," Working Paper no. 107, Stockholm Institute of East European Economies.

Ross, Märten (1994), "Exchange Rate Policy and Inflation," *Bank of Estonia Bulletin* 7: 32–9.

Saavalainen, Tapio (1995), "Stabilization in the Baltic Countries: A Comparative Analysis," Working Paper no. 95-44, International Monetary Fund, Washington, DC.

Sachs, Jeffrey (1995), "Postcommunist Parties and the Politics of Entitlements," *Transition* 6(3): 1–4.

Thornhill, John, and Matthew Kaminski (1995), "Baltic States Shrug Off Bank Crisis Setback," *Financial Times* (11 July), p. 3.

CHAPTER 11

Economic Reform in Ukraine

Oleh Havrylyshyn

Late is better than never – but more difficult.

1. INTRODUCTION

From the time of its independence on 24 August 1991, until at least the autumn of 1994, Ukraine was generally counted among the slowest reformers in the postcommunist group of countries (EBRD 1994, IMF 1995a). The presidential election victory of Leonid Kuchma over Leonid Kravchuk in July 1994 brought about a change in the priority accorded to economic reforms, and we see since October 1994 a comprehensive set of significant measures for stabilization and structural reforms. For outside observers, the dye marker identifying this sea change was the 31 October 1994 approval of the first IMF loan to Ukraine, a $375 million first-tranche of the systemic transformation facility (STF).

While the change in direction is clear, too little time has passed for a meaningful assessment of results. This essay therefore focuses primarily on the first three years under Kravchuk, and an analysis of why reform was delayed so long. In the analysis, I will also attempt to indicate how the delays in reform made the subsequent reform efforts more difficult. In place of a conclusion, I provide a tentative assessment of Kuchma's reform efforts.

One can identify three principal hypotheses explaining the delay of reforms in Ukraine:

(1) intellectual debates about economic transition and the speed of reform;

The views expressed here are my own, and should not in any way be considered as reflecting the position of the Ukrainian authorities or the IMF. I am grateful to the following individuals for their helpful comments: Mario Blejer, Taras Kuzio, Mancur Olson, Gur Ofer, and Jacques Polak. The responsibility for errors of fact or interpretation remains my own.

(2) the priority of nation-building tasks such as establishment of legal, political, military, and social institutions;

(3) the interests of the "new-old" elites in an unreformed (or, more accurately, a half-reformed) economy.

I will argue in this essay that while the first two hypotheses (especially the second) did play a role at the very beginning of Ukraine's independence, the most important factor in delaying real economic reform was the third: the self-interest of a regenerated, capitalist-oriented, communist elite. This view applies not only to Ukraine but to many other transition countries as well. Elsewhere (Havrylyshyn, forthcoming) I have elaborated the notion that a new monopoly- or rent-seeking capitalist elite has risen from the ashes of the old communist "patriarch" elite, and has used its influence to delay real reforms or freeze them in a fledgling state that suits its interests. I shall call this group the post-Soviet *rentier patriarchs*.[1]

The rest of the essay is organized as follows. Section 2 outlines the general thesis of post-Soviet rentier patriarchs – their evolution and their position vis-à-vis reforms. Section 3 gives an overview of major macroeconomic developments since 1991, including preliminary data for early 1995; this will serve as a statistical background for the analysis of the reform process in subsequent sections. Section 4 then demonstrates the principal argument of how reform was delayed in Ukraine by the new rentier interests, and finally Section 5 reviews the recent turn to a reformist direction – its nature, problems, and early results.

2. REFORM AND THE ROLE OF POST-SOVIET RENTIER PATRIARCHS

The popular press is by now replete with stories of the new "mafia" in postcommunist states, correctly noting that a very large part of the new capitalist class in fact comes from the old communist *nomenklatura*. It should not be surprising that, in all former communist states,

---

[1] I use the term "rentier" to reflect the popular public perception (and terminology used in transition economics) that the profits of these new capitalists are very often based not on entrepreneurial skills, but rather on rights and privileges granted by the government. In fact, "rentier" usually means one who earns a fixed income from mere ownership of assets; in the narrowest economic meaning (New Palgrave *Dictionary of Economics*) it is only interest income from financial assets. The correct economic terminology is "rent-seeking capitalist," but the term is awkward in translation and the use of "rentier" in many transition economies leads me to appropriate this term for present purposes.

members of this elite were best positioned to become the first new capitalists working under new quasi-market rules. Of greater relevance
for this paper is the question of how such a new class – with its obviously great political influence – will view the prospects of the following fundamental reform measures: (1) decentralization, (2) privatization, (3) financial stabilization, and (4) liberalization. The answer,
briefly, is: positively for those elements that benefit them (1 and 2),
and more negatively for those that do not (perhaps 3 and definitely
4). To elaborate, let me consider how things evolved, especially in
those economies where sharp, rapid, and comprehensive reform measures were *not* taken.

As central command disappeared, decentralization brought a new
autonomy for the old Soviet patriarchs (directors of enterprises and
state farms, local leaders, high officials). At first, their communist
background discredited them, and the expected reform measures –
privatization, opening up of foreign markets for competition, reduced subsidies – threatened their elite status. In countries where
reform measures were quickly undertaken, members of the elite who
were not pushed aside were at least forced to begin to behave approximately like competitive capitalists. In countries that delayed reform,
the continuing administrative interventions left in place distortions
such as controlled prices and regulated trade; this created the potential for large profits to be made on, for example, the differences between world and domestic prices. The delay also gave the old elites
time to transform themselves into a new, monopolist, capitalist elite
reliant on state financial support and privileges. The economics literature would define them as "rent-seekers" – that is, economic actors
who devote considerable effort to lobbying governments for privileges (such as export or import licenses) that allow them to capture
the profits or rents of their privileged, monopolylike position.[2]

The new economic arrangement is straightforward. The state provides budgetary subsidies and cheap bank credit, allegedly to sustain
the economy and keep people on the job. It also maintains low bread
prices "for the good of the average citizen" and low prices for key raw
materials "for the good of industry." This leads to inflation, but also
provides the directorate both with continuing patriarchal influence
and the funds to engage in such side operations (through commercial
spinoffs from the state factory) as purchasing low-priced titanium,
magnesium, or petroleum, obtaining licenses from their old-boy

[2] Krueger (1974) is the *locus classicus* for the economic theory of rent seeking.

colleagues at the ministry of foreign trade, selling these commodities abroad at higher world prices, and earning thereby a substantial profit. The results are: materials shortages, inflation, corruption, capital flight, new affluence for a few, and popular discontent. Popular discontent is partially quieted as patriarchs fulfill their neofeudal obligation, ensuring the workers have jobs and some privileges (health care, vacations, some consumer goods) and are paid enough to survive as before. Discontent nevertheless finds an outlet in worker behavior: "you pretend even less than in Soviet times to be paying us, and we pretend even less to be working." The result: still more absenteeism, still lower productivity, still less production. More worrisome for the future is that new investment in production capacity is not taking place, since commercial trade operations are far more profitable. Moreover, this powerful new economic elite does not want complete reform, because the transition world *between* a planned and a competitive economic system is ideal for its members.

Post-Soviet rentier patriarchs are most certainly not in favor of a return to central command arrangements. Indeed, the early decentralization (already under Gorbachev in the former USSR) is what gave first life to their improved status. At some point, the elites may recognize that excessive cheap credit and subsidies cause inflation, which in the long run hurts even the new capitalists by eating away at the production potential of the economy. Some efforts at fiscal and credit restraint are then likely. Very soon (and in some cases, already), the new capitalists will see that privatization of even large-scale state enterprises is in their interests because it can, of course, be organized so that they become the major shareholders. Fair or unfair, this would be good for the economy *if* true competition were allowed to work, to sort out the efficient capitalists from the inept; in a competitive environment, it often takes only one generation to go from riches to rags. But it's a big "if" and a questionable one, because allowing competition would mean wholeheartedly pursuing the fourth change, liberalization. While the rentier patriarch elite might eventually consider the first three steps to be in their interest, it is a stretch of the imagination to believe they would ever consider in their interest a liberalization that closes the lucrative potential of cheap raw materials and also removes their monopolistic status[3] by introducing foreign and domestic competition.

---

[3] References to such activities (and to such a situation of new monopoly capitalist interests) are now numerous, and I could easily take the spotlight off Ukraine by giving other examples –

It is popular to attribute a great deal to the role of corruption as a separate explanation of delayed reform. The best way of incorporating this into the explanation of the rentier patriarch model is to consider corruption as the illegal tip of the rentier patriarch iceberg. Indeed, where government distortions such as easy credit, price controls, and export licenses motivate rentier-capitalist activities, it is inevitable that some bribery and corruption of bureaucrats will follow. An old philosophical puzzle asks: If a tree falls in a forest and there is no one there to hear it, will there be a sound? An analogous puzzle may be put as follows: If someone tries to pay a bribe for the rights to pursue a certain economic activity, but there is no government restriction on that activity and hence no government regulator to take the bribe, will there be corruption?

A more important point that must be addressed is the realist counterargument: "corruption and profits from privilege are widespread in history and in today's world, so there is no point in moralizing about them." The moral judgment on what is an acceptable degree of corruption and privilege is for each person to make individually; I have nothing further to say on this matter, for the moralist–realist debate is not the main point of this essay. The main point is that those who benefit from government-granted privileges are fundamentally opposed to the changes that reforms would entail for economic regulation – changes that would remove the basis of their privileges. The more extensive and more deeply entrenched the system of privileges becomes, the stronger the opposition to reform. And since economies do not disintegrate but instead deteriorate by stagnating for long periods of time (as in, e.g., Peronist Argentina, Zaire, pre–Rajiv Gandhi's India), one may wait a long time indeed before the rentier interests realize that their base of profiteering is threatened. In the meantime, reforms continue to be delayed, and economic recovery and restructuring continue to be postponed. This is why extensive rentier profits and associated corruption are serious problems irrespective of moral judgment.

but not without first mentioning the most obvious Ukrainian case of former Prime Minister Zviahilskiy, who is "in hiding" from charges brought by Ukrainian prosecutors. For other examples, consider the Russian firm Nordex and its pamphlet's boast: "We made high margins on our trading activities due to the substantial differences between domestic and world prices" (*Financial Times*, 16/17 April 1994, p. I); or the G-13 conglomerate in Bulgaria (*Financial Times*, 10 April 1994); or the *New York Times* (20 April 1995, p. D2) quoting Andrei Shleifer, a foreign advisor on Russian privatization: "The big worry is that Russia will turn into Latin America 30 years ago."

Table 1. *Ukraine: main economic indicators 1990–96*

	1990	1991	1992	1993	1994	1995	1996[a]
Production[b]							
Industry	41.3	42.4	49.0	52.2	51.0	n/a	n/a
Agriculture	30.3	30.2	19.7	16.4	17.7	n/a	n/a
Real GDP[c]	−3.6	−11.9	−17.0	−14.2	−23.0	−10.0	−8.0
Industrial production	−0.1	−4.8	−6.4	−8.0	−28.2	n/a	n/a
Employment	−0.1	−1.7	−2.0	−2.3	n/a	n/a	n/a
Consumer prices							
Year average within period	4.5	161.0	2,000	10,155	401	182	47
Real wage index (1987 = 100)	125.1	125.1	107.5	63.4	55.0	n/a	n/a
Broad money (end-period)	n/a	101	921	2,103	465	n/a	40
NBU refinance rate (end-period)	n/a	12.0	80	240	240	55	21
State budget[d]							
Revenue	n/a	36.5	41.5	41.1	44.3	39.0	36.4
Expenditure	n/a	50.6	71.9	51.2	52.9	43.4	39.4
Balance	n/a	−14.1	−30.4	−10.1	−8.6	−4.4	−3.0
Trade[b]							
Exports	n/a	n/a	11.3	12.8	12.1	13.6	n/a
Imports	n/a	n/a	11.9	15.3	14.5	16.0	n/a
Exchange rates							
Karbovanets per U.S. dollar (end-period)	1.67	638	12,610	104,000	200,000	185,000	101,176[e]
Increase from previous year	n/a	400×	20×	8×	2×	n/a	n/a

Notes: 1993 population = 51.9 billion; 1993 GDP per capita (PPP) = $1,910 U.S. "n/a" denotes "not available".
[a] Estimated. [b] In billions of U.S. dollars. [c] Percentage change from previous year. [d] As percentage of GDP. [e] Hryvnia per U.S. dollar.
Source: IMF, *Recent Economic Developments in Ukraine* (October 19, 1994); 1995 and 1996, preliminary documents.

The rentier-patriarch theory brings us to a state of frozen transition, a monopolistic, noncompetitive, and highly regulated economy reminiscent of many Latin American and other Third World cases. The theory is perhaps incomplete without consideration of how this Gordian knot may be cut. One answer is: it may continue for a long time (as such regulated mixed economies as India and Argentina went on, little changed for decades) until the performance lag of the economy with respect to the rest of the world becomes so obvious – to rent seekers, other new elites (e.g. a commercial middle class), and the general populace – that the balance of consensus shifts to liberalization.

Another possibility is the "fortuitous happenstance" posited by Mancur Olson in his theory of shifts from warlord anarchy to autocracy to democracy.[4] Olson's model of political economy speaks of "roving bandits" in chaotic societies at some point deciding it is better to become "stationary bandits" (i.e., princes, kings, governments) – replacing looting with taxation. This can easily be modified to tell the rent-seeking story of the preceding pages. What is also useful in Olson's model is the argument about what brings a shift from stationary banditry (with autocratic rule) toward a democratic, open, and market society. His best answer, the fortuitous happenstance of a new leader(s) (through elections, revolution, birth, etc.) may also apply here. It may be the best possible explanation of why some countries such as Poland and Czechoslovakia moved quickly on reforms (including liberalization) and avoided the worst of the rent-seeking effects. It may also be a future explanation given for reform efforts in Ukraine and perhaps elsewhere. Indeed, in Section 4 I argue (somewhat along these lines) that the Ukranian election victory of Kuchma in July 1994 can be considered such a fortuitous happenstance.

3. UKRAINE: MACROECONOMIC DEVELOPMENTS, 1991–95

The statistical indicators of Table 1, for all their shortcomings, leave no doubt about the worsening economic situation in Ukraine over the period 1991–94. The output decline seen in Figure 1 is the most frequently cited indicator of deterioration, but other developments are probably more important. Inflation worsened considerably in the first year of independence (to about 2,000%), accelerated to hyper-

---

[4] See Olson (1993). An analysis of Soviet and post-Soviet corruption in the framework of Olson's concept of "bandits" is found in Olson (1995).

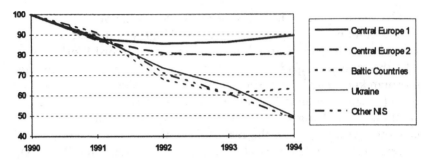

Figure 1. Index of real domestic product for Eastern Europe, the Baltics,
Ukraine, and other NIS countries, 1990–94 (1990 = 100).

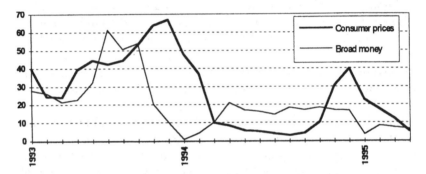

Figure 2. Inflation and monetary policy: monthly percent change
(three-month moving) in prices and money supply.

inflationary levels in 1993 (10,155%), but appeared to be cut back
sharply to 401% in 1994 – though the year-to-year rate was much
higher at 890%. Its relation to the budget deficit and monetary expansion is fairly evident in the data of Table 1, and in Figure 2. As the
budget deficits exploded in 1992 to reach 30.4% of GDP, monetary
expansion was fully accommodating – in fact, it went beyond this to
accommodate also substantial amounts of quasifiscal government
financing via directed credit to enterprises and collective farms. This
tendency for quasifiscal financing became the principal factor behind
monetization and the consequent near-hyperinflation of 1993: the
budget deficit actually fell to 10.1% in 1993, but broad money growth
rose from 921% in 1992 to 2,103% in 1993. It is only in 1994 that we
see an abatement of both the budget deficit needing monetization
(which fell further to 8.6%) and directed credit issues; hence broad
money expansion was kept to a relatively restrictive 361%.

In the meantime, output levels and real wages kept falling. The statistical measure of GDP's decline during "transformational recessions"[5] is of course strongly biased downward. Even if it were accurate it would not adequately reflect standard-of-living changes, both because of grey economy expansion and because of "true" valuation, as Sachs (1993) first argued in reference to Poland (fewer unwanted goods does not constitute less welfare). The development of a grey economy has been analyzed in Kaufman (1994), who makes clear there was substantial (though not easily measured) expansion of informal activity. Measurement biases involve also "new" enterprise management's understating of production to cover for capital flight whereas earlier, as Soviet managers, they would overstate. All of these biases are doubtless applicable to Ukraine; see Section 4.2.

Nevertheless, I refer to output indicators for three reasons. First, despite the foregoing biases, the consensus of analysts is that output declined substantially – at least in the first years of transition. Second, the biases are broadly similar for all these economies and so cross-country comparisons are likely to be valid. Finally (and this is a political economy point), many native politicians and intellectuals have argued for slower reforms plus easy fiscal and monetary policies in order to ease the pain of declines in output and income. Section 4.1 shows that Ukraine was a typical example of how such arguments played a role in decision making. Figure 1 is a simple illustration of the error in these arguments. All fifteen of the newly independent states (NIS) fared much worse than Central European ones except perhaps in the first year (1990–91), when output decline was in fact less strong than in Central Europe. Thereafter, although Central Europe had hit bottom by 1992 and with few exceptions began to recover by 1993, the NIS countries continued to suffer deterioration. Within this group only the three Baltic states, starting stabilization and reform about one to two years after their Central European neighbors, were able to achieve a recovery by 1994. True to the belief that delayed reform measures soften the output decline, we see Ukraine in 1992–93 suffering less decline than the Baltics or even other NIS countries.[6] But the deeper truth is revealed in 1994, when the Baltics recover and Ukraine continues to suffer an output decline

[5] A very useful term coined by János Kornai.

[6] The study from which Figure 1 is drawn categorizes Ukraine along with Belarus as a slow reformer within the NIS; this further emphasizes the point.

far stronger than other NIS countries – in effect, "catching up" to them by 1994.

In a word, slower reforms may at best soften the impact in early years, but only at the cost of substantially delaying the recovery. Although street wisdom about economic matters needs to be taken with caution, the "street index" of the economy's health amongst the populace of transition countries – monthly wage in U.S. dollars – may be closest to the heart of the matter. In the second half of 1994, this figure was about $20/month in Ukraine, compared to about $80 in Russia, over $100 already in the Baltics, and much higher still in Central Europe. Although this number overstates the decline in living standards, it does give a good qualitative sense of the general situation of economic stability and confidence in the economy.

Beyond this general level of developments, further elaboration is merited in two areas: the relation between monetary policy and inflation, and the evolution of the foreign exchange regime. Figure 2 indicates quite clearly that, with little exception, inflationary tendencies followed closely the movements of broad money creation. I noted earlier that monetary policy was itself a direct reflection of budget deficit–financing needs, but starting with 1992 and even more so in 1993, the policy also reflected the success of interest groups in lobbying the central bank to issue to them directed credit carrying strongly negative rates of interest. The monetary stance was less clear starting in early 1994, when a more reformist–oriented central bank governor (see Section 4) resisted these pressures both in public statements and, with varying success, in actual practice. This "isolated monetary squeeze" (including a sharp increase of interest rates) did reduce inflation significantly, but – because this was a period in which other measures of reform were still stalled – at the expense of an even deeper output decline than in 1993.

I am not here suggesting that output decline is an entirely bad thing; a squeeze may be necessary to induce hard budget discipline and the beginning of restructuring. But for reasons more fully described in Section 4, accompanying reforms did not come until late 1994, and monetary policy for the second and third quarters of 1994 reverted to the earlier loose stance – albeit still far more restrictive (15–20% per month) than in 1993. The continued abatement of inflation (CPI below 10% per month from March 1994 to October 1994), and its subsequent jump in the last quarter of 1994, can both be explained by the stance of price controls. Most of 1994 saw continuation

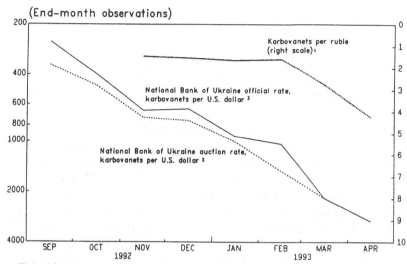

Figure 3. Exchange-rate developments, September 1992 – April 1993.
Source: IMF (1993).

and even strengthening of price controls, but considerable price liberalization occurred in October and November. Hidden inflation may have existed in the middle part of 1994, as suggested by the sharp drop of the exchange rate during this period (see Figure 3). The first quarter of 1994 shows a further monetary tightening, and once the price liberalization pass-through was completed, inflation falls sharply from about 40% in December 1994 to below 10% by April 1995.

In particular, one may note the periodicity of multiple and uniform exchange-rate regimes. A multiple exchange-rate system prevailed from independence until March 1993; a nearly uniform and nearly convertible regime held a brief interlude (about six months); and a return to multiple practices came in August–September 1993. The October 1994 reforms of the Kuchma government included reintroduction of a uniform rate based on essentially open-market operations – though some differences still remain between cash operations of individuals and noncash operations of commercial entities. The distortionary gaps of the multiple-regime periods are clear in Figure 3, as is the tentative stabilization achieved more recently.

4. THE POLITICAL ECONOMY OF NONREFORM
IN UKRAINE, 1991-94

4.1. Exogenous Explanations of Delayed Reform

Of the three competing explanations for delayed reform (see Section
1), the first two – lack of intellectual consensus on the process of economic reform, and the priority needs of nation-building tasks – can
be considered as given factors, as being outside the economic dynamics of the post-Soviet period. They may be viewed as the "initial conditions" Ukrainian leaders faced, just as leaders of other transition
economies had.[7] In contrast, as described by the theoretical model
of Section 2, the economic self-interests of a new rentier elite are an
endogenous element of the process and so carry greater explanatory
potential.

Let me address these "initial conditions" arguments, but first a
note of caution. Although there is certainly a measure of validity to
these arguments, their weight compared to the third ("rentier" explanation) is systematically exaggerated in all public and academic
discussions, for a very simple reason. All who are convinced that economic reform should not proceed rapidly by their sincere belief in
arguments (1) or (2) will strongly voice those arguments. All who are
convinced that economic reform should not proceed rapidly, because
reform runs counter to their personal interests, could not admit as
much and so instead will join the chorus for arguments (1) or (2) or
both. Consequently, public statements are inherently biased toward
the exogenous explanations of delayed reform. Politicians are in all
times and places prone to blame "outside" and "unforeseen" difficulties, but in this situation there is even more incentive to do so.

Intellectual debates about when and how to proceed with economic reform have been closely tied to the popular academic–political theme
of Ukraine's uniqueness and the need for devising a "third way."
Added to this was the global misperception regarding "shock therapy." During the first year of independence (1992) it was perhaps understandable to think that there was no historical experience for such

---

[7] I do not discuss in this essay a third "given": the large terms-of-trade shock coming from
increased energy prices. That this was actually used as a reason for *delaying* price liberalization – despite its obvious indication of the need for such liberalization – is testimony to the
power of rentier interests. The profits made from purchasing imported and state-subsidized
petroleum products and then re-exporting them under license (during critical energy shortages) are an instance *par excellence* of rentier interests dominating national interests.

a large transformation of economy and society, and that Ukraine's colonial inheritance of poor administrative, financial, and international expertise was a big disadvantage.[8] However, by 1993 – when the experiences of Poland, Czechoslovakia, the Baltic States, and even Albania first began to affirm the thesis that radical reforms actually work – intellectual arguments for delay began to sound hollow, as if their proponents were naive captives of the economic interests opposing reform. Moreover, by 1994 – when other former colonies such as Kyrgyzstan, Armenia, and Moldova somehow managed to overcome their provincial inheritance and at least make serious efforts at economic reform – the lack of experience or appropriate expertise became a less and less convincing argument.

Nation-building priorities are a rather more convincing thesis for delayed reforms, though the biases of public statements apply here as well. Nonetheless, I expect many future historians will write that Ukraine's delayed reforms were attributable to the need of first building up the institutions of a new state and a new policy, and to some extent this is correct.[9] Certainly, those in the democratic nationalist movements (Rukh and its descendants) who accepted a deal for the continuation of rule by the partocrats (led by Kravchuk) did so largely out of the belief that they themselves were not strong enough to ensure a victory for independence. In so doing they also accepted the possibility (which became a reality) that the old partocracy and bureaucracy would slow the process of economic reform. This early decision may or may not have been a mistake, and I do not here plan to argue historical counterfactuals of what could have been achieved by the combined forces of independence, democracy, and market movements at a time when the old communist elite was in disarray and unsure of its own future. If it was a mistake, it was an understandable one.

More serious and less understandable were subsequent mistakes of these "democratic" political forces:

not realizing that lack of economic reform increases the economic costs of transition, reverses the favorable attitude of the populace toward markets, and finally undermines support for independence;

---

[8] A succinct glimpse into these debates is provided in volume 2 of *Politichna Dumka* [*Political Thought*] (1994, Kyiv).

[9] An early version of such a thesis can be found in Zviglyanich (forthcoming) and in Kuzio and Wilson (1994).

simplifying the "kovbasna" or "sausage" politics to a crude version
and thereby erroneously dismissing it;[10]
not realizing soon enough that delaying economic reform gives
time for the old elite to recolor itself (politically from red to blue
and yellow, economically from red to green), regroup, and re-
assert its economic (and hence political) primacy; and
not recognizing by the time of elections in 1994 how much damage had been done to the economy, and to their own credibility,
by the Faustian deal of "independence for nonreform."

The strong democratic nationalist support for Kravchuk in the
June 1994 election certainly suggests they were either ignorant of
the damage or unwilling to recognize their error. The deal made with
former members of the now defunct Communist Party of Ukraine in
effect allowed a rapid transformation of the old elite into a new elite,
now rid of its unattractive communist label and freshened by a little
bit of new blood. One can easily associate this new elite with the concept described in Section 2, the post-Soviet rentier patriarchs whose
personal financial interest are best met by a half-reformed economy.

Though one should not completely reject the relevance of nation-
building needs, since indeed the initial conditions in Ukraine provided only a fragile and limited set of state institutions, neither should
one make too much of this. After all, nation-building tasks were
needed to some extent everywhere, and in many cases the needs were
as substantial as Ukraine's but did *not* result in a secondary role for
economic reform; rather, they put reform as a co-equal fundamental
of nation building (the Baltics, Moldova, Kazakstan, Armenia,
Croatia, and Macedonia are a few examples). Perhaps the most sensible interpretation is that the preindependence forces in Ukraine,
unlike those in other countries, did not have (or did not believe they
had) enough political strength of their own to accomplish nation-
building tasks and hence allied themselves with a clearly less reform-
oriented political group – the old communists.[11] The compromise
resulted in an opportunity for this "new-old" elite to hijack the pro-

---

[10]   The popular notion of *kovbasna polityka* [sausage politics] – i.e., people supporting independence because of expectations that Ukraine would do better economically – was derided by
many democratic politicians as being a poor philosophical basis for building a nation. The
worsening economic situation gave substantial meaning to such popular views and put into
question the idealistic basis for nation building.

[11]   Taras Kuzio (pers. commun.) argues that, beyond this, the commitment to economic reform by the pro-independence forces in Ukraine (and many of their emigré backers) was
not as strong as that in the Polish, Baltic, or other cases.

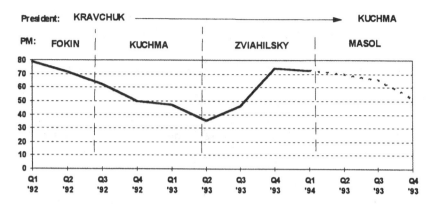

Figure 4. Overall administrative control index for Ukraine, 1992–93.

cess of economic transition and direct it to their preferred destinations, which brings me directly to the third hypothesis and its application in Ukraine.

4.2. An Endogenous Explanation: Rentier-Patriarch Interests

A combination of hesitancy (attributable to intellectual debates over reform speed) plus the lack of serious attention paid to economic issues (because of a perceived priority in nation building) are certainly enough to understand why Ukraine did not jump into a Polish or Czechoslovak style of rapid reform upon independence in December 1991, or even follow Russia's Gaidar-led liberalization of early 1992. The delays in reform during 1992 are best seen in the zig-zag actions summarized in the Appendix: "Chronology of Economic Reforms." I will describe these developments in the framework of "reform" and "anti-reform" interests. A summary view of the ups and downs of reform are shown in Figure 4 (adapted from Kaufman 1994), which shows an index of administrative control (100% = full administrative control; 0% = full liberalization).[12]

Kravchuk President, Fokin P.M. (August 1991 to October 1992). After Gaidar's moves in Russia to free prices, Ukraine's government – led by

[12] The index of the chart is too much of a "summary" to capture the notion of zig-zagging described more fully in the text and the Appendix. Certainly, in both the Fokin and Kuchma period, the movements did not occur smoothly in one direction and did zig-zag. Under Zviahilskiy, a better characterization would be of a sharp reversal from reform to recentralization.

Prime Minister Vitold Fokin, a former head of Derzhplan of Ukraine (Ukrainian central plan committee) – decided not to follow suit, but rather tried to isolate itself by keeping almost all prices regulated, imposing restrictions on exports, issuing consumer-purchase "coupons" as part of salaries, and forbidding key goods to be purchased with rubles (still in circulation alongside the coupons). This zig away from reform was followed by a zag toward reform. In the spring of 1992, plans for economic reform were prepared; a new, young deputy prime minister for economic reform was appointed (Volodymyr Lanovey, who had strong reform credentials); and by the end of March a reform program had been drawn up and approved by Parliament for an historical first presentation to the International Monetary Fund by the minister of finance, Hryhoriy Pyatachenko. The document was not, however, a formal program to be considered for IMF financial support, because Ukraine did not officially become a member of the Fund and World Bank until 3 September 1992. It was meant for a premembership review in Washington, in order to demonstrate the intended direction of policy.

Zigging away from reform, other programs were also being prepared, including one by the short-lived Duma.[13] A bit later, after Lanovey was dismissed, another (less reformist) program was prepared by the cabinet.[14] The Duma document was in some ways more radical and forward-looking than the one presented to the IMF, with rapid introduction of the hryvnia and more rapid privatization, but it was less ambitious in other areas (budget deficit reduction, price liberalization). Perhaps the most important fact behind the Duma plan – whose key leader was V. Yemelyanov, also a former Derzhplan head – was the important role played by Viktor Pynzenyk in its drafting. This, together with the unstinted support of the still influential Yemelyanov, helped push Pynzenyk forward as a key reform thinker and leader.

The period of Fokin's tenure as prime minister of an independent Ukraine (under President Kravchuk) was a little over one year (from August 1991 to October 1992). One cannot say that reforms were not

---

13 From 1992 to 1993, an institution called the Duma was set up, which was essentially an appointed council of experts divided into various colleges of social, political, and economic areas.

14 The author was at this time Deputy Minister of Finance, responsible for establishing Ukraine's relationships with international financial organizations. He was therefore privy to the cabinet meeting that approved this informal document, and privy to comments such as "This is good for the IMF; what we present to Parliament we'll worry about later."

taking place at all, as certainly some liberalization of foreign exchange operations and prices did occur. This is reflected in Figure 3 and the index of Figure 4, which fell slightly in 1992 during Fokin's tenure. But the zig-zagging of pro-reform and anti-reform measures more fully typifies this period – leaving, on balance, a little-reformed and still highly regulated economy.

In the meantime, the re-emerging partocrats began their transformation to rentier capitalists along two key, parallel paths. First, they began to become capitalists through establishment of spinoff private commercial activities known on the street as *pryhvatyzatsia* (from the Ukrainian "pryhvatyty" = to grab and the English "privatization"). Concurrently, as patriarchs they had privileged access to cheap credit from the central bank and to licenses for domestic trade, or for exports and imports. Government use of inflation as a tax is a well-known concept in economics, as is the Tanzi effect: that is, excessive inflation in fact reduces government revenue. This it did in Ukraine (see Havrylyshyn, Miller, and Perraudin 1994). But the near-hyperinflation worked in the private interests of the new elite, providing the necessary credit to be funneled through spinoff enterprises into trading and export activities and to enable maintenance of a minimal level of support for the patriarch's workers' wages and other benefits. Because the foreign operations of any rentier patriarch could not easily be hidden from the people, some sharing was necessary (e.g., funding a trip by the kolkhoz football team to a tournament in Italy).

Data are not readily available to demonstrate statistically the first of these developments, although close observers need no convincing. The second phenomenon is also not easily demonstrable by direct statistics, but three indirect measures clearly reflect it. (1) Although registered exports for 1992 were about $12 billion (U.S.), the National Bank of Ukraine (NBU) showed an end-1992 deficit of $300 million, and government accounts held dollars in amounts not generally exceeding $100 million at any one time; the acute shortage of foreign exchange was universally known and proclaimed. This was a sure indicator of massive capital flight. (2) Even though inflation in 1992 was well over 1,000%, the lending rates to enterprises and kolkhoz (as set by the NBU) were generally below 100%. It need not be emphasized that patriarchal influences affected the destination of these cheap credits. (3) During this period of severe foreign exchange shortages, the exchange rate was set at an official level that was far below any realistic indicator of a market rate, providing a premium to those entitled to purchase dollars from the government at official rates. Until March 1992, the previous USSR official rate of 0.6 R/$ (rubles per dollar) was retained for accounting purposes, a rate of 1.8 R/$ was used for trade, while the market rate was 100 R/$. For the rest of 1992, a market-based official rate was used, but it still was only 60–70% of the rate obtaining in actual market transactions (IMF 1993).

Kravchuk President, Kuchma P.M. (October 1992 to October 1993). When Fokin was eventually forced to resign under pressures of the small democratic and rightist forces in Parliament, Kravchuk's appointment of Leonid Kuchma as prime minister was at first greeted as a reinforcement of the continued role of the old "red directors," as his past was a prime example of this group's influence. But the former director of the USSR's largest missile and aerospace factory turned out to be less comparable to Arkady Volsky in Russia (leader of the directors group in the Russian Duma at the time) and more like Carlos Menem of Argentina: a reformer!

In October 1992 there began an interlude of reformist effort. I have argued (see Havrylyshyn 1994), although many disagree, that Leonid Kuchma was a reformer. It was a surprise to many when in late 1992, with about three months' tenure as prime minister, Leonid Kuchma started talking about reform. When first appointed he was labeled a red director. Some compared him to Arkady Volsky, and suggested that Kuchma was a "reformer" only for the benefit of large-scale industrial enterprises and not for other sectors or for true open-market opportunities. Hence his choice of reform-minded Victor Pynzenyk as vice-premier and his strong support of the latter's clearly reformist actions (note the movement in Figure 4) came as a surprise to many in Ukraine. Why did these reform efforts eventually fail, and what were the consequences?

This effort failed for two reasons. One reason was that the West did not take the opportunity to provide Ukraine with political or financial support in a timely fashion. This led to some disillusionment with the West and with the transition to market reform in the minds of Ukrainian policy makers, including reformers. A second and perhaps more important reason was that Kravchuk's willingness to continue implicit support for Kuchma (never expressing agreement or encouragement for the reform moves but never openly opposing them either) came to an end in May 1993. Historians may determine whether this was because Kuchma went too far in reforms or because (by May 1993) polls showed Kuchma to be more popular than Krav-chuk – or both.

The achievements of Kuchma and Pynzenyk were at first very sig-nificant. The formal exit from the ruble zone in November 1992 and the effort to unify and liberalize foreign exchange operations eventu-ated a considerable closing of the gap between official and market rates by the spring of 1993 (see Figure 3; an auction of foreign ex-change was begun in November 1992). Price decontrols were also sub-stantial; for example, the index of retail price controls fell from 75% in 1992Q3 to 11% in 1993Q3 (Kaufman 1994). On balance, Kauf-man's index shows a steep decline in the degree of administered con-trols, from about 70% in 1992Q2 (under Fokin) to 35% in 1993Q2 (under Kuchma).

Part of the new government's economic strategy included a seri-ous consideration of agreement with the IMF and World Bank on a program to be supported by external funds. Despite the publicly known doubts of P.M. Kuchma about Western willingness to finance Ukraine, he agreed to have his deputy, Mr. Pynzenyk, devote consid-erable efforts in the winter and early spring of 1993 to negotiations with the IMF.[15] The lax monetary policy of this period was a very significant concern of IMF negotiators, but the achievements in exchange-rate and other liberalization, plus the commitment of the prime minister and his deputy for reform, were enough to result in good progress in the negotiations through May 1993.

Reflective of populist, traditionalist, and new rentier-patriarch in-terests, Parliament soon became disillusioned with Kuchma, and by the spring of 1993 was able to overrule the reformist efforts of Kuch-ma and Pynzenyk in one, alas, very important area: provision of di-rected credit by the NBU to "needy" enterprises and kolkhoz. Mon-etary expansion continued explosively[16] (see Figure 2), completely undermining the efforts at exchange-rate stabilization and price de-controls. This certainly did not inspire confidence in the IMF negoti-ators, who were otherwise keen to assist the Kuchma–Pynzenyk gov-ernment to the tune of $350–$700 million for the remainder of 1993.

However, the political turn of events in May brought all programs to a halt. Kuchma turned to Parliament with a request for exten-sion of his emergency powers (limited to certain economic spheres).

---

[15] The author was at this time representing Ukraine's interests as alternate executive director at the IMF Board of Directors, and was therefore directly involved in these efforts.

[16] 1992Q4 = 95%, 1993Q1 = 156%, 1993Q2 = 89%, and 1993Q3 = 420% (Ukraine Ministry of Economy 1993; IMF 1995b).

Although Parliament had not been particularly supportive of Kuch-ma since early 1993 (it was still composed predominantly of former communists), he had continued to enjoy at least the implicit support of Kravchuk. Yet on May 18, when Parliament began to discuss the extension, Kravchuk spoke in Parliament in direct opposition to the request. One immediate consequence was that the IMF mission in Kyiv was advised that political debate over "who's in charge" would for several weeks eclipse economic issues, and that any prospects of a quick agreement were thus sharply reduced. The mission left Kyiv.

The May 18 events in Parliament marked the practical end of the reform efforts of Kuchma and Pynzenyk. Kravchuk's withdrawal of support on the one hand, and the West's slowness on the other hand in seizing earlier opportunities to support Ukrainian reformers (as it had done for Russian reformers in 1992), tilted the balance of the Kuchma administration in the other direction.[17] Already by July 1993, resumption of a more regulated official exchange rate sharply reversed the direction of liberalization (see Figures 3 and 4). In August 1993 Pynzenyk resigned, although Kuchma remained until the political tide had clearly turned against him; Kuchma then resigned in October 1993.

Kravchuk President, Zviahilskiy P.M. (October 1993 to June 1994). The general tendency of reform reversal is clear in Figure 4, showing a rise in the index of administrative controls during Zviahilskiy's ten-ure, essentially back to mid-1992 levels of administrative control. Subsequently there began a reinforcement of the "monopolistic capi-talism" of the post-Soviet era. Managers of monopolistic enterprises reasserted their positions by lobbying government to support them via credit – directly from the budget or indirectly through the bank-ing system.

The reversals came quickly and in particular involved areas where rentier interests were strongest: domestic trade, foreign exchange, and foreign trade.[18] In November 1993, a state decree formally strength-ened the still-existing system of state order and state purchases, effec-tively reinvigorating central plan functions. Connected to this was the decree of 17 December 1993 that reimposed export quotas and corresponding licenses on a wide range of goods (agricultural, ores

---

[17] For example, the substantial delays in U.S. support for Ukraine are documented in Iwan-ciw (1995).

[18] A detailed description of these developments may be found in IMF (1995b).

and raw materials, metals, energy). The quotas and licenses were allocated by the ministry of foreign economic relations.

Under Kuchma, the liberalization of foreign trade had not been particularly strong. The first step, a decree of 12 January 1993, in fact merely clarified the fairly rigid regime that had been practiced. A small liberalization effort on 20 May 1994 was first reversed by the Zviahilskiy government (the 17 December 1993 decree noted previously) and then confounded by a reversal of the reversal in a 29 December 1993 decree. Despite the confusing evidence of official documents, the results on balance are clear: more than 30% of export quotas were sold at auction in 1993 (Kuchma–Pynzenyk), compared to less than 5% in 1994 (Zviahilskiy–Landyk).

It is broadly accepted in economic analysis that auctioning of trade quotas (export or import) is a far more liberal and transparent mechanism than allocation of such quotas. Clearly, allocation increased under Zviahilskiy and with the return to the cabinet of such administratively oriented officials as Oleh Shlepichev (who in preindependence times had been head of the resources allocation committee; under Fokin, minister of economy and deputy prime minister for foreign economic relations; and during Kuchma's tenure, special advisor to Kravchuk on international financial issues).

The other key area of return to administrative procedures and increased powers of central allocation was in foreign exchange – which continued to be in great shortage throughout! The partially successful efforts at unification of exchange-rate operations and market liberalization (with the opening of an auction market whose value determined the official rates) were already reversed under Kuchma in August 1993 with the reintroduction of multiple exchange rates. This was followed quickly by Pynzenyk's resignation. Under Zviahilskiy, a 2 November 1993 decree eliminated the weekly auction market and stopped free interbank transactions in foreign exchange. The open auction was replaced in February 1994 with a limited – some would say "managed" – auction wherein the NBU was the sole seller of foreign exchange.

The return to multiple exchange rates (see Figure 3) – official, NBU auction, cash market (official exchange points for private citizens), and street market – gave full bloom to the opportunities for privileged access to scarce foreign exchange. The prime mechanism for allocation became the newly established Tender Committee ("interministerial committee on the priority of foreign exchange use") set up by a 29 November 1993 presidential decree and consisting of representatives of the NBU and the ministries of finance, the economy, and foreign economic relations.

To recap: the ministry of economy (whose staff and four floors in the main cabinet of ministers building in Kyiv remained those of the former Derzhplan) now was reinvigorated by an informal planning role with state orders back in place; the ministry of foreign economic relations now enjoyed new power over allocation of export quotas and licenses, powers not previously existing in Kyiv during the Soviet period. The predominant role of these two ministries in the Tender Committee completed the circle: power of allocation of foreign exchange. Thus the classical triad of key economic levers on any administered economy – allocation of production resources (through state orders), allocation of foreign trade rights, and allocation of foreign exchange – was back in the hands of government. There was one difference from the Soviet period: a large network of "commercial operations" in private hands (a result of the *pryhvatizatsion* mentioned earlier), with close connections to government structures and with a strong incentive to lobby the government for access to allocated privileges. A better arrangement for rent-seeking activities cannot be imagined.

Two indirect indicators of the rent-seeking environment are (1) the spread between official and street rates and (2) high estimates of capital flight. Consider the evidence of Figure 3. During the Fokin period, the ratio of official rate to street rate ranged from about 0.60 to 0.70. By April of 1993, even before the opening of the interbank auction, the liberalization of foreign exchange operations resulted in a ratio of virtually 1.0, which lasted through July 1993. The July–August policy decrees were immediately reflected in a decline of this ratio to 0.71 in September 1993, and in the period from October 1993 to October 1994 the values ranged between 0.25 and 0.45 – far lower even than under the later part of Fokin's tenure (Ukraine Ministry of Economy 1995).

Popular journalistic estimates of capital flight from Ukraine reach as high as $15–$20 billion. No in-depth studies have yet been attempted, but some very rough counterfactual calculations indicate that such magnitudes are entirely feasible. First, consider the portion fleeing not out of the country but into "mattresses." For example, in pre-1990 Poland this was popularly guessed to be up to $5 billion; convertibility of foreign exchange in 1990 brought out all these hoards, and the flood of personal dollars into the market (through legal bank accounts) quickly confirmed this order of magnitude. Ukraine, with a population 25% higher than Poland's, could certainly expect as much.

The remaining amounts ($10–$15 billion) compare to export and GDP estimates as follows. This figure equals 30–35% of officially recorded exports over the three years 1992–94 (about $12 billion per year), or 10–15% of official GDP (about $100 billion, excluding grey market activity). Inasmuch as the most common mechanism for commercial, large-scale capital flight is underreporting the value of exports, it is useful to note that Ukraine's value of exports before independence is estimated to have been 25–30% of GDP (Koropeckyj 1992, p. 372). Official GDP is now about $100 billion, so a normalized level of exports ought to be about $25–$30 billion. Between recorded exports of $12 billion and potential of $25–$30 billion, there is a lot of room for temporarily reduced exports (attributable to the deep transformational recession in most neighboring economies) *as well as* underreporting on a scale of several billion dollars per year. If actual exports are even 60% of potential (i.e. $16–$19 billion) then a gap remains of $4–$6 billion annually compared to recorded exports, which easily gives a cumulative capital flight of well over $10 billion – or 10% of GDP. I might add that cumulative capital flight from Latin America had by the mid-1980s reached such estimated magnitudes.

5. KUCHMA ELECTED PRESIDENT: FORTUITOUS HAPPENSTANCE OR SYSTEMATIC EVOLUTION?

With the election of Kuchma as president in early July 1994, the opportunity for reform presented itself once again. Although it is too early to see clear results or to be certain that new policies will continue, the direction of change in policy is unquestionable and substantial. The Appendix outlines the key steps taken, and I will note here only briefly some aspects of this second effort at reform in Ukraine.

First, *the measures taken came quickly.* Within days of his inauguration, Kuchma hosted Michel Camdessus (head of the IMF) as his first international visitor. Kuchma agreed on the principles of a first program and a first credit under the so-called systemic transformation facility (SFT), and also agreed on a very short two-month timetable to work out technical details. The timetable was basically met, and the program was initiated before the end of September 1994. Government measures taken before and after the credit was released (on 30 October 1994) were also quick: many prices were liberalized, the budget was cut sharply, export licensing was halved, and – most important – the exchange rate was unified.

With a heady sense of déjà vu, Pynzenyk was brought back by Kuchma (in early October of 1994) as First Deputy P.M. for Reform. This followed a period of internal debates on key policy issues, including the question of whether unification and liberalization of the foreign exchange regime should occur immediately or more gradually. With about the same time lag that had occurred in July–August 1993 between reintroduction of multiple exchange rates and the resignation of Pynzenyk, September–October 1994 saw Pynzenyk rejoining the government followed by elimination of the multiple exchange-rate system.

The pace continued quickly and is best exemplified by the rapid agreement on a much tougher, and financially much larger ($1.96 billion), stand-by program in March 1994. The STF was a temporary financial facility of the IMF, intended to help transition economies get started and move toward the more conventional stand-bys. The expectation had been of a 6–12-month time lag, and in fact most other countries moved at the expected pace. Ukraine's rapid five months was bettered only by Moldova, with a mere three-month lag.

Second, the textbook *policy measures were in general quite substantial:*

a sharp curtailment (if not full elimination) of state orders, especially for grain and export goods;

a tight policy of monetary expansion, with interest rates exceeding inflation levels;

a substantial reduction in the budget deficit to below 10% by end-1994 and to 3.2% for all of 1995;

liberalization of most prices including energy, and replacement of their subsidies with targeted financial support only for the neediest;

virtual elimination of export quotas and licenses; and

unification and liberalization of the foreign exchange market.

Third, while it is much too early to expect results, *some indications of success and some shortcomings* can be noted. Although inflation remains high, it had fallen from nearly 28% in December 1994 to the teens in the first three months of 1995, and is estimated at 5.8% for

April. Even more dramatic was the effective stabilization of the kar-bovanets exchange rate, which remained virtually unchanged for the period January–March at about 135,000 kb/$. Also, the ratio of the official (= auction) to street rate, which ranged from about 0.25 to 0.45 in the Zviahilskiy period, immediately jumped to 0.85 in November 1994; in 1995 the ratio has been about 0.90. A positive consequence of this is already measurable: monthly wages in dollars – a very popular barometer of the economic situation – have risen from the averages of $15–$20 in 1994 to about $30 in 1995.

One shortcoming, apart from the still high inflation (which expert analysts did not expect to fall as quickly as it has), is a hesitancy on export regulations. Although formal export quota and licensing has been substantially eliminated, two kinds of measures remain. For those categories of goods where Western markets present barriers (explicit quotas for agriculture and steel, or threats of countervailing duty measures), Ukrainian authorities have argued that it is necessary to continue quotas and indicative price arrangements. For example, the continued U.S. categorization of Ukraine as a "state planning" economy fortifies the arguments of those favoring oversight regulation of exports, since the penalties for "dumping" are far greater than with countries designated as market economies. Another set of measures involves preregistration of export contracts, the rationale being that large capital flight can be stemmed by the possibility of a precise follow-up of export proceeds.

My final remark on the recent reform efforts concerns *the political-historical question* of the factors behind the Kuchma election. One possibility is that he defeated Kravchuk because the electorate was unhappy with the latter's virtual inaction on economic matters and the associated blossoming of a new, visible class of wealthy elite. In favor of this view is the Kuchma campaign's strong references to economic deterioration and chaos, corruption, and lack of reform. (Recall also his rising popularity as P.M. when he began to undertake some reforms.) Against this view are two facts: Kuchma's campaign sounded an appeal to eastern Ukraine, which favored improving relations with Russia. In eastern Ukraine, where pro-market sentiment is weakest, he won in a big way; in western Ukraine, where pro-market sentiment is strongest, he lost in an even bigger way.

An alternative view falls under the Olson concept of "happenstance." Without needing to specify the doubtless multifaceted and complex political reasons for Kuchma's election, we simply accept that history brought to Ukraine an economic reformer who could undertake to break (or at least loosen) the rentier-patriarch grip on the economy.[19] The main measures of Kuchma's program are aimed at the three key areas of administrative control noted earlier: state orders, foreign trade controls, and foreign exchange allocation. Moreover, some important judicial actions have been aimed at what the populace considers the new capitalists. This includes charges brought against former P.M. Zviahilskiy and some associates in the Damiano Bank affair ($25 million embezzlement) as well as an investigation into Blasco operations. The judicial actions can be viewed as needed political symbols of the struggle against corruption, which I defined earlier as the tip of the rentier iceberg. The economic measures are aimed at the root causes of rentier activities: a regulated, administered economy of privileges.

It is too early to judge if the efforts at reform will continue and so succeed in unthawing the frozen transition. If they do succeed, historians will help clarify the question of whether a reformer like Kuchma was elected because of systematic voter dissatisfaction with burgeoning rentier capitalism and lack of reform, or if the election of a reformer in 1994 should rather be considered a fortuitous happenstance, an unexpected event that broke the interests of rent-seeking lobby groups and hence pushed Ukraine toward a market economy. Either way, the not-so-unique case of Ukraine offers important historical lessons on the political economy of reform.

APPENDIX

CHRONOLOGY OF ECONOMIC REFORMS IN UKRAINE, 1990–94

| To 1990 | *Under Gorbachev and perestroika,* considerable decentralization of planning process: co-op laws allowed first forms of pseudo-private activity; increased autonomy of enterprises, lesser role for Moscow GOSPLAN; increased regionalization to republics, with more enterprises under republic control and therefore greater role for Derzhplan–Kyiv. |

---

[19] To return briefly to the parallel with Carlos Menem, President of Argentina, it may be noted he too was not voted in because Argentinans were tired of hyperinflation and a highly regulated economy. Indeed, his previous record (unlike Kuchma's) did not demonstrate any reformist inclinations. Further, as pointed out by Mario Blejer, after election he at first tried briefly to implement a Peronist-populist policy, and only its evident failure led him to become a reformer. Readers may judge in both cases how applicable is the term "fortuitous happenstance."

| June 1990 | *Declaration of sovereignty* by Ukrainian Parliament: first mention of separate currency; establishment of central bank (National Bank of Ukraine); tax payments to center continually reduced; stated principle of full control of almost all assets on Ukrainian territory. |

November–
December 1990

First reform concept or plan: working group organized by V. Pylypchuk (head of economic reform commission of Parliament) includes parliamentarians as well as local and foreign economists; their market-oriented program remained largely on paper because the government did not act on it.

August 24, 1991

Independence declaration: NBU fully operational but not necessarily effective; currency continues to be USSR ruble; reassertion of principle that all assets on Ukrainian territory are owned by Ukraine (the state, not individuals) and effective implementation of this principle; until December 1991, no actions that could be considered as "reform."

January–
September 1992

First steps of economic independence: introduction of consumption vouchers (coupons) in reaction to shortages of USSR ruble shipments from Russian central bank; NBU by now creating fresh money supply, not only with coupons but with bank credits (denominated in old rubles) to ministry of finance and state enterprises; attempt to continue price controls in face of Russian (Gaidar) price liberalization, resulting in low-priced Ukrainian goods flowing to Russia, exacerbating shortages; government reaction is combination of some price liberalization (on nonkey goods) and export restrictions on other goods; some "spontaneous" privatization by insiders slowly increases size of the pseudoprivate sector; increased subsidies and cheap credit to state sector; state budget deficit exceeds 25% of GDP; inflation surges ahead of Russian levels, inducing government to print more money and raise wages in order to keep up with prices (which are adjusted by administrative decree but are *not*, in general, liberalized); several "programs" of economic reform and stabilization are formulated but remain largely unimplemented; in September 1992, Ukraine officially becomes member of IMF and World Bank.

October 1992

Kuchma appointed Prime Minister.

October– December 1992	*First steps under Deputy P.M. Pynzenyk*: (1) full exit from ruble zone and coupon becomes national currency for both cash and noncash transactions; (2) virtual liberalization of foreign exchange operations, so formal and street market values converge; consequently, "hidden" coupon devaluation is revealed and fiction of 1:1 ratio with ruble is replaced by market values reaching 5 coupons/ruble (1,000 k/$) by year's end.
January– May 1993	*Further steps toward reform*: with Kuchma as P.M. and Pynzenyk as Deputy P.M. for economic reform, a new program is formulated and some partial steps taken, including alternating the foreign exchange measures of November 1992, some further price liberalization, some removal of export controls and licensing, and the first symbolic privatization auctions; inability to hold back budget expenditures, as well as NBU credit creation, exacerbates continued high inflation; negotiations with IMF on first potential credit to Ukraine brought to a halt on 18 May 1993 when Kuchma's request for extension of emergency economic powers does not obtain support of Kravchuk and is hence denied by Parliament.
July 1993	*Reversal of foreign exchange liberalization,* with introduction of "stable" official exchange rate (about 4,000–5,000 k/$); black market quickly surges to about twice official levels.
August 1993	*Vice-P.M. Pynzenyk resigns.*
October 1993	*P.M. Kuchma resigns,* Y. Zviahilskiy appointed acting P.M.
November 1993 – January 1994	*Reintroduction of various administrative controls on economy*: in addition to "official" exchange rate and closing of auction market, other measures include tight export licensing, maintenance of very low interest rates on NBU loans, reintroduction of price controls, return to greater amount of state purchasing orders, no open privatization but plenty of spontaneous insider acquisition of assets; inflation surges to nearly 100% per month in late 1993.
January– June 1994	*Isolated monetary squeeze*: outspoken "tight-money" governor of NBU (Yuschenko) is until January 1994 usually overruled, and credit expansion is based on political considerations; thereafter his views are increasingly applied and a credit squeeze brings

monthly inflation down to single digits; no other reform moves are taken, so economy continues to deteriorate and foreign exchange earnings are hidden; massive capital flight, corruption, and diversion occur, so that Ukraine's "official" foreign exchange reserves number in the tens of millions of dollars, while billions worth of debts go unpaid.

July 1994   *Kuchma elected president*: first high-level foreign guest invited is Camdessus, head of the IMF (July 26); they agree to work quickly to a negotiated program of financial support.

September 30, 1994   *Agreement in principle for an IMF program* (structural transformation facility) of $370 million credit plus other funds to be contributed by World Bank and individual countries, subject to certain steps toward economic stabilization.

October 1994   *Steps taken to meet conditions of IMF program*: exchange rate liberalized and unified as in November 1992; over half of export licenses eliminated, but a new presidential decree imposes "preregistration" requirements (a nontransparent form of export regulation); many prices liberalized, including bread, energy, housing rents, and public transportation, with graduated movement to 100% cost recovery; first steps to contain budget deficit (10% GDP target); STF program officially approved by IMF and credit of $370 million provided; World Bank follows with $500 million.

March 1, 1995   *Stand-by program* ($1.96 billion over 12 months) approved, subject to some prior conditions; government of Ukraine initials an agreement with IMF (ironically, this is one of the last official acts of nonreformist P.M. Masol before his resignation days later).

April 7, 1995   *IMF board approves program for release of funds* (including $600 million from World Bank and $850 million from industrial countries) after all its conditions are met (including a budget deficit for 1995 of 3.2% as measured by international norms); by this time, initial results of reforms since November 1994 show a stabilization of the karbovanets, with auction rate and street rate diverging by less than 10%; stabilized exchange rates increase average monthly wages from $15–$20 (1994) to $25–$30.

REFERENCES

European Bank for Reconstruction and Development [EBRD] (1994), *Transition Report* (October). London: EBRD.

Havrylyshyn, Oleh (1994), "Ukraine's Economic Crisis," *Ukraine Business Review* 2(1): 5–13.

Havrylyshyn, Oleh (forthcoming), "How Patriarchs and Rent-Seekers Hijack the Transition to a Market Economy," in *Perspectives on Contemporary Ukraine*. Cambridge, MA: Harvard University Press.

Havrylyshyn, Oleh, Marcus Miller, and William Perraudin (1994), "Deficits, Inflation and the Political Economy of Ukraine," *Economic Policy* 19: 354–401.

IMF (1993), *Ukraine 1993* (Economic Reviews, no. 10). Washington, DC: International Monetary Fund.

IMF (1995a), *Policy Experiences and Issues in the Baltic Countries, Russia, and Other FSU States*. Washington, DC: International Monetary Fund.

IMF (1995b), *Ukraine 1995* (Economic Reviews, no. 17). Washington, DC: International Monetary Fund.

Iwanciw, Eugene (1995), *United States Foreign Assistance and Ukraine*. Washington, DC: Ukrainian National Association.

Kaufman, Daniel (1994), "Diminishing Returns to Administrative Controls and the Emergence of the Unofficial Economy," *Economic Policy* (suppl.): 51–70.

Koropeckyj, I. S. (1992), *The Ukrainian Economy*. Cambridge, MA: Harvard University Press.

Krueger, A. (1974), "The Political Economy of a Rent-Seeking Society," *American Economic Review* 69(3): 291–303.

Kuzio, Taras, and Andrew Wilson (1994), *Ukraine, Perestroika to Independence*. London: Macmillan.

Olson, Mancur (1993), "Dictatorship, Democracy and Development," *American Political Science Review* 87(3): 567–76.

Olson, Mancur (1995), "Russian Reforms: Established Interests and Practical Alternatives," presented at the conference on "The Dissolution of Power and Societies in Transition" (April, Moscow).

Sachs, Jeffrey (1993), *Poland's Jump to a Market Economy*. Cambridge, MA: MIT Press.

Ukraine Ministry of Economy (1993), *Ukraine in Numbers*, vol. 4. Kyiv, Ukraine.

Ukraine Ministry of Economy (1995), *Ukraine in Numbers*, vol. 14. Kyiv, Ukraine.

Zviglyanich, Vladimir (forthcoming), "The Nationalist and Pragmatist Models in Ukraine," in S. Wolchik and V. Zviglyanich (eds.), *Ukraine in the Post-Soviet World: Building a State*. Central European University Press.

PART III

Afterword

CHAPTER 12

Economic Transformation and the Policies for Long-Term Growth

Vito Tanzi

1. INTRODUCTION

This conference volume has focused mainly, though not exclusively, on issues and experiences related to stabilization attempts of economies in transition during the past five years. The essays presented have been informative and interesting, with conclusions that will be very useful to policy makers. The contributors to this volume have examined the role of monetary and exchange-rate policies; the importance of reducing the fiscal deficit; the relationship between the fiscal deficit, inflation, and the exchange rate; the importance of economic liberalization; and so forth. Thus, much of the analysis and discussion has been directed at the role of *macroeconomic* policy.

I will not try to add to that rich discussion or comment on any particular presentation. Rather, I will address a different and, I hope, complementary, question: What economic issues should worry the economic minister of a country in transition once the macroeconomic situation has been brought into some acceptable balance? By "acceptable balance" is *not* meant that the country has no inflation, no fiscal deficit, and no problems with the balance of payments. Instead, it simply means that the macroeconomic problems have become more or less manageable and not much worse than those prevailing in countries that are not in transition.

Problems such as high inflation and balance-of-payments crises generally require the full and urgent attention of policy makers. Thus, they distract them from focusing on such other important (but less urgent) objectives as long-run growth and equity. However, when the macroeconomic problems are no longer major ones, growth and equity objectives should be pushed to the forefront of policy makers' attention. It is especially important for the transition economies – having recently emerged from a period in which economic policy was

313

not guided by the laws of an open market – immediately to establish
rules of the game and pursue policies that will facilitate or promote
equitable economic growth.

2. THE ROAD TO GROWTH

The role that the government should play, both during and after the
transition, will be particularly difficult to define. That role will necessarily be different from the one that government played throughout
years of central planning. During transition, the government's role
will also differ from the much reduced role that will be appropriate
when the country has become a full-fledged market economy. Yet
during the transition, the role of the government will remain important because: (a) the market will continue to operate imperfectly and
will not be able to perform the allocative and distributional tasks with
the same degree of effectiveness as it does in mature market economies;[1] and (b) many new institutions necessary for an efficient market
economy will need to be created.[2]

The issues discussed here are hardly exhaustive, and are presented
in an informal and impressionistic way rather than rigorously. I shall
start with two general observations.

The first, made in the form of an analogy, is that policy makers
should realize that long-term growth is a marathon race rather than a
hundred-meter dash. The growth race is one that requires stamina, a
lot of work, and constant adapting. It is a race in which the gains from
success come mainly in the distant future even though the costs may
be immediate. The benefits from successful stabilization policies – in
terms of reduced inflation, better balance-of-payment outcomes, and
so on – are immediately visible to everyone and thus can be proudly
claimed by the government.[3] However, policies that make long-term
growth possible are less likely to bring political benefits to their crea-
tors.[4] This bias may explain why, at times, governments that have

---

[1] During the transition, market imperfections will abound. For an interesting discussion of
these imperfections and their consequences for the role of government, see Stiglitz (1995).

[2] I have previously compared the development of a market economy to that of an ecological
system (Tanzi 1990). The economic system is in equilibrium when a kind of ecological balance is achieved among institutions and available skills.

[3] We all know the names of ministers who successfully stabilized their economies. We have
greater difficulty remembering the names of ministers who, through their quiet and competent work, promoted long-run growth.

[4] Thus, governments with a short time horizon may not show much interest in policies that will
bring future growth. The fact that individuals do not change their behavior until the new policies have been in place for some time (and can thus be considered permanent) implies that

shown much energy and imagination in stabilizing the economy seem to become lethargic when the time comes to carry out policies that are consistent with long-term and sustained growth. Because of these biases, successful stabilization is at times followed by stagnation.

The second observation is that there are no miracle recipes for growth. The pursuit of growth is not only less exciting, glamorous, and politically beneficial than that of stabilization – it is also more difficult. In spite of much research over the years, economists still do not fully undersand why and how countries grow.[5] For example, policies that seem to generate a high growth rate in one country may not produce equally positive results in another. Take, for example, policies that result in high capital accumulation. Although many fast-growing economies have high shares of investment in gross domestic product, many economies with high investment shares (including the now extinct centrally planned economies) do not (or did not) experience high growth rates.

This conflicting evidence raises the question of whether it is the high rate of investment that leads to a higher growth rate (as is generally believed) or whether it is the high rate of growth that leads to a higher demand for investment goods (roads, airports, schools, hospitals, power plants, telephone systems, etc.) to reduce or eliminate bottlenecks created by the growing demand for goods or services that accompanies rising incomes.[6] There is a tendency to forget that investment can be highly unproductive. Therefore, until there is some assurance that the economic forces at play will channel available resources into productive areas, it may not necessarily be good policy to promote an increase in the share of investment into GDP, especially when such an increase is financed by debt accumulation.[7] But the assurance that capital will be invested productively can only come when a market economy is fully operating. It is unlikely that bureaucratic decisions will be able to achieve this result.

Economists do not understand what combination of (a) institutional changes, (b) changes in incentives to invest, work, save, and take risk, (c) change in the accumulation of factors of production (capital, labor, human capital), (d) changes in other policies (trade policy, tax policy, monetary policy, etc.), and (e) sheer luck create the

---

there will be a hiatus between the introduction of new policies and their effect on the growth rate.

[5] For a useful contribution to the theory of growth, see Barro and Sala-i-Martin (1995).

[6] Of course, this does not imply that a country could keep growing without additional investment, because the bottlenecks would eventually choke growth.

[7] For an elaboration of this point for centrally planned economies, see Tanzi (1991).

conditions that make a country's economy grow faster than elsewhere.[8] The pursuit of growth is like a game played by a whole nation.
As in soccer or football games, victory requires single-mindedness,
good training, good inputs, efficient use of those inputs, and a coach
who – by giving the right signals – transforms the parts into an efficient whole and thus helps bring victory. After the victory has been
achieved, it is often difficult to single out which was the determining
factor. And, of course, it is impossible to do so before the game is
played. Until the transition is completed, the role of the coach will in-
evitably have to be played by the government because the market will
not have developed enough to reduce the need for governmental intervention to the minimal level advocated by laissez-faire economists.[9]

Ignorance of the precise processes that bring growth should not,
however, become an excuse for governmental inaction. Even though
we do not fully understand what makes countries grow, we have a
fairly good idea of some necessary conditions for growth. I will highlight a few of these conditions, especially those of greater relevance to
economies in transition, together with more general issues.

3. CONDITIONS THAT FACILITATE GROWTH

It is generally agreed that *macroeconomic balance* and *stabilization* are essential conditions for growth. There is now much evidence that supports the view that high inflation is not compatible with growth: no
country has experienced sustained, long-term growth while its rate of
inflation remained very high. The evidence is less clear for lower
(though still positive) rates of inflation. Thus, inflation need not fall
to zero.[10] Dr. Skegro, the Deputy Prime Minister of Croatia, has re-
marked that in countries experiencing high inflation, cost-reducing
technical changes will attract little attention on the part of enterprise
managers. During high inflation, financial decisions and financial
advisors become much more important than technical decisions and
engineers or other individuals concerned with the technical side of

---

[8] In most empirical studies of growth there is an often large residual that defies explanation.

[9] One difficulty evident now in many transition economies is that policy makers with little
exposure to the workings of market economies are those who are assigned the difficult and
important task of leading their economies in that direction.

[10] Some countries with moderate rates of inflation have succeeded in sustaining high rates of
growth for prolonged periods. And of course it must be recalled that the rate of inflation was
negative in many countries during the long period that characterized the Great Depression
of the 1930s. The rate of inflation is just one factor, and in some cases it may not be the most
significant factor.

production. Therefore, it is essential to keep inflation relatively low and prices flexible in order to facilitate the flow of resources to more productive uses. It follows that price controls must be phased out as soon as possible.

In working market economies, the rules that determine the sharing of national income among the factors of production are clear and relatively stable. In these economies, there is little if any confusion about who is entitled to what, because well-established rules guarantee this result. These are rules that assign clear property rights to individuals and to public and private institutions, and rules that guarantee the sanctity of contracts.[11] If property rights are undefined or opaque then the assignment of incomes becomes unclear and erratic, causing many problems to develop. In this situation, the resources, decisions, and efforts needed to promote long-term growth will not be forthcoming.

One of the basic, unresolved problems in many economies in transition – as well as in some (especially African) developing economies – is the lack of clear delineation, or recognition, of *property rights*. At times, assets (land, buildings, machines, natural resources, etc.) seem to be neither privately owned nor publicly owned; they fall in between.[12] When assets are publicly owned, there is confusion concerning what part of the public sector has clear property rights over them. At times the confusion occurs between different levels of government, or between state enterprises and government narrowly defined; at other times, it is between different parts of the same level of government. This confusion in property rights not only slows the decision-making process and prevents some productive investments from being undertaken, it also creates conditions where corruption thrives. Well-placed bribes on the part of foreign enterprises or domestic investors often remove short-run obstacles to the decision-making process, but they do not permanently eliminate the uncertainty created by the confusion in property rights.

Though it is often discussed separately, the *sanctity of contracts* is itself an aspect of the property rights issue – when the latter is interpreted in a broad sense. Contracts establish claims or rights over

---

[11] Thus, the shares going to wage earners, to investors, to savers, etc. are determined by contracts and by well-defined property rights.

[12] In some cases the problem is that the public sector (or some who control that sector) may, with impunity and while offering little or no compensation, expropriate assets owned by private individuals. In other cases, the reverse is true. The experience in some transition economies with asset stripping and with so-called *nomenklatura* privatization is a case in point.

resources or actions. Progress in market economies depends fundamentally on the growth of contracts and on the expectation that contracts will be honored most of the time.[13] Thus, when a worker enters
into a contract with an employer, the worker expects to be paid the
agreed wage after satisfying his or her share of the contract – that is,
after completing the work.[14] When a supplier sells some of its output to others, it expects in exchange a payment, reflecting the agreed
price, within the specified time indicated in that contract. When a
utility company sells electricity or water or telephone services to other
companies, it expects to be paid on time. When a bank lends money
to individuals and enterprises, it generally expects to get the money
back, plus the agreed interest, at the specified time. In all these examples and many others, a major disregard of contractual obligations
has characterized many of the economies in transition.

Contractual obligations are often ignored in transitional economies, and arrears in payments accumulate between enterprises and
workers, enterprises and other enterprises, enterprises and government, government and enterprises, enterprises and banks, and so on.
When this matrix of arrears becomes widespread and the sums involved are significant, even the most successful stabilization policies
are unlikely to lead to growth. In other cases, there may even be a
tradeoff between stabilization and growth if some aspects of the stabilization policies have promoted an increase in these arrears. Those
who are hurt by the accumulation of these arrears often cannot take
effective legal action against those who have not lived up to the terms
of their contracts. The problem is especially serious when it is the
public sector that is in arrears (to wage earners, pensioners, suppliers, etc.).

These problems with the enforcement of contracts and with the
confusion of property rights extend to other relationships among government, individuals, and enterprises. In a way, the tax system represents a form of contract between the government and the private
sector. However, in this case one side (the government) has the power
to change the terms of the contract by changing tax rates or introducing new taxes. A tax system that maintains constant effective tax

---

[13] A likely indicator of a market's sophistication is the number of contracts that are entered
into each year. In a working economy, a large share of these contracts will be honored.

[14] Many contracts in market economies are "implicit"; however, they are still generally
honored.

rates over time is considered more efficient than one that collects the same average revenue but with fluctuating effective rates.[15]

Individuals and enterprises that make decisions whose consequences extend well into the future (investment and saving decisions, choice of careers, etc.) are often deterred by excessive tax uncertainty. It is thus important for countries in transition to introduce as soon as possible an effective tax system that can be taken as more or less permanent by the private sector and so can be regarded as a parameter in their decisions. Of course, such a system will require not only good tax laws but also an *efficient tax administration*. This aspect is particularly important for taxes on the income of individuals and enterprises. Many economies in transition are still far from achieving an adequate tax system: either the legislation keeps changing or the administration remains inefficient.

The implication of the foregoing is that policy makers must pay full attention to the tax system in order to put in place taxes that provide revenue for stabilization purposes *and* are efficient, stable, and well administered. The achievement of this objective requires a lot of detailed (and usually not very exciting) work. So far, policy makers of many countries have been distracted from achieving this objective by the urgent need to stabilize the economy, at times even at the cost of introducing such inefficient taxes as (for example) those on exports.[16]

Of course, one cannot plan on the level of taxation by abstracting from the level of spending. In general, when the countries in transition began their journey toward a market economy, they already had extremely high tax levels, often exceeding 40–50% of GDP. This level was needed to support equivalent levels of public spending. Market economies with per-capita incomes well under $5,000 (U.S.) – the income level in most transition economies – are generally not able to generate tax/GDP ratios higher than, say, 25%. Thus, the transition to a market economy will inevitably lower tax-raising potential to levels not likely to exceed 25% of GDP.[17] This implies that government spending in transition economies must be significantly cut in order to be consistent with lower levels of taxation.

---

[15] This result has often been emphasized in recent literature. For a basic reference see Barro (1979).

[16] This is another area where growth policies and stabilization policies may at times conflict: when stabilization is achieved through the introduction of bad and varying taxes.

[17] In some of the poorer transition economies, the potential ratio of taxes to GDP may be well below 25%.

Public expenditure has in fact been coming down, though in several countries at a slower rate than taxation. However, the reduction in public expenditure has often been neither growth- nor equity-friendly. The cuts have been somewhat indiscriminate, often determined merely by cash available rather than by rational and detailed plans based on the productivity and equity of public spending.[18] For the latter to take place, in addition to hard analysis it is necessary that the fiscal institutions essential to reasonable public expenditure policy – budget offices and the treasury – are developed and can achieve the required level of expertise. Expenditure cuts through sequestration, or through the building up of arrears, must be replaced by expenditure cuts based on a rational process of political economy. Only then will the objectives of growth and equity be respected.

The creation of a good budget office, of sound budgetary procedures, and of an efficient treasury – one that (a) allows the government to keep track not only of actual cash spending but also of commitments made and (b) enables proper cash management – is a time-consuming process that requires financial resources as well as the full attention of relevant policy makers. In several transition countries, such policy makers have shown less patience and interest than is needed to carry this enterprise to its successful end. Once again, one reason is that there is little political gain for the minister who invests time and energy in this activity.

The creation of *fiscal institutions* that would help the government to avoid breaking contracts is certainly necessary for an environment to be conducive to growth; however, it is far from sufficient. For example, effective tax rates may be stable over time, thus satisfying one of the requirements of tax efficiency. Yet, they may be stable *and* excessively high. When it comes to the impact on growth, low rates are clearly better than high rates. But low rates are possible only when expenditure needs are modest. A careful review of the government's role in the economy will be necessary in order to adjust downward its revenue needs. This review would have the objective of removing the government from many activities (such as widespread consumer and producer subsidies) in which its role is not essential or even necessary in a market economy. It will also require some important redirection of spending.

---

[18] As already mentioned, at times the cuts have been made by the simple expedient of delaying payment to pensioners and wage earners during periods of high inflation.

A review of the government's economic role is a politically sensitive matter, but an essential one. Such a review, which ought to involve both the executive and legislative branches of government, should be conducted in the open and with full public participation. It would become part of the process of educating people to the features of a market economy and preparing them for necessary policy changes. The final, ideal outcome would be some (broad?) consensus about what role the government should play in the economy and the implications of that role for the level of spending and taxation. Of course, the actual or current role of the government cannot be changed from one minute to the next, but one can at least define what that role should be over the long run and begin to move in that direction. If the government does not function well or its role remains undefined, long-term growth is unlikely to occur.

Over the longer run, the government must play a limited role yet must operate as efficiently as possible. This objective has implications for: the kind of people the government hires, the wages it pays, the design of social spending, the choice of investment projects, how well the government performs vis-à-vis operation and maintenance of the existing infrastructure, the level of taxation and the structure of the tax system, the regulations that it maintains or eliminates, determining what becomes privatized and what remains public, and so forth. Clearly, growth requires that the relevant ministers allocate a lot of attention to many messy and time-consuming areas, because the road to long-run growth is paved by more than just stabilization successes.

In countries where most assets had been publicly owned, important policies must deal with the extent to which assets will remain in the hands of the public sector. The basic reasoning for confronting the question of ownership is the assumption that, in efficient market economies, assets that are privately owned generally contribute more to production and welfare than assets that are publicly owned. Although this assumption is in some cases highly questionable,[19] in general it is closer to the truth than the opposite assumption. It seems realistic to assume that in transition economies there are many valuable assets that contribute little to the generation of welfare or to measured national income. It is also safe to assume that the government probably

---

[19] Contrast, for example, the welfare created by paintings in public museums, where they can be seen by millions of people, with the welfare created by paintings in private posession, which usually are seen and enjoyed by only a small group of people.

does not have a good account of all these assets. Therefore, one action worth pursuing is to generate a full inventory of everything that is publicly owned, including works of art (some of which may be in basements of museums and may not have been seen by anyone for years), zoos, buildings, land, enterprises, mineral resources, means of transportation, and so forth. This action could be accompanied by a full inventory of the country's liabilities. It is important for a country to know what its future commitments will be under current policy.

This *inventory of assets and liabilities* would provide the rough raw material for making an estimation of the net worth of the public sector, following the example of New Zealand and certain other countries. The information obtained would need to be refined and updated on a regular basis, but it would introduce at least the concept of a public sector's balance sheet; this could eventually become a useful guide for governmental policy. It would also facilitate national policy by encouraging the government to focus on its contingent liabilities, and it just might influence the government to make better use of its available resources.

The inventory of assets would expand the debate over privatization, which in my view has focused excessively on enterprises and has thus ignored other assets. The point is that the public sector owns much more than enterprises, and these other assets should likewise generate the highest feasible return. Assets that cannot be used productively by the public sector should be disposed of – taking care that no insiders benefit disproportionately in the process. This is an area where corruption is likely to play a major role. In many countries, assets have been appropriated by private interest in exchange for very little payment to the public sector. Such an improper transfer may contribute to a rise in national income (if, after the transfer, the asset is used more productively) but at a high cost in terms of equity.

Streamlining regulations is another area where explicit policy action is badly needed. I have yet to see any formal action aimed at clearing the jungle of regulations that have accumulated over the years. Regulations create a most fertile ground for corruption[20] and are often an obstacle to the growth process.[21] Once again, a useful action would be that of assaying a full *inventory of all existing regulations*.

[20] See Tanzi (1995).
[21] In centrally planned economies, one needed permission to do almost anything. In a mature market economy, one should have the freedom to do anything that is not explicitly prohibited. Moving from the first to the second requires a lot of work.

The government could create a working group charged with the task of identifying all regulations that have economic implications. This inventory should include not only the regulations imposed by the national government, but also those imposed by other parts of the public sector. Once again, the final objective should be to get rid of useless or damaging regulations. Obviously, before policy decisions can be made in this area, the basic facts must become known and must be carefully analyzed.

This process (or a parallel one) will surely discover that, although many regulations should be removed, some essential others should be created. These would include supervision over banks, stock markets, insurance companies, and so on. Because many new institutions will be coming into existence, the regulatory activities related to them must be established. What is fundamental is that the new regulations not be simply added to existing ones. In summary, the regulatory role of the government must be fully and openly discussed, must be clearly defined, and must be efficient and resistant to interpretation and abuses. This regulatory policy must be coordinated and closely followed by relevant policy makers (ministers, governing boards of central banks, etc.).

4. CONCLUDING REMARKS

In these short and highly informal remarks I have tried to complement the many important contributions in this book by calling attention to issues and policies that are very important yet receive little explicit attention, especially from macroeconomists. I have pointed out that there may be political biases that reduce the attention that high-level policy makers allocate to some of these issues. I have also emphasized that progress in these areas may be slow because a lot of detailed and, at times, not very exciting work is needed before changes can be made. I have also stressed that our knowledge of what generates growth is somewhat incomplete, so there is far less certainty in this area (than in, say, stabilization) that a given action will lead to growth.

Policy determination or reform in certain areas is likely to promote growth. I have discussed many of the issues involved: (a) macroeconomic balance and stabilization; (b) property rights; (c) the sanctity of contracts; (d) the need for a "parametric" and efficient tax system with reasonable tax rates; (e) the level and composition of public spending and the role of the public sector in general; (f) creation of essential fiscal institutions such as the budget office, treasury, tax administration, etc.; (g) determination of the long-run role of government in the economy; (h) privatization issues; (i) net worth of the public sector; and (j) regulations.

Each item in this rather long list is important for growth, and each deserves a far more comprehensive treatment than I can give here. However, I would like to mention three additional areas to which policy makers should pay particular attention. These are:

(1) the need to emphasize efficiency *within* the public sector;
(2) the pedagogic role of high-level officials; and
(3) the need to worry about equity aspects of economic policy.

Efficiency in the use of public resources generally receives but perfunctory mention, and few countries have explicitly initiated a campaign or even debate aimed at making progress in this area.[22] A little-known law attributed to Pareto claims that, on average, 20% of the employees in public offices perform 80% of the productive work. Perhaps Pareto's percentages are exaggerated, and perhaps there are public offices where all employees work hard and productively. However, my own observation is that, in many public offices, a substantial share of the work force is in fact either doing little or working hard but accomplishing little that is useful. In some cases, efficiency cannot be improved because of the reluctance to reduce the work force through transfers, firing, or early retirement. In other cases, efficiency cannot be improved because of the many existing constraints that prevent reallocation of resources. Explicit and sustained attention to this problem, accompanied by an educational campaign about the cost of public-sector inefficiency, could have beneficial effects over time.

The importance of the role that officials can play in explaining basic economic laws to the general public cannot be exaggerated, especially in countries where most people have no idea about the role that prices, profits, interest rates, or exchange rates play in the economy. Policies need to be explained not only to legislators and to employees of the executive branch, but also to the public at large. Economic illiteracy often leads to misguided economic policies. An articulate finance minister, or even the prime minister or president, can play a

---

[22] Vice President Gore's aim of "reinventing government" in the United States is one example of such a campaign. New Zealand had made major strides in this area.

tremendously important role in explaining new policies, and in explaining why change may be needed. The more economically literate the public becomes, the easier it should be to gain its support for making difficult but necessary policy changes. For example, former U.S. President Reagan (and, to a lesser extent, Menem in Argentina) used his prestige and mass communication (television or radio) to explain policies in terms that even economic novices could understand.

I have focused on issues that must be addressed by transition countries once they have stabilized their economies and started the journey toward long-run or sustained growth.[23] I have focused on issues of efficiency and institution building, largely ignoring the issue of equity. This, however, is not because equity is unimportant. In fact, equity is likely to become central to the policies of transition economies because of the distortions in income distribution reported in many of these countries.

The process of transformation creates enormous opportunity for gains to some and losses to others. These gains will be legitimate to the extent they originate from normal market activities but illegitimate to the extent they are the result of corruption, criminal activity, or special connections that provide privileges to some but not others. Although it will not be possible (nor, perhaps, desirable) to prevent inequitable income distribution entirely, too much inequity will create an environment that will lead to populist policies and will make the transition all the more difficult, thus reducing the prospects for growth for many years to come. This is why the objective of equity cannot be ignored even by a government set on creating a market economy.

REFERENCES

Barro, Robert J. (1979), "On the Determination of Public Debt," *Journal of Political Economy* 87: 940–71.

Barro, Robert J., and Xavier Sala-i-Martin (1995), *Economic Growth*. New York: McGraw-Hill.

Stiglitz, Joseph (1995), *Whither Socialism?* Cambridge, MA: MIT Press.

Tanzi, Vito (1990), "Fiscal Issues in Economies in Transition," in V. Carbo, F. Coricelli, and J. Bossak (eds.), *Reforming Central and Eastern European Economies*. Washington, DC: World Bank, pp. 221–8.

---

[23] This does not imply that the countries should wait for full stabilization before initiating the actions suggested here.

Tanzi, Vito (1991), "Mobilization of Savings in Eastern European Countries," in A. B. Atkinson and R. Brunetta (eds.), *Economics for the New Europe*. London: Macmillan, pp. 175–95.

Tanzi, Vito (1995), "Corruption, Arm's-Length Relationships and Markets," in G. Fiorentini and S. Peltzman (eds.), *The Economics of Organized Crime*. New York: Cambridge University Press, pp. 161–80.

Index

327